POLYCENTRICITY IN THE EUROPEAN UNION

Supranational governance is being challenged by politicians and citizens around the European Union as over-centralised and undemocratic. This book is premised on the idea that polycentric governance, as developed by Vincent and Elinor Ostrom, is a fruitful place to start in addressing this challenge. Assessing the presence of, and potential for, polycentric governance within the EU means approaching established principles and practices from a new perspective. While the debate on these issues is rich, longstanding and interdisciplinary, it has proven difficult to sidestep the 'renationalisation/federalisation' dichotomy. The aim of this Volume is not to reject the EU's institutional structure but to provide a different benchmark for the assessment of its functioning. Polycentric theory highlights the importance of multilevel horizontal relationships within the EU – between states, but also between many sub-state actors, all the way down to individuals. This helps us answer the question: how do we achieve self-governance in an interdependent world?

DR JOSEPHINE VAN ZEBEN is a Fellow at Worcester College, University of Oxford. In 2013, she was a postdoctoral researcher at the Vincent and Elinor Ostrom Workshop in Political Theory and Policy Analysis. Dr van Zeben holds a degree in social sciences from Utrecht University, as well as law degrees from the University of Edinburgh, the University of Amsterdam and Harvard Law School. She has also been a lecturer at ETH Zurich since 2012. Her research focuses on how pluricentric systems – such as the EU – can best be structured to address complex regulatory problems.

DR ANA BOBIĆ is a postdoctoral researcher at the LEVIATHAN research project at the Hertie School of Governance, Berlin. She works on questions of accountability in EU economic governance, with a focus on the role of judicial and constitutional review. At the Faculty of Law, University of Oxford, she completed a DPhil as a Graduate Assistance Fund Scholar and the MJur as the OSI/University of Oxford scholar. She previously obtained a BA LLM *summa cum laude* at the Faculty of Law, University of Zagreb in 2011. Ana was also a lecturer in Constitutional and Administrative Law at Keble College, University of Oxford.

POLYCENTRICITY IN THE EUROPEAN UNION

Edited by

JOSEPHINE VAN ZEBEN
University of Oxford

ANA BOBIĆ
Hertie School of Governance

CAMBRIDGE
UNIVERSITY PRESS

CAMBRIDGE
UNIVERSITY PRESS

Shaftesbury Road, Cambridge CB2 8EA, United Kingdom

One Liberty Plaza, 20th Floor, New York, NY 10006, USA

477 Williamstown Road, Port Melbourne, VIC 3207, Australia

314–321, 3rd Floor, Plot 3, Splendor Forum, Jasola District Centre, New Delhi – 110025, India

103 Penang Road, #05–06/07, Visioncrest Commercial, Singapore 238467

Cambridge University Press is part of Cambridge University Press & Assessment, a department of the University of Cambridge.

We share the University's mission to contribute to society through the pursuit of education, learning and research at the highest international levels of excellence.

www.cambridge.org
Information on this title: www.cambridge.org/9781108437653

DOI: 10.1017/9781108528771

First published 2019
First paperback edition 2026

A catalogue record for this publication is available from the British Library

Library of Congress Cataloging-in-Publication data
Names: Zeben, Josephine A. W. van, 1984–, editor. | Bobic, Ana, 1987–, editor.
Title: Polycentricity in the European Union / Edited by Josephine van Zeben, University of Oxford, Ana Bobic, University of Oxford.
Description: New York, NY : Cambridge University Press, 2019. | Includes bibliographical references and index.
Identifiers: LCCN 2019002559 | ISBN 9781108423540 (alk. paper)
Subjects: LCSH: Legal polycentricity – European Union countries. | Conflict of laws – European Union countries. | International and municipal law – European Union countries. | Legitimacy of governments – European Union countries.
Classification: LCC KJE5076 .P64 2019 | DDC 340.9094–dc23
LC record available at https://lccn.loc.gov/2019002559

ISBN 978-1-108-42354-0 Hardback
ISBN 978-1-108-43765-3 Paperback

CONTENTS

TABLES

CONTRIBUTORS

VIGJILENCA ABAZI Assistant Professor of European Law and Senior Researcher at the Centre for European Research in Maastricht at Maastricht University

ANA BOBIĆ Postdoctoral Researcher at the LEVIATHAN Project, Hertie School of Governance, Berlin

MARTIJN VAN DEN BRINK Postdoctoral Researcher at the Max Planck Institute for the Study of Religious and Ethnic Diversity

FRANCIS CHENEVAL Chair of Political Philosophy at the University of Zurich

LETICIA DÍEZ SÁNCHEZ Postdoctoral Emile Noël Fellow at the Jean Monnet Center at New York University

SACHA GARBEN Professor of EU Law at the College of Europe, Bruges

IRIS GOLDNER LANG Jean Monnet Professor of EU Law and the holder of the UNESCO Chair on Free Movement of People, Migration and Inter-Cultural Dialogue, University of Zagreb

DAMJAN KUKOVEC Senior Lecturer, Middlesex University, London

MICHAEL D. MCGINNIS Professor of Political Science and Associate Dean of the College of Arts and Sciences, Indiana University and former Director of the Vincent and Elinor Ostrom Workshop in Political Theory and Policy Analysis

KALYPSO NICOLAÏDIS Professor of International Relations, University of Oxford

JOSEPHINE VAN ZEBEN Fellow Worcester College, University of Oxford

FOREWORD

I met Josephine van Zeben in 2013 when she was a visiting scholar at the Vincent and Elinor Ostrom Workshop in Political Theory and Policy Analysis, at Indiana University, Bloomington. The Ostrom Workshop was then, and is now, a world-famous research and teaching institution specializing on the application of a unique mode of institutional analysis to a wide range of policy settings. Most outsiders are familiar only with the Nobel Prize-winning research of Elinor Ostrom on community-based management of resource commons. But Josephine realized that Elinor Ostrom's research program had been built upon the foundation laid by Vincent Ostrom's earlier conceptualization of the polycentric governance typical of urban metropolitan areas in the United States.

The key message from both streams of research was that local communities can become and remain self-governing only if they are embedded within a broader political, economic, and social-cultural regime that was supportive of these efforts. Josephine wanted to know if the emerging structures and processes of governance in the European Union can support this same kind of local self-governance, and if not, then what reforms are needed to accomplish that goal?

She faced a huge challenge: nearly all of the examples of this mode of institutional analyses were focused on local policy. Any effort to generalize these same principles to the continental scope and bureaucratic depth of the EU would require considerable care. Although both Vincent and Elinor Ostrom had passed away the year before, their writings remained as a foundation for future development of their ideas. But it was important to avoid getting lost in conceptual cul-de-sacs. For example, whenever Vincent Ostrom wrote about governance in Europe, he expressed particular admiration for the lost complexity of the Holy Roman Empire! And when Elinor Ostrom addressed issues of climate policy, she emphasized the potential benefits of policy changes at the level of cities or other sub-national governments, and changes in consumer behavior, while paying very little attention to the role of international treaties.

For the most part, then, Josephine, her co-editor Ana Bobić, and their colleagues in this project have had to draw their own connections between the abstractions of polycentric governance and the details of the European Union. As a career-long Workshopper, I must say that I am very impressed with the dexterity with which they accomplish that task in this book. I would like to briefly draw a potential reader's attention to a few particularly compelling aspects of their analysis.

Contributors to this Volume recognize that the increasingly complex regulatory apparatus at the EU level remains incomplete (because member states retain control over some important areas of policy) and internally inconsistent (agencies' areas of jurisdiction can overlap to a bewildering extent). Using the concept of polycentricity, they can explain why at least a minimal level of continued ambiguity in governance processes might actually be a desirable condition, rather than a problem to be solved.

I especially appreciated the way the authors shift attention away from stale debates regarding the EU's "democracy deficit" to focus instead on the foundational requirement that local groups need to be able to gain access to information about public policy that can help them identify the sources of the problems they are facing, and to evaluate which institutional options might be available to them. Several chapters highlight the importance of nurturing horizontal ties of community that cut across the nation states that comprise the EU. For example, they investigate the extent to which current EU institutions and procedures make it easier or more difficult for communities of "third-party nationals," especially refugees or immigrant communities from countries outside of the EU, to connect with each other, share information, appeal for help from regional, national, or supranational political authorities, or take direct action to improve their current plight.

Through the lens of polycentricity, they bring into focus a rarely asked but critical question: to what extent does the EU facilitate or hinder the ability of under-resourced or vulnerable groups to govern themselves? In this way, they shine new light on the never-ending search for justice, which is a concern that has rarely been directly addressed in previous institutional analyses done in the style of the Bloomington School.

All of the contributors to this Volume have demonstrated their ability to draw accurate and insightful connections between the detailed operation of the European Union and the Ostroms' deep understanding of polycentric governance. Not only do they identify novel changes in EU processes that might facilitate a fuller realization of the potential benefits of polycentric governance; they also offer astute observations of likely hurdles ahead. Anyone interested in either the EU or institutional analysis more generally should carefully consider the arguments made in this fascinating Volume.

Michael D. McGinnis
Professor of Political Science, Associate Dean of the College of Arts and Sciences, Indiana University and former Director of the Vincent and Elinor Ostrom Workshop in Political Theory and Policy Analysis
July 20, 2018

ACKNOWLEDGEMENTS

The road to completion for this project was long, and not without a few detours. In 2013, a grant from the Niels Stensen Fellowship enabled Josephine to become a visiting fellow at the Vincent and Elinor Ostrom Workshop in Political Theory and Policy Analysis. She set out to consider whether polycentric governance theory could be valuable in understanding the EU's current and future development. It soon became clear that to move successfully from promise to practice would require more time, and more people – neither of which were available at the time.

A few years later, at the University of Oxford, progress on the polycentric research agenda was jump-started when Josephine was introduced to Ana Bobić by a common friend and colleague – Tamara Perišin. Debating and brainstorming the initial findings made it clear that the promise was still there and the topic was still, or perhaps even more, important. Plans for an edited volume were made and accepted by Cambridge University Press. A workshop in Oxford, made possible by the support of the Law Faculty's Research Support Fund, followed in February 2018, as did many discussions with our collaborators in person and over email.

The results of this collective effort are set out in these pages. Different from some edited volumes, this work has become one book, with one story, narrated by several authors. This was a demanding process for all involved and our gratitude to our authors – most of whom were unfamiliar with polycentric theory but all of whom mastered and enriched it – is second only to our gratitude for the intellectual legacy of Vincent and Elinor Ostrom. Their theories, as well as their method of working, inspired this interdisciplinary effort and we hope it makes a valuable contribution to the continuing work of the Ostrom Workshop and scholarly community. Michael McGinnis, former director of the Workshop and longstanding collaborator of Elinor and Vincent, has – in true Ostrom tradition – always provided mentorship and encouragement to young scholars and kindly agreed to contextualise this project in the foreword. We are very grateful for his continuing support.

Bringing together a work with so many different scholars into a coherent whole would not have been possible without the trust of our editors at Cambridge University Press – first Kim Hughes and later Tom Randall – and the vital support of our outstanding research assistants, Roderic Kermarec and Julia Vassileva.

The work on polycentricity in the EU has only just started and we look forward to continuing on this road. Hopefully this Volume can act as a starting point for those interested in this, and related, areas.

Finally, we dedicate this book to our families, with love, gratitude and hope for the future.

Josephine van Zeben
Ana Bobić

LIST OF CASES

European Courts

National Courts

INTRODUCTION

The Potential of a Polycentric European Union

JOSEPHINE VAN ZEBEN AND ANA BOBIĆ

Political and academic debates on the European Union's future move along a continuum between a state-centric free trade zone[1] and federal European state.[2] These debates cumulated in the 2016 Brexit referendum and the anticipated end of the United Kingdom's EU membership on 29 March 2019.[3] Brexit is only one of the myriad of challenges, ranging from fiscal crises to humanitarian tragedies, that the EU faces.[4] The expansion of the Union's mandate and institutional set-up has not been able to prevent, or even reduce, these challenges. The starting point of this Volume is that the solution to these problems does not lie on the well-travelled continuum between renationalisation of powers and a federal Europe. Instead, we take up Vincent Ostrom's challenge to contemplate

1 See e.g. Y. Tamir, *Liberal Nationalism* (Princeton University Press, 1995) and G. Majone, 'Europe's "Democratic Deficit": The Question of Standards', *European Law Journal* 4 (1998), 5. See also R. Schütze, *European Constitutional Law* (Cambridge University Press, 2012), 54.

2 See e.g. J. Habermas, 'Why Europe Needs a Constitution', *New Left Review* 11 (2001), 5; E. Eriksen, J. Fossum, and A. Menéndez (eds.), *Developing a Constitution for Europe* (Routledge, 2004); D. Šiđanski, *The Federal Future of Europe: From the European Community to the European Union* English trans. (University of Michigan, 2000); N. Fligstein, *Euroclash: The EU, European Identity, and the Future of Europe* (Oxford University Press, 2008).

3 P. Craig, '"Brexit": A Drama in Six Parts', *European Law Review* 41 (4) (2016), 447 (showing that the causes for the Leave vote were many and its consequences still unclear); see also P. Craig, 'Brexit, A Drama: The Interregnum', *Yearbook of European Law* 36 (2017), 3.

4 Each of these challenges has given rise to its own subfield of European scholarship, which in turn feeds back into more general debates regarding competences and subsidiarity. See e.g. G. Davies, 'Democracy and Legitimacy in the Shadow of Purposive Competence', *European Law Journal* 21 (1) (2015), 2 (on the interpretation and assigning of EU competence through a study of internal market competences); M. Bartl, 'The Way We Do Europe: Subsidiarity and the Substantive Democratic Deficit', *European Law Journal* 21 (1) (2015), 23 (considering the principle of subsidiarity through a case study of European private law) and F. Scharpf, 'After the Crash: A Perspective on Multilevel European Democracy', *European Law Journal* 21 (3) (2015), 384 (on the future of European integration after the financial crisis).

a system of societal relationships not dominated by 'the state' or 'the government'[5] by exploring the presence of, and potential for, polycentric governance within the EU.

As a descriptive theory of governance, polycentric governance is characterised by the presence of many centres of decision making, which are formally autonomous and may compete and/or collaborate under an overarching shared system of rules. [6] Normatively, polycentric governance accommodates both representative and deliberative models of democracy by placing intrinsic value on individual self-governance without prescribing specific outcomes from the process of governance.[7] The institutional set-up of polycentric systems aims to ensure balance between decision-making centres so as to prevent dominance of certain centres and safeguard continued self-governance.[8] Adopting a polycentric perspective means to conceptualise society as a collection of rule-based interactions between individuals. In this context, self-governance refers to the ability of individuals to determine the rules that underlie these interactions and to set the goals for sustained interactions that result in collective action.

This Volume has a dual ambition: first, and most importantly, by assessing the EU's potential for polycentric governance, it seeks to offer an alternative theory of governance for the EU, as compared to existing pluricentric EU governance theories – specifically federalism, multilevel governance, constitutional pluralism, and multilevel constitutionalism. [9]

[5] V. Ostrom, *The Meaning of American Federalism: Constituting a Self-governing Society* (ICS Press, 1994), i. In this Volume, the importance of non-dominance is contextualised by J. van Zeben in Chapter 1, and further explored by F. Cheneval in Chapter 3.

[6] V. Ostrom, C. Tiebout, and R. Warren, '"The Organization of Government in Metropolitan Areas": A Theoretical Inquiry', *The American Political Science Review* 55 (1961), 831.

[7] M. McGinnis and E. Ostrom, 'Reflections on Vincent Ostrom, Public Administration, and Polycentricity', *Public Administration Review* 72 (2012), 15.

[8] P. Aligica and V. Tarko, 'Polycentricity: From Polanyi to Ostrom, and Beyond', *Governance: An International Journal of Policy, Administration, and Institutions* 25 (2012), 237, 246.

[9] Legal scholarship does propose changes to the EU's constitutional make-up with a view to change its method of governance. However, these legal theories (e.g. constitutional pluralism) must be distinguished from political theories such as multilevel governance. Polycentricity, conversely, acts as a complete theory of governance. For an excellent example of legal writing in this area, see M. Dawson and F. De Witte, 'From Balance to Conflict: A New Constitution to Europe', *European Law Journal* 22 (2) (2016), 204. See also N. Walker, 'Constitutional Pluralism Revisited', *European Law Journal* 22 (3) (2016), 333; I. Pernice, 'Multilevel Constitutionalism and the Treaty of Amsterdam: European Constitution-making Revisited?', *Common Market Law Review* 36 (1999), 703 and A. Jordan, 'The European Union : An Evolving System of Multi-level Governance . . . or

The descriptive nature of some existing theories limits their ability to engage with the democratic concerns that inform much of the binary debate between centralisation and renationalisation of European competences.[10] The strengthening and expansion of the EU's polycentric features with a view to ensuring individual self-governance creates a model of European governance that accommodates different conceptions of European *demos*,[11] as well as the divergent constitutional theories applied to the EU,[12] without having to revert either to a state-centric or federal model of Europe. Moreover, the similarities and overlaps between polycentricity and other EU-related pluricentric theories of governance show that polycentric governance is not foreign to the EU; many of the EU's institutional features already support a polycentricity system. By critically examining which institutional features of polycentricity are missing or incomplete in the current EU framework, targeted suggestions for improvement are possible.

The second aim of this Volume is to expand the scope of application of polycentric theory itself. Developed by Vincent and Elinor Ostrom through the Bloomington School of Institutional Analysis, polycentric theory has thus far primarily been used to explain (local) governance in the United States of America, and natural resource management by local communities worldwide. The application of polycentric theory to the EU has been very limited: Vincent Ostrom commented on the EU several times – going as far as to say that 'the

Government?', *Policy & Politics* 29 (2001), 193. For a detailed comparison and discussion of these theories see, in this Volume, Chapter 1 by J. van Zeben.

10 See e.g. J. Habermas, 'Democracy in Europe: Why the Development of the EU into a Transnational Democracy Is Necessary and How It Is Possible', *European Law Journal* 21 (2015), 546; J. Weiler, 'Democracy without the People: The Crisis of European' (2012), available at www.europarl.europa.eu/RegData/etudes/etudes/join/2013/474438/IPOL-AFCO_ET(2013)474438_EN.pdf accessed 1 on November 2018; M. Kumm, 'Democratic Challenges Arising from the Eurocrisis: What Kind of a Constitutional Crisis Is Europe in and What Should Be Done about It?', in *Challenges of multi-tier governance in the European Union: Effectiveness, efficiency and legitimacy* (Directorate-General on Internal Policies 2013, available at www.lehrstuhl-pernice.de/tl_files/documents/Multi-tier%20governance%20in%20the%20EU.pdf#page=126 accessed on 1 November 2018) (arguing for increased democracy at the European level). Conversely, see G. de Búrca, 'Europe's Raison D'Etre', *New York University Public Law and Legal Theory Working Papers* (2013), 385 (arguing that the EU's current day added value is its influence on interstate relations *outside* of the European Union, not within the EU).

11 See, in this Volume, Chapter 3 by F. Cheneval.

12 For an overview, see S. Bredt, 'Prospects and Limits of Democratic Governance in the EU', *European Law Journal* 17 (2011), 35.

future development of human civilisation turns critically upon the resolutions that are attained in Europe'[13] – but never developing polycentric theory to fit the EU's particular context.[14] Other authors have used the term polycentricity to describe related, but different, issues of EU governance.[15] Through careful examination of the descriptive and normative implications of polycentricity for the EU, we have been able to expand the theoretical foundations of polycentric theory to better fit large polycentric systems, and to flesh out the shape and form of polycentric institutional features.[16] This will hopefully benefit the work of those who seek to study polycentricity in other supranational settings, such as climate change governance.[17]

Structure of the Volume

The foundations of this Volume were laid during van Zeben's yearlong research stay at the Ostrom Workshop in Indiana in 2013. The purpose of this visit was to assess the extent to which the EU is already polycentric and, assuming that this would be desirable, which polycentric features of EU governance should be strengthened. However, it quickly became clear that mapping the full polycentric potential of the EU required expert knowledge of many areas of EU law, and would therefore be better achieved through a collaborative effort rather than through a monograph. This Volume is the product of an interdisciplinary collaboration between the contributors, finetuned by critical discussions of each other's work through a workshop

[13] V. Ostrom, *The Political Theory of a Compound Republic* 3rd edn (Lexington Books, 2007), 223.

[14] V. Ostrom, 'Faustian Bargains', *Constitutional Political Economy* 7 (1996), 303. The most complete attempt by other members of the Bloomington School is the unpublished work by McGinnis and Hanisch: M. McGinnis and M. Hanisch 'Analyzing Problems of Polycentric Governance in the Growing EU' (2005) Paper presented at the Transcoop Workshop on Analysing Problems of Polycentric Governance in the Growing, EU Humboldt University Berlin (on file with the author).

[15] See e.g M. Wind, 'The European Union as a Polycentric Polity: Returning to a Neo-medieval Europe?', in J. Weiler and M. Wind (eds.), *European Constitutionalism beyond the State* (Cambridge University Press, 2003), 103 and R. Dehousse, 'Beyond Representative Democracy: Constitutionalism in a Polycentric Polity', in J. Weiler and M. Wind (eds.), *European Constitutionalism beyond the State* (Cambridge University Press, 2003), 135.

[16] See in detail, in this Volume, Chapters 1 and 2 by J. van Zeben.

[17] D. Cole, 'Advantages of a Polycentric Approach to Climate Change Policy', *Nature Climate Change* 5 (2015), 114; E. Ostrom, 'Polycentric Systems for Coping with Collective Action and Global Environmental Change', *Global Environmental Change* 20 (2010), 550.

in February 2018 and written commentary until the final drafts. This reflective process added greatly to the analysis contained in this Volume and our collective thinking on polycentric theory in the EU. We are hopeful it also cemented opportunities for future collaborative efforts.

The authors in the first part of the Volume set out the theoretical foundations of polycentricity, and the extensions to the existing theory that its application to the EU requires. In the first two chapters, van Zeben positions polycentric theory with respect to other pluricentric theories and proposes an analytical framework through which the polycentricity of governance systems can be identified and assessed (Chapter 1). This general theoretical framework is then tailored to the specifics of the EU (Chapter 2). The remainder of the first part focuses on core concepts of EU integration and their relation to polycentricity: self-governance and *demos* in the EU (Cheneval, Chapter 3); the conceptualisation of the subsidiarity principle in polycentric theory and EU practice (van Zeben and Nicolaïdis, Chapter 4); and the impact of the internal market on polycentricity within the EU (van Zeben and Bobić, Chapter 5).

The second part of this Volume discusses the institutional essentials of polycentric governance and their prerequisites in turn. First, Bobić defines the overarching shared system of rules and considers its enforcement (Chapter 6); van den Brink focuses on the role of EU citizenship and its ability to secure self-governance through free entry and exit within the EU (Chapter 7). Relatedly, Goldner Lang considers the position of third-country nationals in the EU and their potential for self-governance (Chapter 8). Finally, Kukovec examines the possibilities for peaceful contestation of the rules and under the rules (Chapter 9). The three subsequent chapters relate back to the enforcement of the shared system of rules within the EU's polycentric system. Díez Sánchez considers the extent to which access to justice, particularly through the judicial system, is available under the shared system of rules (Chapter 10); and, Abazi and Garben conclude this part of the Volume by setting out the possibilities for access to information, and the ways in which collective and individual capacity to learn is facilitated and/or obstructed in the EU, respectively (Chapters 11 and 12).

This in-depth study of the polycentric features and potential of the EU sets the stage for an alternative model of European governance, which places self-governance at the centre. The concluding chapter will provide an overview of the limits of EU polycentricity, as discussed in the second part of the Volume. In addition, it provides some suggestions on how to best accommodate two intrinsic challenges of polycentric governance – complexity and the risk of fragmentation[18] – in order to improve the likelihood of polycentric success in the EU.

[18] For a more detailed discussion of these challenges in the EU context see, in this Volume, Chapter 2 (Section III) by J. van Zeben.

PART I

1

Polycentricity as a Theory of Governance

JOSEPHINE VAN ZEBEN

The study of polycentric systems lies at the heart of Vincent and Elinor (Lin) Ostrom's work on governance, which forms the foundation for the Bloomington School of Institutional Analysis. Polycentric governance theory supplied the theoretical and normative basis for empirically orientated Workshop tools, such as the Institutional Analysis and Development (IAD) and Social-ecological systems (SES) frameworks,[1] developed by the Ostrom Workshop.[2] In this Volume, polycentricity is used as the descriptive and normative theory by which to analyse governance in the EU. This chapter lays the groundwork for this analysis by mapping the development of polycentricity as a concept and as a theory of governance, and by defining several key concepts within polycentricity (Section I). It then proposes an analytical framework for the examination of the EU as a polycentric system by identifying the essential features of polycentric governance systems (Section II).

I Development of a Theory of Governance

In 1961, Vincent Ostrom, Charles Tiebout and Robert Warren co-authored an article on the organisation of large metropolitan areas in

[1] On the IAD framework, see notably E. Ostrom, 'Institutional Rational Choice: An Assessment of the Institutional Analysis and Development Framework', in P.A. Sabatier (ed.), *Theories of the Policy Process* (Westview Press, 1999); E. Ostrom, 'Background on the Institutional Analysis and Development Framework', *Policy Studies Journal* 39 (1) (2011), 7; M. D. McGinnis, 'An Introduction to IAD and the Language of the Ostrom Workshop: A Simple Guide to a Complex Framework', *Policy Studies Journal* 39 (1) (2011), 169; on the SES framework, see J. M. Anderies, M. A. Janssen, and E. Ostrom, 'A Framework to Analyse the Robustness of Social-Ecological Systems from an Institutional Perspective', *Ecology and Society* 9 (1) (2004), 18; E. Ostrom, 'A General Framework for Analysing Sustainability of Social-Ecological Systems', *Science* 325 (2009), 419; M. D. McGinnis and E. Ostrom, 'Social-Ecological System Framework: Initial Changes and Continuing Challenges', *Ecology and Society* 19 (2) (2014), 30;

[2] https://ostromworkshop.indiana.edu/

the United States.[3] At the time of writing, the multiplicity of political units – federal, state, county, municipal and semi-private – in metropolitan areas was considered highly problematic: a state of 'too many governments and too little government' giving rise to a 'duplication of functions' in 'overlapping jurisdictions'.[4] Put differently, too many cooks in the metropolitan kitchen were suspected of spoiling the public goods broth. However, Ostrom, Tiebout and Warren's article concluded that 'polycentric' governance is not inherently problematic; both polycentric and monocentric systems struggle to accommodate the 'multiplicity of interests in various public goods sought by people in a metropolitan region'.[5] Theoretically, there was no evidence that it would be easier for a central regulator to accommodate all these interests than for a polycentric regulator;[6] empirically, there was little research that could substantiate either claim.

In the 1960s and 1970s, the Ostroms set out an empirical research agenda to test the 'pathology' of US metropolitan areas. Studying several large metropolitan areas in the American Midwest, they found that monocentric systems are not necessarily better placed to deal with public goods provision in metropolitan areas than polycentric systems.[7] In fact, in terms of economic efficiency, polycentric systems often outperformed monocentric ones.[8] The functioning of polycentric systems has been subsequently tested through a multitude of other studies, including water management in the United States.[9] Most notably, Lin Ostrom

[3] V. Ostrom, C. Tiebout, and R. Warren, 'The Organization of Government in Metropolitan Areas: A Theoretical Inquiry'. *The American Political Science Review* 55 (1961), 831.

[4] ibid., at 831.

[5] ibid., at 838.

[6] ibid. ('It is doubtful that sub-optimization in gargantua is any easier to accomplish than supra-optimization in a polycentric political system.')

[7] E. Ostrom, 'Metropolitan Reform: Propositions Derived from Two Traditions' (1972) reprinted in M. D. McGinnis (ed.), *Polycentricity and Local Public Economies: Readings from the Workshop in Political Theory and Policy Analysis* (University of Michigan Press, 1999), 148.

[8] See in detail section I.A.

[9] V. Ostrom, *Water and Politics: A Study of Water Policies and Administration in the Development of Los Angeles* (Haynes Foundation, 1953); V. Ostrom, 'Political Economy of Water Development', *American Economic Review* 52 (2) (1962), 450; V. Ostrom, 'Water Economy and Its Organization', *Natural Resources Journal* 2 (1) (1962), 55; E. Ostrom, *Public entrepreneurship: A case study in ground water basin management* (Unpublished PhD manuscript, 1964, available at http://citeseerx.ist.psu.edu/viewdoc/download?doi=10 1.1.196.3254&rep=rep1& type=pdf; for a recent restatement of this work, see E. Ostrom, 'Beyond Markets and States: Polycentric Governance of Complex Economic Systems', *American Economic Review* 100 (2010), 641.

continued this research agenda into the study of common resource management, which cumulated in the governance rules set out in *Governing the Commons.*[10] Since then, empirical testing and theoretical development of polycentricity has primarily taken place in the context of natural resource management in the light of polycentricity's perceived suitability for the governance of environmental 'commons'.[11] These studies have led commons scholars to attribute a number of potential advantages to polycentric governance systems, including learning, trust, adaptation and the mitigation of risk.[12]

The importance of this empirical work cannot be overstated, and the findings of their studies have been well documented.[13] However, underlining the need for further testing of established hypotheses on the efficiency and effectiveness of fragmented governance systems was only one of the contributions of Ostrom, Tiebout and Warren's seminal article. They also provided the first conceptualisation of a 'polycentric' governance system,[14] on which Vincent Ostrom based his further work on polycentric governance theory. There are however important

10 E. Ostrom, *Governing the Commons: The Evolutions of Institutions for Collective Action* (Cambridge University Press, 1990).

11 For foundational work on the commons, see G. Hardin, 'The Tragedy of the Commons', *Science* 162 (1968), 1243 and H. Scott Gordon, 'The Economic Theory of a Common-Property Resource: The Fishery', *Journal of Political Economy* 62 (2) (1954), 124. More broadly, see E. Ostrom, R. Gardner, and J. Walker, *Rules, Games and Common-Pool Resources* (University of Michigan Press, 1994) and E. Ostrom, J. Burger, C. B. Field, R. B Norgaard, and D. Policansky, 'Revisiting the Commons: Local Lessons, Global Challenges', *Science* 284 (1999), 278; for a comprehensive overview of this literature on polycentricity, see also K. Carlisle and R. L. Gruby, 'Polycentric Systems of Governance: A Theoretical Model for the Commons', *Policy Studies Journal* (2017 -forthcoming)

12 G. R. Marshall, 'Polycentricity, Reciprocity and Farmer Adoption of Conservation Practices under Community-Based Governance', *Ecological Economics* 68 (2009), 1507 as cited in Carslisle and Gruby; see also Carlisle and Gruby (n. 11) 9–21.

13 See notably E. Ostrom, 'Polycentric Systems as One Approach for Solving Collective Action Problems', in M. A. Mohamed Salih (ed.), *Climate Change and Sustainable Development, New Challenges for Poverty Reduction* (Edward Elgar, 2009).

14 Governance is an ambiguous term which has been ascribed many different meanings in different disciplines. An excellent overview of these understandings and a useful typology is provided in O. Treib *et al.*, 'Modes of Governance: Towards a Conceptual Clarification', *Journal of European Public Policy* 14 (1) (2007), 1. On governance in the EU, see also C. Joerges *et al.* (eds.), *Mountain or Molehill? A Critical Appraisal of the Commission White Paper on Governance* (Robert Schuman Centre, European University Institute, 2001); C. Knill and A. Lenschow, 'Modes of regulation in the governance of the European Union: Towards a comprehensive evaluation' (2003) European Integration Online Papers 7, available at http://eiop.or.at/eiop/texte/2003-001a.htm. On the use of governance in international law, see M.-C. Smouts, 'The Proper Use of Governance in International Relations', *International Social Science Journal* 50 (1998), 81.

differences in the normative focus of the initial definition and Vincent's theory. More generally, there is ongoing terminological confusion regarding the term 'polycentricity'. The remainder of this Section will therefore carve out the analytical space that Ostrom's polycentric theory occupies by distinguishing it from other conceptions of polycentricity; discussing the aims of polycentric governance as perceived by Ostrom; and defining several constituent elements of polycentric governance, including self-governance.

A Polycentricity: Definitions and Aims

The term 'polycentricity' is not exclusive to Vincent Ostrom's work. In fact, the use of the term in Michael Polanyi's 1951 book *The Logic of Liberty* is often treated as its first mention.[15] Notably, Ostrom, Tiebout and Warren were not aware of Polanyi's use of the term until after the publication of *The Organization of Government in Metropolitan Areas: A Theoretical Inquiry*, and Ostrom does not directly engage with Polanyi's work until 1994.[16] Nevertheless, the two are almost always discussed in tandem, implying that Ostrom built his theory of polycentric governance on Polanyi's foundation.[17] Notwithstanding some common features – most importantly the presence of multiple centres of decision-making – Polanyi's polycentricity is almost entirely analytically distinct from Ostrom's. The assumption that Ostrom's theory of polycentric governance traces back to Polanyi confuses the descriptive and normative implications of these different concepts of polycentricity.

Descriptively, Ostrom, Tiebout and Warren's polycentric political systems occupy a different space from the polycentricity identified by Polanyi. In the words of Ostrom, Tiebout and Warren,

> Polycentric" connotes many centres of decision-making which are formally independent of each other. Whether they actually function

[15] M. Polanyi, *The Logic of Liberty* (University of Chicago Press, 1951).

[16] V. Ostrom, *The Meaning of American Federalism: Constituting a Self-Governing Society* (ICS Press, 1994), 225.

[17] See e.g. P. D. Aligica and V. Tarko, 'Polycentricity: From Polanyi to Ostrom, and Beyond', *Governance: An International Journal of Policy, Administration, and Institutions* 25 (2012), 237, 238; C. Skelcher, 'Jurisdictional Integrity, Polycentrism, and Democratic Governance', *Governance: An International Journal of Policy, Administration and Institutions* 18 (1) (2005), 89; K. Andersson and E. Ostrom 'Analyzing Decentralized Resource Regimes from a Polycentric Perspective', *Policy Sciences* 41 (1) (2008), 71; R. Oakerson and R. B. Parks, 'The Study of Local Public Economies: Multi-Organizational, Multi-Level Institutional Analysis and Development', *Policy Studies Journal* 39 (1) (2011), 147.

> independently, or instead constitute an interdependent system of relations, is an empirical question in particular cases. To the extent that they take each other into account in competitive relationships, enter into various contractual and cooperative undertakings or have recourse to central mechanisms to resolve conflicts, the various political jurisdictions in a metropolitan area may function in a coherent manner with consistent and predictable patterns of interacting behavior. To the extent that this is so, they may be said to function as a 'system'[18]

This definition shows the adoption of a society-wide, systematic approach, focusing on the provision of public goods within communities. In contrast, Polanyi's polycentricity occurs in 'professional organisation' within which people are motivated by professional duties, not membership of a broader society or community.[19] A key example of this is the legal system; Polanyi's characterises the law as a polycentric system, where justice is more likely achieved through a court-based system which can continuously update its beliefs and consider the specific conditions of each case, than by a central decision maker.[20] Polanyi does suggest that the sustainability of these groups depends on their value to society more broadly, but the provision of these benefits to society can only be incidental to the shared goal of the group, such as the pursuit of justice or truth.[21] However, Polanyi does not address the question as to whether society as a whole can be polycentric.[22]

18 Ostrom, Tiebout, Warren (n. 3) 831.

19 See M. Polanyi (n. 15) 194.

20 Polycentricity in this sense has been used as a strong argument in favour of the Common Law. See L. Fuller, *The Morality of Law* revised edn (Yale University Press, 1969); L. Fuller and K. Winston, 'The Forms and Limits of Adjudication', *Harvard Law Review* 92 (1978), 353; G. F. Gaus, *The Order of Public Reason: A Theory of Freedom and Morality in a Diverse and Bounded World* 1st paperback edn (Cambridge University Press, 2012); J. King, *Judging Social Rights* (Cambridge University Press, 2012). See also more generally, H. Petersen and H. Zahle, *Legal Polycentricity: Consequences of Pluralism in Law* (Avebury, 1995). For a recent application of this view in the area of labour law, see C. Kilpatrick, 'Has Polycentric Strike Law Arrived in the UK? After Laval, After Viking, After Demir?', *International Journal of Comparative Labour Law and Industrial Relations* 30 (2014), 293.

21 M. Polanyi (n. 15) 57.

22 M. Polanyi (n. 15) 115. ('all contacts with spiritual reality have a measure of coherence. A free people, among whom many are on the alert for calls on their consciences, will show a spontaneous coherence of this kind. They may feel that it all comes from being rooted in the same national tradition; but this tradition may well be merely a national variant of a universal human tradition. For a similar coherence will be found between different nations when each follows a national tradition of this type. They will form a community of free peoples. They may argue and quarrel, yet will always settle each new difficulty in the end, firmly rooted in the same transcendent ground.')

Polanyi's polycentricity may be summarised as a process of trial and error and continuous adjustment that are necessary to achieve ideals such as justice (polycentricity in law), beauty (polycentricity in the arts) and truth (polycentricity in science).[23] He stressed that the success of these systems depends on the freedom of its participants to make individual contributions and to structure their activities in the way that they consider best.[24] Despite this broad range of freedom, participants share a common goal that provides a focus for their individual efforts, which in turn provides a set of implicit and explicit (social) norms around which the community can self-organise. This raises a further definitional problem: for Polanyi, the question as to whether a system is polycentric was closely linked to its potential for 'spontaneous self-organisation'.[25]

Self-organisation is often equated with the normative focal point in Ostrom's theory of polycentricity: self-governance. In Ostrom's view, Polanyi's reference to spontaneity, as juxtaposed with 'deliberate' orders, implies an unintentional development.[26] Ostrom strongly disagreed with this reading of 'spontaneity', finding it implausible for democratic society – or polycentric systems of order – to emerge, modify or sustain itself 'spontaneously'.[27] Ostrom considered experimentation and 'spontaneity' – referred to as polycentric 'self-coordination' –[28] to be expressions of successful self-governance, rather than a confirmation of the intrinsic viability of democratic institutions in the absence of clear underlying rules.[29] In essence, polycentricity is the expression of a system's capacity for self-governance, which over time will give rise to a complex system of governance institutions.[30] By making explicit that Polanyi's

23 M. Polanyi (n. 15).

24 See also M. Polanyi (n. 15). ('[S]elf-coordination of independent initiatives leads to a joint result which is unpremeditated by any of those who bring it about. Their coordination is guided as by an "invisible hand" toward the joint discovery of a hidden system of things. Since its end-result is unknown, this kind of cooperation can only advance stepwise, and the total performance will be the best possible if each consecutive step is decided upon by the person most competent to do so . . . Any attempt to organize the group . . . under a single authority would eliminate their independent initiatives and thus reduce their joint effectiveness to that of the single person directing them from the centre. It would, in effect, paralyze their cooperation.')

25 V. Ostrom, *The Meaning of American Federalism* (n. 16) 226.

26 V. Ostrom, *The Meaning of American Federalism* (n. 16).

27 ibid.

28 ibid.

29 ibid.

30 With thanks to Michael McGinnis for capturing our discussion on this topic in one phrase.

claims regarding self-organisation were limited to small groups with shared goals, their beliefs may not have been as contradictory as suggested by Vincent's comments.

Clarifying the different conceptual spaces occupied by Ostrom and Polanyi allows us to distinguish between polycentricity as a dynamic process of experimentation aimed at achieving a common good (as per Polanyi) and polycentricity as a type of governance system that displays certain characteristics with the aim of achieving and maintaining self-governance, which in turn may result in the provision of certain common goods (as per Ostrom).

This characterisation of Ostrom's polycentricity jumps ahead by incorporating a normative focus on self-governance, which was absent from the descriptive definition provided in *The Organization of Government in Metropolitan Areas.* In their co-authored piece, Ostrom, Tiebout and Warren positioned metropolitan areas as public goods providers.[31] Consequently, the justification for choosing a centralised or decentralised polycentric form of government was based on the regulator's ability to capture externalities, increase efficiency and incorporate relevant preferences with respect to public good provision.[32] Their focus on economic efficiency is in line with the key tenets in public administration and public choice scholarship to which Ostrom, Tiebout and Warren were important contributors. It is however not the normative heart of Ostrom's later work on polycentric governance theory; rather, polycentric theory developed in part as a response to limitations that Vincent perceived to exist in public choice scholarship.[33]

Polycentricity's divergence from public choice theory, and specifically its focus on efficiency, reflects Ostrom's fundamentally different understanding of human motivation in the creation and maintenance of institutions.

31 EU integration has similarly been characterised as a 'collective' and/or 'club' good, see G. Majone, 'Rethinking European Integration after the Debt Crisis' (2012) UCL European Institute Working Papers 3.

32 Ostrom, Tiebout, Warren, (n. 3) 835–6. These economic evaluative criteria echo Tiebout's earlier work on local governments, which argues that free riding in local government can be prevented if local governments can tailor their service provision to voter preferences – provided a number of assumptions are met, for example, that voters are perfectly mobile and have full information – they can 'vote with their feet' implying a perfect overlap between preferences and provision, C. Tiebout, 'A Pure Theory of Local Expenditures', *Journal of Political Economy* 64 (5) (1956), 416.

33 V. Ostrom and E. Ostrom, 'Public Choice: A Different Approach to the Study of Public Administration', *Public Administration Review* 31 (2) (1971), 203; M. D. McGinnis and E. Ostrom, 'Reflections on Vincent Ostrom, Public Administration, and Polycentricity', *Public Administration Review* 72 (1) (2012), 15.

Vincent considered individuals to be intrinsically motivated to self-organise, provided that they were taught the skills needed to craft institutional arrangements. This motivation is multi-faceted and individual-specific, whereas the rationality assumption that underlies public choice models only captures one dimension of motivation.[34] Relatedly, Vincent found the benchmark of efficiency as externally imposed to have limited utility, since individuals or communities may decide to prioritise other goals.[35]

Self-governance is both the aim and defining characteristic of polycentric governance. Polycentricity is an expression of society's capacity to self-govern,[36] which over time will give rise to a complex system of governance institutions. Equally, Ostrom's constantly evolving polycentric systems can only be maintained through active participation by its self-governing constituents.[37] However, positioning self-governance as the normative aim of polycentricity poses its own challenges. Arguably not all types of self-governance are benign (e.g. criminal networks) and clearly the goals of different self-organised groups can be at odds with each other. The next subsection sets out Ostrom's thoughts on these issues and the relationship between his views on democracy and polycentric self-governance.

B Self-Governance in Polycentric Systems

Ostrom dedicated several books and hundreds of pages to detailing how we might conceptualise our thinking about society in a way that centres on human society self-governing, rather than relying on the state to rule or government to govern.[38] Much of his work was rooted in American

34 V. Ostrom, 'Some Developments in the Study of Market Choice, Public Choice, and Institutional Choice', in J. Rabin, W. Bartley Hildreth, and G. Miller (eds.), *Handbook of Public Administration* (Marcel Dekker, 1989), 861; V. Ostrom, *The Meaning of Democracy and the Vulnerability of Democracies: A Response to Tocqueville's Challenge* (University of Michigan Press, 1997), 96–9.

35 V. Ostrom, 'Tools for Decision-Making in Resource Planning', *Public Administration Review* 19 (2) (1959), 114; V. Ostrom, 'Epistemic Choice and Public Choice', *Public Choice* 77 (1) (1993), 163.

36 V. Ostrom, *The Meaning of American Federalism* (n. 16) 256. ('The character of a democratic society is revealed by the willingness of people to cope with problematic situations instead of presuming that someone else has the responsibility for them.')

37 ibid., 257. ('Self-governing societies depend upon achieving a capacity to reform themselves.')

38 See, inter alia, V. Ostrom, *The Meaning of American Federalism* (n. 16); V. Ostrom, *The Political Theory of a Compound Republic: Designing the American Experiment* 3rd edn (Lexington Books, 2007); V. Ostrom, *The Intellectual Crisis in Public Administration* (University of Alabama Press, 1973).

traditions of democracy and federalism. Given our ambition to use this work in order to describe and possibly improve European governance, we must explicate the assumptions that drive polycentric self-governance and the context in which they were developed; specifically, the relationship between democracy and self-governance, and the reliance of polycentricity on vertical and horizontal societal relationships.

C *Democracy and Self-Governance*

Ostrom's concept of self-governance is defined by his views on the role of the individual in a democratic society,[39] specifically the United States federal system. To Ostrom, federalism – understood as an expression of polycentric governance that limits the potential negatives of democracy – constitutes a breeding ground for democratic governance, allowing people to participate in several types of association. This may be contrasted with the assumption that democratic government naturally decentralises and becomes federal, or even polycentric.[40] Similarly, democratic rule based on the rule of law tends to provide constitutional guarantees that are needed to ensure self-governance.[41] Ultimately, however, to Ostrom democracy is contingent on polycentric governance (and thus self-governance), while democracy is not a prerequisite for polycentricity. The source of this causal relationship can be traced back to De Tocqueville's treatise on democracy in the United States of America,[42] which heavily influenced Ostrom's work. That said, democracy – as defined by Dahl, not in the US majoritarian sense[43] – appears to be the system of governance most able, and most likely, to espouse the polycentric institutional essentials and prerequisites.[44] It is hard to imagine a dictatorship allowing for peaceful contestation of the shared system of rules or provide meaningful access to justice. Ostrom's rejection of the automatic link between democracy and polycentricity may therefore

39 ibid.; see esp. V. Ostrom, *The Meaning of American Federalism* (n. 16) 226.

40 R. Wagner, 'Self-governance, Polycentrism, and Federalism: Recurring Themes in Vincent Ostrom's Scholarly Oeuvre', *Journal of Economic Behavior & Organization* 57 (2005), 173, 184.

41 V. Ostrom, *The Meaning of American Federalism* (n. 16) 47.

42 A. de Tocqueville, *Democracy in America* (Volume I, 1835; Volume II, 1840, H. Mansfield and D. Winthrop (trans. and eds.), University of Chicago Press, 2000).

43 R. Dahl, A Preface to Democratic Theory (1956), 9–10.

44 See Section II.B. See also P. D. Aligica and V. Tarko, 'Co-production, Polycentricity and Value Heterogeneity: The Ostrom's Public Choice Institutionalism Revisited', *American Political Science Review* 107 (4) (2013), 726, 736.

better be understood as a rejection of the causal relationship between the two, and a critique of US majoritarian politics.[45]

De Tocqueville attributed the success of American democracy to the rich variety of small societal units – townships, churches and other non-state centric forms of organisation – that preceded the federal United States and provided generations of social learning on self-governance.[46] In his view, 'overinvolved' government could undermine people's incentive to manage their own affairs and render them complacent.[47] Cognisant of the historic context of De Tocqueville's work, Ostrom's view on the role of the individual in democracy also relies heavily on responsibility, resilience, ownership,[48] and learning.[49] Despite this framing of self-governance in terms of its effects on society, Ostrom considered the individual to be the basic unit of analysis, relying heavily on methodological individualism.[50] Any collective unit of self-governance may be the subject of subsequent stages of analysis; it is the individual that creates these units through agency relationships with other individuals and therefore forms the basis.[51] However, in order for these individuals to constitute a self-governing

[45] With thanks to Ana Bobić for our critical and stimulating discussions on this topic.

[46] De Tocqueville (n. 42) Vol. I, 40 ('the township was organized before the county, the county before the state, the state before the nation').

[47] De Tocqueville as quoted in Ostrom, *The Meaning of American Federalism* (n. 16) 259. ('With reference to American democracy, my conclusion, then, is that democracy is at risk when "the government" is presumed to "govern". [..] The institutions of government were there to mediate and resolve conflicts and reach out to larger communities of relationships, but not to exercise command and control over all aspects of life.')

[48] Ownership in societal processes is typically created through citizenship – the strongest legal form of membership currently available. For an overview of the problems confronting EU citizenship specifically, see D. Kochenov, '*Ius Tractum* of Many Faces: European Citizenship and the Difficult Relationship between Status and Rights', *Columbia Journal of European Law* 15 (2) (2009), 169. See also, in this Volume, Chapter 7 by M. van den Brink.

[49] V. Ostrom, *The Meaning of American Federalism* (n. 16) 272. ('When the cares of thinking and the troubles of living are left to others, self-government is abandoned, democracy withers away, autocracy emerges, and people being preying upon one another in the name of liberty and equality. The future belongs to those whose covenants are bonds of mutual trust grounded in principles of self-governance and who learn to use processes of conflict and conflict resolution to elucidate information, clarify alternative, stimulate innovation, and extend the frontiers of inquiry to open new potentials for human development.')

[50] V. Ostrom, *The Meaning of American Federalism* (n. 16) 229. ('In a theory of polycentric orders I further assume that individuals are the basic units of analysis.') Lin Ostrom incorporated Vincent Ostrom's theory into her Institutional Analysis and Development (IAD) Framework. For an overview, combined with a discussion of the framework's legal strengths and weaknesses, see D. H. Cole, 'Formal Institutions and the IAD framework: bringing the law back in' (2014) Indiana University Ostrom Workshop, Maurer School of Law, SPEA, Research Paper Number 297.

[51] V. Ostrom, *The Meaning of American Federalism* (n. 16) 227.

society, sustained interaction is needed. It is therefore analytically challenging to conceive of a polycentric society or system as being composed of singular individuals; this is why many consider the groups formed by individuals in order to address certain issues (regardless of their form, rules or aims) the building blocks, and relevant unit of analysis, of complex polycentric governance systems.[52]

Self-governance can thus be considered a selfish *and* selfless exercise where people are trained and incentivized to contribute to the societal groups they belong to; individuals come together 'to seek their own gain, with the knowledge that gain comes through a long-term commitment with other self-interested citizens'.[53] In this state of 'enlightened' self-interest, one's own position is intrinsically linked to that of others in the same group(s) and/or society, which implies a certain level of permanence in terms of group boundary and composition while these common goals are being pursued. At the same time, the dynamic nature of Ostrom's concept of self-governance entails an inherent measure of change, also to social groups and alliances.

What is conspicuously absent from this discussion is clear guidance on what it means to 'govern' oneself. Ostrom refers to the capacity of individuals to 'formulate mutually agreed upon rules that they themselves proceed to enforce'.[54] This definition is echoed in Lin Ostrom's later work on community-based management of common pool resources: self-governance means that the resource users are the ones who define the rules by which the resource is managed.[55] As supported by

[52] This is also recognised by V. Ostrom, see e.g. V. Ostrom, *The Meaning of American Federalism* (n. 16) 229. ('Individuals will occupy positions where decisions are taken on behalf of the interests of others in the exercise of agency and trust relationships. Business firms, units of government, agencies of government, legislative bodies, political parties, courts and nation-states may also be used as units of analysis having to do with relationships at incremental levels of analysis. Societies then become richly nested assemblages of associations that include the diverse forms of association developed within and among units of government. Diverse autonomous units can then be subject to analysis in relation to specifiable rules of association.')

[53] R. Herzberg, 'Commentary on Richard Wagner's "Self-Governance, Polycentrism, and Federalism: Recurring Themes in Vincent Ostrom's Scholarly Oeuvre"', *Journal of Economic Behavior & Organization* 57 (2005), 189, 190.

[54] V. Ostrom, *The Meaning of American Federalism* (n. 16) 226.

[55] S. Colin-Castilo and R. T. Woodward, 'Measuring the Potential for Self-Governance: An Approach for the Community-Based Management of the Common-Pool Resources', *International Journal of the Commons* 9 (1) (2015), 281, 282. Both Elinor and Vincent Ostrom reference Douglas North's work on institutions and his view on 'the rules of the game'. See D. North, *Institutions, Institutional Change, And Economic Performance* (Cambridge University Press, 1990) 3. ('[T]he rules of the game in a society or, more

Ostrom's views on the relationship between polycentricity, democracy and federalism, the specific form that self-governance takes is immaterial; it should be up to the self-governing individuals, rather than a 'higher' authority, to determine the rules, and goals, of their game. The implications of this represent another important departure from the public choice scholarship where Ostrom started his theory, as the individuals and communities involved in polycentric systems are presumed to set their own goals, which may lead to the sacrifice of efficiency for the pursuit of other goals, such as sustainability or equity.[56] This means that efficiency may be a valid external benchmark for polycentric systems' performance, but it is not the benchmark by which to assess whether or not a system *is* polycentric. This in turn begs the question whether there are goals set by polycentric systems that can be considered 'invalid' or 'malignant'. In order to answer this question, closer attention must be paid to another fundamental element of polycentric theory: the relationship between individuals and government, and the relationship between individuals.

D Vertical and Horizontal Relationships in Polycentric Systems

Polycentric systems could be conceptualised as a set of 'games' where each actor is playing multiple games simultaneously and sequentially.[57] In complex polycentric systems, there may be multiple games, taking place at several levels: a certain amount of overlap between the decision-making units is inherent to the system.[58] It would be naïve to disregard the role of the state – and the vertical relationship between individuals and the state – in such games. Ostrom's focus on the individual and her capacity for self-governance should therefore not be understood as hostile towards, or incompatible with, governmental action. In fact, public officials are considered potential allies and teachers in the process of self-governance by supporting communities to identify and solve common problems.[59] Similarly, 'politics [are] the practical process

formally the humanly devised constraints that shape human interaction.') For a more general discussion of conceptualisations of 'institutions', see D. Cole, 'The Varieties of Comparative Institutional Analysis', *Wisconsin Law Review* 2 (2013), 101.

56 See also M. D. McGinnis and E. Ostrom (n. 33) 20–1.

57 See V. Ostrom, *The Meaning of American Federalism* (n. 16) 228.

58 See V. Ostrom, C. Tiebout, and R. Warren (n. 3).

59 M. McGinnis and E. Ostrom (n. 33) 21.

through which communities act to identify and solve their common problems, and to realize shared opportunities.'[60]

The presence of governmental power also facilitates the establishment, and enforcement, of an overarching shared system of rules. Such a system of overarching rules is needed to ensure that the constructive conflict needed to sustain self-governance does not deteriorate into a state of destructive conflict, such as war.[61] Ostrom supported the idea that the law must be effectively enforced – and that both individuals and officials are subject to the rule of law – and that law cannot be self-generating, self-determining or self-enforcing.[62] This means that some measure of inequality in power is necessary for the operation of legal constraints. However, this inequality should be limited in order to prevent dominance.[63] In sum, vertical relationships can support the maintenance of a polycentric system insofar as they do not result in dominance or the concentration of power in one decision-making centre.[64] For a system to achieve and maintain full polycentricity, both horizontal and vertical relations need to become polycentric. This means that there can be no 'monopoly of authority relationships' within the 'whole system of human affairs, public and private'.[65]

In *The Meaning of American Federalism*, Ostrom discussed patterns of polycentricity in competitive market economies, public economies, scientific inquiry, the legal system, systems of governance with separation of powers and checks and balances, and international relations.[66] Taking the market as an example, Ostrom considers entrepreneurs vital for both public and private enterprise. The cross-fertilisation between public and private institutions relates closely to Ostrom's view of the market as a 'complex institutional arrangement'.[67] Competition within markets is

[60] ibid.

[61] Constructive conflict can bring benefits such as learning – as discussed by Garben in this Volume – and already highlighted in the context of natural resource management by T. Dietz, E. Ostrom, and P. C. Stern, 'The Struggle to Govern the Commons', *Science* 232 (2003), 1907.

[62] V. Ostrom, 'Polycentricity' (Part 1) (1972) reprinted in M. D. McGinnis (ed.), *Polycentricity and Local Public Economies: Readings from the Workshop in Political Theory and Policy Analysis* (University of Michigan Press, 1999), 55.

[63] ibid., at 46 and 50. Ostrom also considered this powersharing the mark of a democracy; envisaging a constant process of power distribution and sharing based on constitutional norms.

[64] See in more detail, Chapter 3 by F. Cheneval in this Volume.

[65] See V. Ostrom, *The Meaning of American Federalism* (n. 16) 136.

[66] ibid., at 228 onwards.

[67] M. D. McGinnis and E. Ostrom (n. 33) 20.

crucial to ensure its polycentricity, as is voluntary cooperation between buyers and sellers. If a market functions in equilibrium, benefits such as public information regarding goods and services will emerge.[68] If dominance is allowed to occur, for instance through a monopoly, these benefits will be reduced and/or costs may be imposed on individuals. In this situation, a governmental body can interfere by legally enforcing the shared system of rules. Ensuring a balanced market thus depends on the horizontal relationships between market actors, and on the vertical relationship between market actors and the state which ensures appropriate limits (agreed upon in turn by the market actors through their agency relationship with the state).

II Polycentric Governance: Attributes, Institutional Essentials, and Prerequisites

Ostrom, Tiebout and Warren's initial definition clearly identifies several core characteristics of polycentric systems. However, many of these characteristics – multiple centres of decision making, competitive and cooperative relationships – could also be used to describe other pluricentric systems.[69] A complete framework of polycentric analysis must therefore include those features that distinguish polycentric systems from federal, multilevel or otherwise pluricentric systems.[70] The analytical framework used in this Volume does so by developing polycentric characteristics that allow for continued self-governance.

The building blocks of our analytical system are *attributes* – necessary but non-exclusive features of polycentric systems;[71] *institutional essentials* – the conditions that ensure the continued existence of 'self-generating' polycentricity by ensuring that 'individuals acting at all levels will have the incentives to create or institute appropriate patterns of ordered relationships'.[72] Put differently, institutional essentials ensure

[68] V. Ostrom, *The Meaning of American Federalism* (n. 16) 229–30.

[69] Aligica and Tarko were among the firsts to present a categorisation of polycentric systems through the definition of 'necessary conditions' as those found in all polycentric systems, and 'non-necessary conditions' as variations in polycentric governance, see P. D. Aligica and V. Tarko (n. 17). For a recent alternative structure, see K. Carlisle and R. L. Gruby (n. 11).

[70] For an in-depth comparison with main types of EU pluricentric governance theories see, in this Volume, Chapter 2.I by J. van Zeben.

[71] The term 'attributes' is inspired by Aligica and Tarko, who use it to describe the basic features of a concept under consideration. See P. D. Aligica and V. Tarko (n. 17).

[72] V. Ostrom, 'Polycentricity' (n. 62) 60.

that the system supports and maintains self-governance. These institutional essentials are in turn facilitated by three *prerequisites*: access to information, capacity to learn and access to justice. To speak of a successful polycentric system, all these elements must be in place; if not, it is likely that a polycentric system will revert to a different form of pluricentric governance such as federalism.[73]

A Attributes

Every polycentric system displays three attributes. *First* and foremost, polycentricity requires the existence of many centres of decision making which are formally independent of each other. As already highlighted by Ostrom, Tiebout and Warren's definition in *The Organization of Government in Metropolitan Areas*, the actual independence of these centres is an empirical question which can only be answered on a case by case basis, for instance by assessing de facto or *de jure* autonomy of the centres.[74] While the constellation of these centres is expected to change over time, some measure of permanence in their interactions is required in order for them to function as a 'system'.[75]

Ostrom's theory of polycentric governance also acted as the basis for some of the empirical tools developed in the Ostrom Workshop. There is a cross-fertilization between these empirical methods and polycentric theory, which allows us to further specify the types of decision centres that help constitute a polycentric system. Specifically, the Institutional Analysis and Development (IAD) framework shows that polycentric systems tend to incorporate centres that are *multilevel* (local, provincial, regional, national, global); *multipurpose* (general, issue-specific, and/or cross-jurisdictional); *multisectoral* (public, private, voluntary, hybrid);

[73] See M. D. McGinnis and M. Hanisch, 'Analyzing Problems of Polycentric Governance in the Growing EU' (2005) Paper presented at the Transcoop Workshop on Problems of Polycentric Governance in the Growing EU, Humboldt University Berlin (on file with the author), 22. ('As each system moves away from the polycentric balance, the relevant communities no longer enjoy the benefits of resilience, redundancy, access to local knowledge, adaptability, flexibility, experimentation, accountability, or efficiency in terms of responding to diverse citizens preference.')

[74] See e.g. G. Marshall, 'Polycentricity and Adaptive Governance' (2015) Paper presented to the panel 'The new polycentricity? Conceptual basis and operationalisation for the study of the commons' convened during the 15th Biennial Global Conference of the International Association for the Study of the Commons, Edmonton, Canada, 25–29 May 2015.

[75] V. Ostrom, C. Tiebout, and R. Warren (n. 3) 831.

and *multifunctional* (containing specialised units for, inter alia, the provision, production and financing of goods).[76] This is not to say that there will not be a multitude of single-level and single-purpose units in polycentric systems; rather, a polycentric system will have to be able to deal with policy problems that span multiple levels, sectors and actors, which is most identifiably done through units that incorporate some of this complexity. Crucially, polycentric systems will display overlap between all these units. As phrased by McGinnis and Ostrom:

> Polycentric governance requires a complex combination of multiple levels and diverse types of organizations drawn from the public, private, and voluntary sectors that have overlapping realms of responsibility and functional capacities [...] In addition, private corporations, voluntary associations, and community-based organizations play critical supporting roles in a polycentric system of governance, even if they have not been assigned public roles in an official manner.[77]

A *second* attribute is the presence of continued competition, cooperation and conflict resolution between the centres of decision making. The centrality of competition can be explained by Ostrom, Tiebout and Warren's initial focus on public goods provision in metropolitan areas. Ostrom's later work continues to view a competitive market as central to a polycentric approach to human affairs but recognises that within markets, and in other aspects of society, the focus is on cooperation rather than competition.

In order for both these processes to run successfully, the *third* attribute must be present: an overarching shared system of rules. This system of rules allows for conflict resolution as part of a broader process of continuous readjustment,[78] as it reflects a shared understanding of the core set of values and state of the world, both present and future.[79] Ostrom emphasises the importance of the ability to make 'mutual adjustments for ordering [individuals'] relationships with one another within a general

[76] M. D. McGinnis, 'An Introduction to IAD and the Language of the Ostrom Workshop: A Simple Guide to a Complex Framework', *Political Studies Journal* 39 (2011), 169.
[77] M. D. McGinnis and E. Ostrom (n. 33) 15.
[78] See V. Ostrom, *The Meaning of American Federalism* (n. 16) 231. ('Appropriate constraining institutions are therefore necessary to the maintenance of competitive market conditions.') See also P. D. Aligica and V. Tarko (n. 17) 250. ('It is important to hold in mind that polycentricity involves the existence of multiple centers of decision making *within an accepted set of rules.*' Emphasis in original.)
[79] See T. Dietz, E. Ostrom, and P. C. Stern (n. 61).

system of rules where each element acts with independence of other elements.'[80]

As these attributes are not exclusive to polycentric systems, they must be combined with polycentric institutional essentials and prerequisites aimed at safeguarding continued self-governance, so as to prevent the system from converting into another form of governance.

B *Institutional Essentials*

Ostrom identifies three institutional essentials for polycentric governance. The *first* essential presumes the availability of a range of viable options of self-governance, through reference to 'the conditions for entry and exit in a particular polycentric ordering'.[81] Individuals must be able to freely enter and exit centres of decision making so they can continuously form new relationships. If not, exit from one centre could be the end of the attempt to self-organise around a particular issue; individuals must be able to continue to pursue their shared aspirations through an alternative forum once they decided to exit a given jurisdiction or decision-making unit. Entry and exit may mean a shift to another jurisdiction but could also be done by shifting alliances to another group within the same jurisdiction.

The *second* institutional essential is the enforcement of the overarching shared system of rules. Ostrom considered the shared system of rules as the 'legal framework' of the polycentric system.[82] Their enforcement is a crucial incentive in ensuring individuals act in a polycentricity-reinforcing way. *Finally*, peaceful contestation and revision of the general rules of conduct is needed to encourage individuals to actively engage with governance.[83]

These three institutional essentials can take many different shapes and forms. For example, peaceful contestation could be achieved through an independent and impartial court system. But informal mechanisms for contestation and conflict resolution may prove equally (or, more) important.[84] Similarly, the overarching shared system of rules can be written down in a constitution or be encapsulated in social norms.[85]

[80] V. Ostrom, 'Polycentricity' (n. 62) 57.
[81] ibid., at 59.
[82] ibid., at 60.
[83] ibid., at 63.
[84] M. D. McGinnis and M. Hanisch (n. 73) 22.
[85] See e.g. the United Kingdom where the absence of a written constitution does not signify the absence of an agreed upon overarching body of rules. See e.g. J. Jowell, 'The Rule of

The effectiveness and sustainability of each of these essentials depends heavily on individuals' awareness of, and engagement with, these processes, which brings us to the role of prerequisites.

C *Prerequisites*

Ostrom underscored the importance of *access to information* and the *ability to learn* in achieving a self-governing society.[86] The reasoning here may seem self-evident: people must be aware of, and understand, the shared rules and their consequences in order to revise and enforce them. Learning and access to information are also necessary for individuals to choose properly between alternatives related to their freedom of entry and exit.[87] Moreover, learning allows for 'updating' of relationships in repeated interaction.[88] Finally, *substantive and formal access to justice* is needed in order to ensure peaceful contestation. However, it is important to note that once a polycentric system is in equilibrium, it also ensures better opportunities for learning, and access to information and justice. For example, one can learn from regulatory experimentation and choose those forms of governance that work best.[89]

**

Attributes, institutional essentials and prerequisites are interrelated and are best defined in that way. By means of illustration: in a polycentric order, independent centers of decision making are able to cooperate, compete and resolve conflicts as part of a broader process of continuous readjustment under a generally accepted body of overarching rules.[90] The *attribute* of continuous cooperation, competition and conflict resolution needs peaceful contestation and the enforcement of a shared system of rules (both *institutional essentials*) in order to be maintained. In turn, access to information, the capacity to learn and access to justice

Law', in J. Jowell *et al.* (eds.), *The Changing Constitution* 8th edn (Oxford University Press, 2015), 13.

86 V. Ostrom, 'Polycentricity' (n. 62) 60. See also, in this Volume, Chapter 11 by V. Abazi and Chapter 12 by S. Garben.

87 See also M. D. McGinnis, 'Costs and Challenges of Polycentric Governance' (2005) Paper presented at Workshop on Analyzing Problems of Polycentric Governance in the Growing EU, Humboldt University, Berlin (available at http://citeseerx.ist.psu.edu/viewdoc/download?doi=10.1.1.529.2214&rep=rep1&type=pdf), 17 (on the role of transparency regarding access to information).

88 See also C. Lindblom, *Intelligence of Democracy* (Free Press, 1965).

89 See also S. Garben's discussion of laboratory federalism in Chapter 12 of this Volume.

90 V. Ostrom, 'Polycentricity' (n. 62) 57.

are all *prerequisites* for these two institutional essentials to function, and to prevent the reversal of a polycentric system to another type of pluricentric system.

Each polycentric system will find different ways to incorporate these features, and its success in doing so will determine its ability to accommodate self-governance. This framework is aimed at providing tools that allow us to analyse a system's polycentric ability and potential, including the European Union's.

Table 1.1 *Attributes, Institutional Essentials, and Prerequisites of Polycentric Systems*

Attributes	(i)	Multiple independent centres of decision making
	(ii)	Continuous competition, cooperation and conflict resolution
	(iii)	Overarching shared system of rules
Institutional Essentials	(i)	Freedom and ability to enter and exit
	(ii)	Enforcement of shared system of rules
	(iii)	Peaceful contestation among different (interest) groups
Prerequisites	(i)	Access to information
	(ii)	Capacity to learn
	(iii)	Access to justice

2

Polycentric Features of the European Union

JOSEPHINE VAN ZEBEN

The premise underlying this Volume is that polycentricity provides a descriptive theory of governance for the European Union, as well as a desirable aim for its development. Neither of these claims is without controversy; there are many theories of EU governance and an equal number of divergent views on its preferred future. To meaningfully add to an already rich landscape of EU research, we must first situate polycentricity among existing theories of EU governance and explicate its added value (Section I). By identifying existing polycentric attributes of the EU (Section II) and discussing the potential pitfalls of a fully polycentric EU (Section III), this chapter provides a broad stroke assessment of polycentricity in the EU. This facilitates more detailed analysis of separate polycentric features in the remainder of the Volume, so as to improve our understanding of how, and whether, to unlock the EU's polycentric potential.

I Polycentricity as Distinct Theory of EU Governance

This Volume focuses on formal European institutional arrangements and the extent to which they incorporate the features of a polycentric system.[1] Our focus on legal rules and relationships helps us position our polycentric theory of EU governance within the vast body of European governance scholarship spanning, among others, the work of lawyers, political scientists, and economists.[2] By presenting polycentricity as

[1] It does so to the exclusion of informal methods of organisation. This restriction of scope is necessary to ensure the feasibility of this project but limits its ability to provide a full survey of EU rules and relationships.

[2] Some of the theories that are excluded from our analysis include: network theory (see e.g. G. Peters and J. Pierre (eds.), *Handbook of Public Administration* (Sage, 2003); B Peters, 'Managing Horizontal Government: The Politics of Co-ordination', *Public Administration* 76 (1998), 295; for the relationship between network theory and polycentricity see M. D. McGinnis and E. Ostrom, 'Reflections on Vincent Ostrom, Public Administration, and Polycentricity', *Public Administration Review* (2012), 15); *demoicracy*

a theory of governance through the lens of formal (legally defined) relationships, we place it in the analytical space currently occupied by inter alia theories of federalism,[3] multilevel governance,[4] constitutional pluralism,[5] and multilevel constitutionalism.[6]

The added value of our polycentric approach depends on its distinctiveness ('Does the theory present an original position?'), which in turns must be supported by its descriptive ('How well does a theory describe reality?') and normative ('Does the theory present an attractive picture of

(included through the work of F. Cheneval, Chapter 3, and van Zeben and Nicolaïdis, Chapter 4 in this Volume); as well as executive federalism, differentiated integration and political union light, all discussed in detail in M. Dawson and F. De Witte, 'Self-Determination in the Constitutional Future of the EU', *European Law Journal* 21 (3) (2015), 371.

3 On the role of federalism in the EU, see M. Wind, 'The European Union as a Polycentric Polity: Returning to a Neo-medieval Europe?', in J. H. H. Weiler and M. Wind (eds.), *European Constitutionalism beyond the State* (Cambridge University Press, 2003), 103 (including a historic analysis).

4 For a recent restatement of multilevel governance theory, see L. Hooghe and G. Marks, 'Types of Multi-level Governance', in H. Enderlein, S. Wälti, and M. Zürn (eds.), *Handbook on Multi-level Governance* (Edward Elgar, 2010), 17. See also G. Marks, L. Hooghe, and K. Blank, 'European Integration from the 1980s: State-Centric v. Multi-level Governance', *Journal of Common Market Studies* 34 (1996), 341; G. Marks and L. Hooghe, 'Unraveling the Central State, but How? Types of Multi-level Governance', *American Political Science Review* (2003), 233.

5 For foundational texts on constitutional pluralism, see N. MacCormick, 'The Maastricht Urteil: Sovereignty Now', *European Law Journal* 1 (1995), 259; N. MacCormick, *Questioning Sovereignty: Law, State and Nation in the European Commonwealth* (Oxford University Press, 1999); N. Walker, 'The Idea of Constitutional Pluralism', *Modern Law Review* 65 (2002), 317; M Maduro, 'Contrapunctual Law: Europe's Constitutional Pluralism in Action', in N. Walker (ed.), *Sovereignty in Transition* (Hart Publishing, 2003), 502; N. Walker, 'Postnational Constitutionalism and the Problem of Translation', in J. H. H. Weiler and M. Wind (eds.), *European Constitutionalism beyond the State* (Cambridge University Press, 2003); N. Barber, 'Legal Pluralism and the European Union', *European Law Journal* 12 (3) (2006), 306; M. Maduro, 'Interpreting European Law: Judicial Adjudication in a Context of Constitutional Pluralism', *European Journal of Legal Studies* 1 (2) (2007), 1; M. Kumm, 'The Cosmopolitan Turn in Constitutionalism: On the Relationship between Constitutionalism in and beyond the State', in J. L. Dunoff and J. P. Trachtman (eds.), *Ruling the World? Constitutionalism, International Law and Global Governance* (Cambridge University Press, 2009) 258; N. Krisch, *Beyond Constitutionalism – The Pluralist Structure of Postnational Law* (Oxford University Press, 2010); M. Avbelj and J. Komárek (eds.), *Constitutional Pluralism in the European Union and Beyond* (Hart Publishing, 2012).

6 I. Pernice, 'Multilevel Constitutionalism and the Crisis of Democracy in Europe' *European Constitutional Law Review* 11 (2015), 541; G. della Cananea, 'Is European Constitutionalism Really "Multilevel"?', *ZaöRV* 70 (2010), 283; N. Walker, 'Multilevel Constitutionalism: Looking beyond the German Debate' (2009) LEQS Paper No. 08/2009 (summarising developments in this area).

the future of the EU?') qualities.[7] Polycentricity's distinctiveness as a descriptive theory for EU governance is twofold: first, its analytical structure captures insights of four other important theories of EU governance discussed below. In doing so, it presents a more complete picture of the practice of EU governance. Second, by embracing the dynamic nature of governance and its complexity, polycentricity can better accommodate the ever-evolving nature of the EU system. The second challenge for polycentricity is to provide an appealing normative alternative to existing theories. Its vehicle for doing so is the prioritisation of self-governance as an aim for institutional design. This is both the most promising and most challenging feature of polycentricity as EU theory of governance, as will be discussed in detail below.

A *Polycentricity's Descriptive Distinctiveness*

At first glance, polycentricity's ability to describe the reality of EU governance appears limited by the fact that Vincent Ostrom developed his polycentric theory with almost exclusive reference to the United States and its federal structure.[8] Federalism has been forcefully rejected as a model for European integration – as normative political theory and as a model of governance –[9] although this may be changing as the institutional development of the EU brings it functionally closer to a federation.[10] Nevertheless, the EU continues to differ from the United

[7] On descriptive, normative and distinctive claims, see N. Walker, 'Multilevel Constitutionalism' (n. 6).

[8] P. D. Aligica and V. Tarko, 'Polycentricity: From Polanyi to Ostrom, and Beyond', *Governance: An International Journal of Policy, Administration, and Institutions* 25 (2012), 237, 245. See also V. Ostrom, *The Meaning of American Federalism: Constituting a Self-governing Society* (ICS Press, 1994) 239. ('[D]esigning the American constitution could be viewed as an experiment in polycentricity while federalism could be seen as one way to capture the meaning and to operationalise one aspect of this type of order.') There are, of course, important differences between federal systems. For the distinction between 'highly federalised' systems and 'unitary forms' of federalism drawn by Ostrom see V. Ostrom, *The Intellectual Crisis in Public Administration* (University of Alabama Press, 1973), 22.

[9] Failed attempts to transform the EU into a federal polity (through the Constitution for Europe) may be argued to reduce the descriptive value of federalism as a theory of EU governance. See e.g. V. Giscard D'Estaing, 'The Convention and the Future of Europe: Issues and Goals', *International Journal of Constitutional Law* 1 (2003), 346; A. Borriello and A. Crespy, 'How to Not Speak the F-word: Federalism between Mirage and Imperative in the Euro Crisis', *European Journal of Political Research* 54 (2015), 502.

[10] Particularly the development of EU citizenship rights as well as the development of the Charter of Fundamental Rights and the position adopted by the Court of Justice have

States in important ways: its conception of 'government' and 'governance', and its accommodation of multiple jurisdictions, even in its perception of democracy,[11] to name a few. In essence, polycentricity implies the diffusion of sovereignty over several levels of governance and numerous institutions;[12] a feature it shares with federal systems, and which increases the analytical overlap between federalism and polycentricity. Ultimately, however, polycentricity and federalism are not identical, nor interchangeable. Rather, federalism can be accommodated within polycentric governance, the latter being a broader concept.

As compared to federalism, polycentricity allows for an additional dimension of crosscutting, overlapping 'issue-specific' jurisdictions and envisages an explicit role for non-governmental bodies, such as private and community-based organisations.[13] This role is particularly important in the light of the EU's *sui generis* approach to governance and government, which allows for private actors to shape and enforce rules and incorporate new forms of governance.[14] Polycentricity's explicit

added to this move closer to federalism. See e.g. D. Kochenov (ed.), *EU Citizenship and Federalism: The Role of Rights* (Cambridge University Press, 2017). On the role of the court, see L. F. M. Besselink, 'The ECJ as the European "Supreme Court": Setting Aside Citizens' Rights for EU Law Supremacy', Blog Post, available at https://verfassungsblog.de/ecj-european-supreme-court-setting-aside-citizens-rights-eu-law-supremacy accessed in June 2018. See also K. Lenaerts, 'The ECHR and the CJEU: Creating Synergies in the Field of Fundamental Rights Protection', Speech delivered at the European Court of Human Rights, Solemn hearing for the opening of the Judicial Year 26 January 2018, available at https://www.echr.coe.int/Documents/Speech_20180126_Lenaerts_JY_ENG.pdf accessed June 2018, 2.

11 Particularly as Ostrom's work was inspired by the Federalists and De Tocqueville's work on nineteenth century United States. See V. Ostrom, *The Meaning of American Federalism: Constituting a Self-governing Society* (ICS Press, 1994).

12 Initially, Ostrom treats American federalism and polycentricity as practically interchangeable, as they both allowed for a high level of diversity in levels of government provision. See also R. Herzberg, 'Commentary on Richard Wagner's "Self-Governance, Polycentrism, and Federalism: Recurring Themes in Vincent Ostrom's Scholarly Oeuvre"', *Journal of Economic Behaviour & Organization* 57 (2005), 189, 193. Another shared characteristic is the contestation of government authority: National action can be questioned at the state level, and state action at the federal level, ibid., at 194.

13 M. D. McGinnis and E. Ostrom (n. 2) 15.

14 On governance, see European Commission, '*European Governance: A White Paper*', 25 July 2001, Brussels, COM(2001), 428, 6 ('rules, processes and behaviour that affect the way in which powers are exercised at European level, particularly as regards openness, participation, accountability, effectiveness and coherence'). The distinction between government and governance within the European Union has given rise to its own scholarship, which goes beyond the scope of our current discussion. On governance as a method of regulation, see e.g. Special issue of the *European Law Journal* (*European Law Journal* 8 (1) (2002). More generally, see R. Eising and B. Kohler-Koch (eds.),

focus on self-governance and the incorporation of horizontal relationships within the rule-ordered interactions that make up society allows polycentricity to successfully incorporate non-governmental elements of EU governance. It also distinguishes polycentricity further from federalism, which is focused on vertical transfers of sovereignty, to the exclusion of horizontal relationships.

Multilevel governance theory (MLG), as initially developed by Marks and Hooghe, comes closest to polycentric theory in its conceptualisation of 'governance'; it also involved the sharing of powers between supranational and subnational territorial layers of public *and* private actors.[15] The development of MLG theory has been fundamental to the study of the European Union and many of the insights of this body of scholarship can be used to strengthen polycentric inquiries. MLG theory divides systems in two types:[16] Type I MLG systems strongly resemble classic federal systems, whereas Type II MLG systems are issue-specific special purpose jurisdictions that may cross pre-existing territorial boundaries – for example, an agency that is tasked with cross-border water management. While these two types could exist independently, it is clear that, as polycentric systems, MLG systems are expected to encompass both vertical and horizontal/diagonal partitions.[17]

Multilevel governance theory deals with conflict resolution; MLG theory considers Type I jurisdictions best suited for deliberation about basic value choices in society, while Type II jurisdictions are best suited for problem solving.[18] With respect to the latter, there exists the assumption that 'externalities among jurisdictions are sufficiently limited to sustain compartmentalised decision making'.[19] This assumption is

The Transformation of Governance in the European Union (Routledge, 1999). See also S. Finer, *Comparative Government* (Penguin, 1970) as quoted in ibid (describing governance and government rather as two poles on a continuum of different governing types). See extensively A. Jordan *et al.*, 'The Rise of "New" Policy Instruments in Comparative Perspective: Has Governance Eclipsed Government?', *Political Studies* 53 (2005), 477.

15 G. Marks, 'Structural Policy and Multilevel Governance in the EC: The State of the European Community', in A. Cafruny and G. Rosenthal (eds.), *The State of the European Community: The Maastricht Debate and Beyond* (Boulder, 1993), 392.

16 L. Hooghe and G. Marks, 'Types of Multi-level Governance', in H. Enderlein, S. Wälti, and M. Zürn (eds.), *Handbook on Multi-level Governance* (Edward Elgar, 2010), 17.

17 M. D. McGinnis and M. Hanisch, 'Analysing Problems of Polycentric Governance in the Growing EU' (2005) Paper presented at the Transcoop Workshop on Problems of Polycentric Governance in the Growing EU Humboldt University Berlin (on file with the author), 24.

18 L. Hooghe and G. Marks (n. 16) 28.

19 ibid.

unlikely to hold in the EU context, and means that MLG would find it hard to fully incorporate the dynamic complexity of EU governance when there is an interweaving of issues, which creates different allies and adversaries at different points in time. Polycentricity embraces this time of complexity and thus provides additional tools to analyse these types of processes. The absence of further normative underpinning in MLG theory moreover fails to provide a conflict resolution mechanism for conflicts that are not contained within a Type I or II jurisdiction. The fact that MLG scholarship is primarily descriptive more broadly reduces its ability to provide guidance on improvement of the system to accommodate more self-governance (or other normative aim).[20]

Constitutional pluralism provides another much criticised, but ultimately very influential, view of the EU.[21] Like polycentricity, constitutional pluralism views the EU as composed of multiple centres of authority in continuing constructive conflict.[22] These sites hold independently plausible claims of constitutional authority,[23] which preclude the existence of a single dominant authority.[24] The main tension, and point of divergence between the two theories, is their treatment of the shared

[20] See notably A. J. Jordan, 'The European Union: An Evolving System of Multi-level Governance . . . or Government?', *Policy & Politics* 29 (2) (2001), 193, 201.

[21] For an overview of these critiques and an empirical assessment of its validity, see A. Bobić, 'Constitutional Pluralism Is Not Dead: An Analysis of Interactions between the European Court of Justice and Constitutional Courts of Member States', *German Law Journal* 18 (6) (2017), 1395.

[22] Ibid., at 1421 onwards detailing the incrementalism (regarding law as process, a dynamic) and the auto-correct function of constitutional pluralism, which are comparable to polycentric processes although more court-centric.

[23] The 'constitutional' in constitutional pluralism frequently goes undefined. We subscribe to Shaw's presentation of Treaty provisions and the jurisprudence of the Court of Justice as the four 'pillars of EU constitutionalism', which regulate: (1) the nature of the polity; (2) the rule of law and its systemic properties; (3) key values, principles and norms; and (4) the exercise of power within the EU. See A. Stone Sweet, 'The Structure of Constitutional Pluralism: Review of Nico Krisch, beyond Constitutionalism: The Pluralist Structure of Post-National Law', *International Journal of Constitutional Law* 11 (2) (2013), 491, 493 and J. Shaw, 'Process and Constitutional Discourse in the European Union, *Journal of Law and Society* 27 (2000), 4, 15–18.

[24] N. Walker, 'Constitutional Pluralism Revisited', *European Law Journal* 22 (3) (2016), 333. This position has also been critiqued in the light of the recent *Gauweiler* judgement (Gauweiler and Others, Order of 14 January 2014, 2 BvR 2728/13, available at www.bundesverfassungsgericht.de/SharedDocs/Entscheidungen/EN/2014/01/rs20140114_2bvr272813en.html accessed 8 June 2015 and Case C-62/14 *Gauweiler and Others* ECLI:EU:C:2015:400.); see D. Kelemen, 'On the Unsustainability of Constitutional Pluralism: European Supremacy and the Survival of the Eurozone', *Maastricht Journal of European and Comparative Law* 23 (1) (2016), 136.

system of rules: under polycentricity, the multiple centres of authority and decision-making function under a set of shared generally accepted rules.[25] Under constitutional pluralism, there is disagreement regarding the hierarchy of rules as well – i.e. national vs EU constitutional rules – which begs the question whether we can speak of a shared set of rules. The focus on legal expressions of conflict in constitutional pluralism also leads to a focus on courts at the expense of other institutions.[26] Comparatively, polycentricity takes a broader view of the EU system than constitutional pluralism, which may be better characterised as a legal, rather than governance, theory of the EU.[27]

Multilevel constitutionalism (MLC), as introduced by Pernice,[28] also adopts the idea that the EU is governed by a shared set of rules, composed of the national constitutions, and bound together by the constitutional body that is the EU Treaties.[29] MLC shares with polycentricity its focus on 'the centrality of an interactive process of establishing, organising, sharing and limiting powers'[30] and its characterisation of the constitution as citizen-focused may be seen as supportive of self-governance.[31] Despite sharing these conceptual similarities, polycentricity does not

[25] In fact, the place of law is not self-evident in Ostrom's focus on political theory and empirical work. Early work of Vincent Ostrom on water rights is an important exception, see V. Ostrom, 'The Water Economy and Its Organization', *Natural Resources Journal* 2 (1962), 55 and V. Ostrom, 'The Political Economy of Water Development', *The American Economic Review* 52 (1962), 450. The descriptive value of polycentricity, and part of its distinctiveness, therefore depends on the extent to which one can successfully identify such a shared set of norms within the EU system. See in detail, in this Volume, Chapter 8 by A. Bobić.

[26] N. Walker, 'Constitutional Pluralism Revisited' (n. 24) 336.

[27] While N. Walker, 'Constitutional Pluralism Revisited' (n. 24) 337 hints at the fact that constitutional pluralism may be transitioning into a broader, political, theory of the EU, this is yet to be fully developed.

[28] See I. Pernice (n. 6).

[29] I. Pernice, 'Constitutional Law Implications for a State Participating in a Process of Regional Integration. German Constitution and "Multilevel Constitutionalism"', in E. Riedel (ed.), *German Reports on Public Law Presented to the XV. International Congress on Comparative Law* (1998), 40–65. See also D. Grimm, 'Does Europe Need a Constitution?', *European Law Journal* 1 (3) (1995), 282, commented on by J. Habermas, 'Remarks on Dieter Grimm's "Does Europe Need a Constitution?"', *European Law Journal* 1 (3) (1995), 303. See also N. Reich, 'A European Constitution for Citizens: Reflections on the Rethinking of Union and Community Law', *European Law Journal* 3 (2) (1997), 131. Beyond the EU context, a second stream of MLC has been developed which focuses on the application of constitutional ideas, principles and practices beyond the state, see N. Walker, 'Multilevel Constitutionalism (n. 6) 1.

[30] N. Walker, 'Multilevel Constitutionalism' (n. 6) 4.

[31] ibid.

share MLC's exclusive focus on constitutionalism; while the presence of a shared overarching system of rules is important, rules need not necessarily be labelled 'constitutional' in order to fulfill this role.[32] Polycentric theory is more concerned with a functional division of powers based on the aims determined by citizens than with a legal constitution-based division of powers.[33] Moreover, Ostrom was particularly passionate about moving past the nation state as the reference point for theories of governance.[34] This is particularly relevant in the European context, which some consider as having moved to a post-state non-holistic style of constitutionalism, precisely to accommodate collective action and coordination problems, which cannot be sufficiently addressed within the jurisdictional boundaries of the state.[35]

B Normative Distinctiveness

It is difficult to entirely separate the normative aims of polycentricity – or any theory – from its descriptive features, as the latter are meant to achieve the former. Ostrom viewed sustainable self-governance as polycentricity's ultimate aim.[36] Many of the essential features of polycentric systems are therefore aimed at ensuring that individuals and collectives are able to express normative concerns and attempt to fix injustices, and thereby better able to meaningfully govern themselves. This ability of the system to continuously update and adjust itself in order to accommodate individual and collective pursuits and to enable redress of perceived grievances is a broad reading of self-governance, which must be

[32] This links back to earlier comments regarding the role of informal and non-legal rules in making up the constitutional fabric of a system. Substantive examples may be found in the general principles of EU Law, as developed by the Court of Justice of the EU, see e.g. T. Tridimas, *The General Principles of EU Law* (Oxford University Press, 2016). Behaviourally, actors, specifically courts, can be seen to practice self-restraint when engaging in dialogue about the overarching rules, developing what may be considered a 'constitutional' code of conduct. The constitutional nature of this conduct refers to the fact that such self-restraint and mutual respect can be traced back to the fundamental nature of the principles *and/or* relationships at stake. On this phenomenon in the context of constitutional pluralism, see A. Bobić (n. 21) 23.

[33] See also N. Walker's reference to functional competences in N. Walker, 'The Idea of Constitutional Pluralism' (n. 5) 346.

[34] V. Ostrom, *The Meaning of American Federalism* (n. 11) i. ('We cannot explore these ideas so long as our thinking about order in human societies is dominated entirely by reference to "the state" or "the government".')

[35] See also N. Walker, 'Multilevel Constitutionalism' (n. 6) 25.

[36] See in detail, in this Volume, Chapter 1 by J. van Zeben.

distinguished from goals that the constituents of polycentric systems may set for the system (for example, efficiency, equity, political representation, or economic progress). Moreover, it must be distinguished from external aims by which polycentric systems may be evaluated; polycentric theory does not claim that polycentric systems are by definition more efficient or just than monocentric systems.[37] The comparative strengths of polycentric governance can only be determined with reference to the empirics of a specific system.[38]

In further positioning polycentricity vis-à-vis existing EU governance theories, we find that the normative distinctiveness of polycentricity tends to be a matter of degree and emphasis, rather than a difference in kind. The political theory of federalism echoes polycentricity's aim of self-governance.[39] MLG theory is often normatively neutral, though at times may refer to solutions better suited to effectiveness or efficiency,[40] which is not part of the normative drivers of polycentricity. The normative goal of constitutional pluralism – 'desirable' applications of primacy – is primarily aimed, first, at the avoidance and/or resolution of constitutional conflict within the EU; and, second, at upholding value pluralism – i.e. a balancing of values striving to protect a wide array of both EU and national concerns.[41] While important, these goals do not envisage a direct role for the individual, something which multilevel constitutionalism – like polycentricity – seeks to address; MLC's aim is to improve the EU's supranational processes so as to ensure the

[37] See K. Carlisle and R. L. Gruby, 'Polycentric Systems of Governance: A Theoretical Model for the Commons', *Policy Studies Journal* (2017 - forthcoming).

[38] As is already emphasised by V. Ostrom, C. Tiebout, and R. Warren, 'The Organization of Government in Metropolitan Areas: A Theoretical Inquiry', *The American Political Science Review* 55 (1961), 831.

[39] See e.g. L. Acton, 'Nationality', in J. N. Figgis (ed.), *The History of Freedom and Other Essays* (Macmillan, 1907), 277. ('A great democracy must either sacrifice self-government to unity or preserve it by federalism. The coexistence of several nations under the same State is a test, as well as the best security of its freedom.')

[40] See A. Benz, 'Multilevel Governance in the European Union', in S. Piattoni (ed.), *The European Union: Democratic Principles and Institutional Architectures in Times of Crisis* (Oxford University Press, 2015); T. Conzelmann, 'A New Mode of Governing? Multi-level Governance between Cooperation and Conflict', in T. Conzelmann and R. Smith (eds.), *Multi-level Governance in the European Union. Taking Stock and Looking Ahead* (Nomos, 2008); H. Enderlein, S. Wälti, and M. Zürn (eds.), *Handbook on Multi-level Governance* (Edward Elgar, 2010).

[41] A. Bobić, 'The Jurisprudence of Constitutional Conflict in the European Union', unpublished doctoral thesis, 56. See also M. Kumm, 'The Jurisprudence of Constitutional Conflict: Constitutional Supremacy in Europe before and after the Constitutional Treaty', *European Law Journal* 11 (3) (2005), 262, 286.

empowerment of the individual, which is sidestepped by intergovernmentalism.[42] None of these normative aims is incompatible with, or hostile to, the aforementioned broad reading of self-governance. However, the dynamic and complex ways in which polycentricity foresees self-governance to become a sustainable systemic outcome are unique to polycentric governance theory.

Having set out the normative distinctiveness of polycentric governance theory, we must ask ourselves whether the picture of a polycentric EU aimed at accommodating a high level of self-governance is an attractive one. One way to answer this question would be to consider the ongoing calls for (re)nationalisation of competences within the EU,[43] as well as a simultaneous push for increased centralisation of power at the EU level, in response to the crises of the past decade. These seemingly contradictory 'cures' are the result of a fundamental disagreement as to the EU's disease and its cause. Those advocating renationalisation of processes and powers perceive the EU's democratic deficit – accompanied with a loss of legitimacy – as the disease, and excessive centralisation at the EU level as its cause.[44] Conversely, those who have argued for increased centralisation believe that the EU fails to deliver state-like democracy, caused by insufficient state-like powers.[45]

[42] I. Pernice, 'Multilevel Constitutionalism and the Crisis of Democracy in Europe', *European Constitutional Law Review* 11 (3) (2015), 541, 543.

[43] See the *Gauweiler* case discussed above (n. 24). See J. Weiler, 'In the Face of Crisis: Input Legitimacy, Output Legitimacy and the Political Messianism of European Integration', *Journal of European Integration* 34 (7) (2012), 825; V. Schmidt, 'Democracy and Legitimacy in the European Union Revisited: Input, Output and 'Throughput'', *Political Studies* 61 (2013), 2; K. Lindgren and T. Persson, 'Input and Output Legitimacy: Synergy or Trade-off? Empirical Evidence from an EU Survey', *Journal of European Public Policy* 17 (4) (2010), 449.

[44] A. Wimmel, 'Theorizing the Democratic Legitimacy of European Governance: A Labyrinth with No Exit?', *European Integration* 31 (2) (2009), 181; A. Moravcsik, 'In Defence of the 'Democratic Deficit': Reassessing Legitimacy in the European Union', *Journal of Common Market Studies* 40 (4) (2002), 603; G. Majone, 'Europe's "Democratic Deficit": The Question of Standards', *European Law Journal* 4 (1) (1998), 5; A. Follesdal and S. Hix, 'Why There Is a Democratic Deficit in the EU: A Response to Majone and Moravcsik', *Journal of Common Market Studies* 44 (3) (2006), 533; R. Bellamy, 'Still in Deficit: Rights, Regulation, and Democracy in the EU', *European Law Journal* 12 (6) (2006), 725.

[45] D. Grimm, 'Does Europe Need a Constitution?', *European Law Journal* 1 (1995), 282; for a comprehensive analysis of the relevant literature, see also M. Kumm, 'The Cosmopolitan Turn in Constitutionalism: An Integrated Conception of Public Law', *Indiana Journal of Global Legal Studies* 20 (2) (2013), 605, 607 onwards.

From the perspective of polycentricity, both these positions miss the mark; polycentricity aims to achieve a rule-ordered society that is not premised on the ability of the 'state' to govern. Applied to the predicament of the EU, this means that we must sidestep the EU/Member State dichotomy and are forced to look for solutions that are not dependent on variations of the nation state.[46] Self-governance may take many forms, assuming that the institutional essentials of polycentric governance and its prerequisites are safeguarded.[47] The problem may therefore not be any real or perceived deficit in democratic representation – our perception of which is referenced solely on the national experience of democracy – at the EU level,[48] but rather unequal ability to self-organise and to engage in certain types of collective action, such as those made possible through peaceful contestation and access to justice more broadly.[49] An example of such a process would be that proposed by Dawson and De Witte; their model that would allow for the questioning, rather than entrenchment, of EU objectives through several institutional changes at the EU level, including the creation of a European Senate, and an increased possibility for inclusive political contestation.[50] A polycentric EU would also allow for peaceful contestation of the EU's objectives – and consequent updating of the shared system of rules – as supported by the dynamic changes foreseen in any polycentric system. Different from Dawson and De Witte's model, which is premised on political self-determination, polycentric self-governance refers to all arenas of society, not only the political.

How then, if at all, would the prioritisation of polycentric self-governance change the debate on the legitimacy of EU governance? Successful polycentricity would accommodate a multiplicity of views on how the goals and objectives of the EU are best achieved.

46 This can be contrasted with Chalmers' suggestions for greater self-governance, in which national parliaments play a central role. See D. Chalmers, 'Democratic Self-Government in Europe: Domestic Solutions to the EU Legitimacy Crisis' (2013) Policy Network Paper, available at www.policy-network.net/publications/4399/Democratic-Self-Government-in-Europe. This would also address Weiler's claim that the only actors able to transfer legitimacy are the nation states, see J. Weiler (n. 43) 837.

47 See in detail, in this Volume, Chapter 1 by J. van Zeben.

48 It may well be argued that many Member States suffer from different, but equally severe, threats to democracy at the national level. See J.-W. Müller, 'Should the EU Protect Democracy and the Rule of Law inside Member States?', *European Law Journal* 21 (2) (2015), 141.

49 See P. D. Aligica and V. Tarko (n. 8).

50 See M. Dawson and F. de Witte (n. 2).

Specifically, it would allow self-governance in different forms as long as the methods and objectives of this self-governance respect the shared overarching rules and values. This plurality of views brings its own challenges,[51] and supports an understanding of the EU as a *demoicracy* rather than a democracy.[52] As explained by Nicolaïdis, '[i]f democracy is the rule of *the entire people*, a demoicracy is a polity ruled by *a plurality of peoples* who govern together but not as one'.[53] *Demoicratic* theory and polycentricity differ on the continued importance of the nation state in this process[54] – *demoicracy* awards greater deference to the role of Member States –[55] but they share the crucial concern for self-governance enabled through coordination and aggregation.[56] Importantly, *demoicracy* also prioritises this process of contestation and collaboration between groups over potential functionality concerns.[57] Polycentric theory does not claim that a polycentric EU would be a more efficient or effective one. This is an important departure from the current characterisation of the EU as a polity legitimised by its outputs.[58] Embracing polycentric governance in the EU together with demoicratic citizenship could change the focus away from

[51] See Section III.

[52] See, in this Volume, Chapter 3 by F. Cheneval, and Chapter 4 by K. Nicolaïdis and J. van Zeben; more generally, F. Cheneval and K. Nicolaidis, 'The Social Construction of Demoicracy in the European Union', *European Journal of Political Theory* 16 (2) (2016), 235; K. Nicolaidis, 'Mutual Recognition: Promise and Denial, from Sapiens to Brexit', *Current Legal Problems* 70 (1) (2017), 227. This is not to say that the EU may not pursue values that are traditionally associated with democracy. This is exemplified *inter alia* by its external policies, see e.g. A. Wetzel and J. Orbie, 'With Map and Compass on Narrow Paths and through Shallow Waters: Discovering the Substance of EU Democracy Promotion', *European Foreign Affairs Review* 15 (2011), 705.

[53] K. Nicolaïdis, 'Demoicratic Theory and Europe's Institutional Architecture in Times of Crisis', in S. Piattoni (ed.), *The European Union: Democratic Principles and Institutional Architectures in Times of Crisis* (Oxford University Press, 2015), 138.

[54] A similar disconnect between the nation state and political membership has been advocated in relation to citizenship, see e.g. R. Bauböck, 'Expansive Citizenship – Voting beyond Territory and Membership', *Political Science and Politics* 4 (2005), 683.

[55] C. J. Bickerton, *European Integration: From Nation-States to Member States* (Oxford University Press, 2012) as cited in K. Nicolaïdis (n. 53).

[56] *Demoicratic* theory sometimes uses the term 'self-determination' rather than 'self-governance'. See K. Nicolaïdis (n. 53) 141.

[57] ibid.

[58] J. Weiler (n. 43) 836; T. Isiksel, *Europe's Functional Constitution* (Oxford University Press, 2016) 6, 13, 224; J. Habermas, 'Democracy, Solidarity and the European Crisis', in A.-M. Grozelier *et al.* (eds.), *Roadmap to a Social Europe* (Social Europe Report 2013), available at www.ictu.ie/download/pdf/roadmap_to_social_europe_sej_oct_2013 . pdf#page=9, 4.

formal legitimacy towards an internalised commitment to EU processes and membership independent of 'cost-benefit calculations'.[59]

II Polycentric Features of the EU

This Section provides a preliminary discussion of whether the EU displays the attributes, institutional essentials and prerequisites of polycentric systems (Table 2.1). The complex dynamic nature of polycentric systems and of the EU precludes a comprehensive discussion of all EU processes relevant for these features; many – though not all – will be elaborated upon in the remainder of this Volume. This overview is aimed as demonstrating a preliminary descriptive fit and a starting point for further discussion.

A Attributes

The presence of *multiple independent centres of decision making* is perhaps the least controversial of the EU's polycentric features. Numerous entities exist at the European, regional, national and subnational level with different forms of organisation, longevity and composition. As mentioned above, the fact that EU law explicitly provides for the

Table 2.1 *Attributes, Institutional Essentials, and Prerequisites of Polycentric Systems*

Attributes	(i)	Multiple independent centres of decision making
	(ii)	Continuous competition, cooperation and conflict resolution
	(iii)	Overarching shared system of rules
Institutional Essentials	(i)	Freedom and ability to enter and exit
	(ii)	Enforcement of shared system of rules
	(iii)	Peaceful contestation among different (interest) groups
Prerequisites	(i)	Access to justice
	(ii)	Access to information
	(iii)	Capacity to learn

[59] F. Cheneval and K. Nicolaïdis (n. 52) 253.

inclusion of non-governmental actors distinguishes it from other legal systems,[60] such as international law.

The creation, powers and relative position of these centres to one another are determined by the *shared overarching system of rules*. This includes traditional 'constitutional' elements,[61] such as the European Treaties and the Charter on Fundamental Rights, but extends further to internal market law, which has been the initial and central aim of European integration, and national constitutional law relevant for the relationship between the EU and the national level.[62] The identification of these legal instruments as an overarching system of rules in the EU, and its shared nature, may seem controversial.[63] However, contestations regarding competing claims of sovereignty are to be expected in a polycentric system that includes more than one sovereign. Arguably, the creation of the EU has itself changed the nature of sovereignty.[64] Tensions between, *inter alia*, national and EU constitutional norms are an important part of this ongoing process of adjustment.[65] However, the

[60] On the inclusion of the individual in European government, see Case 26/62, *NV Algemene Transporten Expeditie Onderneming van Gend en Loos* v. *Nederlandse Administratis der Belastingen* [1963] ECR 1; Case 6/64, *Flaminio Costa* v. *ENEL* [1964] ECR 585.

[61] See J. Shaw (n. 23).

[62] See in detail, in this Volume, Chapter 8 by A. Bobić.

[63] Much of this controversy is captured in constitutional pluralism, which attempts to resolve the conflicting views regarding the relative sovereignty of the European Union and the Member States within their respective jurisdictions. See Section I. For further criticism of constitutional pluralism, see D. Kelemen, 'On the Unsustainability of Constitutional Pluralism: European Supremacy and the Survival of the Eurozone', *Maastricht Journal of European and Comparative Law* 23 (1) (2016), 136.

[64] See e.g. *R* v. *Secretary of State for Transport ex. p. Factortame (No. 2)* [1991] AC 603; consider also J.-H. Reestman, 'The Franco-German Constitutional Divide', *European Constitutional Law Review* 5 (3) (2009), 374, 388. ('[W]hile the protection of the German constitutional identity is absolute, that of the French one is not.' Reestman refers here to constitutional identity rather than sovereignty, but it may be argued that the creation of the EU has brought about a perceived need to establish protections for constitutional identity.) See also P. Craig, 'Britain in the European Union', in J. Jowell, D. Oliver, and C. O'Cinneide, *The Changing Constitution* 8th edn (Oxford University Press, 2015); M. Elliott, 'The Principle of Parliamentary Sovereignty in Legal, Constitutional, and Political Perspective', in J. Jowell, D. Oliver, and C. O'Cinneide (eds.) *The Changing Constitution* 8th edn (Oxford University Press, 2015); N. W. Barber, 'The Afterlife of Parliamentary Sovereignty', *International Journal of Constitutional Law* 9 (2011), 144; N. Walker, 'Late Sovereignty', in N. Walker (ed.), *Sovereignty in Transition* (Hart Publishing, 2003).

[65] See A. Bobić, 'Constitutional Pluralism Is Not Dead: An Analysis of Interactions between the ECJ and Constitutional Courts of Member States', *German Law Journal* 18 (6) (2017), 29. Self-adjustment is equally central to polycentric systems, see P. D. Aligica and V. Tarko, n. 8, 245–6. ('It suggests that if one is interested in the conditions preserving

question of the primacy of EU law should not be confused with the question as to whether there is, as a matter of practical and political consensus, an overarching set of rules and values that governs actors within the EU. If there were not, the United Kingdom would not feel bound to leave the EU in order to no longer be governed by these rules.[66]

Constructive conflict between centres of decision making regarding the substance of the shared rules and the centres' positions vis-à-vis each other is a necessary reflection of the ability to self-govern and does not erode the rules' status as shared and overarching.[67] The system of rules contained in the Treaties and the Charter on Fundamental Rights enables *competition and cooperation* by different suppliers of public and private goods, as well as *conflict resolution* between them.

That is not to say that position and abilities of each these centres of decision making are equal; for example, the ability for subnational governmental actors to participate in EU level processes is restricted in many ways.[68] While equality of participation is not a requirement of this polycentric attribute, these limitations can affect actors' ability to engage in continuous competition, cooperation and conflict resolution, and ultimately the ability for self-governance of the individuals organised through these centres. These inequalities speak to the institutional essentials and prerequisites that are needed to maintain polycentricity within the EU as compared with other types of pluricentric governance.

and enhancing the aforementioned "political objectives," one needs to better understand what makes polycentric systems so special. The conclusion was that a polycentric arrangement has a built-in mechanism of self-correction. Self-correction is the crucial functional or operational feature of polycentricity that explains in good measure an important part of its performance.')

66 See European Union Referendum Act 2015, Chapter 36, available at www.legislation.gov.uk/ukpga/2015/36/enacted accessed 19 May 2016.

67 D. Halberstam, 'Constitutional Heterarchy: The Centrality of Conflict in the European Union and the United States', in J. L. Dunoff and J. P. Trachtman (eds.), *Ruling the World? Constitutionalism, International Law, and Global Governance* (Cambridge University Press, 2009) 331; D. Thym, 'From Ultra-Vires-Control to Constitutional Identity Review: The Lisbon Judgment of the German Constitutional Court', in J. M. Beneyto and I. Pernice (eds.), *Europe's Constitutional Challenges in the Light of the Recent Case Law of National Constitutional Courts – Lisbon and Beyond* (Nomos, 2011); M. Claes and J.-H. Reestman, 'The Protection of National Constitutional Identity and the Limits of European Integration at the Occasion of the Gauweiler Case', *German Law Journal* 16 (4) (2015), 917.

68 See e.g. J. van Zeben, 'Local Governments as Subjects and Objects of EU Law: Legitimate Limits', in E. Fahey and S. Bardutszky (eds.), *Framing the Subjects and Objects of Contemporary EU Law* (Edward Elgar, 2017) 123.

B Institutional Essentials

The possibility and manner of participation in the EU system depends on actors' abilities to freely *enter and exit.* Member States experience high costs of entry and exit, even if both are theoretically available.[69] For individuals, the cost of entry and exit depends entirely on which membership is under consideration, and how we measure cost. The free movement rights linked to the internal market and the creation of European citizenship are two ways in which cost of entry and exit has been significantly lowered, and an individual's ability of movement has been increased. Several chapters in this Volume will explore the continued limitations of this mobility; for example, the implications of linking mobility to economic activity in the internal market;[70] the interaction between EU citizenship rights and national citizenship rights;[71] and the difference between third-country nationals and EU nationals.[72] Our focus on formal rules does not incorporate less tangible, but nonetheless important, limitations to entry and exit – for example, those caused by linguistic or cultural differences.[73]

Ostrom's discussion regarding the ability to enter and exit does not explicitly incorporate the role of *voice*. In order meaningfully to enter, it may be assumed that entry entails the possibility to voice one's views and participate in societal processes essential to self-governance. In the setting of the nation state, one could think of 'positive liberties'[74] such as the political rights of participation.[75] Many of these participatory rights are linked to citizenship and are not shared equally among the inhabitants of the European Union. Voting rights of EU citizens have generally increased through the introduction of the concept of EU citizenship

69 On exit, see Article 49 TEU and P. Craig, 'Brexit: A Drama in Six Acts', *European Law Review* 41 (2016), 447; on entry, see e.g. P. Kubicek, 'Turkish Accession to the European Union: Challenges and Opportunities', *World Affairs* 169 (2005), 67.

70 See, in this Volume, Chapter 5 by A. Bobić and J. van Zeben.

71 See, in this Volume, Chapter 7 by M. van den Brink.

72 See, in this Volume, Chapter 8 by I. Goldner Lang.

73 On mobility in the EU, see E. Recchi, 'Cross-State Mobility in the EU: Trends, Puzzles and Consequences', *European Societies* 10 (2) (2008), 197.

74 To be contrasted with Woodrow Wilson's ideal type of governance through the separation of administrative democracy and policy, see W. Wilson, Congressional Government (Meridan Books 1963, 1885 edn). On the distinction between the liberal and republican view of democracy, see J. Habermas, 'Three Normative Models of Democracy', *Constellations* 1 (1) (1994), 1, 2.

75 For corresponding views on the European context, see D. Kochenov (n. 10).

but are not absolute.[76] Participation in national elections continues to be reserved to national citizens, and the possibility to participate in local elections varies due to the Member States' heterogeneous implementation of what constitutes 'local government' under the Municipal Elections Directive.[77] Voting rights vary even more substantially for the significant number of third-country nationals who reside in the EU.[78]

Our discussion of entry and exit distinguishes between the position of Member States and individuals. This difference affects all institutional essentials; the position of Member States within the EU continues to differ from all other actors on account of their claims to sovereignty. As 'masters of the Treaties', Member States continue to have unique power to change the shared system of rules through inter-governmental meetings.[79] While other parties can voice their views in these proceedings and can influence governmental positions indirectly at the national level,[80] the Member States hold exclusive power to sign and ratify the Treaties.[81]

This exclusivity does not extend to the *enforcement* of the shared system of rules. The Treaties also provide opportunities for individuals, EU actors and other groups to challenge behaviour by Member States and

[76] The case law of the Court of Justice has recently received a vast amount of critique concerning the alleged changes in the scope of citizenship rights. See D. Kostakopolou, 'When Citizens Become Foreigners', *European Law Journal* 20 (4) (2014), 447; P. Van Elsuwege and D. Kochenov, 'On The Limits of Judicial Intervention: EU Citizenship and Family Reunification Rights', *European Journal of Migration and Law* 13 (2011), 443.

[77] See Municipal Elections Directive (1994), Council Directive 94/80/EC, laying down detailed arrangements for the exercise of the right to vote and to stand as a candidate in municipal elections by citizens of the Union residing in a Member State of which they are not nationals, Official Journal of the European Communities, L 368/38, 31/12/2014; See also P. Kiiver (ed.), *National and Regional Parliaments in the European Constitutional Order* (Europa Law Publishing, 2006).

[78] See D. Kochenov, '*Ius Tractum* of Many Faces: European Citizenship and the Difficult Relationship between Status and Rights', *Columbia Journal of European Law* 15 (2) (2009), 169, 175 and S. Song, 'Democracy and Noncitizen Voting Rights', *Citizenship Studies* 13 (6) (2009), 607.

[79] For a discussion of the latest treaty revision, see L. Pech, 'The Institutional Development of the EU Post-Lisbon: A Case of Plus ça Change . . . ?' (2011) UCD Dublin European Institute, Working Paper 11–5.

[80] For the role of the regions in the latest Treaty revision, see S. Weatherill, 'Finding a Role for the Regions in Checking the EU's Competence', in S. Weatherill and U. Bernitz (eds.), *The Role of Regions and Sub-national Actors in Europe* (Hart Publishing, 2005), 131. One could also consider the role of individuals in the ratification of treaty revisions, e.g. the Dutch, Spanish, French and Luxembourg referenda on the Constitutional Treaty (2005) and recently the Dutch referendum on the EU Association Agreement with the Ukraine.

[81] C. Closa, 'National Higher Courts and the Ratification of EU Treaties', *West European Politics* 36 (2013), 97.

others that may be seen to undermine the shared system of rules and their enforcement.[82] The de facto ability of these actors to enforce the shared system of rules – also captured with the prerequisite of *access to justice* –[83] is highly differentiated and distinguishes between 'privileged' and 'non-privileged' applicants.[84] The standing before the EU courts of non-privileged applicants is much more restricted compared to privileged parties. In addition, there are issues relating to the enforcement of the shared system of rules – particularly questions pertaining to the extent of the EU's competence – that feed into the controversial debate as to who is the 'final arbiter' of EU law.[85] To ensure the proper working of this institutional essential, the ability of actors to access (primarily legal) avenues for such enforcement, as well as the relationship and position of the arbiters of these questions, must be well defined.[86]

The differentiation between Member States and individuals is also reflected in their ability to engage in *peaceful contestation*. The EU's shared system of rules covers a diverse set of cross-jurisdictional interactions: between the Member States and the European institutions;[87] between EU institutions *inter se*;[88] between the European citizens and the European institutions;[89] between European citizens and their Member States; and between non-EU entities and EU citizens, Member States and institutions.[90] The shared system of rules legally regulates

82 Articles 263 and 267 TFEU; see in detail, in this Volume, Chapter 8 by A. Bobić.

83 See, in this Volume, Chapter 10 by L. Díez Sanchez.

84 See e.g. A Arnull, 'Private Applicants and the Action for Annulment under Article 173 of the EC Treaty', *Common Market Law Review* 32 (1995), 7.

85 This controversy is the starting point of constitutional pluralism. See n. 24.

86 See Section II.C.

87 For the dual role of the European institutions as agent and principal, see P. Lindseth, 'Equilibrium, Demoi-cracy and Delegation in the Crisis of European Integration', *German Law Journal* 15 (2014), 529. On the interaction between the European institutions see S. Meunier, 'What Single Voice? European Institutions and EU–US Trade Negotiations', *International Organization* 54 (2000), 103 and P. Kirchhof, 'The Balance of Powers between National and European Institutions', *European Law Journal* 5 (2002), 225.

88 See C. Reh, 'The Lisbon Treaty: De-Constitutionalizing the European Union?', *Journal of Common Market Studies* 47 (2009), 625, 638 (on the practice of 'institutional balance' between the EU bodies).

89 See e.g. C. Koch, 'Locus Standi of Private Applicants under the EU Constitution: Preserving Gaps in the Protection of Individuals' Right to an Effective Remedy', *European Law Review* 30 (2005), 511.

90 See, in this Volume, Chapter 8 by I. Goldner Lang; see relatedly, G. de Búrca, 'Europe's Raison D'Etre' (2013) New York University Public Law and Legal Theory Working Papers, Paper 385 (arguing that the EU's current day added value is its influence on inter-state relations *outside* of the European Union, not within the EU).

these interactions and provides various national and European judicial avenues for peaceful contestation.[91] There are also numerous non-judicial possibilities for structural and ad hoc contestation,[92] such as the European Ombudsman,[93] the Citizens' Initiative,[94] and the SOLVIT program that provides EU citizens outside of their Member State with advice and support regarding their EU rights.[95]

C Prerequisites

The ability for parties to use these opportunities depends on *access to justice*, *access to information* and their *capacity to learn* about and from these processes.[96] These three prerequisites affect the sustainability of each institutional essential. The information to engage in peaceful contestation may be different from that related to entry and exit but the need to be informed about processes and specific issues remains the same. EU institutions have invested heavily in 'transparency' in the form of access to EU documentation.[97] However, in order meaningfully to engage with this documentation, a lot of information, and learning, must have taken place about processes and policies at the EU level, which is costly, leading to further information asymmetries between individuals and interest groups.[98] Moreover, this obligation to supply information is not shared

[91] For considerations relating to standing, see C. Koch (n. 89).
[92] See in detail, in this Volume, Chapter 9 by D. Kukovec.
[93] On the European Ombudsman, see R. Rawlings, 'Engaged Elites: Citizen Action and Institutional Attitudes in Commission Enforcement', *European Law Journal* 6 (2000), 4.
[94] Similarly, the Citizens' Initiative may foster cross-border cooperation between citizens. See e.g. A. Chytla, 'European Citizens' Initiative – Remedy or Placebo for the Democratic Deficit in the European Union', in R. Grzeszczak and I. Karolewski (eds.), *The Multi-level and Polycentric European Union: Legal and Political Studies* (Lit Verlag, 2012), 151.
[95] See Commission Recommendation of 7 December 2001 on principles for using 'SOLVIT' – The Internal Market Problem Solving Network, OJ L 331 15 December 2001, and http://ec.europa.eu/solvit/what-is-solvit/index_en.htm
[96] See extensively, in this Volume, Chapter 12 by S. Garben. See also C. Paraskevopoulos, 'Social Capital, Learning and EU Regional Policy Networks: Evidence from Greece', *Government and Opposition* 36 (2) (2001), 253.
[97] See e.g. the 'Transparency portal', which allows European citizens access to numerous documents, legislation and proceedings <http://ec.europa.eu/transparency/regexpert/>; and freedom of information laws, e.g. Decision 2005/370/EC and Directive 2003/4/EC. See also A. Héritier, 'Composite Democracy in Europe: The Role of Transparency and Access to Information', *Journal of European Public Policy* 5 (2003), 814.
[98] M. D. McGinnis, 'Costs and Challenges of Polycentric Governance' (2005) Paper presented at Workshop on Analyzing Problems of Polycentric Governance in the Growing EU, Humboldt University, Berlin (on file with the author) at 17 (on the role of transparency regarding access to information), at 13.

by Member States in all areas. Even at the European level, an increasing number of documents are obscured from public scrutiny through their classification as matters of 'public security' or otherwise privileged.[99] The frequent reliance on comitology also complicates individuals' ability to learn and be informed.[100] Learning to self-govern is central to Ostrom's vision of a polycentric society and there are European initiatives that attempt to strengthen civil society building.[101] Similarly, formal and substantive access to justice is a precondition for challenging aims and processes, and thereby for self-governance.[102]

This brief overview is not intended to include every potential expression of each polycentric building block. Instead it aims to highlight how the prerequisites and essentials relate to each other, and what tensions exist between and within these features of polycentric governance. Although polycentric theory presupposes the existence of several levels of government and governance, this multitude of potential relationships complicate our empirical assessment of polycentric governance within the EU. This Volume attempts to meet this challenge through thorough debate of each polycentric feature and its accommodation within the EU governance system. These discussions will help us identify key ways in which the articulation of polycentricity in the EU may be advanced. However, polycentricity brings with it its own challenges.

III Polycentric Potential and Pitfalls in the EU

A polycentric system of European governance would allow for self-governance in a way that the current structure does not. This would address legitimacy concerns and could pave the way to a rule-ordered

[99] See V. Abazi, 'Closed Oversight: European Parliament's Access to Official Secrets', *Cambridge Journal of International and Comparative Law* 5 (1) (2016), 31; D. Curtin, 'Keeping Government Secrecy Safe: Beyond Wack-a-Mole' (2011) *Max Weber Lecture, European University Institute*, available at http://cadmus.eui.eu/bitstream/handle/1814/18641/MWP_LS_Curtin_2011_07rev.pdf?sequence=3, 5.

[100] See e.g. A. Héritier, 'Institutional Change in Europe: Co-decision and Comitology Transformed', *Journal of Common Market Studies* 50 (2012), 38; M. Rhinard, 'The Democratic Legitimacy of the European Union Committee System Governance', *Governance* 15 (2) (2002), 185; J. Mendes, *Participation in EU Rule-making: A Rights-Based Approach* (Oxford University Press, 2011); A. Gornitzka and U. Sverdrup, 'Access of Experts: Information and EU Decision Making', *West European Politics* 34 (1) (2011), 48. See also Council Decision 1999/468 and Regulation 1049/01.

[101] For an overview of programs, visit http://ec.europa.eu/enlargement/tenders/support-for-civil-society/civil-society-facility/index_en.htm

[102] See, in this Volume, Chapter 10 by Leticia Díez Sánchez.

society that does not take the state as a starting point or benchmark; polycentricity allows for the conceptualisation of European governance that leads past, rather than back to, the (Member) State. In doing so, it may create a more resilient and inclusive EU.[103] Functionally, increased self-governance could also provide secondary benefits such as increased participation, efficiency, learning and experimentation. However, polycentricity will also create more *complexity* and a greater risk of *fragmentation*. This concluding section offers some considerations regarding these pitfalls of polycentricity, which may be kept in mind when reading the remaining chapters of this Volume.

Complexity in a polycentric system has dual meaning: complexity of the polycentric system,[104] and complexity of the information needed to self-govern. Polycentric systems of governance themselves are complex, consisting of many different centres of authority with different constituencies, aims, organisational structures and life spans. Polycentricity also presupposes multiple individual memberships of different centres of authority. Many of these centres will be nested in, or across, larger jurisdictions. This adds additional complexity as to which legal rules may apply to certain situations. At the moment, the EU only has a limited mandate to streamline the rules that cover cross-jurisdictional activities.[105] Enabling more self-governance may – somewhat counter-intuitively – depend on further harmonisation of cross-jurisdictional rules. If not, the transaction costs associated with these multiple memberships may be prohibitive and reduce the possibility for self-governance in a larger, geographically dispersed, system such as the EU.[106]

[103] See also D. Chalmers, 'The Reconstitution of European Public Spheres', *European Law Journal* 9 (2003), 127 and G. Falkner, 'European Social Policy: Towards Multi-level and Multi-actor Governance', in R. Eising and B. Kohler-Koch (eds.), *The Transformation of Governance in the European Union* (Routledge, 1999), 93 (referring to the creation of a post-national democracy).

[104] It may also be good to acknowledge the complexity of studying polycentric systems, as phrased by Lin Ostrom, 'I do not introduce complexity lightly. I view scientific explanation as requiring just enough variables to enable one to explain, understand, and predict outcomes in relevant settings' (E. Ostrom, *Understanding Institutional Diversity* (Princeton University Press, 2005), 7).

[105] See, in this Volume, Chapter 5 by J. van Zeben and A. Bobić.

[106] See also, on similar issues in large natural resources systems, D. Huitema, E. Mostert, W. Egas, S. Moellenkamp, C. Pahl-Wostl, and R. Yalcin, 'Adaptive Water Governance: Assessing the Institutional Prescriptions of Adaptive (Co-)Management from a Governance Perspective and Defining a Research Agenda', *Ecology and Society* 14 (1) (2009), 26; C. Wyborn, 'Cross-Scale Linkages in Connectivity Conservation: Adaptive Governance Challenges in Spatially Distributed Networks', *Environmental Policy and Governance* 25 (1) (2015), 1.

This complexity interacts with the complexity of the information needed to self-govern successfully in modern society.[107] The overburdening of active individuals, and free riding by others, becomes likely in the face of this type of complexity.[108] Rather than an increase of debate and deliberation, this could result in the concentration of power in certain expert centres,[109] and/or in policy stagnation and stalemate,[110] both of which can already be witnessed in the EU. Complexity can also manifest as legal uncertainty – uncertainty about what the law is and/or how it applies to (new) situations. While some measure of uncertainty is part of the natural development of any system, excessive legal uncertainty undermines the rule of law – and ultimately the overarching rules of the EU –[111] and is therefore undesirable.

Polycentric governance is furthermore inherently *fragmented* and can give rise to duplication of service-providing functions and corresponding inefficiencies.[112] It can also lead to the undersupply of public goods, as some groups are likely to self-organise much more effectively than others,[113] and may do so to the exclusion of others.[114] Polycentricity's implicit acceptance of functional fragmentation as a natural consequence of accommodating different preferences expressed through self-

[107] The total body of European Union law applicable in the European Member States is currently estimated at over 1 billion words, see http://ipsc.jrc.ec.europa.eu/index.php?id=198.

[108] See B. Frey and R. Eichenberger, 'FOCJ: Competing Governments for Europe', *International Review of Law and Economics* 16 (1996), 315, 324.

[109] See also V. Ostrom, C. Tiebout, and R. Warren (n 38). For an EU-based example, see e.g. J. de Haan and L. Gormley, 'The Democratic Deficit of the ECB', *European Law Review* 21 (2) (1996), 95.

[110] M. D. McGinnis and E. Ostrom (n. 2).

[111] See in detail, in this Volume, Chapter 6 by A. Bobić.

[112] V. Ostrom, C. Tiebout, and R. Warren (n. 38). See also K. Andersson and E. Ostrom, 'Analyzing Decentralized Resource Regimes from a Polycentric Perspective', *Policy Sciences* 41 (1) (2008), 71.

[113] See also D. Chryssochoou 'Civic Competence and the Challenge to EU Polity-Building', *Journal of European Public Policy* 9 (5) (2002), 756. For an example on different abilities of sub-national actors to self-govern, see J. van Zeben, 'A "bottom-up" Perspective on EU–US Relations: The Role and Potential of Subcentral Authorities', in D. Curtin and E. Fahey (eds.), *A Transatlantic Community of Law: Legal Perspectives on the Relationship between the EU and US Legal Orders* (Cambridge University Press, 2014). There are complex social factors that determine an individual's propensity to self-govern, many of which cannot be influenced by legal rules and outwith the scope of this chapter. R. Rhodes, 'The Hollowing out of the State: The Changing Nature of the Public Service in Britain', *The Political Quarterly* 65 (2) (1994), 138.

[114] For examples of this from American local government, see P. Rigos and C. Spindler, 'Municipal Incorporation and State Statutes: A State-Level Analysis', *State & Local Government Review* 23 (2) (1991), 76.

governance may thus create negative societal externalities. This would be in direct conflict with the EU's aim of solidarity between the Member States and the people of Europe.[115] It could lead to situations where increased self-governance creates de facto barriers despite the reduction of legal barriers through, *inter alia*, internal market laws.[116] Fragmentation can also create a dispersion of responsibilities which can make it difficult to hold decision makers accountable,[117] which in turn can lead to lessened legitimacy.

**

This chapter presents a snapshot of the EU through a polycentric lens. It positions polycentricity among other theories of European governance and identifies the EU's polycentric features. It shows that realising a polycentric EU does not only present challenges in terms of ensuring full expression of its polycentric features, but also that a fully polycentric EU creates new challenges. These challenges are especially hard to solve as the solution of one problem may aggravate another. The remainder of this Volume discusses each of the EU's polycentric features in more detail. This multisided and inter-disciplinary approach to polycentric governance is aimed at providing a realistic picture of the strengths and weaknesses of polycentric governance.[118]

[115] See *inter alia* Preamble to the TEU ('Desiring to deepen the solidarity between their peoples while respecting their history, their culture and their traditions.'), Article 2 TEU, Article 3 TEU ('It shall promote economic, social and territorial cohesion, and solidarity among Member States') and specifically the new Article 222 TFEU (on assistance to Member States in case of manmade and natural disasters).

[116] See also M. Dawson and F. de Witte (n. 2) 378.

[117] See D. Huitema *et al.* (n. 106); E. S. Lieberman, 'The Perils of Polycentric Governance of Infectious Disease in South Africa', *Social Science & Medicine* 73 (2011), 676.

[118] For an example of a multisited approach, see for example S. Merry, 'New Legal Realism and the Ethnography of Transnational Law', *Law and Social Inquiry* 31 (4) (2006), 975; G. Marcus, 'Ethnography in/of the World System: The Emergence of Multi-Sited Ethnography', *Annual Review of Anthropology* 24 (1995), 95.

3

Demoicratic Self-Government in the European Union's Polycentric System: Theoretical Remarks

FRANCIS CHENEVAL

Political authority is predominantly conceived and justified as coercive power exercised by a centralised decision unit. In the context of local government, Robert Wood referred to this type of unified political authority as 'Gargantua' (in reference to Rablais' giant).[1] Wood viewed 'Gargantua' as a positive force, the counterweight of decentralised government. Ostrom, Tiebout and Warren questioned the choice of a single unit and site of government at a level that is judged as ideal for governmental actions, be it centralised or decentralised. Specifically, they showed that centralised government, while justified for the provision of some specific public goods in some cases, is not the only and not the best way to conceive of a successful exercise of political authority overall. In 'The Organization of Government in Metropolitan Areas'[2] – the implications of which go well beyond the theory of metropolitan government – the authors show that, in many contexts, political units can produce specific public goods more successfully when they work together at many different crosscutting levels at the same time, but remain formally separate. The authors called this social construct a 'polycentric political system' and they proposed a theoretical framework to assess the scale, structure, and performance of metropolitan polycentric political systems.[3]

As the core criterion for the evaluation of 'success' of political authority, Ostrom, Tiebout and Warren focus on the provision of public goods. Methodological differences notwithstanding, this idea is compatible with many contractualist positions in political philosophy. The latter hold, for instance, that the provision of peace and security[4] or the provision of

[1] R. C. Wood, 'The New Metropolis: Green Belts, Grass Roots or Gargantua?', *American Political Science Review* 52 (1958), 108.

[2] V. Ostrom, C. M. Tiebout, and R. Warren, 'The Organization of Government in Metropolitan Areas: A Theoretical Inquiry', *American Political Science Review* 55 (1961), 831.

[3] ibid., 831.

[4] See, for example, T. Hobbes, *Leviathan* (Cambridge University Press, 1991).

freedom and equality in human coexistence are the fundamental goods. Political authority is legitimate if it provides them and it is necessary for their provision.[5] If my reading is correct, Ostrom *et al.* do not depart from the normative idea that government's purpose is the provision of public goods. They simply consider a wider range of public goods and services, such as education, clean water, waste management, etc., and they construe a more complete organisational theory of political authority in an empirically driven argument, assessing what actually works and how. In order to judge the appropriate 'packaging' or scale of government with regard to specific public goods and services, Ostrom, Tiebout and Warren proposed to consider the standards of control, efficiency, political representation and self-determination, and offered an extremely careful analysis of these standards, their potential conflicts of realisation, as well as examples of how they should be applied. I will not reiterate all these valuable arguments here, nor their further, more recent development by different scholars.[6]

In this chapter, I want to focus on the conceptual and normative implications of polycentricity and self-government in relation to multilateral social constructs such as the EU in its present form. From a conceptual and normative point of view, this implies a more direct necessity to address the popular sovereignty question in the framework of a system of co-decision making and rule-based governmental action of multiple self-governing statespeoples (*demoi*). In order to theorise the specific nature of polycentricity in the context of the EU, I bring together the concepts of polycentricity, self-government, and *demoicracy*. The first Section focuses on conceptual questions regarding the self-governing decision unit and decision competence. I especially explore the conceptual relation between self-government, competence-competence and *demoicracy*. Section II offers an analysis of the relations between the concepts of polycentricity and *demoicracy*. The added value, I propose, is a theory that better accounts for agency and the related claims to self-government. In Section three I apply the concepts to the analysis of the EU and try to offer some more concrete normative guidance that follows from my analysis.

[5] See I. Kant, Metaphysik der Sitten Teil 1. Metaphysische Anfangsgründe der Rechtslehre (Meiner 2009); J. Rawls, *A Theory of Justice* revised edn (Harvard University Press, 1999).

[6] See M. D. McGinnis (ed.), *Polycentricity and Local Public Economies: Readings from the Workshop in Political Theory and Policy Analysis* (University of Michigan Press, 1999); M. D. McGinnis and E. Ostrom, 'Reflections on Vincent Ostrom, Public Administration, and Polycentricity', *Public Administration Review* 72 (2011), 15.

I Self-Governing Decision Units

Starting *in medias res*, I immediately focus the theoretical inquiry on the decision-making competence of the self-governing units. The basic idea is that in a polycentric system, many decision units (neighbourhoods, cities, regions, states, etc.) have the competence to exercise or delegate the provision of public goods, but not all have competence-competence in the strict sense of the term, nor do all have the same competence-competence.

A Competence-Competence

The term competence-competence requires some clarification. In its broader meaning, it should not be conflated with state sovereignty. It has a vast application in (international) arbitration law and in international commercial law.[7] In these matters, competence-competence may refer to the power of an arbitral tribunal to rule on its own jurisdiction. The tribunal is not thereby sovereign in the meaning of the term that is implied when states are declared sovereign. Competence-competence has also been extensively discussed in the context of EU law, where the principle of conferral states that the EU only disposes of competences explicitly delegated in the Treaties (Articles 4 and 5 TEU). This implies, as is held by the Constitutional Court of Germany, that the EU has no competence by right to determine its competences. Furthermore it can lose competences with Treaty revisions.[8] In principle, Member States have the right to exit, and thereby regain competences previously delegated to the EU, or they can take competences away from the EU in a new Treaty if they achieve agreement with all others. Other theories argue that the EU and its member states form one constitutional system in which competence-competence is with the EU and with the EU only.[9]

It is not my intention to interfere with the legal or historical discussion in this matter but to offer some conceptual analysis. Fundamental

[7] G. Born, *International Commercial Arbitration* 2nd edn (Kluwer Law International, 2014), 853.

[8] BVerfGE 89, 155 at 194–9 – Maastricht. See also, P. Lerche, '"Kompetenz-Kompetenz" und das Maastricht-Urteil des Bundesverfassungsgerichts', in J. Ipsen, H.-W. Rengeling, and J. Mössner (eds.), *Verfassungsrecht Im Wandel* (Köln, 1995), 409.

[9] I. Pernice, 'Constitutional Law Implications for a State Participating in a Process of Regional Integration. German Constitution and "Multilevel Constitutionalism"', in E. Riedel (ed.), *German Reports on Public Law* (Nomos, 1998), 42.

political disagreements notwithstanding, there are different definitions at play when the term is used in these debates, which I will try to unpack.

In a Hohfeldian terminology,[10] competence-competence can be more specifically conceived as a bundle of powers and immunities of a decision unit. In what follows, I only refer to formal political units with competence to make generally binding decisions.[11] **A** has a power if, and only if, **A** has the ability to alter his or her own or someone else's components of rights. Actions such as commanding, promising, waiving, sentencing, consenting, selling and abandoning are all examples by which a right-holder exercises a power to change his own or someone else's freedoms, claims, powers and immunities. A specific legal power relevant to our analysis is the right to bind oneself and others by contract, or any form of mutually binding agreement. If **A** lacks the ability to alter **B**'s Hohfeldian components, then **B** has an immunity vis-à-vis **A**. In other words, **B** has an immunity if and only if **A** lacks the ability, i.e. has a legal disability to alter **B**'s privileges, claims, and powers. Therefore, the different uses of competence-competence referred to above imply the following: a decision unit **A** has competence-competence if it has one or more of the legal powers to:

1) determine its own powers
2) constitute a decision unit
3) join a decision unit
4) delegate powers to a decision unit
5) withdraw powers from a decision unit
6) exit a decision unit
7) dissolve a decision unit.

Different meanings of competence-competence follow, depending on how many powers 1–7 are included in the definition. Furthermore, competence-competence can also be defined as consisting of immunities. In the most robust version of this type of competence-competence, these immunities are held towards all other actors. Decision unit **A** has competence-competence if it has immunity against the alteration or withdrawal of the power to:

8) determine its own powers
9) constitute a decision unit

[10] W. N. Hohfeld, 'Fundamental Legal Conceptions as Applied in Judicial Reasoning', *The Yale Law Journal* 26 (8) (1917), 710.

[11] See also, in this Volume, Chapter 6 by A. Bobić.

10) join a decision unit
11) delegate powers to a decision unit
12) withdraw powers from a decision unit
13) exit from a decision unit
14) dissolve a decision unit.

Again, different meanings of competence-competence follow from different bundles of immunities, and from the kind of actors against which the immunities apply. Before explaining this further, I would like to make three preliminary clarifications: first, a system of powers and immunities of many decision units *erga omnes* can be analytically modelled by pairing always two. Second, if a decision unit does not have immunity in relation to **x** (e.g. the power to determine its jurisdiction), it has a liability with regard to **x**. Third, to the immunity of an actor **A** against **B** always corresponds a disability of actor **B** that mirrors **A**'s immunity. In reference to the examples given above, some of the following implications might help clarifying the debate.

First, if an actor (e.g. arbitral tribunal) can determine its own jurisdiction, it thereby disposes of a power of the type 1. But it may not have the other powers 2–7 and it may not have immunities 8–14. It thus has very 'thin' competence-competence. *Second*, a decision unit might hold and exercise powers 1–7 internally, i.e. without binding itself contractually to other decision units holding equal powers. For example, a municipality could subdivide its school districts or set up additional school districts and delegate powers to them. *Third*, a decision unit **A** might also constitute a decision unit **D** together with one or several other decision units holding equal powers, and create a shared system of rules to govern the common institution. It thereby delegates powers. It transfers the powers to **D**, but might hold co-decision rights in **D** depending on the agreement. *Fourth*, if decision unit **A** constitutes a decision unit **D** multilaterally (with two or more other decision units holding the relevant powers) it no longer has the power to dissolve the decision unit **D** unilaterally; it only has a right to exit from **D** but the others might decide to uphold **D**.

Fifth, a decision unit **A** holding powers 1–7 can lose its powers unless it has the corresponding immunities. An arbitral court as well as a treaty-based international organisation can lose powers if international treaties are changed. The same is true for a municipality who can lose its powers to higher level units if they so decide. The EU as such has no veto position against the change of treaties, nor has an arbitral tribunal. The strong condition of not being able to have a power altered or to lose it altogether holds only if a decision unit has certain immunities against the other units to alter or withdraw its powers and/or dissolve it as decision unit. These immunities should not be confused with the power restrictions that apply in multilateral delegation of powers to common decision units. We can infer that competence-competence in the strong sense, akin to sovereignty, means that a decision unit has immunities against others to alter or cancel its powers that no other unit can extinguish. *Sixth*, it is a mistake to understand competence-competence uniquely as sovereignty, in the sense of the existence of a single supreme power that can override others in all cases, especially when a sovereign decision unit has delegated powers to common institutions multilaterally. In this case, its powers 4 and 5 are devolved to a collective decision-making procedure with other sovereign decision units. Power 7 might be shared. Just as the multilateral unit can only be created multilaterally, it can only be dissolved in the same way. Power 6 (exit) is not to be confused with a case by case opt-out within the decision unit to which power has been delegated. If case by case opt-out within the unit were unlimited, this would defeat the purpose of having a common unit and system of shared rules. In this constellation, competence-competence of a decision unit in the sense of a comprehensive bundle of immunities 8–14 means that other decision units cannot annul the power of a decision unit to determine its own jurisdiction and to enter and exit common decision units. It cannot imply that every delegated power can be withdrawn individually by the decision unit while that decision unit remains a member of the joint decision unit, especially when it is a joint decision unit of sovereigns who hold strong immunities against each other. Furthermore, for the concept of competence-competence to be consistent, the powers and immunities do not have to be unrestricted, but can be limited by legal disabilities.[12]

There are thus implications when decision units with full bundle of powers and immunities enter into relations with each other, as in the example of the EU. This is mainly the case because the EU does not have power 1 (the power to determine its own powers);[13] some powers are

[12] H. L. A. Hart, *The Concept of Law* postscript edited by P. A. Bulloch and J. Raz (Oxford Clarendon Press, 1994), 69–71.

[13] See Article 5 TEU and Articles 2 to 6 TFEU. In addition, the German *Bundesverfassungsgericht* placed the principle of conferral as the 'basic feature of the Community legal order'. German Bundesverfassungsgericht Cases 2 BvR 2134/92 and 2159/92 Manfred Brunner and Others, Judgment of 12 October 1993 *Common Market Law Review* 1 (1994), 57, 94. For a discussion on whether the European Union does have

delegated and shared among the members and among the members and the EU, some powers are not delegated to the EU, others are exclusively reserved to the EU, and some immunities of a member decision unit can override the powers of the partners.[14] As far as the joint arrangement is concerned, if a decision unit with the fullest consistent bundle of powers and immunities of members in the EU system is interested in maintaining the institutional status quo of the common decision unit 'EU', it has the competence to veto any change which might result in the creation of a new competence of the EU at its expense. No new arrangement in which competence is further delegated to the common unit can be adopted without consent of a member. An EU member state **A** has immunity against the powers of others to change the arrangement of powers (competences) and thereby exercise their powers 4 and 5 alone or jointly against **A**.

The competence to block change – in the case of the EU, the change of reaties – remains with the decision units holding this immunity. The power to change the shared system of rules, on the other hand, is not a power such a decision unit can exercise unilaterally. If a constitutive decision unit wants to change the allocation of powers within the system of shared powers, then competence resides with all decision units collectively, insofar as they can only move ahead together. It is thus clear that the decision unit that holds competence-competence in the strong sense, e.g. an EU member state, has immunities that other decision units, e.g. the EU, an international arbitral tribunal or an EU agency, do not have. In sum, we can see that both are wrong, those who say that in the EU competence-competence is with the EU and those who say that it resides with the Member State. But they are wrong in different regards. The first group is wrong insofar as the EU has no immunity regarding its powers. The immunities are on the side of the Member State. The second group is wrong insofar as the Member State has no unilateral power to change the powers that have been delegated to the EU. The member state cannot unilaterally withdraw those powers from the EU that it has agreed to delegate to the EU. It can regain immunity with regard to those powers only by withdrawing from the EU altogether.

the power to determine its own powers, see H. Lindahl, 'Sovereignty and Representation in the European Union', in N. Walker (ed.), *Sovereignty in Transition* (Hart Publishing, 2003), 107.

[14] See notably Articles 4 and 5 of the TEU; Articles 2 to 6, 114 and 352 of the TFEU.

B Demoicracy

The main reason for introducing the concept of competence-competence, and the idea of a plurality of units with competence-competence, into the theory of polycentricity is the central role that self-government plays in polycentricity. Vincent Ostrom's theory implies certain normative claims when referring to self-government and polycentricity. Self-government is possible if a decision unit has competences and competence-competence in the sense of certain powers. But in order to be robust, self-government, especially the self-government of smaller units with less physical or market power, needs to be made more credible by the guarantee of certain immunities against the powers of others to cancel or alter its competences. I read the empirical theory of Ostrom as a rationale to delegate and pool competences efficiently, not as a blueprint for domination by cancelling powers of decision units deemed inefficient. The term *demoicracy*, as I use it in this contribution, expresses the assumption that there are not only a plurality of political decision-making units (as in every polycentric political system), but also a plurality of units with competence-competence as a bundle of powers and immunities specified above, which I call the *demoi*, the constitutionalised statespeoples.[15] In the case of the EU, it is the Member States' peoples.

One might want to question this classification of two types of polycentricity by referring to systems in which there is simply no single site or unit that holds competence-competence. In a first objection, competence-competence in the strong meaning of powers and immunities might be systemically diffused across all the organs of government (as some argue is the case in the United States of America), and not in a single decision unit (as is the Queen in Westminster Parliament in the UK). In a second objection, the place of the sovereign might be considered empty. In democracy, sovereignty is a concept without embodiment in any one person, institution or institutional system; rather, it is replaced by the constant struggle for hegemony.[16]

To answer the first objection, we can submit that diffused sovereignty is sovereignty internally and towards others. In the US, supreme power of statehood is exercised against other internal forms of power, even if it is exercised via competition and checks and balances among political

[15] F. Cheneval, *The Government of the Peoples: On the Idea and Principles of Multilateral Democracy* (Palgrave Macmillan, 2011).

[16] C. Lefort, *Democracy and Political Theory* (Polity Press in association with Basil Blackwell, 1988).

institutions, and even if we cannot locate it in any single political institution or person. Sovereignty diffused in an institutional system is what is meant by the sovereignty *of* the people manifested in interaction of organs of democratic government, paired with immunities towards other units holding the same powers. At least in principle, the people is sovereign in the United States, and popular sovereignty is exercised via the governmental organs, and only via the governmental organs.[17] The USA, i.e. the constitutionalised US-American people manifested in its political institutions, holds immunities against other states and citizens hold immunities against the USA (basic rights) since the sovereign can be and is limited by legal disabilities. The second objection is void due to the legal nature of democratic politics. The democratic institutions by which political power is exercised in modern democracies are constituted and identified (parliaments, courts, governments, agencies, etc.) by rules conferring power. And these rules imply that there is a sovereign and that there are subjects.[18] If this were not the case, we could not distinguish the legitimate electorate from a flash crowd, and we do distinguish the two when we try to assess who represents the legitimate collective expression of the authoritative voice of the people, although we do also believe that a flash crowd demonstrating is a legitimate form of voicing demands in democratic politics, but it is not an authoritatively binding voice.

In sum, I hold that polycentric systems are either contained in an institutional system that embodies the sovereignty of the *demos* systemically or in a single institutional expression (unitary state), or they are systems in which we find a plurality of decision units with sovereignty. I call them here the *demoi*. In the latter case, the *demoicratic* case, polycentricity refers to a plurality of formally separate decision units with competence-competence in the strong sense creating overlapping, crosscutting multilevel and multipurpose governmental organizations, in which powers are altered substantively, even the powers of 'sovereign' states, but in which some powers and immunities cannot be cancelled by others. Polycentricity does not need to be accounted for in terms of *demoicracy* in all cases. In municipal polycentricity the subunits cannot be understood as sovereign *demoi* although they can be understood as *demoi* with a certain degree of self-government competences. Inversely, *demoicracy* can always be accounted for in terms of polycentricity. I do not see how *demoicracy* could be non-polycentric.

[17] J. Dewey, 'Austin's Theory of Sovereignty', *Political Science Quarterly* 9 (1894), 31, 49.
[18] H. L. A. Hart (n. 12).

The central problem that any political community faces is the potential conflict between the adequate levels of control and efficiency in providing public goods on the one hand, and political representation and self-determination of the political community on the other. Mere calculations of efficiency will not solve this problem, because the optimisation of efficiency varies with regard to different public goods, and choices need to be made on the basis of value judgements regarding the trade-offs. Furthermore, it is one of the implications of self-government that a political community might decide for a suboptimal level of control and efficiency in a trade-off with accountability and immediacy.[19] But a political community can only totally disregard control and efficiency at its own peril. Many thus accept the pressure to delegate governmental competency to different levels for each specific public good and thereby create multiple publics for each specific set of governmental transactions. These multiple publics are unbundled. Hence, they are no longer coterminous with the formal decision-making body at any level. As far as the act of delegation is concerned, this is not a problem for self-government as long as the delegation takes place in participatory procedure involving the citizens and exit rights are maintained.[20] But the fundamental questions then become 1) which decision-making body has the competence to decide or delegate which kind of public service provision, and which decision-making body has the competence to allocate the competence to decide? 2) How can self-government be maintained in a system with multiple *demoi* for the areas in which the *demoi* act together?

Theorists of polycentricity have addressed the problem of scale (well beyond metropolitan government) but not really the problem of competence-competence in relation to self-government. Some referred to sovereignty in a medieval or neo-medieval setting.[21] The feudalistic features of such systems beg the question of how polycentricity can be realized in the context of modern democracy.[22]

In the next Section, I analyse the concepts of self-government and polycentricity. I try to show how well they fit with the Aristotelian or

[19] V. Ostrom, 'Epistemic Choice and Public Choice', *Public Choice* 77 (1993), 163; see also, in this Volume, Chapter 4 by J. van Zeben and K. Nicolaïdis on the conceptualisation of the subsidiarity principle in polycentric theory and EU practice.

[20] F. Cheneval, *The Government of the Peoples* (n. 15).

[21] A. W. Salter and A. T. Young, 'Market-Preserving Federalism as Polycentric Sovereignty' (2016), Working Paper, available at https://doi.org/10.2139/ssrn.2735963.

[22] For further considerations along these lines of thought, I refer to Chapter 4 on subsidiarity by J. van Zeben and K. Nicolaïdis in this Volume.

citizenship-based conception of politics. The remainder of this chapter will then revolve around the conceptual and normative implications of locating polycentricity in the context of coordination of governmental actions among self-governing *demoi*. I will try to give a theoretical account of polycentric self-government of constitutionalised peoples, and discuss some important similarities and differences of this ideal-type in relation to the EU.

II Self-Government and Polycentricity

Vincent Ostrom insisted on the importance of self-government in his theory of polycentricity but he did not always offer much conceptual and normative guidance. The idea of this first section here is to complement this. It seems reasonable to adopt a relatively undemanding definition of self-government; self-government does not depend on the actual realisation of the common good for the unit. The reason is not that this perfectionist definition would disqualify all real political units from being considered as self-governed. Rather, it is extremely difficult, if not impossible, to determine what the overall common good is substantively, how it relates to different public goods and to the boundaries among political units. I therefore define a political community as self-governing:

1) if, and only if, the relevant binding rules, under which its members and residents live, originate from within the institutions of that community and are applied by officials belonging to its institutions;
2) if, and only if, its governing institutions are appropriated by a sizeable number of members as their *own* institutions.

This second condition implies a minimal form of political equality, understood as the equal value of the act of consent of every member to the existence of the political institutions.[23] Taken together, these conditions imply that government *for* the people or the creation of output-legitimacy by institutions that are not recognised in the sense of appropriated *by* the people are excluded from this definition of self-government. In other words, if for instance clean water is provided by the authoritative actions of totally external and non-appropriated governmental institutions this might fulfil the conditions of efficiency and control, but it does not fulfil the condition of

[23] For a similar account, see C. Bird, 'The Possibility of Self-Government', *American Political Science Review* 94 (2000), 563, 564.

self-government. On the other hand, if those external or higher governmental institutions act on the basis of competence that the political community of citizens has authorised and mandated, be it by delegation, this fulfils the condition of self-government because the act of authorisation has originated from within the institutions appropriated by the political community as their own institutions.

The condition that the binding rules have to originate within the institutions of a political entity conceptually implies that self-government includes a high degree of powers 1–7, or at least a high degree of stability of delegated competence by a rule conferring power. Furthermore, a unit cannot be self-governing in the sense of the above definition if higher-level units can easily cancel most of its powers, and if it does not control entry and exit of the governmental units to some reasonable extent. The self-governing political unit needs to dispose of the competence to realise the production of public goods, or to delegate the production of public goods to collaborative enterprises if judged necessary for reasons of control and efficiency, and it needs to dispose of the competence to recall delegation if judged necessary. Furthermore, it needs to have the guarantee that other entities with which it enters into relations of provision of public goods also dispose of the competence to do so in a stable manner. If a unit has no immunities, in the sense that we described in Section I of this chapter, it would have to exist under rules made by institutions, which it may no longer accept. Hence, it could no longer be considered as self-governed.

The conceptual relation between the self-governing people and the democratic people has been called into question.[24] According to our non-demanding notion of self-government, the self-governing people can decide or accept to be governed undemocratically, provided that this happens by its *own* institutions. As soon as one adds government *by* the people to the definition of self-government, implying participatory procedures in which freedom of political association and the possibility of political activity of all members of the *demos* constitutes the political 'self' (as opposed to government *of* the people only), the relation between self-government and participatory democracy becomes conceptually necessary. This is true even for a Rikerian liberal democracy in which elections are not seen as expressing the aggregated will of the people, but simply as

[24] W. H. Riker, *Liberalism against Populism: A Confrontation between the Theory of Democracy and the Theory of Social Choice* reissue (Waveland Press, 1988).

a control of the governmental elites by electoral competition. I adopt such a 'participatory' definition of self-government (populist or liberal). However, I do not make the realisation of a common good the ultimate condition for self-government, which would correspond to Bird's third understanding of self-government.[25]

A Polycentricity and 'Politics'

In order to assess the conceptual relation of polycentricity and self-government, it is helpful to reflect on the more fundamental concept of politics, to which they both relate, and their treatment by political philosophy and theory. Polycentricity is a term that is still relatively unfamiliar to mainstream political philosophy and theory. Two mutually exclusive reasons might account for this. First, one could argue that there is a redundancy or a large degree of overlap between polycentricity and well-established terms such as multilevel governance, decentralisation, subsidiarity, separation of powers, checks and balances, federalism, consociationalism, and so forth.[26] The second reason for the disregard of political philosophy for the term could be that polycentricity does indeed have a substantively different meaning than the concepts just mentioned, but that this meaning is distinctly non-political or even anti-political.

Polycentricity is indeed a term some philosophers of science and economists, since Michael Polanyi's *Logic of Liberty*,[27] have used to describe productive spontaneous orders.[28] Such orders are characterised by processes of self-adjustment in the absence of a centralised authority. According to Polanyi, the success of science, i.e. the approximation of the truth, is due to the 'polycentric organization' of research activities. Actors freely participate, freely choose the area of contribution. They freely structure their activities while converging on the goal to search for objective truth and to recognise the objective truth, or at least the best approximation thereof when it becomes evident. In such a setting, in which serendipity and a trial and error evolutionary process of a multitude of agents interacting freely produce the best results,

25 See C. Bird, 'The Possibility of Self-Government', *American Political Science Review* 94 (2000), 563, 564.

26 I do not go into this matter because the distinctiveness of polycentricity and/or overlap with other terms is dealt with in the introduction of this Volume.

27 M. Polanyi, *The Logic of Liberty* (Routledge, 1951).

28 See notably P. D. Aligica and V. Tarko, 'Polycentricity: From Polanyi to Ostrom, and Beyond', *Governance* 25 (2012), 237.

centralised hierarchical command is not only unnecessary; it defeats the purpose.

If one assumes, as do most political philosophers from Hobbes to Rawls, that political authority is to be conceived as vertical coercive command, as monopoly of force, as centralised authority over a certain domain of action within a circumscribed territory, then polycentricity is a term that clearly falls outside the realm of the political. It is an anti-political term. Any extension of the realm of polycentricity implies a decrease of the realm of the political in this account.

B Verticality and Horizontality

However, if one considers the original meaning of 'political', this purely vertical and centralistic notion of politics is inadequate. In fact, the contrary is the case: The polis is an association of citizens who recognise each other's status-equality and establish governmental authority via communication and cooperation, take turns in holding governmental office and in exercising this authority. I hold that the adjective 'political' specifically denotes vertical or coercive relations of subjection *and* horizontal relations of mutual recognition of equal status of citizens and/or political units. This two-dimensional understanding of political authority is the very point of the Aristotelian meaning of *politeia*. Many other conceptions of generally binding authority, crafted in languages other than Greek, separate the dimension of vertical subjection from horizontal recognition, and consequently engage different terms for governmental authority on the one hand, and social recognition of membership status on the other. But Aristotle wrote that in the regime of the *polis* called *politeia*, the citizens, who mutually recognise each other as equals, take turns in exercising the office of political authority; they need to be able to rule and to be ruled.[29] In this conception of politics,[30] it is inadequate to account for political relations only in terms of centralisation, coercion and subjection (Gargantua, Leviathan), just as it is inadequate to account for political relations only in terms of flattened transactional relations of free exchange among individuals. The art of doing politics well consists in the way in which a community is able to transform the tension between the vertical exercise of authority and the horizontal recognition of equal status into a functional social equilibrium that produces public goods.

[29] Aristotle, *Politics* (VII 14, 1332b25).
[30] Notwithstanding the inconsistent exclusions from citizenship in the time of Aristotle.

Politics, as I understand the term in the Aristotelian heritage, is about accounting for vertical authoritative relations in terms of free associational processes of recognition. The prime political good in this understanding is the peaceful, free and broad social acceptance of binding collective action. This conception of politics contains the idea of self-government at its core, i.e. the government of a society by the participation of its members, whereby the members recognise each other as equals with regard to their status as citizens and the political action that is related to it, whatever their personal and categorical inequalities otherwise might be. Polycentricity relates well to the core meaning of 'political'. First, it accounts for the combination of the horizontal and associational dimension of politics, both descriptively and normatively, with the vertical dimension via the conception of differentiated structures of separate and joint structures of government.[31] Second, it accounts for the empirical fact that political units are not self-contained but inter-connected in their provision of public goods by overlapping boundary conditions.[32]

Polycentricity is especially pertinent in a plurality of political authorities that, for various reasons, are engaged in common acts of government regarding a certain set of goals, such as the EU.[33] There is a close relation between the concepts of *demoïcracy* and polycentricity, because both share in the idea of self-government and multiple spheres of joint government. Furthermore, both are pertinent for an adequate understanding of the EU. As mentioned above, *demoicracy* simply adds another dimension of plurality to the notion of polycentricity, namely the plurality of *demoi* with competence-competence and immunities against the cancellation of competencies. It has also become clear from my conceptual analysis of competence-competence in Section I how competence-competence and *demoicracy* as joint endeavour of self-governing decision units with competence-competence (statespeoples) is compatible with a shared system of rules.[34]

It would however be an error to apply polycentricity to politics by negation or suppression of the vertical dimension of politics altogether. Gargantua is a system that has *only one* dominant centre of power in relation to all public goods and services that are provided, while

31 See, in this Volume, Chapter 1 by J. van Zeben.

32 ibid.

33 See, in this Volume, the Introduction and Chapter 1 by J. van Zeben, and Chapter 5 by J. van Zeben and A. Bobić.

34 For a more thorough analysis, see A. Bobić, Chapter 6 in this Volume.

polycentricity has many. Any political arrangement in which polycentricity plays an important role will also be characterised by vertical relations of authority and by a plurality of dominant centres of power. The point is not that the latter do not exist in a polycentric model of politics. The point of politics, including polycentricity, is that the vertical exercise of authority is accounted for via processes that are based on mutual recognition of equal status of the joint actors. Such vertical authority is therefore limited and horizontally as well as vertically differentiated, and it might be cooperatively upheld in many contexts.[35]

In the *demoicratic* account of polycentricity that I propose, the constituent actors of self-government and dominant centres of legitimate authority are the *demoi*. In the *demoicratic* variation of polycentricity, the relevant 'centres' of government are the different *demoi* which are self-governed and which jointly produce public goods that they cannot produce without the cooperation of other *demoi*.

III Polycentricity and Self-Government in the EU – Conceptual and Normative Underpinnings

In its normative underpinnings, the EU as *demoicracy* is a system of multiple types of recognition.[36] In a setting like the EU, reduced to its normative core of joint self-government, citizens of each self-governing polity recognise:

a) each other as citizens of different *demoi* engaged in a joint governmental endeavour;
b) each other as citizens of the joint governmental endeavour;
c) the institutions of the joint governmental endeavour as appropriated by them as members of a constituent *demos* of the EU.

In addition, the *demoi* collectively recognise:

a) each other as members of a common *demos* of *demoi*;
b) the institutions of the joint governmental endeavour as appropriated by them as *demoi*.

The citizens and *demoi* thereby accept, in principle, that they are engaged in a process in which their self-government and competence-competence

[35] V. Ostrom, *The Meaning of American Federalism: Constituting a Self-Governing Society* (ICS Press, 1991), 29–52.

[36] K. Nicolaïdis, 'Mutual Recognition: Promise and Denial, from Sapiens to Brexit', *Current Legal Problems* 70 (1) (2017), 227.

cannot be cancelled by other *demoi*, individually or collectively, but in which they engage in various, functionally differentiated transnational and national, transregional and regional, transmetropolitan and metropolitan governmental organisations simultaneously, in view of the most efficient provision of public goods that they are willing to choose. All this implies the acceptance of delegating certain powers, and the acceptance of a system of co-decision making to determine a shared system of rules.[37]

The Ostroms and a wider group of Workshop scholars furnished the behavioural and rational basis for a polycentric theory of politics for metropolitan, regional and up to federal and international governmental levels.[38] They argued against a dominant position, which held that a city, metropolitan region, or even the federal system as a whole, should be a community of integrated economic and social relationships under a single (vertically orientated) authority. The initial argument was developed on the basis of the fact that the optimum scale of production is not the same for all public goods and services, that this has behavioural consequences and that these behavioural consequences crystallise into institutional arrangements.[39] Some services may be provided more efficiently on a large scale, while other services may be provided more efficiently on a small scale.[40] This questions the conventional wisdom that the multiplicity of political units is always bad because of too many governments and not enough government, that there is inefficient duplication of functions by overlapping jurisdictions. The imperative of centralisation and unification deduced from these assumptions was refuted by the Ostroms and their associates.[41]

If we apply this theory to the discussion on the final goal of EU integration, the idea of an ever-closer union in the sense of the upscaling of the production of certain public goods to the EU level and also of the competence-competence to the EU is put in a very critical light. Ostrom

[37] See, in this Volume, Chapter 6 by A. Bobić regarding the overlapping nature of a shared system of rules with domestic rules and on how the judicial implementation impacts the very content of the shared system of rules.

[38] https://ostromworkshop.indiana.edu/

[39] V. Ostrom, C. M. Tiebout, and R. Warren (n. 2); V. Ostrom, *The Meaning of American Federalism* (n. 35); V. Ostrom and E. Ostrom, 'A Behavioral Approach to the Study of Intergovernmental Relations', *Annals of the American Academy of Political and Social Science* 359 (1965), 137.

[40] P. D. Aligica and V. Tarko (n. 28) 241.

[41] P. D. Aligica and P. J. Boettke, *Challenging Institutional Analysis and Development: The Bloomington School* (Routledge, 2009); P. D. Aligica and V. Tarko (n. 28).

and colleagues can remind us of two critical statements. First, the idea 'that a government is too large or too small to deal with a problem overlooks the possibility that the scale of the public and the political community need not coincide with that of the formal boundaries of a public organisation'.[42] Second, given the multiple number of public goods to be provided and the cross-cutting cleavages of the boundary conditions of these provisions, the one-to-one mapping of the affected public, the formal public organisation providing the public goods and the political community is highly 'impracticable'.[43] In other words, the 'best' regime is not necessarily to upscale or downscale the level of unified decision making and political representation to the ideal unified level. The best regime may be one in which the organisation of public goods provision can constantly reconstitute itself, in which political communities cooperate on a voluntary basis in the constant search for the appropriate fit among the conflicting tendencies of control, efficiency, political representation and self-government. They may do so separately for the provision of different public goods and services according to a polycentric notion of *demoicracy*. In the gist of this argument, the addition of the idea of *demoicracy* expresses the point that competence-competence as bundle of powers and immunities described above should not be simply upscaled to the highest level if polycentricity is to be upheld. The normative condition of such polycentric government is that there is a prohibition to locate competence-competence to one single unit at the highest level, i.e. the creation of domination by declaring the anullability of all immunities referred to above.

Secondly, it implies that the *demoi* engaged with each other do not claim supreme authority unilaterally, they recognise each other's bundle of immunities.[44] The mutual recognition of immunities is the safeguard against the establishment of a single supreme authority, be it the one of the EU or of the Member States of the EU. 'If the nations of Europe exist as single centers of supreme authority, then there can be no European Community. Conversely, if the European Community were organized by reference to a single center of supreme authority, there could be neither national nor local autonomy. So long as such a concept of sovereignty is presumed necessary to a system of government, I cannot imagine how it

[42] V. Ostrom, C. M. Tiebout, and R. Warren (n. 2) 837.

[43] ibid.

[44] In this respect, polycentricity rests on similar tenets as the theory of constitutional pluralism, recognising multiple coexisting sites with competence-competence. For a difference between the two theories see, in this Volume, Chapter 2 (I) by J. van Zeben.

is possible for democracies to exist in domains that reach out to continental proportions.'[45] From a behavioural point of view the risk that powerful units will seek domination cannot be excluded, but if they are successful there will no longer be a polycentric EU at all. The normative core of *demoicracy* necessarily excludes such a move due to the dissolution of self-government of other decision-making units, as well as the lack of recognition of the non-annullable immunity. Given that trust can be quickly lost, it is questionable if such a strategy of large powerful *demoi* can be successful even from a strictly behavioural point of view.[46]

Furthermore, in the theory of *demoicratic* polycentricity, there is no *a priori* determination of the ideal level or unit where the competence-competence and self-government of the political community should be located. But location in a single highest unit monopolising all powers and immunities defeats polycentricity. We can say that the concept of polycentric *demoicracy* presupposes the competence-competence to be at the level of the *demos*, but this can be below the nation-state level as every *demos* of the interconnected *demoi* can hold a limited set of powers and non-annullable immunities. In line with the theory is also the assumption that *demoi* in the real world reconstitute themselves in adaptation to changing boundary conditions and processes of changing appropriation of political institutions and changing identification with political institutions.[47]

It is of course important to pay attention to the conditions under which the polycentric system can be empirically shown to work and under which the EU can work as a *demoicracy*. This question is beyond the remit of this chapter, in which I limit myself to a few essential theoretical remarks. Other publications have adopted a more empirical approach to *demoicracy*, but obviously a lot remains to be investigated.[48]

[45] V. Ostrom, *The Meaning of American Federalism* (n. 35) 8. I am thankful to Josephine van Zeben for bringing this passage to my attention. I think my focus on competence-competence reinforces Ostrom's position. As bundle of immunities that the *demoi* hold against each other and against the EU, competence-competence makes polycentricity more robust.

[46] V. Ostrom, *The Meaning of American Federalism* (n. 35) 239. ('Any such system of polycentric order is, however, vulnerable to the pursuit of strategies in which some will take advantage of opportunities to gain dominance over others.')

[47] F. Cheneval, 'Demoicracy. A Democracy of Democracies', in H. Kriesi and L. Müller (eds.), *Democracy: An Ongoing Challenge* (Lars Müller Publishers, 2013) 492; see also G. de Búrca, 'Developing Democracy beyond the State', *Columbia Journal of Transnational Law* 46 (2) (2008), 101, 133.

[48] F. Cheneval, S. Lavenex, and F. Schimmelfennig, *European Democracy as Demoi-cracy* (Taylor & Francis Ltd, 2015).

An important point is that the theory of polycentricity has been tested successfully regarding local government and the provision of public goods, such as for instance security. The overall result of the studies is that 'polycentric' arrangements with small, medium, and large departmental systems outperform unitary departments.[49]

As van Zeben shows,[50] the EU can be interpreted and more adequately understood as an ongoing experiment of polycentric government at the regional level. Therefore, the point is not that international relations are intrinsically polycentric – international relations become polycentric when structured by certain institutions that enable productive processes of self-governed mutual adjustment. Further, I define 'productive' as successful in the provision of public goods, such as for instance security, public health and systemic economic stability. In other words, an international polycentric system is an arrangement in which rule-based inter-organisational action replace ad hoc agreements, without creating a singular state writ large.[51] It contains institutions that enable the social management of multiple realms of political organisation.

But it is important to factor in the normative underpinnings of this quest for better efficiency implied by the conditions of self-government and representation that are part of the Ostroms' concept of polycentricity. The 'best' system is the most efficient system *as chosen by the constituent parts*, not simply the most efficient system. And the 'best' constituent parts are the ones that are self-governed according to the criteria I identified in Section II, and that recognise the un-annullable immunities of others. To interpret the EU on the basis of the conception of an ideal-typical polycentric system of self-government implies to conceive of the member *demoi:*

1) as formally distinct and not subject to a single centre of comprehensive, non-annullable powers and immunities;
2) as sites of self-government guaranteed by externally non-annullable immunities;
3) as constituent members of the EU and its polycentric governance arrangements.

[49] M. D. McGinnis (ed.), *Polycentric Development and Governance: Readings from the Workshop in Political Theory and Policy Analysis* (University of Michigan Press, 1999); M. D. McGinnis (ed.), *Polycentricity and Local Public Economies: Readings from the Workshop in Political Theory and Policy Analysis* (University of Michigan Press, 1999).

[50] See, in this Volume, Chapter 2 by J. van Zeben.

[51] See Plato, *The Republic*.

The EU member *demoi* are subject to their own internal processes of recognition. They might also be subdivided in further constituent *demoi*.[52] The *demos*, understood as the unit of self-government, is constituted by rules (constitutive rules), which establish institutional facts. These rules need to be accepted by a sizeable majority of members. They have the form 'X counts as Y in Z'.[53] The *demoi* are institutional facts that are themselves composites of other institutional facts, which depend on certain processes of individual and collective acknowledgment and recognition.[54] In the case of the EU, the internal acceptance of the constitutive rules depends on individual citizens acting collectively at the level of the constituent *demoi* of the EU. The external actors of acceptance are the non-members: citizens of non-member *demoi* and the non-member *demoi*, whereby this process of external acceptance can be informal and more like tacit toleration or it can be more formal, such as in the international recognition of states or membership in international organisations or, as in the case here discussed, the EU.

The institutional facts that constitute a *demos* are manifold. They need to be manifold according to the legitimacy criteria of self-government, because legitimate self-government implies processes of representation and control, which in turn call for institutional differentiation. Even a radial democratic theorist as Rousseau makes the *demos* depend on constitutive rules and institutional separation of powers in which law-making on the one hand, and the application of the law to individual cases and adjudication on the other hand are in the competency of different institutions. These institutions can all be understood as different institutional manifestations of the *demos*. The self-governing *demos* has no primordial existence independent from these institutional manifestations, the constitutive rules that establish them and the social acceptance of these constitutive rules. The *demos* is not a brute fact,[55] its sole ontological grounds are the institutional facts established by socially accepted constitutive rules. Without these institutional features, the *demos* as a site of political authority and legitimate site of self-

52 F. Cheneval, 'Demoicracy. A Democracy of Democracies' (n. 47) 492.

53 As Josephine van Zeben thankfully pointed out to me in a written comment, this social ontology inspired by Searle can be related to E. Ostrom's institutional analysis and development framework for empirical explanatory purposes, but this is beyond the remit of this paper (see E. Ostrom, 'Background on the Institutional Analysis and Development Framework', *Policy Studies Journal* 39(1) (2011), 7).

54 F. Cheneval and K. Nicolaïdis, 'The Social Construction of Demoicracy in the European Union', *European Journal of Political Theory* 16 (2) (2016), 235.

55 See J. R. Searle, *The Construction of Social Reality* (Free Press, 1995).

government has no existence and is unable to act authoritatively as self-governing entity. The *demos* becomes an institutional fact on the basis of constitutive rules that a sizeable majority accepts and enacts over time. A *demoicracy* might have an overarching *demos*, but in this case the overarching *demos* becomes an institutional fact by constitutive rules that all constituting *demoi* accept, and it does not dispose of the immunities of the constituent *demoi*.

The multitude on the town square of Glarus, a small town in Switzerland, assembled according to constitutive rules of the canton of Glarus, is the closest we can come to directly perceive the concrete existence of the *demos* of the canton of Glarus; the *demos* that acts authoritatively and whose acts can be clearly and sustainably identified as authoritative acts of the *demos* of Glarus. The constitutive rules answer the question of what counts as the political entity called the canton of Glarus and what counts as the decision or authoritative voice of the people in the canton of Glarus. Again, the social construction of this reality has an external and internal dimension: the internal dimension being the constitution of the canton of Glarus and the external dimension being the Swiss constitution and international legal recognition of Switzerland. The social processes of recognition need to be reciprocal, the people of Glarus need to accept the external constitutive rules of Glarus and the outside world needs to accept, or at least not reject, the existence of the canton of Glarus and of its constitutive rules.

I am using the canton of Glarus as the most graphic model to exemplify the social ontology of self-government. But popular assembly is of course not the only way to theorise the constitution of a self-governing *demos*. The institutional manifestations necessary to constitute a self-governing *demos* are necessarily manifold and that also is the case for Glarus. Constitutive rules that establish a self-governing *demos* need to establish relations of control and of mutual adjustment that reflect the polycentricity of law and politics. Hence, the self-governing *demos* needs to manifest itself institutionally at least in a body of rule making (legislature), in a body of rule application (administration, executive), and in a body of adjudication (judiciary). But it will find many other institutional manifestations in different agencies and in the cross-cutting, overlapping governmental organisations the canton of Glarus is engaged in. Self-government further necessitates rules of election of office holders, temporal limitation of office, and democratic self-government will base those rules on some idea of universal suffrage at least for the legislature, and possibly on direct voting in form of referenda on laws which the law-making body has decided upon (right of the people to refuse), and eventually direct popular initiatives (right of the people to statute). In addition, as exposed in the first part of this paper, self-government implies that the self-governing entity holds a high degree of competence-competence to exercise, delegate or regain governmental competencies.

In the logic of the social construction of the *demos*, it is conceivable and it is also a political reality on the ground, in some countries and in the EU, that we find a vertically and horizontally structured plurality of *demoi* in a sovereign state (e.g. Switzerland) and among sovereign states (e.g. the EU). In other words, there might be a (more or less accepted) overarching (national or supranational) *demos* that is constituted via the horizontal recognition of a multitude of (subnational or national) *demoi*. Each of these *demoi* has its institutional manifestations, i.e. parliaments, executives, judiciaries, direct voting procedures with circumscribed powers and immunities.

Following the main idea of a political concept of polycentricity understood as joint government of self-governed *demoi*, the system will need to be conceived in terms of processes of mutual adjustment based on formal and informal rules that connect all or many of the institutional manifestations of the *demoi*. If one stresses the polycentric nature of such an ideal-typical system, the horizontal relations of the institutional manifestations of the *demoi* become important. In other words, the logic of integration into a polycentric system will not be to upscale vertical relations of authoritative command to ever-higher supranational levels, but to account for verticality of command by horizontally connecting the institutional manifestations of the *demoi*.

A *demoicratic* polycentric system will be characterised by formal and informal rules that foresee governmental procedures of cooperation and decision making involving the law-making bodies, governments, high courts, and voting procedures of member *demoi* of the demoicratic polity. In this volume, Ana Bobić highlights the 'non-hierarchical' and 'sincerely cooperative' judicial enforcement of the shared system of rules in a polycentric system.[56] In a polycentric *demoicracy*, the decisions of vertical command, besides being limited by legal disabilities of the overarching bodies, are to be accounted for via institutional manifestations of the *demoi* embodied in councils or joint decision making procedures of the executives, legislative, high-courts and popular votes. These bodies or procedures can be conceived as instances of control and co-decision

[56] See, in this Volume, Chapter 6 by A. Bobić.

making in relation to vertical (national or supranational) manifestations of the overarching *demos* or as the main bodies that enact decisions. They also embody the overlapping nature of the shared system of rules of common rules and domestic rules.[57]

We see that the EU's current institutional form is strongly involving the national executives at the EU level and moderately involving the national parliaments in co-decision making, while leaving virtually no role to joint decision making of national constitutional courts (individually the constitutional courts of course do take a stand and exert influence) and joint direct voting. I contend that this only very partially corresponds to the ideal-type of *demoicratic* polycentricity. One might say that while polycentricity is upheld in the EU by a variable geometry of functional governance organisations, the self-government aspect is still underdeveloped due to excessive intergovernmental centralism opposed by individual nationalisms.[58] Furthermore, elements of direct effect in the common market and especially the common currency structure, in combination with intergovernmental centralism, seem to tilt the EU more towards classic statehood with centralised structures of command and control.[59] Depending on what is being stressed and how future developments are anticipated, the EU is either a 'half-full' or 'half-empty' polycentric *demoicracy* given the ideal-type proposed in this chapter. The more concrete institutional features and competencies of the institutions of a polycentric *demoicracy* cannot be determined on a purely theoretical basis; they are the object of concrete negotiation within the given boundary conditions of the public good that is supposed to be provided. The remaining part of this chapter will therefore prioritise the discussion of fundamental questions regarding conflict and conflict control in a polycentric *demoicracy*, over attempting to predict the outcome of these processes.

One question concerns the inclusion of direct voting as a necessary institutional feature of polycentric *demoicracy*. Many representative democracies do not count direct voting as a necessary institutional manifestation of the *demos*, so why should it be necessary in *demoicracy*? There is no absolutely compelling answer to this question, but there are

[57] Again, I refer to A. Bobić's Chapter for a comprehensive description of the overlapping nature of these rules.

[58] For the relation to democratic deficit literature in the EU, see F. Cheneval and F. Schimmelfennig, 'The Case for Demoicracy in the EU', *Journal of Common Market Studies* 51 (2) (2013), 334.

[59] See, in this Volume, Chapter 5 by J. van Zeben and A. Bobić.

a couple of good reasons why in a polycentric *demoicracy* there should be instruments of control via referendums (the right to refute). Firstly, direct voting is the 'missing link' of a composite polycentric structure of *demoi*, such as the EU, in which many fundamental competences are delegated to higher levels in multiple chains of delegation. The problem here is not delegation – as this is done by unanimity – but accountability to the constituent *demoi*. The accountability that is inbuilt in representative democracy as accountability to a single electorate is fragmented in *demoicracy*. The *demoi* need some common institutional power to hold the organs to which public good provision competences have been delegated accountable. This can be done by a right of veto exercised by a sizeable majority of national parliaments or by the right to referendum.

There is a second reason that makes the choice tilt in favour of the referendum solution. One may enquire how citizens in a *demoicracy* are supposed to construct their status as part of a polycentric structure of multiple *demoi*. Their role is defined by a bundle of rules which organise their *joint* governmental action. Multilayeredness as such is not the problem with regard to the collective identity that is supposed to underpin joint governmental action. According to Eurobarometer, 20 years after the Maastricht Treaty, around 50 per cent of the citizens combine both a national and European identity, 40 per cent express only a national identity, and less than 10 per cent feel primarily 'European' (either only or in combination with nationals).[60] These distinctions are critical, but they suggest a dichotomous vertical structure of identity that does not capture the point that in an ideal-typical polycentric *demoicracy* of overlapping shared system of rules, citizens need to identify horizontally as connected with other peoples in multiple organisations of public good provision in cross-cutting cooperative structures.

This horizontal connection to other member *demoi* is different from the vertical identification to the higher level of political integration. In this sense, *demoicratic* self-government implies a sense of *demoicratic* belonging based on mutual recognition and formal norms capable of shifting the centre of gravity among multiple *demoi*.[61] And this form of identification in turn has implications for the rules of institutional design. The *constitutive rules* of *demoicracy* need to foresee procedures, in which the positions of the *demoi* regarding common issues of government are

[60] F. Cheneval and M. Ferrín, 'EU Citizenship: Integrating Multi-layered Identities?', in S. Seubert, O. Eberl, and F. van Waarden (eds.), *Reconsidering EU Citizenship. Contradictions and Constraints* (Edward Elgar, 2018), 187.

[61] F. Cheneval and K. Nicolaïdis (n. 54).

identifiable and comparable over time. Procedures need to deliver results that can be interpreted on the overarching aggregated level, and as appropriated by the *demoi* at the same time. I see no better way of assuring these conditions than by repeated issue-centred voting in which every time new lines of cohesion and division appear among the citizens of the different *demoi*.[62]

The kind of 'schizophrenia' implied in having to take a 'national' vs a 'European' point of view or in having a national parliament voting against a European parliamentary decision, or in which a national constitutional court expresses itself on EU matters, can be achieved by a rule of bottom-up dual aggregation of votes on the different levels in different institutions. One cannot take part in a decision-making process against oneself, just like one cannot play chess against oneself, but one can aggregate a single vote of a citizen at different levels of integration at the same time.[63] In a polycentric polity of interconnected self-governing peoples, the challenge to maintain self-government is to identify, compare, and integrate constantly and to various degrees depending on issues, the positions of citizens with their own respective opinions. The inter-connection of procedures of direct voting according to a rule of dual aggregation of one and the same citizen vote is a possibility to achieve this goal. Last but not least, referring back to complexity and fragmentation as the potential pitfalls of polycentricity, identified by van Zeben earlier in this Volume,[64] one could theorise that the referendum as a simple right to refute of the citizens and *demoi* would represent a simple democratic device of ultimate joint control in a cumbersome multilevel, polycentric system of decision making and hence mitigate the pitfalls van Zeben rightly points to.

IV Conclusion

In this chapter, I analysed the concepts of self-government and polycentricity in relation to the setting of polycentric government of multiple sovereign *demoi*. I showed that the notion of polycentricity is not anti-political; quite to the contrary, it fits well with a certain Aristotelian conception of the political, specifically one that embraces horizontal as well as vertical relationships. Subsequently, I gave a theoretical account of

62 F. Cheneval and M. Ferrín, 'Referendums in the European Union: Defective by Birth?', *Journal of Common Market Studies* (2018, forthcoming).

63 F. Cheneval and K. Nicolaïdis, (n. 54).

64 See, in this Volume, Chapter 2 by J. van Zeben.

a special ideal-type of polycentric self-government of constitutionalised peoples, and discussed some important institutional similarities and differences of this ideal-type in relation to the EU. An essential idea is horizontal connection of all or most of the institutional manifestations of the *demoi* in joint consultation or decision-making bodies, which in turn exercise horizontal checks and balances on each other. I pointed to some deficiencies of the actual EU in this respect, and highlighted referendums with double aggregation of votes as one means to assure self-government for the joint legislative acts of the *demoi*.

4

Polycentric Subsidiarity

JOSEPHINE VAN ZEBEN AND KALYPSO NICOLAÏDIS*

'Taking back control' is not only a mantra for Brexiteers these days. Supranational governance is being challenged by politicians and citizens around the EU as overly centralised, coercive and undemocratic. This book is grounded on the belief that the idea of polycentric governance developed half a century ago by Vincent and Elinor Ostrom is a fruitful place to start if we are to address this challenge. Assessing the presence of, and potential for, polycentric governance within the EU means approaching established principles and practices from a new perspective. While the debate on many of these issues is rich, longstanding and interdisciplinary, it has proven difficult to sidestep the 'free trade area/European federal state' dichotomy.[1] The polycentric perspective offered here aims to add another voice to theories that advocate a 'third way' of understanding EU governance.[2] Such a third way does not reject the EU's institutional structure – the EU already displays all the attributes of a polycentric system, as well as many of its institutional essentials and prerequisites –[3] but provides a different benchmark against which to assess its functioning. Ultimately the question remains: how do we achieve self-governance in an interdependent world?

* The authors would like to thank Dan Cole for his initial thoughts on this topic. He bears no responsibility for the findings of, and opinions expressed in, this piece.

1 See in this Volume, Introduction by J. van Zeben and A. Bobić, 1.

2 See in this Volume, Chapter 1 by J. van Zeben.

3 See in this Volume, Chapter 2 by J. van Zeben. Obstacles to the full expression of polycentricity in the EU remain, particularly when considering individuals' access to the processes that are fundamental to self-governance. These obstacles to, *inter alia*, the enforcement of shared rules, peaceful contestation of the rules, as well as access to justice, information, and learning are detailed in Part II of the Volume. Some of these obstacles can be traced back to the formal rules that govern the EU, others are caused by practical restraints related to resources and information. For a comprehensive summary see Conclusions to this Volume.

Polycentric theory highlights the importance of horizontal relationships within the EU on multiple scales – between states of course, but also between many actors below the states, all the way down to individuals. This is a departure from established EU legal scholarship which focuses primarily, though not exclusively,[4] on vertical relationships: relationships between the EU and its Member States, and between the EU and its citizens. Reconceptualising the European Union as a polycentric system that explicitly includes vertical and horizontal relationships is not a normatively neutral exercise;[5] Vincent Ostrom's theory of polycentricity is built on strong normative claims regarding the role of individuals, self-governance and the nature of democracy,[6] all of which have long been the subject of intense debate within the EU.[7] Sovereignty is a similarly controversial topic, with most Member States maintaining claims to the last word on competence division ('Kompetenz-Kompetenz'),[8] notwithstanding the ever-expanding competences of the EU and the Court-declared primacy of EU law.[9]

[4] On horizontal relationships between Member States/other EU actors, see F. Naert, 'The New EU Economic Governance: Vertical and Horizontal Power Shifts', *Journal of Self Governance and Management Economics* 2 (4) (2014), 77; R. Csehi, 'Horizontal Coordination in Federal Political Systems – Non-Centralization in the European Union and Canada Compared', *Journal of European Public Policy* 24 (2017), 562; on horizontal relationships between the courts, see M. Claes and M. de Visser, 'Are You Networked Yet? On Dialogues in European Judicial Networks', *Utrecht Law Review* 8 (2) (2012), 100.

[5] Some of these consequences are discussed in this Volume by F. Cheneval, Chapter 3.

[6] See also, in this Volume, Chapter 1 by J. van Zeben.

[7] See e.g. V. A. Schmidt, *Democracy in Europe: The EU and National Polities* (Oxford University Press, 2006).

[8] S. Weatherill, 'Competence Creep and Competence Control', *Yearbook of European Law* 23 (1) (2004), 1; G. Beck, 'The Lisbon Judgment of the German Constitutional Court, the Primacy of EU Law and the Problem of *Kompetenz-Kompetenz*: A Conflict between Right and Right in Which There Is No *Praetor*', *European Law Journal* 17 (4) (2011), 470; M. Kumm, 'Who Is the Final Arbiter of Constitutionality in Europe: Three Conceptions of the Relationship between the German Federal Constitutional Court and the European Court of Justice', *Common Market Law Review* 36 (1999), 351; F. C. Mayer, 'The Debate on European Powers and Competences: Seeing Trees But Not the Forest?' (2003) Walter Hallstein-Institut für Europäisches Verfassungsrecht Paper 18/03, available at www.whi-berlin.eu/documents/whi-paper1803.pdf; M. Kumm, 'The Jurisprudence of Constitutional Conflict: Constitutional Supremacy in Europe before and after the Constitutional Treaty', *European Law Journal* 11 (3) (2005), 262.

[9] See Chapter 3 by F. Cheneval, in this Volume. See also, *inter alia*, A. Bobić, 'Constitutional Pluralism Is Not Dead: An Analysis of Interactions between the European Court of Justice and Constitutional Courts of Member States', *German Law Journal* 18 (6) (2017), 1395; N. MacCormick, 'The Maastricht Urteil: Sovereignty Now', *European Law Journal* 1 (1995), 259; O. Garner, 'The Borders of European Integration on Trial in the Member

Ever since the Maastricht Treaty, the EU has apprehended issues of legitimacy and levels of competence under one label: subsidiarity, or the formal directive in EU law to govern at the lowest level possible. Subsidiarity is meant to police the vertical division of power between the European Union and its Member States, particularly in the many areas of competence that are not exclusive to the EU, where the principle of conferral applies.[10] More generally, EU subsidiarity is meant to achieve efficient and effective government through 'governance close to the people',[11] with the appropriate level of government varying along with the scale and scope of the problem to be resolved. Subsidiarity could thus be said to aim at fulfilling two functions: efficient governance, and legitimate governance, including through accountability, by maintaining the greatest proximity possible between the governed and the governing.

Polycentric governance theory similarly emphasises efficiency, aiming at the highest possible level of social welfare, by matching governance to the scale and scope of the regulatory problem at hand.[12] But it balances this concern for efficiency more explicitly than the EU's subsidiarity frame with a concern for self-governance starting with the individual, and moving up to include all forms of collective action, subnational entities and ultimately nation states. This interpretation comes to the fore in Ostrom's later work.[13] Classically subsidiarity traces back to Roman Catholic Social Theory, for which subsidiarity reflected the 'intrinsic value of social forms like the family, the private school,

States: Dansk Industri, Miller and Taricco', *European Journal of Legal Studies* 9 (2) (2017), 1.

10 Article 5(3) TFEU. Member States continue to be the default legislator on all issues, unless detailed otherwise in the EU Treaties. The principle of conferral means that all powers exercised by the EU can be traced back to the Treaties; a doctrine of implied powers would be incompatible with the idea of continued Member State sovereignty. Unsurprisingly, delineating the division of powers in areas of shared competence has proven problematic, despite the presence of the principles of subsidiarity and proportionality. See also F. C. Mayer (n. 8).

11 This is not reflected only in the principle of subsidiarity but also in the common goals of the EU as stated in Article 1 TEU: 'This Treaty marks a new stage in the process of creating an ever closer union among the peoples of Europe, in which *decisions are taken as openly as possible and as closely as possible to the citizen*' (emphasis added).

12 V. Ostrom, C. Tiebout, and R. Warren, 'The Organization of Government in Metropolitan Areas: A Theoretical Inquiry', *The American Political Science Review* 55 (1961), 831; A. Portuese, 'Principle of Subsidiarity as Principle of Economic Efficiency', *Columbia Journal of European Law* 17 (2011), 231; J. Dewey, *The Public and Its Problems* (Henry Holt, 1927), 15–16.

13 See in detail Section II. B.

churches, and labor unions',[14] this intuition is shared by many in the social world whether Catholic or not.

At first glance, the subsidiarity principle seems to reinforce our perception of the EU as a polycentric system.[15] After all, the EU brings Member States together to work out their differences, leaving much political power in national capitals rather than in Brussels. Its single market is managed by agencies across European cities and is predicated on the mutual recognition of national legal and regulatory systems.[16] Judicial and police cooperation, including the single arrest warrant,[17] involves a web of horizontal transfers of sovereignty. And yet, the EU seems to overlook the horizontal dimension of subsidiarity operating at different scales – from individuals and non-state actors to states – and, despite the explicit mention of local and regional governments,[18] provides very limited ways to meaningfully incorporate subational entities. Horizontality in our normative debates around levels of governance is simultaneously pervasive and undertheorised; self-governance, sovereignty and democracy tend to be conceived in relation to vertical distribution of power. Instead, polycentric subsidiarity emphasises the relationship between self-governance and horizontal distribution of power.

This chapter proposes a reconceptualisation of subsidiarity in the EU context enriched by the insights of polycentricity. In a nutshell, we argue

14 R. Hittinger, 'Social Pluralism and Subsidiarity in Catholic Social Doctrine', *Annales Theologici* 16 (2002), 385, 388.

15 The recent restatement of the subsidiarity principle also refers explicitly to local and regional governments.

16 See *inter alia* K. Nicolaïdis, 'Mutual Recognition: Promise and Denial, from Sapiens to Brexit', *Current Legal Problems* 70 (1) (2017), 227; K. Nicolaidis, 'The Cassis Legacy: Kir, Banks, Plumbers, Drugs, Criminals and Refugees', in B. Davies and F. G. Nicola (eds.), *European Law Stories: Critical and Contextual Histories of European Jurisprudence* (Cambridge University Press, 2017); K. Nicolaïdis, 'Mutual Recognition of Regulatory Regimes: Some Lessons and Prospects' (1996) in *Regulatory Reform and International Market Openness* (OECD Publications; Reprinted as part of the *Jean Monnet Paper Series*, Harvard Law School, 1997).

17 See https://e-justice.europa.eu/content_european_arrest_warrant-90-en.do; D. Sarmiento, 'European Union: The European Arrest Warrant and the Quest for Constitutional Coherence', *International Journal of Constitutional Law* 6 (1) (2008), 171; see also (n. 112).

18 Embodied in Article 5(3) TEU: 'Under the principle of subsidiarity, in areas which do not fall within its exclusive competence, the Union shall act only if and insofar as the objectives of the proposed action cannot be sufficiently achieved by the Member States, *either at central level or at regional and local level*, but can rather, by reason of the scale or effects of the proposed action, be better achieved at Union level' (emphasis added).

that self-governance can be reconciled with the management of interdependence through horizontal as well as vertical transfers of authority, and question the ways in which the latter is generally privileged above the former. Polycentric subsidiarity calls for two kinds of reconsiderations of EU legal debate. First, on the EU's own terms, it is questionable whether the principle of subsidiarity, as operationalised through the Commission pre-legislative assessments and Court *ex post* reviews, indeed results in governance 'close to the people'; its efficiency criterion is so easily satisfied that it has proven hard to find cases where EU action would be less effective or efficient than decentralised action.[19] Second, the EU may pay greater homage to individuals as compared to other state-led organisations,[20] but it is undoubtedly a state-centric organisation. Polycentric subsidiarity enlarges our analytical gaze to systematically include actors other than states as part of the subsidiarity landscape.[21] In short, polycentric governance in the EU requires a multiscale principle of subsidiarity that acknowledges the possibility of horizontal competence sharing, as we are already witnessing in EU practice, between and below the state.

The remainder of the chapter is structured as follows: Section I contrasts the interpretations given to subsidiarity by EU law and practice, as opposed to polycentric theory and suggests ways in which differences between the two may be bridged. Section II lays out the basic building blocks of polycentric subsidiarity. Section III concludes by considering applications and implications of polycentric subsidiarity within the EU.

I Redefining Subsidiarity

The term 'subsidiarity' can be traced back to the Roman *subsidium*,[22] and its use as a political principle as far as St. Thomas of Aquinas' work in the thirteenth century.[23] In the centuries that followed, the term and

[19] For an overview of the judicial testing of the subsidiarity principle, and the role of efficiency, see D. Wyatt, 'Could a "Yellow Card" for National Parliaments Strengthen Judicial as well as Political Policing of Subsidiarity?', *Croatian Yearbook of European Law & Policy* 2 (2006), 1.

[20] On this, see also in this Volume Chapter 6, by A. Bobić.

[21] See in more detail Section I.

[22] P. Donati, 'What Does "Subsidiarity" Mean? The Relational Perspective', *Journal of Markets & Morality* 12 (2009), 211.

[23] T. Aquinas, *On the Governance of Rulers (De regimine prinicipu)* G. B. Phelan trans. (University of Toronto Press, 1935), 1265–6.

principle of subsidiarity developed in multiple directions, both theoretically and normatively.[24] The contrast between two such interpretations, that of EU law and polycentric theory, currently occupy separate analytical spaces. This Section sets out their core features and suggests how they may be bridged.

A *Subsidiarity in the EU: The Principle in Practice*

The principle of subsidiarity has been part of the EU's constitutional fabric since the Treaty of Maastricht, which incorporated the principle into the Treaty establishing the European Community.[25] Before this, it had already been applied in EU environmental policy, though not specifically referred to as such.[26] The period between subsidiarity's inclusion in the Maastricht Treaty and its restatement in the Lisbon Treaty (1992–2009) was one of significant frustration and uncertainty regarding the status, application and purpose of the principle.[27] Despite the adoption of an additional protocol on the application of the principles of subsidiarity and proportionality with the Treaty of Amsterdam, the Laeken Declaration of 2001 made clear that serious shortcomings still existed.[28] The Lisbon Treaty introduced a rephrased subsidiarity

[24] Restrictions of space prevent us from providing a detailed overview of the development of subsidiarity. Useful resources include A. Føllesdal, 'Survey Article: Subsidiarity', *Journal of Political Philosophy* 6 (2) (1998), 190; R. Hittinger (n. 14); R. K. Vischer, 'Subsidiarity as a Principle of Governance: Beyond Devolution', *Indiana Law Review* 35 (2001), 103; A. Portuese (n. 12).

[25] Treaty on European Union, Maastricht 7.02.1992.

[26] See J. van Zeben, 'Operationalizing Subsidiarity: Power-sharing in EU Environmental Law', *Harvard Environmental Law Review* 38 (2) (2014), 415.

[27] A sample of the rich academic literature on this topic includes R. Schütze, 'Subsidiarity after Lisbon: Reinforcing the Safeguards of Federalism', *Cambridge Law Journal* 68 (2009), 525. See also K. van Kersbergen and B. Jan Verbeek, 'The Politics of Subsidiarity in the European Union', *Journal of Common Market Studies* 32 (1994), 215; J. Golub, 'Sovereignty and Subsidiarity in EU Environmental Policy', *Political Studies* 44 (1996), 686; D. Benson and A. Jordan, 'Understanding Task Allocation in the European Union: Exploring the Value of Federal Theory', *Journal of European Public policy* 15 (2008), 78.

[28] Laeken Declaration, available at www.cvce.eu/content/publication/2002/9/26/a76801d5-4bf0-4483-9000-e6df94b07a55/publishable_en.pdf. Additional procedural standards were introduced in the Edinburgh Guidelines but these were ultimately not included in the Lisbon revisions and are currently found only in the Impact Assessment Guidelines – a source of soft law applicable to the European Commission in executing its legislative duties. European Commission, Impact Assessment Guidelines, Jan. 15, 2009, SEC(2009) 92, available at http://perma.cc/3NHF-G4WK (part of the European Commission's Smart Regulation agenda).

principle and a refreshed Protocol on the application of the principles of subsidiarity and proportionality.[29]

The reframing of subsidiarity within the Lisbon Treaty must be seen in the light of other changes to the constitutional fabric of the EU, including the categorisation of competences as 'exclusive', 'shared' and 'supporting',[30] as part of an effort to more clearly delineate the division of competence between the EU and its Member States. All these areas are subject to the principle of proportionality, which leaves EU institutions duty-bound to refrain from actions beyond those 'necessary to achieve the objectives of the Treaties'.[31] The principle of subsidiarity only applies to those areas of competence that are not within the exclusive competence of the EU,[32] which continues to comprise the majority of policy areas.[33] Important areas of shared competence include the internal market, economic, social and territorial cohesion policy, environment and consumer protection.[34] As Union action has a pre-emptive effect,[35] the principles of subsidiarity and proportionality are considered important backstops to the expansion of Union competence.

Article 5(3) TEU sets out criteria on which to base our decision as to which level of government is better suited to perform certain tasks.[36] This subsidiarity 'test' has two steps: first, according to the text of Article 5(3), '*the Union shall act only if and insofar as the objectives of the proposed action cannot be sufficiently achieved by the Member States*, either at central level or at regional and local level' (emphasis added). In determining whether it is 'necessary' for the EU to act, account should be taken not only of national parliamentary reports, but also of the position of regional and local actors.[37] Second, it must be shown that

29 Article 5(3) TEU & Protocol No. 2.

30 Articles 3, 4 and 6 of the TFEU.

31 Article 5(4) TEU.

32 Although there is some controversy as to the categorisation of 'exclusive implied organisational powers' of Union institutions and the possible application of the subsidiarity principle to these powers – see R. Schutze, 'Dual Federalism Constitutionalised: The Emergence of Exclusive Competences in the EC Legal Order', *European Law Review* 32 (2007), 3, 5.

33 *Compare* Consolidated version of the Treaty on the Functioning of the European Union Article 3(1), Oct. 26, 2012, 2012 OJ (C326) 55 [hereinafter TFEU] *with* TFEU Article 4(1) *and* TFEU Article 4(2).

34 TFEU Article 4(2).

35 TFEU Article 2(2). ('Member States shall exercise their competence to the extent that the Union has not exercised its competence.')

36 These two goals represent two historical normative underpinnings of the subsidiarity principle, see A. Føllesdal (n. 24) 41–6.

37 Article 2, Protocol No. 2. While this is a formal requirement, the extent to which this happens in practice is limited.

the action, '*by reason of the scale or effects of the proposed action, [can] be better achieved at Union level*' (emphasis added).[38] Yet, with the restatement of Article 5(4) TEU and introduction of the 'early warning system' in Protocol 2,[39] the concentration of competences at the EU level has dramatically increased with the euro crisis.[40] Why?

In a nutshell, the two conditions outlined in Article 5(3) aim at achieving the complementary goals of effectiveness and efficiency: the EU shall act only where its involvement, and not that of the Member States, is likely to produce the intended result (effectiveness), and at lower cost (or 'better') than Member States acting alone (efficiency). In other words, it is about doing the right thing, the right way. Given the desirability of internalising externalities and pervasive economies of scale in managing interdependence, most state action ought arguably be taken or at least coordinated beyond the state. Moreover, where an action ought to be taken beyond the state, and even if it would be desirable to act at the global level, the EU level can arguably provide a first step where global action is not available.[41]

There are two ways of explaining why this definitional approach has not proven a safeguard against the centralisation of competence. First, one could argue that EU action can be explained by the kind of issues faced by the EU; for every issue with a cross-border dimension, it is easy to show *a priori* that the EU *might* be better placed than individual Member States to regulate it. Second, one could counter that efficiency and effectiveness are too narrowly defined by the interpreters of subsidiarity because the 'intended results' (effectiveness) do not include considerations of who governs, who decides who is empowered, and because the relative EU vs Member States' 'costs' do not include the cost of overriding or homogenising the heterogeneous preferences of the Member States, or indeed lower levels of aggregation.[42] If one gives

[38] Article 5(4) TEU.

[39] Protocol No. 2; see also Protocol No. 1.

[40] See A. Alesina, I. Angeloni, and L. Schuknecht, 'What Does the European Union Do?', *Public Choice* 123 (2005), 275 (providing empirical evidence on the expansion of the policy-making role of the European Union in the years between 1971 and 2000); D. Hodson, 'Policy-Making under Economic and Monetary Union – Crisis, Change and Continuity', in H. Wallace, M.A Pollack, and A. R. Young (eds.), *Policy-Making in the European Union* 7th edn (Oxford University Press, 2014).

[41] See Case C-377/98 *Netherlands* v. *Parliament and Council ('Biological patents')* [2001] ECR I-7079 (in this case the Netherlands unsuccessfully challenged a directive on biological patents on the basis that international action was forthcoming).

[42] G. Davies, 'Subsidiarity: The Wrong Idea, in the Wrong Place, at the Wrong Time', *Common Market Law Review* 43 (2006), 63.

some credence to the second type of argument, then substantial harmonisation in areas with strong variations in preferences, like social protection or agricultural policy, is suboptimal.[43] And subsidiarity, as practised in the EU, is merely a rhetorical figleaf which undercuts the Union's aim to regulate as closely as possible to the citizen.[44] The alleged neutrality of the subsidiarity principle as to the preferred level of governance is then also purely theoretical.[45] No wonder that resistance to centralising competences has increased on the part of Member States,[46] and resentment grown among EU citizens.[47]

Neither of the two tangible methods of 'enforcement' of the subsidiarity principle with respect to legislative measures has succeeded in countering such a trend. First, the early warning system introduced in Protocol 2 empowers national parliaments to receive and review EU draft legislative acts,[48] by including 'detailed statements making it possible to appraise the compliance with the principles of subsidiarity and proportionality'.[49] Depending on the amount of reasoned opinions that parliaments submit in response to draft legislation,[50] a draft act may be reviewed, maintained, amended or withdrawn by the Commission. But this 'subsidiarity' check is subject to several limitations: it only applies to certain legislation proper to the exclusion of delegated and implementing acts; and there is no guarantee that objectionable drafts are meaningfully amended or withdrawn. Thus far, the effect of objections on draft legislation has been limited.[51]

43 ibid.

44 Article 1 TEU.

45 See W. Vandenbruwaene, 'The Judicial Enforcement of Subsidiarity: The Quest for an Appropriate Standard', in P. Popelier, A. Mazmanyan, and W. Vandenbruwaene (eds.), *The Role of Constitutional Courts in a Context of Multilevel Governance* (Intersentia, 2012) 144 ('subsidiarity legally understood is a neutral regulative principle').

46 R. Vilipsauskas, 'Eurozone Crisis and European Integration: Functional Spillover, Political Spillback?', *Journal of European Integration* 35 (3) (2013), 361.

47 See K. Nicolaïdis, 'Mutual Recognition: Promise and Denial, from Sapiens to Brexit' (n. 16).

48 Article 12(b) TEU.

49 Protocol No. 2, Article 5. This assessment should include the proposal 'financial impact' as 'the need for any burden, whether financial or administrative, falling upon the Union, national governments, regional or local authorities, economic operators and citizens to be minimized.'

50 There can be individual support (of a specific national parliament or chamber), collective opinions (representing 1/3 of the votes awarded to national parliaments in the Union) and special legislative opinions (simple majority of the votes available).

51 See e.g. T. Raunio, 'Destined for Irrelevance? Subsidiarity Control by National Parliaments' (2010) Real Instituto Elcano Working Paper 36/2010, available at

The second method of enforcement, at the other end of the legislative process, is through judicial review by the Court of Justice. Early case law of the Court of First Instance shows that it was of the opinion that the principle of subsidiarity was not a general principle of law against which the legality of EU action could be tested, at least until the TEU entered into force.[52] Since then, failure to respect the subsidiarity principle makes the legislative act in question susceptible to an invalidity challenge.[53] In these cases, while taking into account both elements of the test set out in Article 5(3), the Court appears to prioritise the 'better achieved at Union level' element (efficiency),[54] rather than the necessity of Union action in the face of Member State inability to successfully address the relevant regulatory problem (effectiveness). Significantly, very few cases since have argued substantive breach of the subsidiarity principle, and only one successfully.[55] On their part, and arguing before the Court, Member States are more likely to point at procedural shortcomings by EU institutions in the legislative process, such as insufficient reasoned support for the subsidiarity requirement.[56]

The Court's reluctance to provide substantive review of the subsidiarity principle has been heavily criticised, as it is viewed to render judicial review of the principle toothless.[57] Others suggest that the principle of subsidiarity may be better understood as a political principle that plays

http://perma.cc/G34K-FZQY; but see I. Cooper, 'A "Virtual Third Chamber" for the European Union? National Parliaments after the Treaty of Lisbon', *West European Politics* 35 (2012), 441; D. Jancic, 'The Game of Cards: National Parliaments in the EU and the Future of the Early Warning Mechanism and the Political Dialogue', *Common Market Law Review* 52 (4) (2015), 939.

52 Case T-29/92, *Bouwnijverheid* v. *Commission* [1995] ECR II-289, paras. 330–31.

53 See Articles 263 and 267 TFEU.

54 See e.g. Case C-58/08 *Vodafone* v. *Secretary of State for Business, Enterprise and Regulatory Reform* [2010] ECR I-4999, para. 78.

55 Case C-376/98 *Tobacco Advertising I* [2000] I-8419.

56 Case C-426/93, *Germany* v. *Parliament and Council* [1995] I-3723.

57 See A. Estella, 'The EU Principle of Subsidiarity and Its Critique' (Oxford University Press, 2002), 156 ('Prudence . . . best summarizes the [European] Court's doctrine on the principle of subsidiarity'); see also R. H. Fallon, 'Judicially Manageable Standards and Constitutional Meaning', *Harvard Law Review* 119 (2005), 1274, 1331 (advocating an activist approach: 'When a constitutional norm is not a judicially manageable standard, it becomes the function of courts to attempt to devise or select one.'); See W. Vandenbruwaene (n. 45) (presenting an analysis of the European case law). See also T. Horsley, 'Subsidiarity and the European Court of Justice: Missing Pieces in the Subsidiarity Jigsaw?', *Journal of Common Market Studies* 50 (2) (2011), 267; F. Sander, 'Subsidiarity Infringements before the European Court Of Justice: Futile Interference With Politics or a Substantial Step Towards EU Federalism?', *Columbia Journal of European Law* 12 (2006), 517.

a role in the legislative process, and that the Court is correct in respecting the democratic progress that precedes adoption of the act.[58] In theory, this is what the early warning system was meant to achieve but as we just saw, it has not done so in practice.

As a result, the EU's interpretation of the principle of subsidiarity meant to restrain the expansion of EU competences has not been able to stop the expansion of EU competence – and has arguably facilitated it, despite pre-legislative and post-legislative controls. This is why, we argue, it needs to be redefined.

B Subsidiarity in Polycentric Theory

The Organization of Government in Metropolitan Areas was written in response to the widely supported, but often unsubstantiated, claim that 'fragmented' government led to inefficiencies, particularly in the local provision of public services.[59] The assumption was that centralisation (and consequent uniformity) of service provision would automatically lead to economies of scale and scope and was therefore preferable to decentralisation. Ostrom, Tiebout and Warren presented a testable hypothesis of potential diseconomies of scope and scale in the centralised production and/or provision of certain public services, which members of the Ostrom Workshop later verified through empirical studies.[60]

[58] P. Craig, 'Subsidiarity: A Political and Legal Analysis', *Journal of Common Market Studies* 50 (2012), 72.

[59] V. Ostrom, C. M. Tiebout, and R. Warren (n. 12), 831.

[60] See in detail, in this Volume, Chapter 1 by J. van Zeben. See also V. Ostrom, 'Polycentricity' (Part 2) Reprinted in M. McGinnis (ed.), *Polycentricity and Local Public Economies* (University of Michigan Press, 1999), 119–138. These hypotheses were tested by E. Ostrom, 'Size and Performance in a Federal System', *Publius: The Journal of Federalism* 6 (1976), 33; E. Ostrom, 'Why Do We Need Multiple Indicators of Public Service Outputs?' In *National Conference on Nonmetropolitan Community Services Research* (US Government Printing Office, 1977), 277–86; E. Ostrom and G. P. Whitaker, 'Does Local Community Control of Police Make a Difference? Some Preliminary Findings', *American Journal of Political Science* 17 (1) (1973), 48; E. Ostrom and G. P. Whitaker, 'Community Control and Governmental Responsiveness: The Case of Police in Black Neighborhoods', in D. Rogers and D. Halley (eds.), *Improving the Quality of Urban Management* (Urban Affairs Annual Reviews No. 8 1974); E. Ostrom, R. B. Parks, and G. P. Whitaker, 'Defining and Measuring Structural Variations in Interorganizational Arrangements', *Publius: The Journal of Federalism* 4 (1974), 87; E. Ostrom and R. B. Parks, 'Neither Gargantua Nor the Land of Lilliputs: Conjectures on Mixed Systems of Metropolitan Organization', in M. D. McGinnis (ed.), *Polycentricity and Local Public Economies* (University of Michigan Press, 1999); W. Blomquist and R. B. Parks, 'Fiscal, Service, and Political Impacts of Indianapolis-Marion County's

In setting out the framework of their 'polycentric political system', Ostrom, Tiebout and Warren never explicitly refer to 'subsidiarity'. Rather they find that the 'problem' of municipal governance 'is to recognise the variety of smaller sets of publics that may exist within its boundaries'. Many of the interests of smaller publics, they argue, 'might be more properly negotiated within the confines of a smaller political community without requiring the attention of centralised decision makers concerned with the big system'.[61] Though not always. They emphasise that the people affected will vary for each set of transactions and problems, and that depending on factors such as information, technology and communication, there may be a different optimal scale of public organisation for each public good.[62] Optimally differentiated production and consumption of public goods are thus positioned as the key potential benefit of polycentric governance, and the potential competitive advantage over monocentric governance.

Ostrom, Tiebout and Warren found that 'patterns of local autonomy and home rule constitute substantial commitments to a polycentric system', capable of 'supplying a variety of public goods with many different scales of organisation and of providing optimal arrangements for the production and consumption of public goods'.[63] Local self-determination could thus be seen as a strong support, if not prerequisite, for polycentric governance.

A year after the publication of *The Organization of Metropolitan Government*, the economist George Stigler issued a resounding defence of the principle of subsidiarity, which echoed Ostrom, Tiebout and Warren's hypothesis:

> If we give each government activity *to the smallest governmental unit* which can efficiently perform it, there will be a vast resurgence and revitalization of local government in America. [...] [B]oth public

Unigov.', *Public: The Journal of Federalism* 25 (1995), 37; R. B. Parks and E. Ostrom, 'Complex Models of Urban Services Systems', in T. N. Clark (ed.), *Urban Policy Analysis: Directions for Future Research* (Urban Affairs Annual Reviews No. 21 1981). The findings tended to support the existence of multiple, smaller, service providers, such as police services. See e.g. 'In terms of immediate response to citizens' calls for service, the existence of *a fairly large number* of autonomous, small- to medium-sized police departments is associated with lower victimization rates, faster response, and higher response capability in the neighborhoods served by those agencies' (E. Ostrom and R. B. Parks in M. D. McGinnis 1999, 292, emphasis added).

[61] V. Ostrom, C. M. Tiebout, and R. Warren (n. 12), 837–8.

[62] ibid., at 836.

[63] ibid., 837, 839.

> functions and private citizens would benefit from the increased participation of citizens in political life. An eminent and powerful structure of local government is a basic ingredient of a society which seeks to give to the individual the fullest possible freedom and responsibility.[64]

Since then, economists have developed numerous ways of mapping governance onto the heterogeneous preferences held at various degrees of aggregation and much has been written on multilevel governance and federalism as a frame for respecting the diversity of preferences in a polity. Indeed, Vincent Ostrom's later work on polycentric theory often returns to the importance of local government, often extrapolating from the municipal level upwards to the federal, as envisioned by Madison and Hamilton in *The Federalist Papers*.[65] This process of positioning higher level decision-making units as subsidiary to lower ones – a kind of 'inverse subsidiarity' – links polycentric self-governance to the principle of subsidiarity.[66] In other words, the default authority should always be at lower level even while that authority might willingly decide to cooperate with others, possibly at a higher level of governance.[67]

In applying Vincent and Elinor Ostrom's theoretical work to polycentric environmental governance, Ostrom scholars have suggested that the principle of subsidiarity may be an appropriate starting point for assigning decision-making rights across the various levels of governance.[68] However, proposing to stimulate polycentric self-

[64] G. J. Stigler, 'The Tenable Range of Functions of Local Government', in E. S. Phelps (ed.), *Private Wants and Public Needs*, ed. with an introduction by E. Phelps (W.W. Norton, 1962), 167–76.

[65] V. Ostrom, 'Polycentricity' (Part 1), reprinted in M. D. McGinnis (ed.), *Polycentricity and Local Public Economies* (University of Michigan Press, 1999); see also V. Ostrom, *The Political Theory of the Compound Republic: Designing the American Experiment* (University of Nebraska Press, 1971).

[66] See also K. Andersson and E. Ostrom, 'Analyzing Decentralized Resource Regimes from a Polycentric Perspective', *Policy Sciences* 41 (2008), 71.

[67] See, for instance, Elinor Ostrom's design principles for successful governance of common-pool resources which requires that 'the rights of appropriators to devise their own institutions are not challenged by external government authorities'. E. Ostrom, *Governing the Commons: The Evolution of Institutions for Collective Action* (Cambridge University Press, 1990).

[68] I. Reeve, G. R. Marshall, and W. Musgrave, *Resource Governance and Integrated Catchment Management.* (Institute for Rural Futures, 2002); M. B. Lane, G. T. McDonald, and T. H. Morrison, 'Decentralisation and Environmental Management in Australia: A Comment on the Prescriptions of the Wentworth Group', *Australian Geographical Studies* 42 (1) (2004), 103; G. R. Marshall, *Economics for Collaborative Environmental Management: Renegotiating the Commons* (Earthscan 2005); G. R. Marshall, 'Nesting, Subsidiarity, and Community-Based Environmental Governance Beyond the Local Level',

governance through 'top-down subsidiarity', rather than allowing local self-governance to function as the foundation of systemic polycentricity and self-governance ('inverse subsidiarity'), risks reversing the exact process that polycentricity is meant to encourage. The possibility or even preference for local governance should not be confused with prescribing the exercise of these powers at a given level, no matter how local or decentralised.

The principle of subsidiarity, as conventionally understood, is a hierarchical and vertical principle. It is meant to counterbalance the powers of dominant decision units, such as the federal or national level of government, by imposing a preference for governance through local decision-making units unless such action is evidently inefficient or otherwise undesirable. Vincent Ostrom based much of his views on democracy and governance on the fundamental belief that governing should be left to the people, not to 'government'.[69] He found that most theories of government had sacrificed this principle in order to make sense of the perceived need for one body that exercises 'supreme authority', typically referred to as 'sovereignty'.[70] Even when federalists state that within federations sovereignty resides with the people who then delegate it to the state or federal level,[71] they largely fail to incorporate the practice of shared sovereignty beyond units of government, to include governance

International Journal of the Commons 2 (1) (2008), 75; M. Moran and R. Elvin, 'Coping with Complexity: Adaptive Governance in Desert Australia', *GeoJournal* 74 (2009), 415; W. Steffen, A. A. Burbidge, L. Hughes, R. Kitching, D. Lindenmayer, W. Musgrave, M. Stafford Smith, and P. A. Werner, *Australia's Biodiversity and Climate Change* (CSIRO Publishing, 2009); G. R Marshall and D. M. Stafford Smith, 'Natural Resources Governance for the Drylands of the Murray-Darling Basin', *The Rangeland Journal* 32 (3) (2010), 267; R. P. Bixler, 'From Community Forest Management to Polycentric Governance: Assessing Evidence from the Bottom Up', *Society and Natural Resources* 27 (2) (2014), 155; G. R. Marshall, M. J. Coleman, B. M. Sindel, I. J. Reeve, and P. J. Berney, 'Collective Action in Invasive Species Control, and Prospects for Community-Based Governance: The Case of Serrated Tussock (Nassella trichotoma) in New South Wales, Australia', *Land Use Policy* 56 (2016), 100. All references as quoted in G. R. Marshall, 'Polycentricity, subsidiarity and adaptive efficiency' Paper presented to the International Workshop on Polycentricity, Ostrom Workshop in Political Theory and Policy Analysis, Indiana University, Bloomington, Indiana, USA, 14–17 December, 2015, available at www.researchgate.net/profile/Graham_Marshall/publication/311405734_Polycentricity_ sub sidiarity_and_adaptive_efficiency/links/58448c1008ae2d217566d349/Polycentricity-subsi diarity-and-adaptive-efficiency.pdf

69 V. Ostrom, The Meaning of American Federalism: Constituting a Self-Governing Society (1994), 261.

70 ibid., 94, 96.

71 ibid., 8 ([Federalism] 'enables people to break out of the conceptual trap inherent in a theory of sovereignty that presumes there must exist some single center of supreme authority that rules of society.').

by individuals and collectives.[72] If we are to speak of the sovereign, Vincent Ostrom famously argued, it should always be the citizen-sovereign.

Under a polycentric view, the concepts of sovereignty, democracy and governance must incorporate references to all relationships in society, vertical as well as horizontal. Most interpretations of American federalism, in Ostrom's view, prioritised the vertical delegation of sovereignty (from individuals to state and federal government) over the potential horizontal sharing and transfer of sovereignty between individuals or localities.[73] Paradoxically, the very virtues we ascribed to *vertical* fragmentation – especially the prevention of authoritarianism –[74] require *horizontal* connections among the various centres of governance which retain ultimate authority, all the way down to individuals and groups.

It is thus unsurprising that when, at the end of his life, Vincent Ostrom turned his gaze to the European Union, he was not impressed. 'Principles of subsidiarity', he reminded EU technocrats in 1996, 'need to be extended to family, neighborhood, and community far beyond the realm of nation-states as contemplated by the Maastricht Accord.'[75] How can the Ostroms' injunction be resurrected?

C *Bridging the Gap with* Demoicratic *Theory*

Ostrom's polycentricity was developed against the backdrop of US federalism and scholarship, and later applied extensively to natural resource management. To argue as we do that its emphasis on horizontal relationships can be inspiring in the EU context, we need to distinguish between two levels. First, within the scope of subsidiarity as used in EU parlance, that is regarding the vertical division of competence between the Member States and the EU in areas of shared and supportive competence, we can speak of polycentric subsidiarity as a way of emphasising

72 ibid., 89.

73 Ostrom believes that the interpretation of the founding documents of the United States – including crucially *The Federalist* written by Alexander Hamilton, John Jay and James Madison – has often been mistaken, which has distorted our understanding of federalism. Whereas federalism does indeed foresee a sharing of sovereignty between multiple units of government, Ostrom submits that the writers of the Philadelphia Convention of 1787 aimed to include a role for individuals.

74 V. Ostrom, 'Polycentricity' (Part 1) (n. 65) 68.

75 V. Ostrom, 'Faustian Bargains', *Constitutional Political Economy* 7 (4) (1996), 303, 307.

horizontal relations as partial substitutes for vertical one.[76] Second, beyond the state, the scope of EU subsidiarity needs to be enlarged in order to take into account the wider range of actors involved in governance. The analogy between these actors and state actors is not fully operative but nevertheless fruitful.

In order to clarify this distinction and drawing on Francis Cheneval in this Volume, we find it useful to draw on conceptualisations of the EU as a polity in the making which provide both a descriptive and a normative heuristic, namely demoicratic theory.[77] At the same time, however, there is also room to enrich demoicratic theory with the conceptual lenses provided by polycentric governance theory.

Demoicratic theory was developed under the conviction that the traditional political science categories pertaining to democracy, discussed in the Introduction to this Volume, needed to be rethought to apply to the EU as a new kind of democracy. As MacCormick so aptly put it:

> For this is a new form of political order, a new kind of 'commonwealth', which offers the hope of transcending the sovereign state rather than simply replicating it in some new super-state . . . It creates new possibilities of imagining, and thus of subsequently realizing, political order on the basis of a pluralistic rather than a monolithic conception of the exercise of political power and legal authority.[78]

This is what demoicratic theory seeks to do. It was developed to account for the polycentric nature of the EU, not simply in the way the United States does between federated states, but to the extent that a plurality of separate peoples, belonging to separate states, constitute its centres, centres which can only function together through freely chosen modes of mutual recognition.[79] Cheneval refers to the constituent *demoi* as separate holders of competence-competence: a bundle of powers and immunities against others to alter or cancel their powers.[80] Hence, these separate political bodies can create a multipurpose multilevel union, to

[76] This also explains the symbolic nature of the inclusion of regional and local bodies in the Lisbon text of Article 5(3) TEU: while they are now included, they are not the ones who transfer competence to the EU.

[77] F. Cheneval and F. Schimmelfennig, 'The Case for Demoicracy in the European Union', *Journal of Common Market Studies* 51 (2) (2013), 334; K. Nicolaïdis, 'European Demoicracy and Its Crisis', *Journal of Common Market Studies* 51 (2) (2013), 351.

[78] N. MacCormick, *Questioning Sovereignty* (Oxford University Press, 1999), 191.

[79] K. Nicolaïdis, 'Our European Demoi-cracy', in S. Weatherill and K. Nicolaïdis (eds.), *Whose Europe? National Models and Constitution of the European Union* (Oxford University Press, 2003).

[80] See also, in this Volume, Chapter 3 by F. Cheneval.

which powers may be delegated, but ultimately a state's powers cannot be cancelled by others. But – and this is where the normative take comes in – the praxis of polycentric government can be eroded through centralising tendencies over time, as we have seen during the euro crisis.

The shared affinity between *demoicratic* theory and polycentric governance theory lies with their respective emphasis on the horizontal dimension of governance. But *demoicracy*, as the term indicates, is centred on the idea of the people, which is not central to the original polycentric scheme. Nevertheless, while Ostrom's municipal units are not *demoi*, the analogy stands.

Yet, in spite of the non-centrality of the idea of people in original *demoicratic* theory, it itself might provide a dual anchor for our polycentric subsidiarity. Recall that if democracy is the rule of *the entire people*, a *demoicracy* is a polity ruled by *a plurality of peoples*, who govern together but not as one.[81] In this definition, 'peoples' refers both to the *demoi* or peoples which have historically constituted states and thus structures of governance within which majorities and minorities can coexist; and 'peoples' also refers to the aggregated yet direct expressions of individual citizens expressing their democratic rights, demands and struggles within and across these states but not reducible to these states. In a *demoicracy*, in other words, states matter insofar as they are themselves the democratic expression of their people, but not only they matter, as we cannot only count on governments to most faithfully express the preferences of their peoples. If this is the case, *demoicratic* theory seeks to conceptualise the ways in which peoples can govern their affairs together most effectively through their respective states but also around them. This is the double agenda set out above regarding the import of polycentric subsidiarity.

In this sense, the difference between *demoicratic* theory and theories of multilevel governance (MLG) analysed by Benz is a matter of emphasis as to whether we should care about the precise nature of the polities or 'jurisdictions' to be aggregated as well as the nature of the whole. The *demoicratic* frame privileges a *specific* level and emphasises the 'nation statist' nature of the constituent units and indeed their very unique quality as 'member states'.[82] Moreover, the *demoicratic* frame is not neutral normatively, concerned as it is with whether modes of

[81] K. Nicolaïdis, 'The Idea of European Demoïcracy', in J. Dickson and P. Eleftheriadis (eds.), *Philosophical Foundations of European Union Law* (Oxford University Press, 2012), 254.

[82] C. Bickerton, *European Integration: From Nation-states to Member States* (Oxford University Press, 2012).

coordination and aggregation protect the self-determination of separate peoples more or less effectively, while MLG privileges the functional requirements of finding the appropriate scale of governance and identity formation in social communities to ensure supranational policy effectiveness, as with the traditional subsidiarity frame described above.[83] This is not therefore a disagreement over input vs output legitimacy, but one about the normative primacy of the political over the functional.[84] The critical point here is that even while national *demoi* remain the dominant political unit where bargains are struck and compulsory solidarities institutionalised, the EU needs to be a space where *demoi* can access each other directly politically rather than simply relying on their government to do so.[85]

In this light, polycentric subsidiarity needs to be developed on two fronts. In the narrow sense introduced above, it serves to emphasise the way in which shared EU competences can be best exercised either by allowing for the right resources and incentives at the state level, or by encouraging and enforcing horizontal cooperation between states rather than the delegation of authority upwards. And given this, we then must ask what is the minimal delegation upwards needed in order for such horizontal cooperation to function, under the adjacent principle of equality between Member States set out in Article 4(2) TEU.[86]

In the second broader sense introduced above, polycentric subsidiarity serves to indicate where and how non-state actors can be better empowered in their separate or joint act of governance. For '*demoi*-cracy' to be constructed and entrenched in a way that is stable and sustainable, it needs to be 'constructed' as a social reality, so as to lead to a lived version

[83] A. Benz, 'Multilevel Governance in the European Union: Loosely-Coupled Arenas of Representation, Participation and Accountability', in S. Piattoni (ed.), *The European Union* (Oxford University Press, 2015); T. Conzelmann, 'A New Mode of Governing? Multi-level Governance between Cooperation and Conflict', in T. Conzelmann and R. Smith (eds.), *Multi-level Governance in the European Union: Taking Stock and Looking Ahead* (Nomos, 2008) 11; H. Enderlein, S. Wälti, and M. Zürn (eds.), *Handbook on Multi-Level Governance* (Edward Elgar, 2010).

[84] K. Nicolaïdis, 'Demoicratic Theory and Europe's Institutional Architecture in Times of Crisis', in S. Piattoni (ed.), *The European Union* (Oxford University Press, 2015), 141.

[85] ibid., at 142.

[86] Article 4(2) TEU "The Union shall respect the equality of the Member States before the Treaties as well as their national identities, inherent in their fundamental structures, political and constitutional, inclusive of regional and local self-government. It shall respect their essential State functions, including ensuring the territorial integrity of the State, maintaining law and order and safeguarding national security. In particular, national security remains the sole responsibility of each Member State."

of 'joint sovereignty'.[87] This is the mission to which polycentric subsidiarity can contribute.

II Mapping Polycentric Subsidiarity

How then do we operationalise polycentric subsidiarity? We suggest it has three core characteristics which are both functional and normative.

First, polycentric subsidiarity must maintain and support *self-governance*; second, it must incorporate, and sometimes privilege, *horizontal* relationships; and third, it must allow for the *organic* development of, and changes to, self-governance. These elements are mutually reinforcing and, in many ways, interlinked.

Under each of these categories, we need to identify the different logics pertaining to the various realms in which polycentricity may apply. Polycentric subsidiarity is about individuals, intermediary bodies, cities and regions as well as Member States. Do we observe and advocate congruent patterns at different scales? How different is it to discuss polycentric subsidiarity among states vs the role of individuals in decision making?

A Self-Governance

The first attribute of polycentric subsidiarity is a bias for self-governance. How should self-governance then be mitigated under conditions of interdependence?

The virtues ascribed to subsidiarity in the European context are very similar to those ascribed to devolution in American federalism.[88] Federalism after all has been about 'self-determination and accountability, political liberty, flexibility, preservation of identities, diversity and respect for internal division of component states'.[89] Naturally, the aim of

[87] F. Cheneval and K. Nicolaïdis, 'The Social Construction of Demoicracy in the European Union', *European Journal of Political Theory* 16 (2) (2017), 235, 239–40.

[88] As summarised by Justice O'Connor, federalism means to assure a decentralised government that will be more sensitive to the diverse needs of a heterogeneous society, increase opportunity for citizen involvement in democracy, allows for more innovation and experimentation, a more responsive government, and, most importantly, a check on abuses of government power. *Gregory* v. *Ashcroft*, 501 U.S. 452, 458 (1991) (citations omitted). See also K. Nicolaidis and R. Howse, *The Federal Vision: Legitimacy and Levels of Governance* (Oxford University Press, 2001).

[89] G. L. Neuman, 'Subsidiarity, Harmonization, and Their Values: Convergence and Divergence in Europe and the United States', *Columbia Journal of European Law* 2

'diversity and the preservation of identities' carries different weight and meaning in a coalition of sovereign nations, or federal union, as compared to a federal state.[90] Similarly, the relationship between individual citizens and the European Union – and the role of individuals within the 'democratic' process of the European Union –[91] is distinct from that of a 'national' citizen and its government in the United States.[92] The politics of Brussels appear distant and democratically inaccessible to most European citizens even as they perceive its growing effects on their daily lives.[93] The *demoicratisation* challenge has been about bridging this gap through injunctions for the EU both to respect and enhance democracy at the national level, and to explore ways to open up these national practices to transnational logics.[94] Polycentric subsidiarity constitutes an additional tool in this arsenal.

Obviously, self-governance is not synonymous with decentralisation, and more decentralisation does not automatically ensure more or better self-governance.[95] Depending on the scale and nature of the issue, it may be far more effective for individuals to organise at the regional or national level. While, in the narrow sense above, self-governance refers to the

(1996), 573, 574 (quoting G. Bermann, 'Taking Subsidiarity Seriously: Federalism in the European Community and the United States', *Columbia Law Review* 94 (1994), 331, 343).

90 G. L. Neuman, ibid., at 575. See also K. Nicolaïdis and R. Howse (n. 88).

91 See also M. Bartl, 'The Way We Do Europe: Subsidiarity and the Substantive Democratic Deficit', *European Law Journal* 21 (1) (2015), 23, on the link between the EU's original functionalist institutional design and its substantive democratic deficit.

92 The formalisation of public authority beyond the nation-state through an increase of formal laws – the European institutions exercise public power in ways similar to nation states – is *the* 'post-national' feature of the European Union that many consider definitive of the EU's *sui generis* nature. See e.g. G. Falkner, 'European Social Policy: Towards Multi-level and Multi-actor Governance', in R. Eising and B. Kohler-Koch (eds.), *The Transformation of Governance in the European Union* (Routledge, 1999), 93–4 (referring to the creation of a post-national democracy).

93 S. A. H. Denters, 'Participation and Democratic Accountability: Making a Difference for the Citizens', (2017) in C. Schwab, G. Bouckaert, and S. Kuhlmann (eds.), *The future of local government in Europe: Lessons from research and practice in 31 countries* (*Modernisierung des öffentlichen Sektors, No. Sonderband 47*, NOMOS 2017).

94 ibid. See also L. Donatelli, 'A Pan-European District for the European Elections? The Rise and Fall of the Duff Proposal for the Electoral Reform of the European Parliament' (2015) Bruges Political Research Paper 44/2015.

95 S. A. H. Denters, 'Active Local Citizenship: A Resource for EU Support?' (2017 – on file with the author); the 1979 Welsh devolution referendum is an example of a situation where possibility for increased self-governance was rejected, see e.g. www.bbc.co.uk/news/special/politics97/devolution/wales/briefing/79.shtml. For a comparative analysis of the situation in 1979 and 1999, see R. W. Jones and B. Lewis, 'The Welsh Devolution Referendum', *Politics* 19 (1) (1999), 37.

Member States – as the only decision unit to have competence-competence and legal immunity against the power encroachment by others as per Cheneval – it needs to apply to other actors in different ways. In short, polycentric subsidiarity requires two moves:

1) Broadening the definition when applied to Member States – Assigning intrinsic value to self-governance in a polycentric subsidiarity assessment goes beyond the instrumental rationale for decentralisation as a way of increasing democratic legitimacy, or enhancing the likelihood that collective decisions will stick. It implies that the efficiency and economies of scale criteria need to be supplemented, or counterbalanced, with considerations of the intrinsic value of self-governance to reflect the intrinsic worth of closeness and immediacy, even at the cost of (some) efficiency. Short of such a move, the principle of subsidiarity fails to bite – a reason is always found why an action must be taken at a higher level. In the EU context, we have seen that once the case for efficiency and effectiveness is made ('*the objectives of the proposed action cannot be sufficiently achieved by the Member States*' and '*can rather, by reason of the scale or effects of the proposed action, be better achieved at Union level*'),[96] there is little to counterbalance it. Polycentric subsidiarity sees self-governance, even if less 'efficient' in certain respects, as this counterbalance.
2) Broadening the definition beyond the state – Where citizen efforts are channelled through existing governmental entities at the local and regional level, they are not meaningfully incorporated in EU subsidiarity assessments: the division of competences below the state remains a matter for the Member States.[97] In the context of polycentric governance, this means that instances of bottom-up, organic, self-governance are almost entirely absent from subsidiarity decisions within the EU; they are only incorporated insofar that their effects are taken into account by national parliaments and/or national representatives in the Council during subsidiarity assessments.[98] In addition to creating a blind spot for instances of organic self-

[96] Article 5(3) TFEU.

[97] See Case C-359/92 *Germany* v. *Council ('Product Safety')* [1994] ECR I-3681; R. Schütze, 'Subsidiarity after Lisbon: Reinforcing the Safeguards of Federalism', *Cambridge Law Journal* 68 (2009), 525.

[98] Some authors believe this problem to be one of principle, rather than of fact, see B. S. Frey and R. Eichenberger, 'FOCJ: Competitive Governments for Europe', *International Review of Law and Economics* 16 (3) (1996), 315 at 323. ('Even if subsidiarity were taken seriously, it would not lead to a real federal structure, because many (actual or prospective)

governance, this practice puts pressure on existing relationships, and hard-won compromises[99] between the Member States and their subsidiaries. Tellingly, the pre-Lisbon subsidiarity test included an assessment of the efficiency of the *national* level to achieve a certain goal and the comparative efficiency of the European level to reach the same objective.[100] While this language was not included in the Lisbon Protocol on subsidiarity, the Commission stated that it would continue to apply these guidelines also after the entry into force of the Lisbon Treaty.[101]

The absence of local and regional government in EU subsidiarity assessments – even though their de facto role in the implementation and enforcement of EU policy is significant –[102] is only half the picture: in order to meaningfully incorporate organic development of self-governance, our focus needs to be expanded to include non-governmental organisations, churches, community groups and other non-state based centres of decision making.

Of course, problems arise when and if the aims identified through self-governance contradict shared values or the overwhelming interest of others.[103] As we revisit this traditional subsidiarity, we must ask why and by whom self-governance needs to be encroached on. Following Vincent Ostrom's reasoning, self-governance could only be overridden by another aim, if such an aim is the result of a process of self-governance.[104] This of course raises the question of what EU level self-

members of the European Union are essentially unitary states without federal subunits of significant competence.')

99 See J.-W. Muller, 'Should the EU Protect Democracy and the Rule of Law inside Member States?', *European Law Journal* 21 (2) (2015), 141; J. Loughlin, *Subnational Democracy in the EU* (Oxford University Press, 2001).

100 Protocol No. 30 on the Application of the Principles of Subsidiarity and Proportionality, annexed to the Treaty on the European Community (1997), Article 13, OJ C 321 E, p. 308. Arguably, a third part of the test should consider the cross-border nature of the activity the EU aimed at regulating, see in Case C-58/08 *The Queen* v. *Secretary of State for Business, Enterprise and Regulatory Reform* [2010] ECR I-4999, Opinion of the Advocate General, para. 24. More generally, see www.ies.be/files/8.16.5_European%20Public%20Prosecutor_Wieczorek_FINAL.pdf

101 Report from the Commission on Subsidiarity and Proportionality, 18th Report on Better Law-Making Covering the Year 2010, COM (2011) 344 final (10.06.2011), at 2,

102 See J. van Zeben, 'Local Governments as Subjects and Objects of EU Law', in E. Fahey and S. Bardotszky (eds.), *Subjects and Objects of EU Law* (Edward Elgar, 2017).

103 For shared values in the EU see, in this Volume, Chapter 6 by A. Bobić.

104 M. D. McGinnis and E. Ostrom, 'Reflections on Vincent Ostrom, Public Administration and Polycentricity', *Public Administration Review* 72 (1) (2012), 15, 20.

governance may look like within the broader global context or rule-bound globalisation – a question beyond this chapter.

Most importantly for our purposes here, the question is how should aims resulting from self-governance be balanced with concurrent requirements, in order to deal with actual or potential externalities when they arise, so as to continue to maximise its import? This brings us to the second attribute.

B Horizontality

Self-governance, as per Ostrom, embraces many different centres and levels of governance, without presuming a hierarchical relationship between them. Horizontal relationships – between actors at the same level of governance and/or with the same competences – are therefore equally relevant as vertical relationships – between actors with different powers at different levels of governance.[105] While the Treaties explicitly recognise the equality of the Member States *inter se* and vis-à-vis the Union (as captured in Article 4 TEU, which describes the relationship as one of 'full mutual respect' and 'equality'),[106] horizontal relations between actors arise in practice under conditions of asymmetric power.

Polycentric conceptualisations of subsidiarity must therefore address the problem of dominance within vertical and horizontal relationships. Dominance can be purposive or structural, it can be the result of political dynamics, and/or a consequence of practical realities, including the ability to provide human capital, goods, information or other resources. Vertical authority can be necessary in order to mitigate horizontal asymmetries of power, and horizontal relations can serve to balance a drift to power centralisation. In the words of Cheneval, '[t]he art of doing politics well consists in the way in which a community is able to transform the tension between the vertical exercise of authority and the horizontal recognition of equal status into a functional social equilibrium that produces public goods.'[107]

To a great extent of course, the EU, more than any federal system, does rest on horizontal relations. Polycentric subsidiarity is therefore not an alternative to subsidiarity as understood in the EU but a matter of emphasis. If rule-based societies are to dampen the monopoly of the

[105] On 'power' in polycentric systems see also, in this Volume, Chapter 3 (Section I.A) by F. Cheneval on competence-competence.

[106] Article 4(3) and 4(2) TEU, respectively.

[107] See, in this Volume, Chapter 3 by F. Cheneval.

state, and if transnational relations between them are to avoid a single centre of dominance, they need to perfect horizontal relationships among them, based on a changing mix of mutual respect, mutual trust, and mutual spying. To simplify, privileging horizontal approaches over their centralising/harmonisation alternatives, we can distinguish between three paradigmatic approaches to doing so:

(1) *Other-regarding domestic/local institutions or habits*: this is of course the cradle of self-governance in an inter-dependent world, where each party would govern itself with personal or institutional empathy, as a result of different degrees of spontaneous adaptation, and different degrees of knowledge of each other.[108] More formally, institutions may be created to internalise externalities at the national or state level even in the absence of compulsion from above (like national fiscal councils under EMU reforms).

(2) *Horizontal coordination*: in this spirit, the EU spent much of its energy in the 2000s developing the Open Method of Coordination, but much of it has since been abandoned.[109] More generally, horizontal cooperation between intermediary bodies in the EU or between national agencies is one expression of polycentric subsidiarity to the extent that this avoids creating centralised bodies. Efforts to coordinate primary, secondary and tertiary education systems between the Member States, assisted by the EU, through the Bologna Process are an illustration of such coordination.[110]

(3) *Horizontal transfers of authority/sovereignty*: only in these cases do we see a unit binding itself contractually to other decision units. In some cases, recognising the extraterritorial application of the rules of other countries or entities on one's territory (mutual recognition) is the price to pay for self-governance, as opposed to harmonisation of standards and centralisation of their enforcement. Mutual recognition paradoxically is intended to protect the space for self-governance while making this space one where alternative standards or standards of enforcement may compete. The second guessing of other Member States' standards can lead to conflict in this setting

[108] K. Nicolaïdis, 'My EUtopia – Empathy in a Union of Others', in M. Segers and Y. Albrecht (eds.), *Re:Thinking Europe – Thoughts on Europe: Past, Present and Future* (Amsterdam University Press, 2016).

[109] See, in this Volume, Chapter 12 by S. Garben.

[110] S. Garben, *EU Higher Education Law: The Bologna Process and Harmonization by Stealth* (Kluwer Law International, 2011).

> and needs to be managed in complex ways.[111] Outside of the internal market, Member States increasingly, though not indiscriminately, accept the judicial systems of Member States with respect to criminal justice, as evidenced by the European Arrest Warrant.[112] This horizontality extends beyond national governments, with Member State constitutional courts routinely cross-referencing each other's judgments, even though there is no legal obligation to do so, or formal precedential effect of such foreign judgments.[113]

Clearly then the relationship between vertical and horizontal relations of cooperation or delegation are multifaceted. To simplify there are instances where the two can be considered functional substitutes but where some degree of centralisation is nevertheless necessary as with the standardisation of product requirements; there are areas where horizontal cooperation and delegation can be elected on grounds of the intrinsic value of self-governance, as in the field of education where the EU facilitates processes of coordination between the Member States, and any powers it holds in this area are also on basis of equality with the Member States.[114]

111 See M. Hazelhorst, *Free Movement of Civil Judgments in the EU and the Right to a Fair Trial* (Springer, 2017): 'Mutual recognition can be seen as the practical application of mutual trust: if one Member State trusts another, then it should recognize judicial decisions and other acts of the Member State without second-guessing whether it conforms to its own national standards'.

112 At first, exceptions were possible in case of systemic flaws: see M. den Heijer, 'Joined Cases C-411 & 493/10, *N. S.* v. *Secretary of State for the Home Department* and *M. E. and Others* v. *Refugee Applications Commissioner, Minister for Justice, Equality and Law Reform*, Judgment of the Court', *Common Market Law Review* 49 (5) (2012), 1735 (note); Now, exceptions can also be invoked on a case by case basis: see G. Anagnostaras, 'Mutual Confidence Is Not Blind Trust! Fundamental Rights Protection and the Execution of the European Arrest Warrant: *Aranyosi and Caldararu*', *Common Market Law Review* 53 (6) (2016), 1675 (note). Recently, the question was raised as to whether the current situation in Poland endangers fair trial and independent judging. The AG has said it could indeed be a valid basis for rejecting Polish decisions if real risk is demonstrated: https://curia.europa.eu/jcms/upload/docs/application/pdf/2018-06/cp180095en.pdf

113 A. Bobić, 'Constitutional Pluralism Is Not Dead: An Analysis of Interactions between the European Court of Justice and Constitutional Courts of Member States', *German Law Journal* 18 (6) (2017), 1395. Specifically note 117 in that article.

114 See S. Garben, *EU Higher Education Law: The Bologna Process and Harmonization by Stealth* (Kluwer Law International, 2011).

C Organic Change

How then is such an emphasis on self-governance to be managed over time? We start from the assumption that in a robust self-governing society, individuals organise around shared interests and goals in ever-changing and dynamic ways. Polycentricity stimulates and protects this *organic development* through the institutional essentials and prerequisites of polycentric governance, which are aimed at ensuring access to processes of creation, enforcement and contestation of the shared rules, as well as to essential opportunities for learning, information and paths to justice.[115] According to Ostrom, self-governance refers to individuals' capacity to 'formulate mutually agreed upon rules that they themselves proceed to enforce'.[116] Defined as such, self-governance is inherently social, aimed at achieving a rule-ordered society where rules are not (exclusively) imposed by the state,[117] and where individuals *organically* self-organise based on their needs and preferences.

What then are the different organic trajectories offered by the various modes of self-governance and horizontal relations outlined above? And for each trajectory, what are some of the questions that arise?

1) *Vertical function:* Each approach may be supported, supplemented, managed or policed in different ways by elements of vertical delegation, e.g. bundles of institutions, rules and standards. The extent of vertical delegation chosen to support horizontal relations ought to be more easily changeable over time, including through formal sunset clauses with respect to EU law, as well as more general multi-stakeholder review processes.
2) *Heterogeneous relationships:* The relevant relations may be between centres which are all of the same kind/same level (say states, or cities) or polycentricity may refer to diagonal relations, i.e. relations among different levels/types of centres, such as states, regions, non-state actors. Simultaneous homogeneity vs heterogeneity of levels may reflect the fact that in different countries or regions, the most effective type of actor for a given action changes over time. Organic change implies a better mirroring between such evolutions and formal competences.

[115] See, in this Volume, Chapters 1 and 2 by J. van Zeben.
[116] V. Ostrom, *The Meaning of American Federalism* (n. 69) 226.
[117] V. Ostrom, *The Meaning of American Federalism* (n. 69) 4.

3) *Temporal differentiation:* Units involved in a relationship may exercise certain functions simultaneously and equally or these functions can be subject to rotation over time. Reasons of expertise and capacity building may dampen the likelihood of rotation, which in turn could be countered by shifts in preferences combined with technological change, which may facilitate access to certain types of expertise or information.
4) *Structural differentiation:* Different kinds of cooperation may be universally desired and applied to all equivalent units holding equal powers, or conversely subject to differentiation, e.g. applied to some but not others, in other words may be subject to differentiated integration.[118] As preferences and technologies change over time, the modes of inclusion in various configurations of players should be subject to flexible arrangements. Conceptually, one could bring the idea of differentiation which initially pertains to different 'clubs of States' all the way down to the individuals, for example, by enabling individuals to provide utility services that had been the prerogative of corporations, such as energy production.[119]
5) *Functional differentiation:* The balance of different types of horizontal relations (as outlined in subsection B) may not apply in the same way for the design of rules/law/standards, their implementation and their enforcement. Directives in every area of EU law illustrate how horizontal agreement between Member States can lead to common standards, which are subsequently implemented and enforced by the Member States – at various levels – incorporating vertical checks on such implementation and enforcement, but also allowing for

[118] One example of this could be a 'multi-speed' Europe. However, in this model, the focus is on the difference in national preferences, which continues to bypass the individual – a classic pitfall of the existing EU narratives. See M. Avbelj, 'Differentiated Integration – Farewell to the EU 27?', *German Law Journal* 14 (2013), 191; J. C. Piris, *The Future of Europe: Towards a 2-speed EU?* (Cambridge University Press, 2012); G. Majone, *Rethinking the Union of Europe Post-Crisis* (Cambridge University Press, 2014); C. Jensen and J. Slapin, 'Institutional Hokey-Pokey: The Politics of Multi-Speed Integration in Europe', *Journal of European Public Policy* 19 (2012), 6; M. Dawson and F. De Witte, 'Self-Determination in the Constitutional Future of the EU', *European Law Journal* 21 (3) (2015), 371, 377.

[119] G. Walker, 'What Are the Barriers and Incentives for Community-Owned Means of Energy Production and Use?', *Energy Policy* 36 (12) (2008), 4401; L. W. Li, J. Birmele, H. Schaich, W. Konold, 'Transitioning to Community-owned Renewable Energy: Lessons from Germany', *Procedia Environmental Sciences* 17 (2013), 719.

processes of horizontal learning, competition and cooperation on implementation and enforcement.[120]

**

To the extent that subsidiarity applies to relationships between political actors, there are many dimensions along which its design can vary. We suggest that such variance needs to be considered in two steps. First, to the extent that polycentric subsidiarity calls for privileging horizontal approaches over their centralising/harmonisation alternatives, we can distinguish between three paradigmatic approaches to doing so: first, by creating or reinforcing domestic institutions, and procedures, that are other-regarding; second, through horizontal coordination; and finally, through horizontal transfers of authority and/or sovereignty.

Within a polycentric system, a number of variables will affect these approaches simultaneously, reflecting the dynamic nature of polycentric governance. These variables of organic change interact with each of these approaches and also reflect the complexity of polycentric governance and the high level of information and learning which is necessary to maintain it.[121]

Table 4.1 *Constituent Elements of Polycentric Subsidiarity*

Actors	Relationships	Variables of organic change
• Member States • Regional governmental actors • Local authorities • Non-governmental organisations • Individuals	• Vertical • Horizontal • Other-regarding institutions/ processes • Coordination • Transfers of authority/ sovereignty	• Vertical Function • Heterogeneous centre • Temporal differentiation • Structural Differentiation • Function differentiation (design implementation, enforcement)

[120] See also, in this Volume, Chapter 12 by S.Garben.
[121] See, in this Volume, Chapter 11 by V. Abazi and 12 by S. Garben.

To illustrate, take the idea of a reformed refugee regime in the EU based on polycentric subsidiarity. This would start with the acknowledgement that refugee management involves fundamental value trade-offs that may be struck differently across states (e.g. the difference in approach to refugee intake between Sweden and Poland; the ways in which different countries balance internal vs border control of people, etc.). Countries could coordinate how their policies are designed, while simply be expected to be other-regarding in implementation, and delegate power to the EU to ensure enforcement. There could also be horizontal transfers of authority through mutual recognition pacts as to the status of refugees, or the creation of compensation mechanisms for accepting additional refugees.

These Member State-centric processes would be balanced by the involvement of cities, regions, together with individuals, families and neighbourhoods, that can replicate processes of horizontal coordination, but also involve transfers of authority and create other-regarding institutions that strengthens the implementation and enforcement of the overarching system of refugee management. The inclusion of these actors at all stages of regulation also prevents a mimetic bias, where different levels of governance simply try to copy each other's processes, thereby limiting responsiveness to heterogeneous preferences and conditions among these centres. While the aim of preventing free-riding by individual Member States, calls for an EU wide system of rules and values to ensure that differentiated preferences and abilities are not used to simply justify free-riding, the practical translation of shared commitments can be differentiated over time.

III Concluding Remarks

This chapter introduced the notion of polycentric subsidiarity as a revised understanding of subsidiarity in the EU. Polycentric subsidiarity supplements the EU's core vertical problematic with both a greater emphasis on the horizontal transfers of power between governments as well as between governmental and non-governmental actors, and with a greater emphasis on subsidiarity 'all the way down'. We argue that while the criteria of effectiveness and efficiency need to remain part of the picture, polycentric subsidiarity aims to facilitate the organic development of self-governing collectives and individuals. In order to do so, expanding the species and levels of governance that form part of a subsidiarity assessment is insufficient; polycentric subsidiarity must also include various forms of horizontal transfers of power, and accommodate the dynamic nature of polycentricity by recognising the variables that affect vertical and horizontal power sharing.

As a result, the EU's political and legal ecosystem must resist the temptation of identifying the characteristics of a subsidiarity 'winner' for a given policy, privileging instead process and possible shifts of locus of governance and authority as circumstances and actors change. Actors within the system could then determine the goals of governance regarding a particular issue, and allow for rules, processes and institutions to develop organically. At first glance, this appears to strip the subsidiarity principle as traditionally understood from its prescriptive function by failing to incorporate a preference for a given level of governance. In practice, the kind of imperatives implied by the idea of polycentric subsidiarity can allow all the actors involved to use the worthy principle of subsidiarity as a genuine normative safeguard for self-governance and self-determination in contemporary politics. The EU, embattled as it is by multifaceted calls to 'take back control', needs to heed this call.

5

Polycentricity and the Internal Market

JOSEPHINE VAN ZEBEN AND ANA BOBIĆ

The internal market is at the core of European integration, with economic interdependency meant to ensure peaceful relations between the Member States. The EU's constitutional set-up reflects the centrality of the market's four freedoms – the free movement of goods, services, capital and persons.[1] Initially, the EU's role was to remove barriers to the internal market but over the years, European integration has become increasingly 'positive', creating common rules in many trade-related areas. As a result, EU competence now extends to policy areas that are not exclusively, or even tangentially, economic.[2] Notwithstanding the EU's important role in other policy areas, the internal market continues to be fundamental. As evidenced by Brexit, many national constituencies still view the internal market as the most important 'pull factor' of EU membership with the most tangible benefits (and costs).[3]

The internal market is a political and legal construct; it has been, and continues to be, shaped by a rich body of primary and secondary EU law, accompanied by the Court of Justice's jurisprudence. As the EU created the market, the market in turn enabled further growth of the EU, with the creation of many EU competences initially justified through their links to the Union's market responsibilities.[4] This interconnectedness between the market and the broader governance system is also emphasised in polycentric governance theory: Vincent Ostrom strongly believed that cross-fertilisation between public and private actors was possible, and necessary, in order to create better institutions. He emphasised that

[1] See notably Article 21, Article 26, Titles II and IV of the Treaty for the European Union ('TFEU').

[2] This is notably the case with regard to EU's shared competences (Article 6 TFEU), encompassing areas such as freedom, security and justice.

[3] See e.g. www.theguardian.com/politics/2017/jul/17/majority-of-brexiters-would-swap-free-movement-for-eu-market-access, accessed July 2018.

[4] See for example Council Directive 67/548/ EEC of 27 June 1967 on the approximation of laws, regulations and administrative provisions relating to the classification, packaging and labelling of dangerous substances [1967] OJ Spec Ed 234.

entrepreneurs' ability to self-organise could be taught to governmental counterparts and other individuals in order to increase levels of self-governance beyond the economic sphere.[5] Similarly, Ostrom found that 'the market' was better conceptualised as a 'complex institutional arrangement',[6] than as a separate or competing force to that of the government.

Polycentric governance requires a dynamic balancing act of many different interests through a complex system of vertical and horizontal interactions.[7] In envisaging such a system, our focus is automatically drawn to political institutions and the rules of engagement with, and shaped by, governmental power. However, this focus may lead us to overlook the vital importance of achieving polycentricity in other arenas – such as judicial affairs and economic life – for realising and maintaining polycentric governance.[8] Simply stated, this implies that the internal market has to be polycentric in order for EU polycentric governance more generally to be successful. Equally, the internal market can only be polycentric if the institutional structure in which the internal market functions allows for polycentricity. This Chapter therefore examines to what extent the EU's internal market is a polycentric system, contained within the larger polycentric order of the EU.[9]

The aim of this Chapter is to explicate connections between polycentric features of the market, complete and incomplete, and EU polycentric governance in general. To facilitate this inquiry, we set out the polycentric attributes of the market to help conceptualise the market as a polycentric system (Section I). We then move on to study if, how, and to what extent, the EU laws governing internal market are able to accommodate the institutional essentials and prerequisites needed for polycentric governance within the internal market (Section II). The final part

[5] M. D. McGinnis and E. Ostrom, 'Reflections on Vincent Ostrom, Public Administration, and Polycentricity', *Public Administration Review* 72 (1) (2012), 15.

[6] ibid., 20.

[7] See, in this Volume, Chapter 1 by J. van Zeben and Chapter 4 by J. van Zeben and K. Nicolaïdis.

[8] V. Ostrom, 'Polycentricity' (Part 1) (1972) reprinted in M. D. McGinnis (ed.), *Polycentricity and Local Public Economies: Readings from the Workshop in Political Theory and Policy Analysis* (University of Michigan Press, 1999), 56.

[9] This positioning of the market is in line with the idea that there is a need for the study of nested systems – systems within systems – even if this introduces a necessary level of complexity to our analysis. See also A. R. Poteete, M. A. Janssen, and E. Ostrom, *Working Together: Collective Action the Commons, and Multiple Methods in Practice* (Princeton University Press, 2010).

of the Chapter examines the effect of complete, and incomplete, polycentric features of the market on EU polycentricity more broadly (Section III).

I The Internal Market as a Polycentric Structure

Competitive markets are open systems where anyone is free to enter as a trader and to engage in exchanges with others through mutual agreements.[10] When functioning successfully, competitive markets present opportunities to create information about prices and quality of services and goods, and the potential for financial rewards can lead to successful innovation.[11] Defined in this way, a prima facie case for the characterisation of the internal market as a polycentric system at the hand of polycentric attributes is quickly made: each individual, consumer group, company or other groups with shared interest can organise themselves as an *independent centre of decision making*. In order to ensure that the market remains competitive and to facilitate the making and honouring of voluntary agreements between the parties, an *overarching shared system of rules* is put in place that prevents problems such as potential dominance in the form of cartels or other monopolistic behaviour, through competition law (or breaches of contract), contract law or consumer protection law. *Continuous competition* is intrinsic to competitive markets and in order to ensure healthy competition, *conflict resolution* strategies are made available to market participants. However, the economic ideal of a competitive market is seldom reflected in the practice of actual markets. Unsurprisingly, therefore, while the EU's internal market does display all the attributes of a polycentric system, there are some important 'ifs, ands or buts'.

First, the identification of independent centres of decision making shows a broader range, and different constellation, of parties as compared to polycentric governance, as membership of the market is not conditioned on citizenship.[12] It also brings out different allegiances between parties; for

[10] V. Ostrom, *The Meaning of American Federalism: Constituting a Self-Governing Society* (ICS Press, 1994), 229.

[11] ibid., at 231.

[12] A strong case can be made that polycentric societies equally do not require citizenship for participation. Citizenship does continue to be the standard for nation states, and also in the EU, the position of citizens and non-citizens differs starkly. On the citizen/non-citizen distinction see, in this Volume, Chapter 7 by M. van den Brink and Chapter 8 by I. Goldner Lang.

example, the interests, decision making and rights of the individual-as-consumer can be distinguished from those of the individual-as-citizen.[13] Parties are also potentially able to assume positions of economic power that translate into the ability to set rules. For instance, the market power of some individual companies allows them to act as independent decision units – i.e. capable of creating rules or standards – without the need to combine forces with others through actions such as price-setting due to a monopoly position, or the unilateral adoption of environmental or social standards for business practices or products. The actual ability of companies to act in this way is regulated, and severely limited, through mechanisms such as competition law aimed at preventing dominance on the market.[14] These controls support the polycentric nature of the market as the emergence of dominance, governmental or private, would be a threat to polycentricity. The unilateral adoption of standards – for example through corporate social responsibility practices – is permitted insofar as they foster competition instead of de facto market foreclosure.[15]

As mentioned above, some shared rules – and common understandings – are needed in order for voluntary exchanges to take place and for competition and coordination to occur without the emergence of dominance. Depending on our level of analysis and the body of rules under consideration, the overarching system of rules can be used both as a support and threat to polycentricity. Negative harmonisation in the internal market creation aligns with this: those rules that created obstacles to competition or collaboration between the independent units (actors of the internal market) are removed,[16] without necessarily pre-empting entirely the creation of rules by Member States and professional organisations.[17] Thus, negative harmonisation appears to be prima facie supportive of polycentric governance within the internal market.

[13] M. Sagoff, 'On the Value of Endangered and Other Species', *Environmental Management* 20 (6) (1996), 897.

[14] As is discussed in detail in Section II.

[15] This is to be distinguished from companies lobbying for the adoption of market-wide changes in standards that do lead to de facto market foreclosure, e.g. higher environmental standards that reward those actors with the newest clean technologies. See notably D. Vogel, *Trading Up: Consumer Protection and Environmental Regulation in a Global Economy* (Harvard University Press, 1995).

[16] For a comprehensive overview of the history of the internal market, see S. Micossi, '30 Years of the Single European Market' (2016), College of Europe, Bruges European Economic Policy Briefings (BEEP) 41/2016.

[17] Moreover, social partners are to be consulted on internal market legislation with social implications, see Article 2 of Commission Decision 98/500/EC of 20 May 1998 on the

Positive harmonisation, where EU legislation is used to create common rules to govern certain processes,[18] is not as obviously compatible with a polycentric market. The danger here, particularly with rules of maximum harmonisation,[19] is one of over-centralisation and the undermining of competition and coordination between the units that constitute the polycentric internal market. In doing so, the potential of the market to create coherence, even in the absence of centralised state-based rule-making, is reduced.[20] In some cases, this type of regulation has tangible benefits – better consumer protection, environmental protection, public health – which raises a higher-level question: can we opt out of polycentricity (at least in some parts of the market) in order to achieve desired or desirable outcomes? Perhaps. However, where this is not our intention, undermining polycentric governance – which effectively means reducing or taking away the ability to self-govern – in order to achieve other aims needs to be a conscious decision, not an accidental side-effect.

In sum, the internal market displays all the attributes of a polycentric system. However, this does not necessarily mean that it also maintains all the institutional essentials and prerequisites that would ensure polycentricity within the market.[21]

II Institutional Essentials in the Internal Market

Institutional essentials help ensure that 'individuals acting at all levels will have the incentives to create or institute appropriate patterns of ordered relationships'.[22] These rules can also be – and often are – informal, but for reasons of feasibility, our focus continues to be on formal rules,

establishment of Sectoral Dialogue Committees promoting the Dialogue between the social partners at European level (notified under document number C(1998) 2334).

18 See e.g. P. Caro de Sousa, 'Negative and Positive Integration in EU Economic Law: Between Strategic Denial and Cognitive Dissonance?', *German Law Journal* 13 (2012), 979.

19 See notably S. Weatherill, 'Maximum versus Minimum Harmonization: Choosing between Unity and Diversity in the Search for the Soul of the Internal Market', in N. Nic Shuibhne and L. W. Gormley (eds.), *From Single Market to Economic Union: Essays in Memory of John A. Usher* (Oxford University Press, 2012).

20 V. Ostrom, *The Meaning of American Federalism* (n. 10) 224. ('If the whole system of human affairs is capable of being organised on principles of polycentricity rather than monocentricity, we could have human societies that no longer depend upon a unity of power to achieve coherence.')

21 See also, in this Volume, Chapter 1 by J. van Zeben.

22 V. Ostrom, 'Polycentricity' (n. 8) 60.

primarily at the European level, that allow for incentives to translate into successful self-organisation. In keeping with the structure of this Volume, the institutional essentials are discussed in turn. Further, the polycentric prerequisites of *access to information*; *access to justice* and *capacity to learn* will be discussed alongside.

A *Freedom and Ability to Enter and Exit*[23]

Free entry and exit to multiple centres of decision making is one of the institutional essentials necessary for a polycentric system to function.[24] Free movement is similarly central to the internal market, which Article 26 TFEU defines as an area of free movement of goods, services, persons and capital without internal borders. These free movement rights are detailed further in a rich body of Treaty provisions, secondary EU legislation, and the jurisprudence of the Court of Justice. Several things become immediately clear when considering these rules: first, there is limited, but important, variation between Member States' adherence to free movement rights in some areas; second, while the internal market is formally homogeneous, the specific rules on entry and exit vary between freedoms; so much so that some have argued these differences warrant viewing the internal market as four distinct internal markets.[25] The latter observation supports the conceptualisation of the market as a polycentric system and requires us to include separate discussions on *rules* of entry with respect to free movement of (i) person, services and establishment; and (ii) of goods and capital. This discussion then forms the basis for our analysis of actors' *ability* to enter and exit the internal market (iii).[26]

[23] The ability to enter the internal market partially depends on national Member State citizenship (linked to European citizenship). A more detailed account of the interaction between EU citizenship and freedom to enter and exit the EU more broadly is presented by M. van den Brink in Chapter 7 of this Volume. The derivative and autonomous rights of non-members (third country nationals) are explored by I. Goldner Lang in Chapter 8 of this Volume.

[24] See V. Ostrom, 'Polycentricity' (n. 8) and P. D. Aligica and V. Tarko, 'Polycentricity: From Polanyi to Ostrom, and Beyond', *Governance: An International Journal of Policy, Administration, and Institutions* 25 (2012), 237, 246.

[25] S. Weatherill, 'The Several Internal Markets', *Yearbook of European Law* 36 (1) (2017), 125.

[26] While not specified throughout this section, references to internal market rights of EU nationals can be read as including nationals from EEA countries and Switzerland. (Indeed, 'the EEA Agreement provides for the inclusion of EU legislation in all policy areas of the Single Market [...] The EEA Agreement guarantees equal rights and

i Free Movement of Persons, Services, and Establishment

The EU's inclusion of non-governmental actors as protagonists, as well as rights holders, can be traced back to the internal market.[27] During the creation of the European Coal and Steel Community in 1951, the creation of rights of workers in the coal and steel industry acted as a catalyst, which eventually led to rights for all citizens to move freely within the territory of the EEC to pursue economic activities.[28] Today, any national of an EU Member State can profit from free movement rights and EU law protection as long as they are economically active,[29] and engage in an activity outside of one's home Member State.[30] Individuals can be protected as workers, in the case of non-independent remunerated work,[31] or as self-employed individuals,[32] under the services and establishment provisions in Articles 49 and 56 TFEU.[33]

The efforts to remove barriers to free movement of workers have been far-reaching, touching on the regulation of entire professions (e.g. the legal profession),[34] harmonising work-related benefits, such as maternity

obligations within the Single Market for citizens and economic operators in the EEA'. See www.efta.int/eea/eea-agreement/eea-basic-features accessed 5 November 2018.)

27 See Article 4(2) of the Treaty on European Union ('TEU'): 'The Union shall respect the equality of Member States before the Treaties as well as their national identities, inherent in their fundamental structures, political and constitutional, inclusive of regional and local self-government'; see also, in this Volume, the Introduction by J. van Zeben; S. Bardutzky and E. Fahey (eds.), *Framing the Subjects and Objects of Contemporary EU Law* (Edward Elgar, 2017).

28 See Article 48 of the Treaty of Rome. ('Freedom of movement for workers shall be secured within the Community (...) such freedom of movement shall entail the abolition of any discrimination based on nationality between workers of the Member States as regards employment, remuneration and other conditions of work and employment.') In their latest reiteration, these rights can be found in Article 45 TFEU. ('Freedom of movement for workers shall be secured within the Union.')

29 Case 263/86 *Humbel and Edel* [1988] ECR 5365, para. 17; Case C-169/08 *Regione Sardegna* [2009] ECR I-10821, para. 23. The Court interpreted this to also include the activity of looking for work. Case C-292/89 *Antonissen* [1991] ECR I-745, para. 13.

30 Joined Cases C-64/96 and C-65/96 *Uecker and Jacquet* [1997] ECR I-3171, para. 16; Case C-211/08 *Commission v Spain* [2010] ECR I-5267, para. 48.

31 For example, Case C-107/94 *Asscher* [1996] ECR I-3089, para. 25.

32 Activities which fall in the scope of exercise of public power are considered to lack an economic character. See, for example, Joined Cases C-159/91 and C-160/91 *Poucet and Pistre* [1993] ECR I-637, paras. 19–20.

33 The difference between the two freedoms is based on the temporary as opposed to permanent economic activity in another Member State, established by the Court of Justice in Case C-55/94 *Gebhard* [1995] ECR I-4165, para. 39.

34 Directive 2006/123/EC of the European Parliament and of the Council of 12 December 2006 on services in the internal market [2006] OJ L376/36 ('Services Directive'); for the example of the legal profession, see Directive 98/5/EC of the

leave,[35] and extending to family members of EU workers to ensure that workers' rights are not indirectly hindered through restrictions on the movement of their family members.[36] Nevertheless, some limits to free movement are allowed – e.g. for employment of a 'public service' nature –[37] and indirect restrictions continue to exist – for instance the continuing lack of social services harmonisation.[38]

Since 1990, the creation of EU citizenship ensures that nationals of all Member States can move freely within the territory of the EU, regardless of their economic activity.[39] This has shifted the focus from removing obstacles to economic mobility within the internal market to ensuring non-discrimination in social rights.[40] The importance of EU citizenship for free movement in the EU, and its polycentric potential, cannot be overstated. Citizenship rights opened the doors for individuals to actively seek optimal economic and associated opportunities across all Member States, thereby significantly fostering conditions for self-governance.[41] However, EU citizenship only has limited explanatory power for the purposes of understanding the polycentricity of the internal market. EU citizenship has broadened the ability to enter and exit *Member*

European Parliament and of the Council of 16 February 1998 to facilitate practice of the profession of lawyer on a permanent basis in a Member State other than that in which the qualification was obtained [1998] OJ L 77/36; for a good example of the debates triggered by early drafts of the Services Directive, see E. Grossman and C. Woll, 'The French Debate over the Bolkenstein Directive', *Comparative European Politics* 9 (3) (2011), 344.

35 For a recent development, see Proposal for a Directive of the European Parliament and of the Council on work-life balance for parents and carers and repealing Council Directive 2010/18/EU, Brussels 6.4.2017, COM/2017/0253 final, 2017/085 (COD).

36 Council Directive 2003/86/EC of 22 September 2003 on the right to family reunification [2003] OJ L251/12. See also Case C-256/11 *Dereci* [2011] ECR I-11315. Third country residents can also hold independent rights, typically linked to their own economic activity, however, the focus of the current chapter is EU nationals. For further discussion of third-country national ('TCN') rights see also, in this Volume, Chapter 8 by I. Goldner Lang.

37 Article 45(4) TFEU.

38 For a general critique, see S. Garben, 'The Constitutional (Im)balance between "the Market" and "the Social" in the European Union', *European Constitutional Law Review* 13 (1) (2017), 23.

39 See Article 20 TFEU.

40 See N. Nic Shuibhne, 'Limits Rising, Duties Ascending: The Changing Legal Shape of Union Citizenship', *Common Market Law Review* 52 (2015), 889.

41 An example of this is the citizenship-related interest groups that have sprung up. See e.g. the European Citizens' Rights, Involvement and Trust Foundation (https://ecit-foundation.eu/ accessed 5 November 2018); see also the3million organisation aimed at securing EU citizens' rights in the UK post-Brexit (www.the3million.org.uk/ accessed 5 November 2018); and conversely, British in Europe, advocating UK citizens' rights in the EU post-Brexit (https://britishineurope.org/ accessed 5 November 2018).

States for economically inactive citizens. Yet, the scope of rights of economically active citizens *within the internal market* continues to differ from economically inactive citizens.[42]

Finally, freedom of establishment allows EU citizens to open (subsidiaries of) companies outside of their own Member State.[43] Similar to other freedoms, non-discrimination is a touchstone for any potential restrictions on establishment: there can be no discrimination against nationals of one Member State when they want to engage in economic activities elsewhere.[44] However, freedom of establishment can be limited; for example through EU competition law,[45] and other regulations aimed at maintaining a market with high consumer protection.[46]

ii Free Movement of Goods and Capital

Articles 34 and 35 TFEU regulate the free movement of goods by liberalising imports and exports among Member States. Free movement of goods has, moreover, been decisively shaped by the jurisprudence of the Court of Justice.[47] The Court has defined the meaning of 'goods' for the purposes of application of EU law;[48] made cross-border movement a prerequisite for the application of EU law;[49] and, most importantly, interpreted the scope of Article 34 TFEU very broadly so as to encompass all rules with any effect on intra-EU trade.[50] Later, jurisprudence has restricted the potential scope of

[42] See Section III.

[43] Article 49 TFEU.

[44] Article 49(2) TFEU.

[45] Articles 101-106 TFEU.

[46] Article 3(3) TEU. See also S. Weatherill, 'Justification, Proportionality and Consumer Protection', in P. Koutrakos, N. Nic Shuibhne, and P. Syrpis (eds.), *Exceptions from EU Free Movement Law: Derogation, Justification and Proportionality* (Hart Publishing, 2016); D. Leczykiewicz and S. Weatherill (eds.), *The Images of the Consumer in EU Law: Legislation, Free Movement and Competition Law* (Hart Publishing, 2016).

[47] See, for example, K. Alter and S. Meunier-Aitsahalia, 'Judicial Politics in the European Community. European Integration and the Pathbreaking *Cassis de Dijon* Decision', *Comparative Political Studies* 26 (4) (1994), 535, 536.

[48] Goods are 'products which can be valued in money and are capable, as such, of forming the subject of commercial transactions.' Case 7/68 *Commission* v. *Italy* [1968] ECR 423, paras. 428–429; Case 7/78 *Thompson* [1978] ECR 2247; Case C-358/93 *Bordessa and Others* [1995] ECR I-361; Case C-318/07 *Persche* [2009] ECR I-359, para. 29; Case C-393/92 *Almelo* v. *Energiebedrijf Ijsselmij* [1994] ECR I-1477; Case C-159/94 *Commission* v. *France* [1997] ECR I-5815; Case 155/73 *Sacchi* [1974] ECR 409.

[49] Case 266/81 *SIOT* [1983] ECR 731, para. 16; Case 229/83 *Leclerc and Others* [1985] ECR 1; Case C-320/03 *Commission* v. *Austria* [2005] ECR I-9871, para. 65.

[50] Case 8/74 *Dassonville* [1974] ECR 837, para. 5.

this definition,[51] with the current test being one of 'hindering market access to importers from other Member States'.[52] Furthermore, the Court created the concept of 'mandatory requirements',[53] an additional set of justifications available to Member States when they indiscriminately[54] restrict free movement of goods, in the absence of harmonising EU legislation,[55] and subject to the proportionality test.[56]

The rules on entry concerning the free movement of capital are set out in Article 63 TFEU, which prohibits all restrictions on the movement of capital between Member States and between Member States and third countries, thus having a wider geographical scope of application.[57] This freedom is perhaps the least debated within legal scholarship and practice – although the potential loss of 'passporting rights' for London City firms after Brexit may change this –[58] and also the least relevant for the current discussion.[59]

[51] For a more detailed overview of this development, see C. Barnard, 'What the Keck Are We Doing?' *Revue Trimestrielle de Droit Européen* (2014), 878; L. Prete, 'Of Motorcycle Trailers and Personal Watercrafts: The Battle over *Keck*, *Legal Issues of Economic Integration* 35 (2) (2008), 133.

[52] 'Any other measure which hinders access of products originating in other Member States to the market of a Member State [. . .].' Case C-110/05 *Commission* v. *Italy (Trailers)* [2009] ECR I-519, para. 35. See also, G. Davies, 'Understanding Market Access: Exploring the Economic Rationality of Different Conceptions of Free Movement Law', *German Law Journal* 11 (2010), 671.

[53] For a further analysis, see B. de Witte, 'Non-market values in internal market legislation', in N. Nic Shuibhne (ed.), *Regulating the Internal Market* (Edward Elgar, 2006).

[54] Measures which discriminate between domestic and imported products can only be justified on grounds listed in Article 36 TFEU. See, for example, Joined Cases C-1 and 176/90 *Aragonesa* [1991] ECR I-4151, para. 13; Case 2/90 *Commission* v. *Belgium* [1992] ECR I-4431, para. 34.

[55] Case C-456/10 *ANETT* [2012], paras. 50–51.

[56] Case C-120/95 *Decker* [1998] ECR I-1831; Case 72/83 *Campus Oil* [1984] ECR 2727; Case 120/78 *Rewe-Zentral AG* [1979] ECR 649.

[57] Further on this specificity of free movement of capital, see J. Snell, 'Free Movement of Capital: Evolution as a Non-linear Process', in P. Craig and G. de Búrca (eds.), *The Evolution of EU Law* (Oxford University Press, 2011).

[58] See M. Lehmann and D. Zetsche, 'How Does It Feel to Be a Third Country? The Consequences of Brexit for Financial Market Law', *CIGI & BIICL series* – Brexit: The Legal implications, Paper No. 14, (2018).

[59] See S. Weatherill, n. 25: 'Capital has become the largely forgotten freedom, not least as a result of the emergence of the Eurozone, and this paper will do little to remedy that forgetfulness, but it too is based on a targeting of restrictions on the free movement of capital in Article 63 TFEU'.

iii Free Movement and the Practice of Enter and Exit

Rules on internal market entry combine into a complicated web, tangled with exceptions in both EU and national law. As a consequence, a person's or a business's actual ability to enter the internal market is determined partly by the EU's harmonisation agenda, and partly by its national implementation. The latter can vary not only among Member States but also at regional or local level.[60] The freedom of entry to the internal market is thus shaped by three parameters: citizenship of a Member State – a precondition of EU citizenship – or a registered seat in a Member State;[61] EU free movement rights as defined in the Treaties, secondary legislation, and case law; and a variety of national rules.

These parameters lead to a differentiation in the ability to enter the internal market across four lines: first, nationals of Member States can access the internal market more easily than third-country nationals. The same applies to companies with a registered seat in a Member State. Second, among nationals and companies of Member States, only those engaged in an economic activity with a cross-border element have access to the internal market and associated rights.[62] Third, the ability to enter, and be active in, the internal market can vary depending on the specific Member State and its implementation of free movement rules. Fourth, the ability to enter the internal market varies by sector of the economy, or type of economic activity. For example, 'services of general economic interest' are treated differently than those exercised with mainly a private economic interest.[63]

[60] For regional differentiation, see, for example, Case C-212/06 *Walloon* [2008] ECR I-1683, where the care insurance scheme was regulated differently in the Flemish region.

[61] Except for free movement of capital, as explained in the previous Section.

[62] The Court's inconsistent case law in this area has created a degree of uncertainty regarding the scope of internal market rules. See, for example, Case C-34/09 *Ruiz Zambrano* [2011] ECR I-1177, para. 42; joined cases C-297/88 and C-197/89 *Dzodzi* [1990] ECR I-3763, para. 36; Case C-28/95 *Leur-Bloem* [1997] ECR I-4161, para. 25; Case C-130/95 *Giloy* [1997] ECR I-4291, para. 21; and Case C-1/99 *Kofi sa Italia Srl* [2001] ECR I-207, para. 32. For a critique of the cross-border rule with a special emphasis on inconsistencies in its application, see M. Mataija, 'Internal Situations in Community Law: An Uncertain Safeguard of Competences in the Internal Market', *Croatian Yearbook of European Law and Policy* 5 (2009), 31.

[63] Commission Staff Working Document, 'Guide to the application of the European Union rules on state aid, public procurement and the internal market to services of general economic interest, and in particular to social services of general interest', Brussels, 29.4.2013 SWD(2013) 53 final/2.

The ability to exit, while very important in a political and practical sense, is not governed by internal market rules in the same way.[64] In theory, exit from the internal market itself could be achieved without exit from the EU (or Member State territory) in a relatively straightforward way. All that is necessary is to leave the scope of provisions on free movement as set out above.[65] In practice, however, it is difficult to imagine a scenario under which an actor would be able to completely exit the market, or what this might look like.

Exiting the internal market as a provider of economic activity, an individual or a company, may be said to happen if an actor ceases their economic activity or confines it to a single Member State. Nevertheless, in the latter case the economic provider may still be subject to competition law within the Member State, which is almost entirely shaped by EU law. In addition, actual,[66] as well as potential,[67] consumers from other Member States may bring the situation back in the scope of EU law, and consequently hinder the actual ability to completely exit the internal market as a provider of services and/or goods. A consumer's ability to exit appears even more restricted; the buying of products imported from another Member State (even unknowingly) immediately places the consumer within the scope of EU law through consumer protection laws. This is also true for the consumption of (online)[68] services from another Member State.[69]

64 See notably Article 4(2) of Directive 2004/58/EC of the European Parliament and of the Council of 29 April 2004 on the right of citizens of the Union and their family members to move and reside freely within the territory of the Member States [2004] OJ L229/35. Article 4(1) states that: 'Without prejudice to the provisions on travel documents applicable to national border controls, all Union citizens with a valid identity card or passport and their family members who are not nationals of a Member State and who hold a valid passport shall have the right to leave the territory of a Member State to travel to another Member State'. And Article 4(2): 'No exit visa or equivalent formality may be imposed on the persons to whom paragraph 1 applies'.

65 Cease an economic activity, confine it to a single Member State, etc.

66 This applies to tourists, individuals receiving medical treatment and those travelling for the purpose of education and business. Joined Cases 286/82 and 26/83 *Luisi and Carbone* [1984] ECR 377, para. 16.

67 See Case C-384/93 *Alpine Investments* [1995] ECR I-1141, para. 39, and more extremely Case C-98/14 *Berlington Hungary* [2015] para. 27, where the Court held that 'it is *far from inconceivable* that operators established in Member States other than Hungary *have been or are interested* in opening amusement arcades in Hungary' (emphasis added).

68 Concerning online commerce, see specifically Case C-108/09 *Ker Optika* [2010] ECR I-12213.

69 See, for example, Joined Cases C-34/95 to 36/95 *De Agostini* [1997] ECR I-3843.

Brexit proves to be an interesting test case as to the practical meaning of exit. The Court of Justice has already been asked a preliminary reference on the question of whether British citizens resident in other Member States will be able to retain their EU citizenship rights post-Brexit.[70] If so, this could also include membership of the internal market for British citizens, regardless of the fact that their home Member State is no longer an EU Member, i.e. that they are no longer citizens of an EU Member State. Thus far, the academic discussion[71] concerning the status of UK nationals after Brexit revolved predominantly around the findings of the Court of Justice in cases of *Rottmann*[72] and *Lounes*.[73] It remains to be seen whether these cases, which refer to rules on Member State nationality which come within the jurisdiction of the Court of Justice, can influence a situation concerning a future non-Member State, and the rights of future non-EU nationals.[74]

**

A truly polycentric market requires a sustained practice of free entry and exit. The free movement rules of the EU's internal market as presented above show a varying degree of ability to enter and exit. On the one hand,

[70] The decision of the Dutch court can be accessed here (in Dutch): https://uitspraken.rechtspraak.nl/inziendocument?id=ECLI:NL:RBAMS:2018:605 accessed 5 November 2018. The decision is currently under appeal before superior Dutch courts. See J. Shaw, 'EU citizenship: Still a fundamental status?' (2018) EUI Working Paper RSCAS 2018/14, 9.

[71] Shaw, ibid; see also G. Davies, 'Lounes, Naturalisation and Brexit' (2018) European Law Blog, available at https://europeanlawblog.eu/2018/03/05/lounes-naturalisation-and-brexit/ accessed 5 November 2018; G. Davies, 'The State of Play on Citizens' Rights and Brexit' (2018) European Law Blog, available at https://europeanlawblog.eu/2018/02/06/the-state-of-play-on-citizens-rights-and-brexit/ accessed 5 November 2018; J. Maugham, 'Why I helped bring the Dutch case over Britons' EU rights' (2018), available at www.theguardian.com/commentisfree/2018/jan/18/dutch-case-britons-eu-rights-brexit-uk-citizens accessed 5 November 2018.

[72] Where the Court found that loss of national citizenship, which would result in the loss of Union citizenship, falls in the scope of EU law and must be proportionate. Case C-135/08 *Rottmann* [2010] ECR I-1449.

[73] Where the Court stated that naturalisation in the host Member State does not deprive the person concerned of rights previously held as an EU free mover. Case C-165/16 *Lounes* [2017].

[74] UK-based scholars appear to be promoting new forms of citizenship, or free movement rights, which would benefit UK nationals after Brexit. See C. Barnard and S. Fraser Butlin, 'Free Movement vs. Fair Movement: Brexit and Managed Migration', *Common Market Law Review* 55 (2018), 203; for an overview of the debate on associate-citizenship, see M. van den Brink and D. Kochenov, 'A Critical Perspective on "Associate EU Citizenship"' (2018) Dublin City University Brexit Institute, available at http://dcubrexitinstitute.eu/2018/05/a-critical-perspective-on-associate-eu-citizenship/ accessed 5 November 2018.

the continued differentiation between freedoms and their national implementation, and between actors, presents a chequered view of the ability to *enter*. On the other hand, the ubiquitous nature of the free movement rules and their wide scope makes it hard to imagine actual freedom to *exit*.[75]

This is not to say that fragmentation and differentiation in regulation across Member States, and of different economic sectors within the internal market, are inherently negative or preclude polycentricity within the internal market. McGinnis has suggested that the homogenisation of economic institutions hinders the ability of EU citizens to take full advantages of national and local communities and their resources.[76] Moreover, these national, regional and local differences are likely to represent preferences of the relevant populations, which is welcomed in a polycentric system.[77] National and local institutions can also function as learning grounds for upscaled economic activity within the internal market.[78] However, while fragmentation and differentiation are not intrinsically problematic, they imply similar restrictions in access to information, learning, justice and most importantly contestation and cooperation with other market actors. This in turn results in a lessened ability to self-govern for these groups, which does undermine the polycentric nature of the market.

B Enforcement of a Shared System of Rules

Individuals' ability to enforce the shared system of rules is an institutional essential necessary for polycentric systemic functioning.[79] The internal market's polycentric potential is thus partly dependent on actors' abilities to enforce the market's free movement rules.[80] There are two main ways through which enforcement takes place: judicially through the Court of Justice and national courts, and through arbitration. The former is subject to institutionalised processes at, and is

[75] S. Weatherill, 'The Several Internal Markets' (n. 25) 127–8.

[76] M. D. McGinnis, 'Costs and Challenges of Polycentric Governance: An Equilibrium Concept and Examples from US Health Care' (2011), available at https://papers.ssrn.com/sol3/papers.cfm?abstract_id=2206980 accessed 5 November 2018, 5.

[77] C. M. Tiebout, 'A Pure Theory of Local Expenditures', *The Journal of Political Economy* 64 (1956), 416.

[78] See, in this Volume, Chapter 12 by S. Garben.

[79] See P. D. Aligica and V. Tarko (n. 24) 246.

[80] This set of rules should be viewed as distinct from the overarching shared system of rules that covers the entire EU system. See in detail, in this Volume, Chapter 6 by A. Bobić.

shaped by, the EU level (i).[81] Arbitration practices, on the other hand, continue to be mostly regional and national.[82] Some key examples of EU level arbitration with the internal market will be discussed in (ii) below.

i Judicial Enforcement

The analysis below considers by which courts, and against which parties, violations of free movement rules can be judicially enforced.

Vertical and Horizontal Relationships Traditionally, international organisations place obligations on states, design their enforcement mechanisms accordingly, and only seldom envisage a role for the individual. When they do, this is an indirect obligation, based on national implementation of international obligations, not international law itself.[83] Conversely, the introduction of the concept of direct effect by the Court of Justice enables individuals to directly enforce their free movement rights, and any other EU rights, against Member States and other individuals, before any national court.[84] This 'legal revolution',[85] which includes the individual in the process of enforcement, is also a necessary step towards achieving a polycentric European Union.

The Court of Justice distinguishes between vertical and horizontal direct effect, the former enabling enforcement of free movement rights against state actors, and the latter allowing enforcement against private parties. In terms of the different market freedoms, free movement of

81 S. Weatherill, 'The Several Internal Markets' (n. 25) 131. This is also true in countries where judicial review has traditionally been marginal. See, for example, J. E. Rytter and M. Wind, 'In Need of Juristocracy? The Silence of Denmark in the Development of European Legal Norms', *International Journal of Constitutional Law* 9 (2) (2011), 470, 471. For a comprehensive list of what is entailed in the duty of national courts to review national law, see M. Claes, *The National Courts' Mandate in the European Constitution* (Hart Publishing, 2006) 67–68.

82 See www.europarl.europa.eu/RegData/etudes/STUD/2015/509988/IPOL_STU(2015)509988_EN.pdf accessed 5 November 2018, at 13.

83 See T. Schilling, 'The Autonomy of the Community Legal Order: An Analysis of Possible Foundations', *Harvard International Law Journal* 37 (2) (1996), 389; and in response, J. H. H. Weiler and U. R. Haltern, 'The Autonomy of the Community Legal Order – Through the Looking Glass', *Harvard International Law Journal* 37 (2) (1996), 411.

84 Case 26/62 *Van Gend en Loos* [1963] ECR 3, establishing the principle of direct effect of EU Law. Each national court must apply EU law to cases within their jurisdiction and protect the rights that it accords to citizens in their entirety (see M. Claes (n. 81) 108). Furthermore, national courts must disregard diverging jurisprudence of superior courts (Case 166/73 *Rheinmühlen* [1974] ECR 33, para. 4).

85 J. H. H. Weiler, 'A Quiet Revolution: The European Court of Justice and Its Interlocutors', *Comparative Political Studies* 26 (4) (1994), 510.

goods is only enforceable against the state, whereas free movement rights relating to services, establishment and workers are enforceable against both the state and collective private entities such as sports federations and trade unions.[86] The Court has further found that the general principle of non-discrimination on the basis of nationality, sex and age can be enforced against all private individuals, in particular in relation to workers' rights,[87] which is particularly important as it strengthens horizontal enforcement. National courts have, however, not uniformly accepted the obligation to apply general principles to horizontal relationships,[88] reducing the scope of horizontal direct effect both in absolute terms and vis-à-vis vertical direct effect.

The polycentric ideal emphasises horizontal relationships, resulting in an order where '[the] many autonomous elements or units seek to order their relationship with one another rather than by reference to some external authority'.[89] This ideal is not reflected in the enforcement of shared internal market rules, as the individual's ability to horizontally enforce internal market rules is limited in terms of the direct effect of these rules. Moreover, national courts further restrict the scope of horizontal enforcement, by limiting the application of general principles of law in horizontal situations.[90]

Moving away from judicial enforcement of shared rules, EU law also empowers individuals and businesses to complain to the European Ombudsman for maladministration by EU institutions, and to petition the European Parliament on matters of implementation of EU law.[91]

86 Case 36/74, *Walrave and Koch*, [1974] ECR 1405; Case C-438/05 *Viking Line ABP* [2007] ECR I-10779; Case C-341/05, *Laval* [2007] ECR I-11767. See also S. Weatherill, 'The Several Internal Markets' (n. 25) 13.

87 Case 43/75, *Defrenne* v. *SABENA*, [1976] ECR 455; Case C-144/04 *Mangold* [2005] ECR I-9981; Case C-555/07 *Kücükdeveci* [2010] ECR I-365; Case C-441/14 *Dansk Industri* [2016].

88 Danish *Højesteret* (Supreme Court) Case 15/2014 *Dansk Industri*, 6 December 2016 (available at www.supremecourt.dk/supremecourt/nyheder/pressemeddelelser/Pages/TherelationshipbetweenEUlawandDanishlawinacaseconcerningasalariedemployee.aspx accessed 5 November 2018). For an analysis, see A. Eriksson, 'European Court of Justice: Broadening the Scope of European Nondiscrimination Law', *International Journal of Constitutional Law* 7 (4) (2009), 73; Editorial Comment, 'The Scope of Application of General Principles of Union Law: An Ever Expanding Union?' *Common Market Law Review* 47 (2010), 1589; M. de Mol, 'The Novel Approach of the CJEU on the Horizontal Direct Effect of the EU Principle of Nondiscrimination: (Unbridled) expansionism of EU law?', *Maastricht Journal of European and Comparative Law* 18 (1–2) (2011), 109.

89 V. Ostrom, *The Meaning of American Federalism* (n. 10) 227.

90 See (n. 88).

91 Article 24 TFEU.

Both these mechanisms can trigger European institutions to 'enforce' against other institutions, and/or Member States.[92]

Access to justice The national court is the individual's first avenue of enforcement,[93] and is obliged to disapply any national law that contravenes an EU law obligation.[94] However, in cases of uncertainty regarding the interpretation of EU law, or its validity, the national court may, or must,[95] refer to the Court of Justice through the preliminary reference procedure. Moreover, when deciding whether or not to disapply a national law that restricts free movement, national courts have to apply the Court of Justice's proportionality test.[96] However, the division of labour between the national court and the CJEU is inconsistent; the Court sometimes carries out the entire proportionality test itself,[97] other times it gives instructions to the national court – of varying levels of detail – to make the assessment itself.[98] This type of heterogeneity 'provides more opportunity for citizens and their officials to innovate and to intervene so as to correct maldistributions of authority and

92 See www.ombudsman.europa.eu/en/atyourservice/infosheet.faces, and for more information about the Petition to the European Parliament, see https://petiport.secure.europarl.europa.eu/petitions/en/home both accessed 5 November 2018.

93 Case 106/77 *Simmenthal* [1978] ECR 629, paras. 18–22.

94 Case 6/64 *Costa* v. *ENEL* [1964] ECR 1141. Even provisions of national constitutions ('rules of national law, however framed') cannot override obligations stemming from EU law. See Case 11/70 *Internationale Handelsgesellschaft* [1970] ECR 01125, para. 3.

95 Article 267(2)-(3) TFEU provides that when a question of interpretation of EU law is raised before a national court, it may submit a preliminary reference to the Court of Justice. In contrast, this is an obligation for national courts against whose decisions there is no further judicial remedy.

96 There are three steps that the Court employs to determine whether the restriction of free movement is proportionate: first, the measure must pursue a legitimate aim; second, the measure must genuinely contribute to that aim; third, the suitable measure must be the least restrictive of free movement; and, finally, the measure must be proportionate to the interest protected by the Member State. In the words of Advocate General Maduro: '[The] greater the degree of detriment to the principle of free movement of goods, the greater must be the importance of satisfying the public interest on which the Member State relies.' Opinion of Advocate General Maduro in Case C-434/04 *Leppik* [2006] ECR I-9171, para. 27.

97 Case C-36/02 *Omega* [2004] ECR I-9609, para. 39; Case C-208/09 *Sayn-Wittgenstein* [2010] ECR I-13693, para. 93.

98 T. Tridimas, 'Constitutional Review of Member State Action: The Virtues and Vices of an Incomplete Jurisdiction', *International Journal of Constitutional Law* 9 (3–4) (2011), 737, 739. For a more detailed and incremental analysis of the case law, see J. Zglinski, 'Europe's passive virtues: The margin of appreciation in EU free movement law' doctoral thesis, (available at http://cadmus.eui.eu/handle/1814/43946). See e.g. Case C-391/09 *Runevič-Vardyn* [2011] ECR I-3787, para. 91.

outcomes'.[99] However, national courts cannot control the degree of deference accorded to them by the Court of Justice in applying the proportionality test, which moreover varies between cases and courts. Therefore, their ability to adjust internal market rules to their specific local, regional or national context remains limited, and more importantly, unpredictable.

As illustrated by the proportionality example, decentralised enforcement of free movement rules through national courts can be friendly to a polycentric market, as it allows for different centres of decision making, while the final authority to interpret the rules in the hands of the Court of Justice ensures the overarching nature of the rules.[100] However, the validity of this impression hinges on the de facto ability of actors to access courts. For example, there may be problems at the national level with delays, costs and representation.[101] Moreover, it is hard for courts to capture the full intricacy of the mutual relationships between different centres of decision making in a single case.[102] Similarly, individuals who decide to challenge EU acts directly before EU courts must show that the relevant act is of a 'direct and individual concern'.[103] The requirement of individual concern has proven an almost unsurmountable obstacle for many (potentially important) claims.[104]

This is not to say that the dominance of judicial enforcement regarding internal market rules is inherently contrary to the ideal of self-

[99] See P. D. Aligica and V. Tarko (n. 24) 246.

[100] On the currently disputed position of the Court of Justice as the final authority for interpretations in the shared system of rules see, in this Volume, Chapter 6 by A. Bobić.

[101] As Prechal underlines, national judicial enforcement is so vast that it still remains largely unknown how EU law is applied before national courts in practice. See S. Prechal, 'Community Law in National Courts: The Lessons from Van Schijndel', *Common Market Law Review* 35 (1998), 681.

[102] L. L. Fuller, 'The Forms and Limits of Adjudication', *Harvard Law Review* 92 (1978), 353, as cited in P. D. Aligica and V. Tarko (n. 24) 239–240.

[103] Article 263(4) TFEU.

[104] On the question of *locus standi* before European Courts, see notably Case 25/62 *Plaumann* [1963] ECR 9; Case C-309/89 *Codorníu* [1994] ECR I-1853; Case T-585/93 *Greenpeace* v. *Commission* [1995] ECR II-220; Case T-177/01 *Jégo-Quéré* v. *Commission* [2002] ECR II-2365; Case C-50/00 P, UPA [2002] ECR I-6677; T. Tridimas and S. Poli, 'Locus Standi of Individuals under Article 230(4): The Return of Euridice?', in P. Moser and K. Sawyer (eds.), *Making Community Law* (Edward Elgar, 2008); S. Enchelmaier, 'No-one Slips through the Net? Latest Developments, and Non-Developments, in the European Court of Justice's Jurisprudence on Art. 230 (4) EC', *Yearbook of European Law* 24 (1) (2005), 173; C. Koch 'Locus Standi of Private Applicants under the EU Constitution: Preserving Gaps in the Protection of Individuals' Right to an Effective Remedy', *European Law Review* 30 (2005), 511.

governance. Scott and Sturm see a new role for courts in forms of new governance as catalysts.[105] They give examples from the jurisprudence of the Court of Justice on how courts can contribute to new forms of governance, which aligns with Vincent Ostrom's ideals of structures of conflict resolution to 'elucidate information, clarify alternative, stimulate innovation, and extend the frontiers of inquiry to open new potentials for human development'.[106] These include a rethink of standing rules to more closely reflect the design of EU acts under review, such as the expansion of standing to those that had the right to be consulted in the decision-making process itself. Furthermore, Scott and Sturm add that courts' interpretations can have an additional epistemic role by way of focusing on the quality of the information gathering and the peer review process used to justify EU action and policies. Finally, they underline the reflexive role that jurisprudence can have on future design of policy making and decision making by emphasising the importance of the inclusive, deliberative and participatory nature of new forms of governance,[107] including also polycentric self-governance.

At present, these potential benefits are not reaped by the EU's system. Moreover, non-judicial enforcement mechanisms at the EU level are similarly limited and top-down; for example, the role of the European Commission is to safeguard the implementation and application of EU law in the Member States.[108] While the enforcement of the shared system of rules as between the EU institutions *inter se*, and the EU institutions and the Member States, does not suffer from access obstacles, it is subject to a real capacity constraint on the side of the European Commission in terms of comprehensive oversight over Member State implementation.[109]

Finally, meaningful access to justice presupposes the availability of a remedy. In terms of vertical relationships – specifically the violation of an individual's free movement rights by a Member State – individuals can

[105] J. Scott and S. Sturm, 'Courts as Catalysts: Re-thinking the Judicial Role in New Governance', *Columbia Journal of European Law* 13 (2006), 565.

[106] V. Ostrom, *The Meaning of American Federalism* (n. 10) 272.

[107] See J. Scott and S. Sturm (n. 105) 573-4.

[108] See Article 17 TEU, setting out the role of the Commission, and Article 258 TFEU, outlining the enforcement powers of the Commission.

[109] On 1 December 2017, 664 Single Market infringement proceedings were pending. Most of the 132 cases launched between 1 December 2016 and 1 December 2017 concerned the environment and the free movement of goods. On average, Member States were taking 23 months and 18 days to comply with a Court ruling. See https://ec.europa.eu/info/sites/info/files/justice_scoreboard_2017_en.pdf accessed 5 November 2018.

be awarded damages.[110] However, remedies against private parties are determined by national rules, in line with the principle of national procedural autonomy.[111] That said, the Court of Justice has made it clear that also in horizontal situations, a remedy should be available. In the context of the internal market, Article 101 TFEU on anti-competitive behaviour has been interpreted as being enforceable between private parties, and as implying the reward of a remedy when infringed.[112] Moreover, notwithstanding considerable national discretion, the enforcement of EU law rights cannot be made more difficult than the enforcement of rights stemming from national law.[113]

ii Arbitration

Arbitration is perhaps the most important possibility for the horizontal enforcement of shared rules. The process can be tailored to the needs and preferences of the parties and does not rely on governmental intervention, even though this option remains available should the decision not be followed by either party.[114] Unsurprisingly, arbitration practices within the EU vary widely.[115] In the absence of harmonisation, national law determines much of the regulatory context for arbitration. Some jurisdictions have limited the ability to establish arbitral institutions,[116] whereas others limit the judicial enforceability of arbitral decisions,[117] or have established a central administrator with mandatory arbitration laws.[118] As parties are free to choose their forum, these differences are not problematic and can be tailored to local preferences and needs. Although there have been no attempts to harmonise arbitration practices within the EU, arbitration and EU law do not live in separate spheres; the enforceability of arbitration decisions can be restricted if they conflict

[110] Cases C-6 & 9/90 *Francovich* [1991] ECR I-5357; Case C-48/93 *Factortame (No. 3)/ Brasserie de Pêcheur* [1996] ECR I-1029.

[111] Case 45/76 *Comet* [1976] ECR 2043, para. 13; Case 33/76 *Rewe-Zentralfinanz* [1976] ECR 1989; see also C. N. Kakouris, 'Do the Member States Possess Judicial Procedural "Autonomy"?', *Common Market Law Review* 34 (1997), 1389.

[112] Case C-453/99 *Courage* [2001] ECR I-6297; Joined Cases C-295/04 to C-298/04 *Manfredi* [2006] ECR I-6619.

[113] Case 45/76 *Comet* [1976] ECR 2043, para. 13. Case 33/76 *Rewe-Zentralfinanz* [1976] ECR 1989.

[114] See, *inter alia*, 1958 New York Convention.

[115] See (n. 82) at 13.

[116] For example, the Czech Republic, Greece, and Hungary.

[117] See e.g. Latvia.

[118] Such as, e.g., Malta and the Malta Arbitration Centre.

with fundamental legal norms or 'public policy' more broadly, policy which the Court of Justice has interpreted rather widely.[119]

Within the context of the internal market, there has been an important move towards the inclusion of arbitration (and other forms of 'out-of-court dispute resolution') in a number of Directives.[120] The Commission's support of arbitration could lead to relative convergence in domestic arbitration practices, or it may exacerbate divergences between them. The latter scenario could shift the power in arbitration towards businesses and powerful private stakeholders, who might start to manipulate these schemes for their own benefit and to the detriment of consumers and citizens.[121] These concerns have led the Court of Justice to adopt special provisions regarding consumer arbitration,[122] which prompted Member States to follow one of two approaches. Some jurisdictions prevent *ex ante* consumer arbitration agreements in the form of arbitration clause, which are null and void; arbitration agreements can only be made after the dispute has arisen. Others allow for these *ex ante* arbitration agreements, but only if individually negotiated. The latter ensures that the consent to the main contract is separated from the consent to arbitration, thus ensuring that consumers are not forced to waive their right to access state courts in order to conclude the main contract.[123] These two

[119] See (n. 82) at 15. See also Case C-126/97, *Eco Swiss* [1999] ECR I-3055. ('A national court to which application is made for annulment of an arbitration award must grant that application if it considers that the award in question is in fact contrary to Article 85 of the EC Treaty (now Article 81 EC), where its domestic rules of procedure require it to grant an application for annulment founded on failure to observe national rules of public policy.')

[120] For example, Directive 2000/31/EC of the European Parliament and of the Council of 8 June 2000 on certain legal aspects of information society services, in particular electronic commerce, in the Internal Market ('Directive on electronic commerce') [2000] OJ L178/1; Directive 2002/21/EC on a common regulatory framework for electronic communications networks and services with further amendments [2002] OJ L108/33; Directive 2008/48/EC of the European Parliament and of the Council of 23 April 2008 on credit agreements for consumers and repealing Council Directive 87/102/EEC [2008] OJ L133/66; Directive 2009/72/EC of the European Parliament and of the Council of 13 July 2009 concerning common rules for the Internal Market in electricity and repealing Directive 2003/54/EC [2009] OJ L211/55; and Directive 2009/73/EC of the European Parliament and of the Council of 13 July 2009 concerning common rules for the Internal Market in natural gas and repealing Directive 2003/55/EC [2009] OJ L211/94.

[121] See http://cadmus.eui.eu/bitstream/handle/1814/44226/LAW_2016_23.pdf?sequence=1&isAllowed=y accessed 5 November 2018, at 3.

[122] Case C-168/05 *Mostaza Claro* v. *Centro Móvil Milenium* [2006] ECR I-10421.

[123] See (n. 82) at 53. See also Directive 2013/11/EU of the European Parliament and of the Council of 21 May 2013 on Alternative Dispute Resolution for Consumer Disputes and

approaches show that even within this horizontal enforcement mechanism, there can be a facilitating role for governmental actors.

**

Our analysis of judicial enforcement shows an emphasis on vertical relationships in enforcement, heterogeneity between the four freedoms, and uncertainty stemming from the jurisprudence of EU and national courts, all of which undermine the ability to judicially enforce shared rules. Member States remain at the centre of the implementation and enforcement of internal market rules. Individual actors are able to enforce the shared rules of the market against Member States that are in violation or fail to implement. However, there are problems with standing that preclude these actors from being on equal footing with the Member States. With respect to those rules that apply directly to other non-state actors, there are limited possibilities for enforcement. Even when individuals can bring claims against other private parties, they are heavily reliant on Member State implementation of the relevant EU rule; the willingness of national judges to apply those rules and/or engage in the preliminary reference procedure with the Court of Justice; and national procedural rules on available remedies. The overall picture is one of narrow inclusion of individuals in enforcement, which curbs opportunities for polycentric self-governance. Compared to judicial enforcement, arbitration provides far greater opportunity for individuals to shape the method of enforcement. Particularly in the context of the internal market, the potential of arbitration appears to be significant. Actions taken by the Commission and the Court in ensuring continued equal access to arbitration for consumers and industries alike are crucial in this respect.

C *Peaceful Contestation of Shared Rules*

Self-governance requires a measure of citizen independence and self-reliance with respect to resolving conflicts and other obstacles. In the words of McGinnis, self-governance is contingent upon individual agency and consequently the investment of 'considerable amounts of

amending Regulation (EC) No. 2006/2004 and Directive 2009/22/EC (Directive on consumer ADR) [2013] OJ L165/63; Regulation (EU) No. 524/2013 of the European Parliament and of the Council of 21 May 2013 on Online Dispute Resolution for Consumer Disputes and Amending Regulation (EC) No. 2006/2004 and Directive 2009/22/EC (Regulation on consumer ODR) [2013] OJ L165/1.

time and energy in seeking out a commonly acceptable solution'.[124] In order for this process to function sustainably, (access to judicial) enforcement of internal market rules alone is insufficient; all market participants must have access to methods of peaceful contestation of the substance of shared rules, not their implementation or enforcement. The size and scope of internal market rules, as well as the rule-making process itself, make it difficult for individual actors to contest existing rules. The polycentric ideal would be for all actors to be able to engage in rule creation, and for conflicts regarding the existing rules to be peacefully resolved. This Section provides an overview of the means through which market participants can contest and influence EU rules;[125] specifically, the European Citizens' Initiative (ECI),[126] public consultation and lobbying.

European Citizens' Initiative[127] Successful ECIs are proposed by a Citizens' Committee, which includes at least seven EU citizens of voting age, living in at least seven different Member States.[128] Assuming a basic threshold is met, the Commission registers the Initiative, after which one million statements of support (signatures) – including a minimum number from at least seven Member States – are collected within 12 months of registration. Hereafter, the Initiative can be submitted to the Commission. The Initiative is subject to discussion before the European Parliament, and the Commission is given three months to adopt a formal response, detailing which action it will be taking, or will not be taking,[129] in response to the Initiative. Should the Commission decide to present

[124] M. D. McGinnis (n. 76) 2.

[125] Given our focus is on the 'shared' internal market rules, means of peaceful contestation of national implementation is excluded from our analysis. These rules are by their very nature not 'shared' as the discretion awarded to Member States for implementation is supposed to allow for differentiation. To the extent that national implementation can lead to a violation of the shared rules, we refer to this dynamic in the preceding section on the enforcement of the shared rules. For an analysis of peaceful contestation in the EU more broadly see, in this Volume, Chapter 9 by D. Kukovec.

[126] Article 24 TFEU.

[127] See, in this Volume, Chapter 10 by L. Diéz Sánchez for an analysis of the subsequent judicial review of ECIs from the perspective of access to justice in a polycentric system.

[128] See Regulation (EU) No. 211/2011 of the European Parliament and of the Council of 16 February 2011 on the citizens' initiative [2011] OJ L65/1; see also http://ec.europa.eu/citizens-initiative/public/welcome accessed 5 November 2018.

[129] As was the case of the European Citizens' Initiative 'One of Us', which did not lead to further action from the Commission. See European Commission, 'Communication on the European Citizens' Initiative "One of Us"', 28 May 2014 COM(2014) 355 final.

a legislative proposal in response to an ECI,[130] the normal legislative procedure applies.[131]

As a means of peaceful contestation, an ECI can lead to a more general increase in bottom-up participation and influence on decision making, which was found by the Commission as one of the main democratic imperatives for improving EU governance.[132] ECIs both empower the individual and contribute to the creation of a European political community.[133] Still, the Commission's discretion as to its response to ECIs means there is not necessarily a direct link between the ECI and rule creation.[134] Furthermore, even if the Commission does decide to pursue an initiative, the Parliament and Council are able to reject the proposed legislation during the legislative procedure. Moreover, even if an initiative is successful in collecting the necessary EU-wide support, the final content of the rule is outside the hands of the citizens. Thus far, the only successful internal market-related initiative concerned food safety.[135] The ECI led the Commission to change the existing rules by proposing the regulation of the use of pesticides through increased control by the

[130] The Commission is, so long as it provides reasons, free to reject the initiative all together. See Case T-646/13 *Minority Safe Pack and Others* v. *Commission* [2017].

[131] For a detailed overview of the procedure, see http://ec.europa.eu/citizens-initiative/public/how-it-works/answer accessed 5 November 2018.

[132] Commission of the European Communities, 'European Governance – A White Paper', Brussels 25.7.2001, COM(2001) 428 final, available at https://ec.europa.eu/europeaid/sites/devco/files/communication-white-paper-governance-com2001428-20010725_en.pdf accessed 5 November 2018, 4, 10.

[133] E. Monaghan, 'Assessing Participation and Democracy in the EU: The Case of the European Citizens' Initiative', *Perspectives on European Politics and Society* 13 (2012), 285, 296. See also, J. de Clerck-Sachsse 'Civil Society and Democracy in the EU: The Paradox of the European Citizens' Initiative', *Perspectives on European Politics and Society* 13 (2012), 299, 300.

[134] A. Karazia, 'The European Citizens' Initiative and the EU Institutional Balance: On Realism and the Possibilities of Affecting EU Lawmaking', *Common Market Law Review* 54 (2017), 177, 178. See also, L. Boussaguet, 'Participatory Mechanisms as Symbolic Policy Instruments?', *Comparative European Politics* 14 (2015), 1.

[135] 'Ban glyphosate and protect people and the environment from toxic pesticides' (http://ec.europa.eu/citizens-initiative/public/initiatives/successful/details/2017/000002 accessed 5 November 2018). A further internal market-related initiative that has been registered and is open for signature concerns the elimination of wage inequalities across the EU, 'Let us reduce the wage and economic differences that tear the EU apart!' (http://ec.europa.eu/citizens-initiative/public/initiatives/open/details/2017/000006 accessed 5 November 2018). Other open initiatives only have indirect baring on the internal market: see 'Stop Extremism' (http://ec.europa.eu/citizens-initiative/public/initiatives/open/details/2017/000007 accessed 5 November 2018) and 'Minority SafePack – One million signatures for diversity in Europe' (http://ec.europa.eu/citizens-initiative/public/initiatives/open/details/2017/000004 accessed 5 November 2018).

European Food Safety Agency, and decided to re-evaluate existing legislation on the matter.[136]

Perhaps one of the most well-known Citizens' Initiatives was the now withdrawn ECI 'Stop TTIP',[137] which requested the Commission to recommend that the Council repeal the negotiating mandate for the Transatlantic Trade and Investment Partnership (TTIP), and not to conclude the Comprehensive Economic and Trade Agreement (CETA).[138] The TTIP ECI was an important test case as to the type of action citizens could request from the Commission; the Commission initially rejected registration of 'Stop TTIP', arguing that an ECI could not entail a negative obligation.[139] The CJEU rejected this argument,[140] and the ECI was duly registered.[141] However, as the registration of the initiative did not take place until 4 July 2018 – almost two years after the adoption of the CETA – this part of the initiative is now devoid of purpose.[142] On 9 July 2018, the initiative was officially withdrawn.[143] While there has not yet been an official response from the initiators as to the withdrawal, the long time period between attempted registration, the Court decision and eventual registration, lays bare another weakness in the ECI process and the ability of citizens to contest EU rule-making in a timely manner.

Public Consultations and Other Dialogue-Based Initiatives The Commission's Better Regulation Agenda underlines its dedication to including civil society and relevant stakeholders by focusing on participatory mechanisms.[144] Public consultations are the main way through

136 For more information, and relevant documents, see: http://ec.europa.eu/citizens-initiative/public/initiatives/successful/details/follow-up/2017/000002/en?lg=en accessed 5 November 2018.

137 See http://ec.europa.eu/citizens-initiative/public/initiatives/obsolete/details/2017/000008 accessed 5 November 2018.

138 'Stop TTIP' http://ec.europa.eu/citizens-initiative/public/initiatives/obsolete/details/2017/000008 accessed 5 November 2018.

139 Commission Decision C(2014) 6501 of 10 September 2014.

140 Judgment of the General Court (First Chamber) of 10.05.2017, Case T-754/14 [2017].

141 Commission Decision (EU) 2017/1254
of 4 July 2017 (notified under document C(2017) 4725).
[2017] L 179/16.

142 ibid.

143 See (n. 137).

144 https://ec.europa.eu/info/law/law-making-process/planning-and-proposing-law/better-regulation-why-and-how_en accessed 5 November 2018; See also, Communication from the Commission to the European Parliament, the Council, the European Economic and Social Committee and the Committee of the Regions Completing the Better Regulation

which citizens can influence agenda setting and rule-making: the Commission has set up an online portal where citizens are able to give feedback to all stages of Commission's legislative activity – from providing ideas and gathering evidence, to commenting on impact assessments and to legislative drafts.[145] While the fact that the Commission is not required to act on feedback limits the actual power of contestation through consultation, it is also helpful in bringing the citizen closer to the legislative process, and adds considerations that the Commission may later be called upon to address, for example, by a review of the use of impact assessments in subsequent court proceedings.[146]

The Commission also organises 'Citizens' Dialogues' – town hall-like debates on broad topics such as the future of the EU, cohesion and the EU budget.[147] Similarly, EU citizens can start an online debate about a certain topic with EU representatives, as well as participate in existing debates.[148] The Dialogues allow for direct debate with the European Commissioners on a number of topics and are open to anyone (including non-EU citizens). It is however not clear what, if anything, is done with the outcome of these Dialogues and whether they could legitimately be considered as the 'contestation' of, specifically, internal market rules.

Public consultations represent a necessary step towards increasing self-governance of EU citizens in their market behaviour, as they require an active approach from the citizen to influence and contest rules. The citizen can subscribe to notifications concerning policies of interest and search for open initiatives and procedures currently taking place. Self-governance here is both conditioned by and benefits from learning.[149] First, citizens must know about the existing mechanisms

Agenda: Better Solutions for Better Results, SWD(2017) 675 final, available at https://ec.europa.eu/info/sites/info/files/completing-the-better-regulation-agenda-better-solutions-for-better-results_en.pdf> accessed 5 November 2018, 3.

145 See https://ec.europa.eu/info/law/contribute-law-making_en and https://ec.europa.eu/info/law/better-regulation/have-your-say both accessed 5 November 2018.

146 Impact assessments are becoming more widely used in judicial review by EU courts to ensure the proportionate use of EU competences. See A. Alemanno, 'Impact Assessment before Courts Evidence-Based Policymaking Meet Judicial Review', in C. Radaelli and C. Dunlop (eds.), *Handbook on Regulatory Impact Assessment* (Edward Elgar, 2016).

147 Currently one Dialogue has been planned and one has occurred: The latter concerning the EU budget for the future and cohesion policy (Riga, Latvia in July 2018), the former to discuss the future of Europe, without any further specification (in Essen, Germany). For more information, see https://ec.europa.eu/info/events/citizens-dialogues accessed 5 November 2018.

148 See https://www.debatingeurope.eu/ accessed 5 November 2018.

149 See in detail, in this Volume, Chapter 12 by S. Garben.

and how to use them in a meaningful way. Equally, learning about different policies helps the citizen to use these instruments of contestation more effectively. It also underlines the Commission's self-imposed commitment to increasing bottom-up influence of citizens on policy making and regulation.

Lobbying Lobbying takes place in all EU institutions.[150] That said, each institution attracts different interest groups[151] and has different preferences in terms of the information it is willing to receive.[152] The Commission's agenda is filled with EU-wide issues, which primarily attract the attention of large individual firms. This is not the case for the European Parliament and Council, which are most commonly approached by European and national associations, respectively.[153] The most prominent feature of lobbying practices in the EU is that they are dynamic and take place in ever-changing constellations, indicative of polycentric practice.[154]

Large corporations appear to hold a natural advantage with respect to lobbying as a method of contestation, given their size, financial resources, and research and development capacities. Nevertheless, smaller groups and businesses may also benefit from the possibility of lobbying at EU level – as compared to the national level – as it allows them to pool their (more limited) resources.[155] Equally, Bouwen shows that most private

[150] Before the adoption of the Single European Act (SEA) in 1987, lobbying in the EU institutions was limited due to well-established national paths, the relatively limited mandate of the Commission, and widespread free-riding by industries in the light of the perceived small gains that could be obtained from active lobbying. See in detail, D. Coen, 'The Evolution of the Large Firm as a Political Actor in the European Union', *Journal of European Public Policy* 4 (1) (1997), 91, 92–93.

[151] These can be individual firms, associations, or Brussels-based lobbying consultants, who reduce costs for smaller firms that would otherwise not have access to EU institutions. See P. Bouwen, 'Corporate Lobbying in the European Union: The Logic of Access', *Journal of European Public Policy* 9 (3) (2002), 365, 373.

[152] This can also be context information about sectors, national domestic conditions and other factors that influence regulation. P. Bouwen, ibid., 369.

[153] ibid., 383.

[154] See D. Coen (n. 150) 98.

[155] In the field of environmental law, see T. Brenton, *The Greening of Machiavelli: The Evolution of International Environmental Politics* (Royal Institute of International Affairs, 1994), at 356–7, as cited in J. B. Wiener, 'On the Political Economy of Global Environmental Regulation', *Georgetown Law Journal* 87 (1999), 749; R. Stewart, 'Pyramids of Sacrifice? Federalism Problems in Mandating State Implementation of Federal Environmental Controls', *Yale Law Journal* 86 (1977), 1196, 1213–14;

interests are able, to some extent, to provide relevant information to EU institutions in order to gain access to lobbying.[156]

The polycentric prerequisite, and benefit, of learning is crucial for successful lobbying: mutual information exchange between the EU institutions and businesses is based on, and creates, knowledge around market conditions and the effect of proposed regulation. Lobbying can increase input legitimacy, as well as a better fit of proposed legislation, thereby contributing to higher levels of compliance after rule adoption.[157] However, in order for these benefits to materialise, dominance by one interest group must be prevented; if not, regulatory capture will replace lobbying.[158]

**

A common concern in relation to participatory mechanisms that enable peaceful contestation of rules, such as ECI and lobbying, is that they may reinforce elitism and existing discrepancies among citizens and their ability to influence decision making.[159] However, while larger corporations and more affluent individuals naturally have more resources to influence rules, smaller interests are nevertheless represented. For example, the one million signatures required for a successful ECI, while considerable, is still significantly lower than comparable efforts at the national level.[160] The use of new technologies has also allowed for participatory mechanisms to become more widely accessible at low to no costs, for instance through online platforms.

Voting at both European and national elections may be considered an indirect method of contestation. From a polycentric perspective, voting problematically does not allow for any targeted contestation of a particular rule or issue; it is a blunt instrument that forces individuals to vote for a package of issues, not all of which they may support or care about. Additionally, and perhaps more importantly, voting forces the voter to rely on her agent (the relevant MP or MEP) to contest the

M. Olson, *The Logic of Collective Action: Public Goods and the Theory of Group* (Harvard University Press, 1971), 5–65.

156 P. Bouwen (n. 151) 371.

157 ibid., 382.

158 For a comprehensive overview of literature on regulatory capture, see E. Dal Bó, 'Regulatory Capture: A Review', *Oxford Review of Economic Policy* 22 (2) (2006), 203.

159 For example, see P. Magnette, 'European Governance and Civic Participation: Beyond Elitist Citizenship?', *Political Studies* 51 (1) (2003), 144; E. Monaghan (n. 133) 290–291.

160 See http://eu-buergerbegehren.org/download/2006-12-eci-studie-englisch.pdf accessed 5 November 2018, 7.

existing rules. It is therefore hard to imagine how voting – however important for issues such as democratic legitimacy – facilitates peaceful contestation of existing rules in a way that enables meaningful self-governance.

In order for polycentricity to be maintained, all market participants must have access to peaceful contestation.[161] The above demonstrates that while not all have equal access, there is no formal exclusion and, importantly, domination in contestation is extremely unlikely. The different ways of contestation complement each other by allowing for a multi-scale response; what begins in a town hall debate may develop into an ECI. Overall, the most effective method of contestation is undoubtedly the judicial route of challenging the validity of a rule. However, access to this route is limited by issues of standing, similar to those related to judicial enforcement.[162] Particularly in a market setting that is subject to continuous change, the dynamic nature of polycentric governance could be an asset in terms of allowing for rules with the best possible fit, following the crucial input from market participants. It would similarly support processes of continued learning and information exchange. These benefits are currently not optimised.

III Polycentric Internal Market within a Polycentric EU

Examining the polycentric features of the internal market explicates the challenge of analysing large polycentric systems, particularly those nested in other polycentric systems. The internal market clearly displays all the attributes of a polycentric system, but to maintain the institutional essentials ensuring self-governance within the market proves to be very difficult. This can partially be explained by some of the characteristics of the internal market, especially the large degree of governmental and EU oversight with the aim of achieving certain social goals,[163] which limits

[161] We are grateful to Michael McGinnis for his contributions to our discussions on this topic.

[162] See Section II.B.ii.

[163] As detailed in Article 3(3) TEU. ('The Union shall establish an internal market. It shall work for the sustainable development of Europe based on balanced economic growth and price stability, a highly competitive social market economy, aiming at full employment and social progress, and a high level of protection and improvement of the quality of the environment. It shall promote scientific and technological advance. It shall combat social exclusion and discrimination, and shall promote social justice and protection, equality between women and men, solidarity between generations and protection of the rights of the child. It shall promote economic, social and territorial cohesion, and

the ability for self-governance with respect to these, and conflicting, individual and governmental goals. However, as illustrated by our analysis of the freedom and ability to enter and exit, these limitations need not be fatal for polycentricity; a measure of differentiation and restriction is acceptable, and perhaps necessary, to prevent other pitfalls, such as the creation of non-state dominance.

For a large part, problems regarding institutional essentials can be traced back to the larger institutional setting of the EU. This is particularly visible with respect to the formal processes available for enforcement and peaceful contestation, which are not internal market-specific and are dominated by judicial processes. These crowd out horizontal interactions, and instead provide individuals with circular processes that continue to position national and European courts – in the position of governmental institutions – as gatekeepers for enforcement and contestation. Rather than replacing these institutions, their mandates could be extended or changed for them to encourage the development of horizontal processes in their shadow. For example, courts could mandate inclusion of previously excluded groups in participatory processes, recognise contributions of individuals in the consultation stage, or recognise arbitration outcomes.

Increased polycentricity in the internal market would have a knock-on effect on the EU as a whole: multi-scale horizontal processes in a dynamic market provide key opportunities for learning and self-governance that would provide actors with the networks and skills necessary to scale up such processes to address bigger issues across larger geographical areas. To this end, policy changes should be made to embrace two developments: first, differentiation within the internal market should be expected and encouraged – under the umbrella of shared rules – in order to allow for bottom-up governance regarding the specific issues. Second, harmonisation is helpful in the creation of procedures that would allow for increased horizontal enforcement and contestation; there is no reason why these processes cannot be facilitated by governmental actors – particularly those with existing expertise about either substantive or procedural issues – as long as they do not dominate these processes to the exclusion of horizontal actions.

solidarity among Member States. It shall respect its rich cultural and linguistic diversity, and shall ensure that Europe's cultural heritage is safeguarded and enhanced.')

PART II

6

The Shared System of Rules in a Polycentric European Union

ANA BOBIĆ

The shared system of rules – itself an identifying attribute of polycentric systems[1] – directly relates to the institutional essentials that are necessary to ensure the sustained functioning of the system by setting out the framework that either enables or restrains them.[2] Ways of entering and leaving the system, as well as enforcing and contesting the shared system of rules, need to be in place and to offer the possibility of dynamic and permanent self-correction.[3] In order to facilitate these institutional essentials, the shared system of rules also needs to accommodate provisions for the polycentric prerequisites.[4] Learning, access to information and access to justice all contribute to creating a more active citizenry, able to make meaningful and efficient[5] use of the institutional essentials. The challenge of identifying the shared system of rules within the EU's system runs parallel to the challenge of identifying what 'overarching set of shared rules' can be considered essential for the existence of polycentric systems generally.[6]

However, the attribute of a shared system of rules lacks detailed conceptualisation. Identifying this system for the European Union therefore necessitates a re-examination of the definition of the shared system of rules as a first step. This chapter will propose a definition of the shared system of rules with contributions from legal research into constitutional

1 See, in this Volume, Chapter 1 by J. van Zeben; P. D. Aligica and V. Tarko, 'Polycentricity: From Polanyi to Ostrom, and Beyond', *Governance: An International Journal of Policy, Administration, and Institutions*, 25 (2) (2012), 237, 245.

2 Chapter 1, in this Volume.

3 P. D. Aligica and V. Tarko (n. 1) 245–6.

4 Chapter 1 in this Volume has importantly further detailed the central position of prerequisites in polycentric systems, rendering them in consequence an indispensable part of the shared system of rules.

5 V. Ostrom, C. Tiebout, and R. Warren, 'The Organization of Government in Metropolitan Areas: A Theoretical Inquiry', *American Political Science Review*, 55 (1961), 831, 842.

6 For a review of the existing literature, see D. H. Cole, 'The Varieties of Comparative Institutional Analysis', *Wisconsin Law Review* (2013), 383.

theory in transnational contexts. In doing so, it will first discuss the role and interpretation of a shared system of rules in a polycentric system through its relationship with other institutional essentials and prerequisites of polycentric governance (Section I). This will provide the analytical framework to allow us to identify the shared system of rules in the EU (Section II). The chapter will then highlight challenges to the shared system of rules through the lens of polycentric theory (Section III). Section IV concludes.

I A Shared System of Rules in Polycentric Systems

Reference to 'rules' implies a natural link to laws and legal research; however, this perspective was not present in the work of Vincent and Elinor Ostrom. Nevertheless, Vincent Ostrom viewed polycentric systems as systems grounded in the rule of law,[7] a value to be achieved through an understanding of democracy as something qualitatively different from the mere majority rule constituted through elections.[8] To Vincent Ostrom, democratic society consists of a certain moral fabric striving to avoid command and control, relying on the due process of law.[9] The constitutional level of analysis for him entails the unanimous establishment of the fair rules of the game.[10] As a consequence, in viewing polycentric political systems as embodying the rule of law,[11] Vincent Ostrom defined them as systems where 'many officials and decision structures are assigned limited and relatively autonomous prerogatives to determine, enforce and alter legal relationships'[12] with the aim of sustaining the interactions between the decision-making centres and individuals.[13] However, he provides no further definition, not least from a legal perspective, of the shared system of rules that is meant to help us identify and sustain polycentric governance.

[7] V. Ostrom, *The Meaning of Democracy and the Vulnerability of Democracies: A Response to Tocqueville's Challenge* (University of Michigan Press, 1997), 3–4.
[8] ibid.
[9] ibid., 11.
[10] ibid., 23.
[11] P. D Aligica and V. Tarko (n. 1), 245.
[12] V. Ostrom, 'Polycentricity' (Part 1) (1972) reprinted in M. D. McGinnis (ed.), *Polycentricity and Local Public Economies: Readings from the Workshop in Political Theory and Policy Analysis* (University of Michigan Press, 1999) 55–6.
[13] M. D. McGinnis and E. Ostrom, 'Reflections on Vincent Ostrom, Public Administration, and Polycentricity', *Public Administration Review* 72 (1) (2012), 15, 20.

Along similar lines, Elinor Ostrom introduces the rule of law as a substantive element of a shared system of rules.[14] However, her concept of the rule of law has a primarily functional focus: a society governed by the rule of law bases the legitimation and parameters of action on written and unwritten rules[15] that need not be created through formal legal processes.[16] She defines rules as 'shared understandings by participants about *enforced* prescriptions concerning what actions (or outcomes) are *required, prohibited* or *permitted*.'[17] For the *shared* system of rules to be in place, all the actors involved must accept it as binding on them.

While neither of the Ostroms clearly articulated a definition of the shared system of rules, their work clearly suggests that any polycentric system can only exist if it has 'rules, constitutions, fundamental political values, and cultural adaptability in maintaining them.'[18] Aligica and Tarko, in restating the Ostroms' theory, in some way equate the rule of law with the existence of an overarching set of rules.[19] In polycentric systems, they emphasise, a shared system of rules is one which is created and observed by all centres of decision making and is considered useful and binding for all.[20] Importantly, Elinor identifies a specific group of 'institutional rules' that are created by individuals who engage with each other in repetitive situations in order to improve the outcome of these situations.[21] Elinor Ostrom and Crawford show that unwritten rules can take the form of 'institutional statements' which can be written, spoken or implied and do not rely on a legislative or administrative process for their acceptance.[22] The inclusion of non-written rules into our perception of a shared system of rules is crucial for a complete understanding of the rules which apply in the European Union.

[14] E. Ostrom, Understanding Institutional Diversity (Princeton University Press, 2005), 20.
[15] ibid., 20.
[16] ibid.
[17] ibid., 18 (italics in original). Vincent Ostrom has never defined in more detail the concept of rules, remaining on the surface level of the rule of law as a principle informing the conduct of democratic societies.
[18] P. D. Aligica and V. Tarko (n. 1) 246.
[19] ibid., 245–6.
[20] ibid., 254.
[21] E. Ostrom, *Understanding Institutional Diversity* (n. 14) 18.
[22] S. E. S. Crawford and E. Ostrom, 'A Grammar of Institutions', *American Political Science Review* 89 (3) (1995), 582, 583.

For Vincent Ostrom, self-governance was both the start and end point – a system of shared rules ensuring self-governance sustains a polycentric system.[23] However, self-governance may also lead to problematic outcomes that do not coincide with fundamental democratic values.[24]

Building on the discussion on the relationship between democracy (ensured through the rule of law) and self-governance in Chapter 1, this chapter proposes a more value-based approach to the shared system of rules. While it should provide for mechanisms of participation that ensure conditions for self-governance, both individual and collective, the shared system of rules should also determine a set of shared values that act as a limit to potentially problematic aims pursued through self-governance.

A final contribution of polycentric theory relevant for the shared system of rules is its characteristic of permanent self-correction.[25] According to Aligica and Tarko, self-correction is a 'built-in mechanism'[26] of polycentric systems and those systems inherently provide more incentives for self-correcting change than monocentric systems.[27] In legal literature, self-correction may be considered synonymous with the concept of incrementalism. It accentuates the gradual development of institutional interactions, and the creation of rules and principles.[28] Incrementalism may be regarded as stemming from an understanding of law as a dynamic (rather than static) and developing body of rules, where the use of analogy and contextual interpretation take

[23] V. Ostrom, *The Meaning of American Federalism: Constituting a Self-Governing Society* (ICS Press, 1994), 47; M. D. McGinnis and E. Ostrom (n. 13) 20.

[24] As rightly pointed out earlier in this Volume – see Chapter 1 by J. van Zeben.

[25] With thanks to M. D. McGinnis for putting forward the dynamic nature of polycentric systems as their crucial feature.

[26] P. D. Aligica and V. Tarko (n. 1) 245–6.

[27] E. Ostrom, 'The Comparative Study of Public Economies' Paper presented upon acceptance of the 1997 Frank E. Seidman Distinguished Award in Political Economy (P. K. Seidman Foundation, 1998), 17–18.

[28] L. R. Helfer and A. M. Slaughter, 'Toward a Theory of Effective Supranational Adjudication', *The Yale Law Journal* 107 (1997), 273, 314; N. Krisch, Beyond Constitutionalism: The Pluralist Structure of Postnational Law (Oxford University Press, 2010) 247; G. de Búrca, 'Developing Democracy beyond the State', *Columbia Journal of Transnational Law* 46 (2) (2008), 101, 157; K. Nicolaïdis, 'Demoicratic Theory and Europe's Institutional Architecture in Times of Crisis', in S. Piattoni (ed.), *The European Union: Democratic Principles and Institutional Architectures in Times of Crisis* (Oxford University Press, 2015), 153.

centre stage.[29] In that sense, a shared system of rules needs to ensure conditions for permanent readjustment and correction are present.

Legal scholars, on the other hand, may be tempted to equate an 'overarching' and 'shared' system of rules with 'constitutional' law, created through a collective act of constituting and determining power relations in a political community. Such an approach is, however, underinclusive for polycentric systems. As mentioned, the rule of law has a primarily functional focus: a society governed by the rule of law founds legitimation and parameters of action on written and unwritten rules from several sources.[30] As polycentric systems are sustained by a multiplicity of actors, the rules of each of these actors logically contribute to the rules of the game. Content, rather than source, is therefore considered decisive in determining the scope of the polycentric system's *overarching* system of rules.

Keeping the previous conclusion in mind, the definition of the shared system of rules aims to contribute to the current literature on polycentricity. It seeks to flesh out the concept of the shared system of rules beyond its use as a synonym for the abstract principle of the rule of law.[31] However, it aims equally to broaden the imagination of legal research in conceiving of a system of rules on a level that reinforces 'consistent and predictable patterns of interacting behaviour'[32] on multiple levels of decision making in a polycentric organisation, but also encourages self-governance.[33] In that sense, the argument is one aimed at bridging the divide between polycentricity and legal research.

In moving beyond traditional legal categories such as constitutional and public international law, this chapter relies on contributions in the research on constitutional theory relating to transnational systems.[34] The argument is that the transnational context provides for a sufficient

[29] R. Higgins, *Problems and Process: International Law and How We Use It* (Clarendon Press, 1995) 10. See also M. Claes,*The National Courts' Mandate in the European Constitution* (Hart Publishing, 2006) 713.

[30] E. Ostrom, *Understanding Institutional Diversity* (n. 14) 20.

[31] Acknowledging this point, see M. Stephan, G. Marshall and M. D. McGinnis, 'An Introduction to Polycentricity and Governance' (on file with the authors) p. 11.

[32] M. D. McGinnis and E. Ostrom (n. 13), 15.

[33] M. D. McGinnis, 'Legal Pluralism, Polycentricity, and Faith-Based Organizations in Global Governance', in M. Sproule-Jones, B. Allen, and F. Sabetti (eds.), *The Struggle to Constitute and Sustain Productive Orders* (Lexington Books, 2008) 48.

[34] This is not to say that the transnational context is an ideal type of a polycentric system, rather that the contributions of that literature may inform the current debate on the shared system of rules in polycentric systems more generally.

level of abstraction for it to be applicable to a plethora of diverse polycentric systems. Equally, the transnational context provides a platform for a wider range of non-state decision-making units, in line with the polycentric questioning of the unchallenged centrality of the nation state.[35] The shared system of rules may thus be defined as one that determines 'the nature of the polity, substantive rules and rules concerning the institutional structure'[36] clarified further through key values, principles and norms.[37] In the words of McGinnis, 'this denotes a rule-based structure that manifests a shared sense of connection among these actors.'[38]

II Defining the Shared System of Rules in the EU

The nature of the European Union as a polity can be described as *sui generis* for a number of different reasons (e.g. its aims, its institutional framework or the extent of harmonisation of the legislation of its Member States). However, what appears to capture the imagination of legal scholarship most is the autonomy of the EU's legal system,[39] and the diverse ways in which it is received and transposed into the legal systems of Member States.[40] This diversity complicates the identification of the sources that form the shared overarching system of rules of the EU as a polycentric polity. Keeping these concerns in mind, the subsequent analysis seeks to identify those rules considered shared as well as overarching in prescribing (that is requiring, prohibiting or permitting) actions and outcomes, both written and unwritten.

In the previous Section, the overarching shared system of rules was defined as including the nature of the polity, substantive rules and rules concerning the institutional structure, as well as key values and principles. Identifying these for the European Union will include consideration of the nature of the EU legal order, the EU and Member State rules that

35 V. Ostrom, *The Intellectual Crisis in American Public Administration* (University of Alabama Press, 1989) 68; V. Ostrom, The Meaning of Democracy and the Vulnerability of Democracies (n. 7) 240.

36 N. Walker, 'Late Sovereignty in the European Union', in N. Walker (ed.), Sovereignty in Transition (Hart Publishing, 2003) 28.

37 J. Shaw, 'Process and Constitutional Discourse in the European Union', *Journal of Law and Society* 27 (4) (2000), 15–18.

38 M. Stephan, G. Marshall and M. D. McGinnis (n. 31) 11.

39 M. Maduro, 'Interpreting European Law: Judicial Adjudication in a Context of Constitutional Pluralism', *European Journal of Legal Studies* 1 (2) (2007), 137.

40 See Section III-C for a further analysis of this point.

determine the division of powers in the polity and limits to EU and state action, the parallel EU and national systems for the protection of fundamental rights, rules on national citizenship;[41] and, rules on judicial structure which influence individuals' access to courts and their participation in the EU preliminary reference procedure. It will also reflect upon self-correction as a necessary feature of the shared system of rules.

A *Identifying the Shared System of Rules*

i The Nature of the European Union

There are perhaps only a handful of topics in European Union studies as frequently debated as the question of the nature of the European Union.[42] This is a consequence of the inherent and almost natural assumption that sovereignty belongs to nation states only, whereas it became clear early on in the integration process that the EU cannot be characterised as an international organisation either.[43] Nevertheless, while the source and development of EU sovereignty differs substantially from the classic notion of state sovereignty – and its nature is debatable[44] – there seems to be a consensus around its existence,[45] and

41 A prerequisite for EU citizenship which is additional to and derived from national citizenship. Article 20(1) TFEU states: 'Citizenship of the Union is hereby established. Every person holding the nationality of a Member State shall be a citizen of the Union. Citizenship of the Union shall be additional to and not replace national citizenship.'

42 For some of the most famous pieces addressing this issue, see K. Lenaerts, 'Constitutionalism and the Many Faces of Federalism', *The American Journal of Comparative Law* 38 (2) (1990), 205; E. Stein, 'Lawyers, Judges, and the Making of a Transnational Constitution', *The American Journal of International Law* 75 (1) (1981), 1; M. Kumm, 'The Cosmopolitan Turn in Constitutionalism: An Integrated Conception of Public Law', *Indiana Journal of Global Legal Studies* 20 (2) (2013), 605; J. H. H. Weiler, The Constitution of Europe: 'Do the New Clothes Have an Emperor?' and Other Essays on European Integration (Cambridge University Press, 1999); N. MacCormick, Questioning Sovereignty (Oxford University Press, 1999); K. Tuori, European Constitutionalism (Cambridge University Press, 2015).

43 For a debate on this issue, see T. Schilling, 'The Autonomy of the Community Legal Order: An Analysis of Possible Foundations', *Harvard International Law Journal* 37 (2) (1996), 389. Weiler offers a critique of his reading of EU law through an international law prism in J. H. H. Weiler, ibid., Chapter 9.

44 G. de Búrca, 'Sovereignty and the Supremacy Doctrine of the European Court of Justice', in N. Walker (ed.), *Sovereignty in Transition* (Hart Publishing, 2003) 449.

45 N. Walker, 'Late Sovereignty in the European Union', in N. Walker (ed.), ibid., 12; H. Lindhal, 'Sovereignty and Representation in the European Union', in N. Walker (ed.), ibid., 107; G. de Búrca, ibid., 451 onwards. Conversely, the Latvian Constitutional Court concluded the EU does not have sovereignty in the classic Westphalian sense. Its subsequent analysis points to a clear struggle to fit the EU into the category of a classical

ultimately on the specific nature of the European Union as a supranational type of polity with characteristics pertaining both to nation states and international organisations. The sovereignty of the EU – although never explicitly mentioned – can be discerned from the early case law of the Court of Justice of the European Union, where it stated that:

> Community constitutes a new legal order of international law for the benefit of which the states have limited their sovereign rights, albeit within limited fields, and the subjects of which comprise not only Member States but also their nationals.[46]

The Court of Justice addressed the characteristics of the newly established legal order, asserting a claim to ultimate legal authority in the limited fields of its competence, albeit not in the classical sense usually associated with nation states.[47] In addition to the case law asserting the autonomy, primacy and direct effect of European Union law, Article 1 and Article 47 TEU state that the European Union is a successor to the European Community, and now has legal personality, resulting from the merging of the earlier second and third pillars with the Community.

De Búrca argues that while the EU certainly does not establish its ultimate authority in the same manner as states do, the Court of Justice's development of a self-referential system of the Treaties, grounded in the doctrines of primacy and direct effect, not only restrict Member States' sovereignty[48] in the classic Westphalian sense, but also render the EU legal order 'independent, autonomous and non-derivative.'[49] She concludes that this makes the EU sovereign. Lindahl is in agreement, as he finds the EU's sovereignty rooted in the creation of the autonomous, independent and self-referential nature of the system of Treaties.[50]

international organisation. *Satversmes tiesa (Latvia) Case No. 2008-35-01 Treaty of Lisbon,* Decision of 7 April 2009, paras. 17–18.

46 Case 26/62 *Van Gend en Loos* [1963] ECR 1, 12. The same was reiterated by the Court in Case 6/64 *Costa* v. *ENEL* [1964] ECR 585, 593.

47 See also, Opinion of Advocate General Kokott delivered on 11 November 2004 in Case C-105/03 *Pupino* [2005] ECR I-5285, para. 32: '[The] Treaty on European Union includes not only inter-governmental cooperation, but also joint exercise of sovereignty by the Union.'

48 Stated explicitly by the Court of Justice as early as *Van Gend en Loos* and *Costa* v. *ENEL* (n. 46).

49 G. de Búrca, 'Sovereignty and the Supremacy Doctrine of the European Court of Justice' (n. 44), 453.

50 H. Lindahl, 'Sovereignty and Representation in the European Union', in N. Walker (ed.), (n. 45) 107.

The doctrines of primacy and direct effect were not uniformly accepted across Member States. National constitutional and supreme courts have consistently claimed final authority in their territory, particularly in relation to their role of protecting the national constitution as hierarchically the highest law applicable in a Member State,[51] and underlining sovereignty as the ultimate limit for European integration and the reach of the principle of primacy.[52] National constitutional courts have also put forward limits to the principle of primacy of EU law, reasserting the untouchable character of the constitutional core.[53] However, these limits to the principle of the primacy of EU law have not caused any serious disturbance to its operation, but rather represent an important point of contestation regarding its scope of application, a point to which I return in Section III.

ii Vertical and Horizontal Institutional Relationships

Article 5 TEU sets out the foundation for the division of competences between the European and the national level, introducing the principles of conferral, subsidiarity and proportionality as conditions for the

[51] For example, *Ústavní Soud* (Czech Republic) Case Pl. ÚS 19/08 *Treaty of Lisbon I*, Judgment of 26 November 2008, www.usoud.cz/en/decisions/20081126-pl-us-1908-treaty-of-lisbon-i-1/ accessed 1 May 2016, para. 216; *Højesteret* (Denmark) Case I 361/1997 *Carlsen*, Judgment of 6 April 1998 [1999] 3 *CMLR* 854; *Bundesverfassungsgericht* (Germany) Case 2 BvR 2661/06 *Honeywell*, Order of 6 July 2010, www.bundesverfassungsgericht.de/SharedDocs/Entscheidungen/EN/2010/07/rs20100706_2bvr266106en.html accessed 1 May 2016, para. 68]; National report – The Constitutional Court of the Republic of Lithuania (2014), 5; *Trybunał Konstytucyjny* (Poland) Case *Accession Treaty*, para. 11; Supreme Court Case (United Kingdom) *Pham* [2015] UKSC 19, 90.

[52] For example, *Ústavní Soud* (Czech Republic) Case *Sugar Quotas III*, headnote para. 8; *Bundesverfassungsgericht* (Germany) Cases 2 BvR 2134/92 and 2 BvR 2159/92 *Maastricht Treaty*, Judgment of 12 October 1993, www.judicialstudies.unr.edu/JS_Summer09/JSP_Week_1/German%20ConstCourt%20Maastricht.pdf accessed 1 May 2016, para. C. II.1.a; *Tribunal Constitucional* (Spain) Case *Constitutional Treaty*, para. II-2.

[53] *Ústavní Soud* (Czech Republic) Case *Lisbon Treaty II*, para. 150; *Conseil Constitutionnel* (France) Case 2006–540 DC *Information Society*, Decision of 27 July 2006, para. 19; *Bundesverfassungsgericht* (Germany) Case 2 BvE 2/08 *Treaty of Lisbon*, Judgment of 30 June 2009, www.bverfg.de/e/es20090630_2bve000208en.html accessed 6 June 2017, para. 240 onwards; *Bundesverfassungsgericht* (Germany) Case 9/2014 *Gauweiler*, Press release of 7 February 2014, www.bundesverfassungsgericht.de/SharedDocs/Pressemitteilungen/EN/2014/bvg14-009.html accessed 4 November 2015, 2.a; *Corte Costituzionale* (Italy) Case 183/1973 *Frontini*, Judgment of 27 December 1973, (1974), 2 *CMLR* 372; *Satversmes tiesa* (Latvia) Case 2008-35-01 *Treaty of Lisbon*, Decision of 7 April 2009, paras. 16.3, 17; *Trybunał Konstytucyjny* (Poland) Case *Treaty of Lisbon*, para. 1.1.2; *Cour Constitutionnelle* (Belgium) Case 62/2016 *Stability Pact*, Judgment of 28 April 2016, www.const-court.be/cgi/judgments_popup.php?lang=en&ArrestID=4097 accessed 16 July 2017, summary.

exercise of competence on the Union level. Title I TFEU determines in more detail the areas in which the EU is able to legislate, dividing them into three categories,[54] which reflect the extent to which the EU is able independently to regulate a certain area.[55] In line with polycentric theory, the division of competences between different centres of decision making is based on functional rather than territorial criteria.[56]

The rules of the EU's institutional structure and the division of powers among these institutions also form part of the shared overarching system of rules in the EU.[57] Inspired by the tradition of representative democracy in Member States' constitutional orders, Article 10 TEU places it at the epicentre of the functioning of the European Union.[58] However, the EU's institutional structure only partially reflects the institutional structure of national representative democracies, predominantly through the directly elected European Parliament, and through the European Commission whose competences somewhat resemble those of a national government. The rules on the EU's institutional architecture are complemented by the rules referring to the role of the institutions of Member States and their role in the functioning of the EU.[59]

54 The exclusive, shared and complementing EU competences.

55 For example, the EU is able to regulate the customs union independently of the Member States, as part of its exclusive competence. On the opposite side of the spectrum is the example of education, where the EU is not allowed to harmonise Member States' rules, but is only able to support, coordinate or complement Member State action.

56 P. D. Aligica and V. Tarko, 'Co-Production, Polycentricity, and Value Heterogeneity: The Ostroms' Public Choice Institutionalism Revisited', *American Political Science Review* 107 (4) (2013), 726, 734; M. D. McGinnis and E. Ostrom (n. 13), 15; N. Walker, 'The Idea of Constitutional Pluralism', *Modern Law Review* 65 (3) (2002), 317, 347; L. Hooghe and G. Marks, 'Unraveling the Central State, But How? Types of Multi-level Governance', *American Political Science Review* 97 (2003), 233, 237; N. Chowdhury and R. A. Wessel, 'Conceptualising Multilevel Regulation in the EU: A Legal Translation of Multilevel Governance?', *European Law Journal* 18 (2012), 335, 340.

57 See Title III of the Treaty on European Union.

58 Where the representative qualities of the European Parliament, the Council of the European Union and the European Council are presented.

59 Such as, for example, the Protocol No. 1 on the Role of National Parliaments in the European Union, 7 June 2016, OJ C202/203, determining the powers of national parliaments in ensuring the principle of subsidiarity is respected in the legislative procedure of the EU. Another example is the role of national courts in the preliminary reference procedure set out in Article 267 TFEU.

It is important to refer in particular to the role of the European Committee of the Regions ('CoR'),[60] which is the only EU institution to represent subnational interests through regional and local authorities. The role of the CoR is mostly advisory,[61] and it can submit cases to the European Court of Justice for alleged breaches of the principle of subsidiarity.[62] The position of the CoR is also important in reinforcing the obligation of the EU to respect the national identities of Member States, inclusive of their regional and local governments,[63] and this complementarity is an important indicator that the EU is composed of multiple, diverse decision-making centres. Equally their interactions occur in a more complex way than that captured by the classic division between the national and the EU level. However, the work of the CoR appears to function along party political lines,[64] depends on the power of the local or regional unit in their domestic context,[65] and the presence in Brussels more generally is dominated by larger and richer regions of the EU.[66] It can be concluded that the work of the CoR offers little in the way of encouraging local and individual self-governing tendencies.

60 Its functions, competences and composition are set out in Article 13(4) TEU, Articles 300, 305–307 TFEU, Council Decision 2014/930/EU of 16 December 2014 determining the composition of the Committee of the Regions [2014] OJ L365/143, and Council Decision (EU) 2015/116 of 26 January 2015 appointing the members and alternate members of the European Committee of the Regions OJ L31/25.

61 The Commission followed 45.5 per cent of the opinions submitted by the Committee. See M. I. Neshkova, 'The Impact of Subnational Interests on Supranational Regulation', *Journal of European Public Policy* 17 (8) (2010), 1193, 1202. The role of the Committee itself is to safeguard the principle of subsidiarity and provide the EU institutions with important information regarding the regional and the local level. See https://cor.europa.eu/en/about/president/Documents/The%20State%20of%20the%20European%20Union%20-%20the%20View%20of%20Regions%20and%20Cities%202018/SOTREG18_Broch_adress_EN_web.pdf accessed 15 October 2018.

62 Prior to the Lisbon Treaty, the Committee did not have the status of a privileged applicant to the Court of Justice. Article 8(2) of the Protocol No. 2 on the application of the principles of subsidiarity and proportionality, 9 May 2008, OJ C115/206 now provides: 'In accordance with the rules laid down in the said Article, the Committee of the Regions may also bring such actions against legislative acts for the adoption of which the Treaty on the Functioning of the European Union provides that it be consulted.'

63 Article 4(2) TEU.

64 M. Callanan and M. Tatham, 'Territorial Interest Representation in the European Union: Actors, Objectives and Strategies', *Journal of European Public Policy* 21 (2) (2014), 188, 206; T. Christiansen and P. Lintner, 'The Committee of the Regions after 10 Years: Lessons from the Past and Challenges for the Future', EIPASCOPE 2005/1, available at http://aei.pitt.edu/5940/1/scop05_1_2.pdf, 8.

65 M. Callanan and M. Tatham, ibid., 202.

66 See generally, C. Moore, 'A Europe of the Regions vs. the Regions in Europe: Reflections on Regional Engagement in Brussels', *Regional & Federal Studies* 18 (5) (2008), 517.

iii Key Values and Principles

Key values underpinning the EU's system represent the substantive foundation of the EU as a legal order. Article 2 TEU is instructive in this regard, identifying values such as human dignity, freedom, democracy, equality, the rule of law and the respect for human rights as EU's aims. Furthermore, as already mentioned, Article 10 TEU highlights the importance of representative democracy, as well as the right of every citizen to participate in the decision making of the EU, and decisions to be taken at the level as close to her as possible. This provides some basis for introducing mechanisms promoting self-governance, albeit to a limited extent.[67] Importantly, within the EU context, the values from Article 2 TEU act as a safeguard for core values that self-governance cannot interfere with.

The Court of Justice of the European Union ('CJEU') has also introduced several key principles of EU law, such as the principles of direct effect and primacy of EU law,[68] through its exclusive jurisdiction to interpret EU law.[69] These principles have established rights for individuals based in EU law, regardless of national implementation. Similarly, the Court has placed fundamental rights alongside general principles of EU law, even before the creation of the EU Charter of Fundamental Rights.[70] The CJEU's central position in the development of the EU's shared system of rules, and the introduction of the said principles, empowered national courts as decision-making centres with respect to EU law. The preliminary reference procedure,[71] and the ensuing progressive case law of the Court of Justice[72] included them as important conduits in ensuring the application and dynamic development of EU law across the Member States.

iv EU Citizenship

A further overarching provision is Article 9 TEU, guaranteeing the equality of all European Union citizens, and introducing the concept of

[67] See in particular Chapter 5 and the analysis on the limited ability of individuals to influence rule-making in the EU's internal market, in particular Section II.C.

[68] In particular, see *Van Gend en Loos* and *Costa* v. *ENEL* (n. 46).

[69] Article 19 TEU.

[70] The Court first mentioned fundamental rights as part of the general principles of Community law back in 1969 in the Case 29/69 *Stauder* [1969], para. 7.

[71] Article 267 TFEU.

[72] See, for example, J.E. Rytter and M. Wind, 'In Need of Juristocracy? The Silence of Denmark in the Development of European Legal Norms', *International Journal of Constitutional Law* 9 (2) (2011), 470.

EU citizenship. EU citizenship is regulated through Treaty provisions,[73] as well as by the Citizenship Directive,[74] which *inter alia* regulates free movement of EU citizens and their family members.[75] The Directive relies heavily on definitions and provisions of civil status and family law enacted in the Member States, which explicitly draw these national rules into the 'overarching system of rules'. The CJEU has been tasked with the interpretation of citizenship rights, particularly their scope.[76] For example, while the Treaty provisions and the Citizenship Directive take the cross-border movement and economic activity[77] of the citizen as a starting point for the enjoyment of the rights, the Court has accorded the right of residence to family members of EU citizens even in the absence of an economic activity/cross-border movement where 'the substance of the rights' would have been impaired.[78]

v Rules on the Internal Market

Moving away from the rules that are considered 'constitutional' in the traditional Nation State-centred sense, the rules regulating the internal market come into play – the EU's initial mandate and still-central aim.[79] The bottom-up participation of non-governmental actors in the functioning of the EU's internal market is perhaps the most vivid example of the EU's polycentric features.[80] From a polycentric perspective, internal market rules are therefore a key part of the shared system of rules in the

[73] Articles 20–25 TFEU.

[74] Directive 2004/38/EC of the European Parliament and of the Council of 29 April 2004 on the right of citizens of the Union and their family members to move and reside freely within the territory of the Member States and repealing Directives 64/221/EEC, 68/360/EEC, 72/194/EEC, 73/148/EEC, 75/34/EEC, 75/35/EEC, 90/364/EEC, 90/365/EEC and 93/96/EEC [2004] OJ L158/77 ('Citizenship Directive').

[75] See, in this Volume, Chapter 7 by M. van den Brink and Chapter 8 by I. Goldner Lang for more information on entry and exit.

[76] For a comprehensive overview of the case law, see D. Kostakopolou, 'Ideas, Norms and European Citizenship: Explaining Institutional Change', *Modern Law Review* 68 (2) (2005), 233; N. Nic Shuibhne, 'Limits Rising, Duties Ascending: The Changing Legal Shape of Union Citizenship', *Common Market Law Review* 52 (2015), 889.

[77] Articles 20–21 TFEU, Articles 3, 6 and 7 of the Citizenship Directive.

[78] See in particular Case C-135/08 *Rottmann* [2010] ECR I-1449, para. 42; Case C-34/09 *Ruiz Zambrano* [2011] ECR I-1177, para. 42.

[79] One might even go as far as assuming that in the European Union as a specific polity, the rules on the internal market also form part of its constitutional rules as they form part of its initial mandate and *raison d'être*. I am grateful to Josephine van Zeben for pointing this out.

[80] For a more detailed analysis of the polycentric features of the internal market see, in this Volume, Chapter 5 by J. van Zeben and A. Bobić.

EU. Most fundamental provisions are found in the Treaties,[81] introducing the free movement of goods, services, persons and capital. An important (but somewhat contested) role in the development of the internal market rules was played by the Court of Justice by further interpreting these provisions which ultimately led to an expansion of their scope.[82]

vi National Constitutions

In analysing the constitutional rules of the EU, legal scholarship often neglects the role of national constitutional law in the more general constitutional architecture of the EU.[83] In order to give a complete answer to the question '*What* does the overarching system of rules regulate?', the legal systems of Member States must be included. An important example of national relevant laws are so-called 'EU clauses', inserted into national constitutions to allow for the penetration of EU law into national law.[84] The importance of the EU clauses lies in their ability to depict the diversity of Member States' legal systems and their method of incorporating the shared system of rules within the EU. Simultaneously, the reliance on national constitutional constructs for the reception of EU law potentially erodes the shared

[81] Article 3(2) TEU; Part III Title I TFEU.

[82] For an overview of the Court's case law in the area of free movement of goods, see I. Lianos, 'In Memoriam Keck: The Reformation of the EU Law on the Free Movement of Goods', *European Law Review* 40 (2015), 225; M. Jansson and H. Kalimo, 'De Minimis Meets Market Access: Transformations in the Substance – and the Syntax – of EU Free Movement Law', *Common Market Law Review* 51 (2014), 523. For a more general overview of the Court's influence in the internal market, see L. Azoulai, 'The Court of Justice and the Social Market Economy: The Emergence of an Ideal and the Conditions for Its Realisation'. *Common Market Law Review* 45 (2008), 1335.

[83] A mere skim through some of the most famous textbooks on EU law depicts rather clearly how national constitutional law is consistently below the radar of these works. See, for example, P. Craig and G. de Búrca, *EU Law: Texts, Cases and Materials* (Oxford University Press, 2015); S. Weatherill, *Cases & Materials on EU Law* (Oxford University Press, 2016). More specific volumes also omit to address national constitutional law when discussing EU constitutionalism. See for example, J. H. H. Weiler and M. Wind (eds.), *European Constitutionalism beyond the State* (Cambridge University Press 2003); G. de Búrca and J. H. H. Weiler, *The Worlds of European Constitutionalism* (Cambridge University Press, 2012).

[84] Examples can be found in Article 23 of the German Basic Law, the UK's European Communities Act 1972, or Article 10a of the Constitution of the Czech Republic. More generally, see A. Albi, '"Europe" Articles in the Constitutions of Central and Eastern European Countries', *Common Market Law Review* 42 (2005), 399; M. Claes, 'Constitutionalizing Europe at Its Source: The "European Clauses" in the National Constitutions: Evolution and Typology', *Yearbook of European Law* 24 (1) (2005), 81.

system of rules as it opens up space for their heterogeneous application, which might hinder all members of the system from being able equally to rely on them.

The substantive constitutional rules of Member States relating to fundamental rights are also part of the overarching system of rules in the European Union. These fundamental rights act as a shield against EU law in those national systems, which have on occasion indicated that they will not apply EU law if it would diminish the protection of fundamental rights within their jurisdiction.[85] At different times, Member States have used the CJEU's fundamental rights jurisprudence as a sword in defence of fundamental rights protection in the national context.[86] Finally, the case law of national courts has informed the development of general principles and fundamental rights at the European level.[87]

B *Self-Correction of the EU's Shared System of Rules*

As presented in Section I, one of the main features of polycentric systems is its ability of permanent self-correction. In the European Union, self-correction manifests itself through two specific characteristics: first, it is carried out informally, in a manner that Elinor Ostrom referred to as 'institutional rules' created by individuals engaging with each other in repetitive situations in order to improve the outcome of these situations;[88] second, it is carried out dominantly, but not exclusively, in the judicial arena, given the centrality of judicial review in the structure of the EU legal framework.[89]

The role of the judiciary in the European Union cannot be overstated. Contrary to initial expectations of the Member States,[90] the European Court of Justice has interpreted EU law progressively, resulting in an

[85] See the judgment 26/2014 *Melloni* of 13 February 2014 of the Spanish Constitutional Tribunal, where it accepted the interpretation of the protection of fundamental rights in criminal proceedings differently from that required by the Spanish Constitution.

[86] Case C-617/10 *Åklagaren* v. *Hans Åkerberg Fransson* [2013].

[87] For a comprehensive overview, see M. de Visser, *Constitutional Review in Europe. A Comparative Analysis* (Hart Publishing, 2014), and M. Bobek, *Comparative Reasoning in European Supreme Courts* (Oxford University Press, 2013).

[88] E. Ostrom, *Understanding Institutional Diversity* (n. 14), 18.

[89] See above, Section II B.

[90] E. Benvenisti and G.W. Downs, 'The Premises, Assumptions, and Implications of Van Gend en Loos: Viewed from the Perspectives of Democracy and Legitimacy of International Institutions', *European Journal of International Law* 25 (1) (2014), 85, 87.

incremental extension of the influence of EU law, and the Court itself. This has caused tensions with the Member States' constitutional courts, which had enjoyed exclusive jurisdiction over the interpretation of national constitutions.[91] This has led to the so-called 'contested or negotiated normative authority'[92] of EU law, which gives rise to interpretative competition among the judicial instances, and creates fertile ground for the self-correction of the system to take place.

In the polycentric EU, issues concerning the shared system of rules arise regularly in the different centres of decision making. All the centres have equal ability to influence this issue through their respective procedural avenues. There are also two legal imperatives driving this dynamic in two opposite directions: the principle of primacy of Union law on the one hand,[93] which would result in a pro-EU solution; and the obligation to respect the national identity of Member States on the other,[94] which would give way to the lower level of decision making. An explicit primacy clause that would serve as a resolution of this inherent conflict failed to come into force as part of the Treaty establishing a Constitution for Europe after its signature in 2004, implying that the sentiment among Member States was and is against any such

[91] The case law of some constitutional courts in the European Union points to the conclusion that they still regard themselves as unrestricted by EU law. For cases where constitutional courts define national sovereignty as the ultimate limit to European integration, see Czech *Ústavní Soud (Czech Republic)* case Pl. ÚS 50/04 *Sugar Quotas III*, Judgment of 8 March 2006, available at www.usoud.cz/en/decisions/20060308-pl-us-5004-sugar-quotas-iii-1/ accessed 1 May 2016, headnote §8; German *Bundesverfassungsgericht* cases 2 BvR 2134/92 and 2 BvR 2159/92 *Maastricht Treaty*, Judgment of 12 October 1993, available at judicialstudies.unr.edu/JS_Summer09/JSP_Week_1/German%20ConstCourt%20Maastricht.pdf accessed 1 May 2016, para. C.II.1.a; Spanish *Tribunal Constitucional* case DTC 1/2004 *Constitutional Treaty*, Declaration of 13 December 2004, Ground 2. In addition, some constitutional courts have unconditionally underlined the hierarchical superiority of their national constitutions, for example Czech *Ústavní Soud* case Pl. ÚS 19/08 *Lisbon Treaty I*, Judgment of 26 November 2008, available at <http://www.usoud.cz/en/decisions/20081126-pl-us-1908-traeaty-of-lisbon-i-1/> accessed 1 May 2016, §216; Danish *Højesteret* case *Carlsen* v. *Rasmussen*, Judgment I 361/1997 of 6 April 1998; German *Bundesverfassungsgericht* case 2 BvR 2661/06 *Honeywell*, Order of 6 July 2010, available at bundesverfassungsgericht.de/SharedDocs/Entscheidungen/EN/2010/07/rs20100706_2bvr266106en.html accessed 1 May 2016, para. 68; National report – The Constitutional Court of the Republic of Lithuania (2014), 5; Polish *Trybunał Konstytucyjny* case K 18/04 *Accession Treaty*, Judgment of 11 May 2005, available at http://trybunal.gov.pl/fileadmin/content/omowienia/K_18_04_GB.pdf accessed 9 March 2016, para. 11; UK Supreme Court case: *Pham* [2015] UKSC 19, para. 90.

[92] M. Maduro (n. 39).

[93] Introduced by the Court of Justice in *Costa* v. *ENEL* (n. 46).

[94] Article 4(2) TEU.

a conclusive provision.[95] Furthermore, the jurisprudence of national constitutional courts and the Court of Justice on this matter showed no unequivocal answer for all circumstances. Through incremental development at both the EU and national level, the Court of Justice recognised that concerns of constitutional importance for Member States may take priority before an EU obligation, subject to the proportionality test: invoking national identity as a legitimate aim benefits from a wider margin of discretion being accorded to the Member State,[96] in particular as the Court stressed that the values protected need not be uniform across Member States.[97] With the introduction of the Lisbon Treaty in 2007, the provision on the obligation of the EU to respect national identities of Member States was expanded in its wording, but it also henceforth fell under the jurisdiction of the Court of Justice.[98] It can be said that the interactions between decision-making centres concerning the scope of application of the principle of primacy and the need to respect national identity has – through the self-correcting feature – developed into a new provision in the Treaties.[99]

The self-correcting feature does not put into question or undermine the right of all decision-making centres to have their say in the correction of the shared system of rules. It is precisely in the acknowledgment of these claims that the self-correction takes centre stage: each of the centres of decision making (national systems and the EU) has inbuilt conditions for the application of self-correction, such as the principle of EU-friendly interpretation on the national level,[100] or the national identity clause in

[95] This is not to diminish the importance of the principle of primacy in the case law of the Court of Justice, but rather to emphasise the importance of the 'political' in relation to the 'legal'. Moreover, it also serves to reiterate the importance of other institutions in the national constitutional setting and its ability to constrain national constitutional jurisdictions.

[96] See also, B. Guastaferro, 'Beyond the Exceptionalism of Constitutional Conflicts: The Ordinary Functions of the Identity Clause' (2012) Jean Monnet Working Paper 01/12, 43.

[97] Case C-36/02 *Omega* [2004] ECR I-9609, para. 31; Case C-208/09 *Sayn-Wittgenstein* [2010] I-13693, para. 87.

[98] B. Guastaferro (n. 96) 4.

[99] Article 4(2) TEU. For a more detailed analysis on the incremental development of judge-made principles in the EU's shared system of rules through permanent conflict and self-correction, see A. Bobić, 'Constitutional Pluralism Is Not Dead: An Analysis of Interactions between the European Court of Justice and Constitutional Courts of Member States', *German Law Journal* 18(6) (2017), 1395.

[100] Italian *Corte Costituzionale* case *Granital* No. 170 of 8 June 1984, 7-3; Judge of the German Federal Constitutional Court A. Voßkuhle, 'Multilevel Cooperation of the European Constitutional Courts: Der Europäische Verfassungsgerichtsverbund', *European Constitutional Law Review* 6 (2) (2010), 175, 188; German *Bundesverfassungsgericht* Cases: 2 BverfGE 2661/06 *Honeywell*, Order of 6 July 2010, paras. 100, 111; 2 BVerfG 2/08 *Lisbon Treaty*, Judgment of 30 June 2009, para. 221; Polish *Trybunał Konstytucyjny* case K 32/09

EU law.[101] However, it is only through interactions between the systems that the self-correction occurs. The self-correction prevents outright conflict between decision-making centres. Over time, this 'code of conduct'[102] will inherently work to self-correct any imbalance and prevent the rise of conflict. It also ensures that the result achieved is conducive to a heterarchical constellation among decision-making centres, where at different times different centres succeed in changing the shared system of rules.[103]

The self-organisation of multiple actors in different centres of decision making that can be characterised as polycentric carry within them the self-correcting ability,[104] and the one described above further demonstrates the polycentric character of the European Union. This behaviour, when regarded in its entirety and as dynamic, rather than static, ultimately represents another source of the overarching system of rules in the polycentric European Union.

**

The overarching shared system of rules in the European Union is one characterised by idiosyncrasy, complexity and dynamism, which from a polycentric perspective each in their own way presents both an advantage and a challenge. The European Union has, on the one hand, opened up space for new institutional solutions ensuring the functioning of a multilevel, multipurpose network of decision-making centres. On the other hand, however, the novelty of the EU's legal framework has resulted in new challenges in identifying the shared system of rules, specifically due to its focus on the internal market as

Treaty of Lisbon, Judgment of 24 November 2010, para. 3.1; General Report, Conference of European Constitutional Courts (2014), 2–4 [this and all the following national reports may be accessed at www.confeuconstco.org/]; National Report – The Supreme Court of Cyprus (2014), 3; National Report – The Constitutional Court of the Czech Republic (2014), 4; National Report – The Federal Constitutional Court of the Republic of Germany (2014), 2; National Report – The Constitutional Court of Hungary (2014), 3; National Report – The Constitutional Court of the Republic of Latvia (2014), 8; National Report – The Constitutional Court of the Republic of Lithuania (2014), 15, 26; National Report – The Portuguese Constitutional Court (2014), 23.

[101] Cases C-36/02 *Omega* and C-208/09 *Sayn-Wittgenstein* (. 97); Case C-391/09 *Runevič-Vardyn* [2011] ECR I-3787.

[102] See also the Introduction to this Volume by J. van Zeben, 6.

[103] Heterarchy can be defined as 'the relation of elements to one another when they are unranked or when they possess the potential for being ranked in a number of different ways.' C. L. Crumley, 'Heterarchy and the Analysis of Complex Societies', *Archaeological Papers of the American Anthropological Association* 6 (1995), 1, 3.

[104] P. D. Aligica and V. Tarko (n. 1), 246.

the driving force behind integration and the disproportionate prominence of market concerns in the shared system of rules. Further, the complexity of the system, while important in order to be able to accommodate for the multifaceted realities of the EU, equally presented an obstacle in identifying the rules as they are located across a variety of sources on different levels and in different forms. Finally, the dynamic character of the shared system of rules is what connects it so tightly to polycentric theory. Decision-making centres are in an incremental fashion contesting the rules and influencing their content, which contributes to their development. However, this practice makes it more difficult to identify the rules that all decision-making centres are continuously considered as both overarching *and* shared.

III Obstacles in Achieving the Full Polycentric Potential

Having presented the existing shared system of rules in the European Union, several issues must be addressed in order for us to be able to imagine the shared system of rules of a fully polycentric European Union. The first issue pertains to the dominance of the top-down approach in the creation and operation of the shared system of rules and the consequences this has for self-governance. The second issue concerns the self-correcting character of the system of rules as it is carried out by the decision-making centres. I will address each of these in turn.

First, it is evident from the analysis above that the dominant method for creating and changing the shared system of rules is a top-down one, where the relevant decision-making centres are, primarily, European and national governmental institutions. Self-governance as an aim cannot be found in the shared system of rules, whereas the tendencies of the EU to promote it more actively can only indirectly be found in Article 10 TEU which focuses on participatory mechanisms for EU citizens.[105] Despite the fact that the Treaties create participation rights for EU citizens, and that the principle of subsidiarity was introduced with the aim that decisions be taken as close

[105] As presented by J. van Zeben and A. Bobić in Chapter 5 of this Volume, although the Commission has taken up initiatives to increase the level of participation of citizens in the political life of the EU, as well as to encourage new forms of governance with a bottom-up character, these do not yet form part of the overarching shared system of rules.

as possible to the citizen,[106] there is little space for a meaningful influence being exerted bottom-up.[107] Individuals can impact the system of rules mainly through elections of their representatives in national and EU institutions, and may bring their issues before national and EU courts seeking redress and indirectly encouraging the system to self-correct.[108] Under such conditions, self-governance has little practical significance. Without a principled dedication to self-governance identified in the shared system of rules, it subsequently and expectedly lacks the institutional essentials and prerequisites in place that would enable, or at least stimulate, self-governing tendencies.

The central role of institutional essentials is to ensure the dynamic nature of the shared system of rules through contestation, enforcement and a freedom of entry and exit available to all under equal conditions. The entry and exit conditions for creating and changing the shared system of rules need to be reformed so as to open up space for more bottom-up participatory decision making – currently they are opened up exclusively to public institutions. Further spaces of contestation, such as the European Citizens' Initiative,[109] could be afforded greater weight and be given binding effect for the decision making centres. In addition, due to the centrality of top-down decision making in the creation and change of rules, polycentric prerequisites are currently equally focused on public institutions. Chapters 10 to 12[110] of this Volume have shown that institutions have privileged access to all polycentric prerequisites. Given that institutional essentials and prerequisites feed back into the shared system of rules, the resulting image is one of a clear-cut dominance of the public over the private, regardless of the EU's market-oriented nature.

Second, the ability to influence the self-correcting characteristic of the shared system of rules is not equal among all decision-making centres. For example, contesting the scope of application of the

[106] Preamble to Protocol No. 2 to the Lisbon Treaty. See also, in this Volume, Chapter 4 by J. van Zeben and K. Nicolaïdis for a more detailed analysis of the shortcomings of the current status of the principle of subsidiarity.

[107] See also, in this Volume, Chapter 5 by J. van Zeben and A. Bobić for an analysis of this issue in matters of the internal market.

[108] See, in this Volume, Chapter 10 by L. Díez Sánchez.

[109] For further detail on the Initiative see, in this Volume, Chapter 5 by J. van Zeben and A. Bobić and Chapter 10 by L. Díez Sánchez.

[110] Sections I, III and III respectively.

principle of primacy has without a doubt led to its limited application when the national constitutional value proportionately restricts an EU law obligation. From a polycentric perspective, such a development is positive as it allows for differentiation and better adjustment to local preferences. However, the dominance of judicial contestation has resulted in asymmetries in influence within certain domestic courts. For example, the German Federal Constitutional Court is seen as the dominant instigator of contestation of the case law of the Court of Justice – being one of the most cited courts EU-wide as well as the most prominent in questioning the decisions of the Court of Justice,[111] and seen as pushing the ordo-liberal agenda in the EU's economic policy.[112] This ultimately means that the extent of differentiation in fact depends on the behaviour of national courts, which evidently do not equally participate in the self-correction of the shared system of rules.

IV Conclusions

This chapter set out to determine the scope and content of the concept of the shared system of rules, specifically in the context of the European Union, with a view to testing the extent to which a shared system of rules can be identified within the EU and what gaps may remain.

The analysis has shown that there is a shared system of rules in place that covers EU and Member State actions and interactions. This system of rules is composed of written and unwritten rules originating from the EU institutions and the Member States. The written rules can be found in primary and secondary EU and national law, while the unwritten rules are created by repeated interactions between European actors, including for instance the judicial interactions between the European and national courts. These rules are connected through shared substantive

[111] General Report, Conference of European Constitutional Courts (2014), 9; G. Anagnostaras, 'Activation of the Ultra Vires Review: The Slovak Pensions Judgment of the Czech Constitutional Court', *German Law Journal* 14 (7) (2013), 959; R. D. Kelemen, 'On the Unsustainability of Constitutional Pluralism. European Supremacy and the Survival of the Eurozone', *Maastricht Journal of European and Comparative Law* 23 (2016), 136; F. C. Mayer, 'Rashomon in Karlsruhe: A Reflection on Democracy and Identity in the European Union: The German Constitutional Court's Lisbon Decision and the Changing Landscape of European Constitutionalism', *International Journal of Constitutional Law* 9 (3) (2011), 757.

[112] C. Joerges, '"Brother, Can You Paradigm?"', *International Journal of Constitutional Law* 12 (3) (2014), 772, 780.

requirements, such as the protection of fundamental rights, equality and democracy.

A lack of consensus as regards the proper scope and meaning of the EU's shared system of rules should not, however, be confused with a lack of consensus as to the existence of the system. It was evident from the analysis that the shared system of rules is continuously contested by a wide range of decision-making centres, especially courts, which causes the system of rules to self-correct. The self-correcting feature of the EU's system is a crucial characteristic which reinforces the dynamic nature of the shared system of rules which, under certain conditions, adjusts to the preferences of the decision-making centres.

The analysis of the relevant rules shows a lack of emphasis on self-governance, which is logically accompanied by a lack of rules concerning institutional essentials and prerequisites that would enable and/or encourage self-governance. Instead, the institutional essentials and prerequisites focus on public institutions and top-down processes. A drastic change in the shared system of rules that would clearly prioritise self-governance and bottom-up processes is unlikely to take place in the context of recent proposals for EU reform.[113] A more likely alternative is the emergence of conditions for self-governance at lower levels of governance through national and subnational processes, with proper recognition of, and room for, these developments within the shared system of rules.

[113] Reuters, 'Highlights of Merkel interview on Europe', 3 June 2018, available at www.reuters.com/article/us-europe-merkel-highlights/highlights-of-merkel-interview-on-europe-idUSKCN1IZ0KN last accessed 25 July 2018.

7

The Promises and Drawbacks of European Union Citizenship for a Polycentric Union

MARTIJN VAN DEN BRINK

Citizenship remains essentially contested. Rival theories offer alternative perspectives to contemporary political problems and place emphasis on different values. Liberal theories of citizenship, for example, prioritise the protection of the individual from the state by granting them a fairly elaborate set of rights, while republican theories seek to foster the active political participation of the citizenry. Distinctions between different conceptions, however, are easily exaggerated; both theories treat citizenship as a status that places citizens in a position to participate in and contribute to practices of political self-governance.[1] There is therefore a clear parallel between the importance of self-governance to contemporary conceptions of citizenship and its centrality in polycentric theory.[2] This Chapter connects both debates and explores the potential citizenship holds for self-governance within a polycentric European Union.

I will draw attention to the different levels of citizenship within the European Union, arising from the different centres of decision making – European, national, and local,[3] and shall argue that our conception of European Union citizenship must be compatible with and respect this multiplicity of decision-making centres. That is, as Joseph Carens said, 'our conceptions of citizenship and political community should grow out of, rather than determine, the political and social arrangements that we choose'.[4] Hence, a more polycentric understanding of citizenship is required within the EU, which recognises the existence of and

[1] For an extensive discussion of liberal and republican accounts, their disagreements and similarities, I. Honohan, 'Liberal and Republican Conceptions of Citizenship', in A. Shachar and others (eds.), *The Oxford Handbook of Citizenship* 1st edn (Oxford University Press, 2017).

[2] See, in this Volume, Chapter 1 by J. van Zeben.

[3] R. Bauböck, 'The Three Levels of Citizenship within the European Union', *German Law Journal* 15 (2014), 751.

[4] J. H. Carens, *Culture, Citizenship, and Community: A Contextual Exploration of Justice as Evenhandedness* (Oxford University Press, 2000), 162.

demonstrates respect for the dispersion of authority within the EU and processes of self-governance at the different levels of government. This distinguishes my argument from more fashionable perspectives on EU citizenship, which place great emphasis on individual free movement and prefer the homogenisation of rights to constitutional divisions of authority and local governance processes. In contrast, I argue that differentiations of rights are inevitable in a Union that divides authority between different centres and shall emphasise the benefits of collective self-governance, whereby 'society as a whole manages the full array of its political, economic, and social affairs'.[5] Our accounts of citizenship within the EU should not devalue the latter.

I should clarify immediately that I include in my definition of citizenship not only legal statuses recognised in national constitutions but treat it as political membership of a particular community. Since local communities – municipalities, federal regions, etc. – have their own democratically controlled governments, they also have their own citizens.[6] Considering self-governance, my focus will be on the challenges posed by the legal construction of EU citizenship for self-governance within the EU and the options for improvement, whereby I will assume – following Cheneval earlier in this volume –[7] a necessary relation between self-government and democracy. My argument is structured around *Walloon*,[8] a case that demonstrates like no other how the complex interplay of different levels of government affects the governance of citizenship, and by citizens, within the EU.

Section I introduces the *Walloon* decision and highlights the consequences of the judicial characterisation of territorial boundaries demarcating different centres of decision making as barriers to free movement. Based on a conception of EU citizenship that privileges individual free

[5] M. D. McGinnis and M. Hanisch, 'Analysing Problems of Polycentric Governance in the Growing EU' (2005) Paper presented at the Workshop on Analyzing Problems of Polycentric Governance in the Growing EU, Humboldt University, Berlin (on file with the author), 6.

[6] This definition follows that of Bauböck (n. 3), but also of polycentric theorists. According to McGinnis, 'each individual is a citizen of one township, the one county that contains that township, the one state that includes that county, and, ultimately, of the nation as a whole'. M. D. McGinnis, 'Costs and Challenges of Polycentric Governance' (2005) Paper presented at the Workshop on Analyzing Problems of Polycentric Governance in the Growing EU, Humboldt University, Berlin, 7. Of course, within the EU, individuals can be citizens of two or more Member States.

[7] See, in this Volume, Chapter 3 by F. Cheneval.

[8] Case C-212/06 *Walloon* [2008] ECR I-1683.

movement and the homogenisation of rights over national constitutional divisions of authority and local self-governance, the Court challenged Belgium's federal arrangement. Section 2 offers an alternative polycentric conception of European Union citizenship that respects divisions of power between different centres of decision making within the EU. That mandates a different understanding of two of the key characteristics of EU citizenship – free movement and non-discrimination. While currently both are employed to undermine the existence of different centres of decision making within the EU, I argue that EU citizens' freedom of entry and exit can be operationalised with respect for practices of collective self-governance within these centres and the system of general rules be enforced so as to overcome barriers to cooperation between them. The principle of non-discrimination on grounds of nationality requires deference to the substantive content of national and local citizenship, and free movement law allows for the connection of the different localities in a way that respects self-governance within the EU. Section 3 moves from the ambition to shape EU citizenship law so that it respects principles of self-governance to thinking through the position of EU citizens itself in processes of self-governance within the EU. It offers some tentative thoughts on the political rights of EU citizens and criticises the long-term to permanent exclusion of foreigners from the national franchise on grounds of democratic justice.

I Walloon

According to Carens, 'talk about citizenship sometimes presupposes, as a background assumption, an idealized (and misleading) conception of the nation-state as an administratively centralized, culturally homogeneous form of political community in which citizenship is treated primarily as a legal status that is universal, equal, and democratic'.[9] That presupposition is inadequate, he explained, because citizenship is often multi-dimensional and divided, and recognising these divisions 'may be essential to fulfil the commitment to equality that is often expressed in the language of citizenship'.[10] That the EU constitutes a system of governance that belies the idea of universality and homogeneity, where full equality between citizens is the norm, appears self-evident. The EU divides decisional authority between different institutions at (at least)

[9] J. H. Carens (n. 4) 161.
[10] ibid.

three levels of government – supranationally, nationally, and locally – and each of these authorities is permitted to define, within the confines of their powers, the substantive content of their policies. Yet, while citizenship within the EU is multi-dimensional, the background assumption of universality and equality continues to inform conceptions of EU citizenship. The decision by the Court of Justice of the European Union (Court of CJEU) in *Walloon* and the relevant literature[11] keenly demonstrate this.

Walloon shows how a complex interaction between different jurisdictions defines the regulation of citizenship within the EU. The governments of Walloon and the French community in Belgium challenged a care insurance scheme established by the Flemish government, which covered non-medical expenses of individuals resident within the Dutch-speaking region or the bilingual region of Brussels. The latter could join on a voluntary basis.[12] Following a Commission challenge – to make the legislation compatible with Regulation 1408/71 EEC – its scope was extended to individuals working within the Dutch-speaking region or bilingual region of Brussels, but residing within the territory of another EU Member State.[13] Excluded were residents of Walloon who worked in Flanders or Brussels, irrespective of their nationality.

The case revolved around the three levels of citizenship within the EU. As *Walloon* demonstrates, authority over policies' substantive content can be local, while national and EU legal rules simultaneously condition access to local benefits. Moreover, these rules were of a different kind: As is common in federal systems,[14] the relevant legislation in Belgium employed the principle of *lex loci domicilii*, which conditions access according to the location of residence.[15] EU legislation, on the other hand, applied the principle of *lex loci laboris*, which assigns as the responsible Member State the country where the Union citizen is employed.[16] While meant to guarantee equal working conditions for

[11] See the literature in footnotes 30-33 below.

[12] *Décret portant organisation de l'assurance soins* (*Moniteur belge* of 28 May 1999) 19149.

[13] *Décret modifiant le décret du 30 mars 1999 portant organisation de l'assurance soins* (*Moniteur belge* of 9 June 2004) 43593.

[14] H. Verschueren, 'The Impact of EU Law on the Devolution of Social Powers in the Member States', in E. Cloots, G. de Baere, and S. Sottiaux (eds.), *Federalism in the* European Union (Hart Publishing, 2012) 265.

[15] *Cour constitutionnelle de Belgique*, 11/2009 (21 January 2009) para. B.12.1-B.14.

[16] Regulation 883/2004 EC on the coordination of social security systems [2004] OJ L 166/1. For the general rule and the many exceptions see: F. Pennings, *European Social Security Law* 6th edn (Intersentia 2010) chapter 6.

employees, the fact that the principle of *lex loci laboris* applied to benefits governed by the *lex loci domicilii* principle according to national law generated discrimination between EU citizens resident within another Member State and those whose place of residence was Walloon. That is, an EU citizen economically active within the Dutch-speaking region was entitled to coverage when resident in Germany, but not when in Walloon. The Flemish care insurance scheme excluded all residents of Walloon and did not distinguish between Belgian nationals and non-Belgian EU citizens.

Reaffirming the 'purely internal' rule, according to which situations lacking a cross-border element (hence, purely internal to one Member State) are beyond the reach of the EU citizenship provisions on free movement,[17] the Court held that the exclusion of Belgian nationals fell outside the scope of EU law and was a matter for Belgian law.[18] Those with a nationality of a Member State other than Belgium, however, fell within EU law's ambit, because those EU citizens had exercised their right to free movement.[19] Moreover, the loss of social advantages, as a result of the exercise of this right, was considered to be an impediment to the right to free movement.[20] The legislation at issue created such an effect, because those:

> pursuing or contemplating the pursuit of employment or self-employment in one of those two regions, might be dissuaded from making use of their freedom of movement and from leaving their Member State of origin to stay in Belgium, by reason of the fact that moving to certain parts of Belgium would cause them to lose the opportunity of eligibility for the benefits which they might otherwise have claimed.[21]

[17] On the purely internal rule, see M. P. Maduro, 'The Scope of European Remedies: The Case of Purely Internal Situations and Reverse Discrimination', in C. Kilpatrick, T. Novitz, and P. Skidmore (eds.), *The Future of Remedies in Europe* (Hart Publishing, 2000); S. O'Leary, 'The Past, Present and Future of the Purely Internal Rule in EU Law', in M. Dougan, N. Nic Shuibhne, and E. Spaventa (eds.), *Empowerment and Disempowerment of the European Citizen* (Hart Publishing, 2012); C. Ritter, 'Purely Internal Situation, Reverse Discrimination, *Guimont, Dzodzi* and Article 234', *European Law Review* 31 (2006), 690; A. Tryfonidou, 'Reverse Discrimination in Purely Internal Situations: An Incongruity in a Citizens' Europe', *Legal Issues of Economic Integration* 35 (2008), 43.

[18] *Walloon* (n. 8) para. 39.

[19] ibid., para. 41.

[20] ibid., para. 46.

[21] ibid., para. 48.

The Flemish government invoked the federal division of powers within Belgium as justification, but the judges resolutely rejected that justification, deciding 'that a Member State cannot plead provisions, practices or situations prevailing in its domestic legal order, including those resulting from the constitutional organisation of that State, to justify the failure to observe obligations arising under [EU] law'.[22]

The Court reasoned that because eligibility is 'dependent on the condition of residence in either a limited part of national territory . . . or in another Member State',[23] the national measures constituted an obstacle to free movement. If plausible, that argument should have far-reaching consequences, as it implies that domestic principles of multilevel organisation constitute unjustifiable limitations to EU free movement law virtually by definition. Federalism, after all, presupposes a set of overlapping levels of authority, with considerable autonomy for the regions to decide substantive policy. The judges thus did not only turn Belgian federal boundaries of welfare into unacceptable barriers to free movement, but also challenged an essential feature of federalism. Moreover, the matter has implications for non-federal states, because also centralised nation states are divided into multiple administrative jurisdictions, creating local rights divisions.[24] Those residing and working in Amsterdam will be subject to a different local regime of benefits and taxation than those employed in Amsterdam but resident in Rotterdam. Following *Walloon*, this could dissuade free movement, because 'moving to certain parts of [the country] would cause [EU citizens] to lose the opportunity of eligibility for the benefits which they might otherwise have claimed'.[25]

While recognising the existence of local centres of decision making, the Court did not acknowledge their importance and failed to take seriously regional and national territorial boundaries of welfare. The prospect of taking up residence within Walloon may be less attractive if it diminishes welfare coverage, but that, of course, is 'an unavoidable by-product of the choice not to harmonise social security schemes'.[26]

[22] ibid., para. 58.
[23] ibid., para. 47.
[24] W. Maas, 'Equality and the Free Movement of People: Citizenship and Internal Migration', in W. Maas (ed.), *Democratic Citizenship and the Free Movement of People* (Martinus Nijhoff Publishers, 2013), 10.
[25] *Walloon* (n. 8) para. 48.
[26] N. Rennuy, 'The Emergence of a Parallel System of Social Security Coordination', *Common Market Law Review* 50 (2013), 1221, 1227.

In case the competence to decide on social welfare arrangements belongs to local authorities, a change of residence in one Member State is supposed to have the same implications as the decision to move to another Member State. It affects one's social entitlements, sometimes for the better, sometimes for the worse. Free movement rights were never premised on the idea that every potential place of residence had to be as attractive as possible, because that would turn existing federal borders into quasi-automatic barriers to free movement. If the rationale behind *Walloon* were to become the norm, certainly Member States constituted along federal lines (or alternative multilevel arrangements) would find themselves in violation of EU law on a constant basis, the only remedy against which is the harmonisation of social welfare systems and the elimination of national, regional and/or local divisions of authority.

Many EU lawyers appear to find this an attractive perspective. Most legal commentary did not fault the case's argumentative shortcomings, nor argued against the characterisation of federal boundaries of welfare as unjustifiable barriers to free movement but submitted that the Court's delineation of EU law's scope was insufficiently far-reaching.[27] It should not have stopped with the inclusion of non-Belgian EU citizens, they argued, but have extended the coverage of the Flemish insurance scheme to Belgian nationals resident in Walloon as well. Many believed thus that the Court should have rendered Belgium's federal boundaries entirely irrelevant, given their potential restraining effect on benefits.

The reasoning behind this position is straightforward; *Walloon* resulted in so-called 'reverse discrimination' between EU citizens. Reverse discrimination arises if EU law demands Member States to offer preferential treatment to nationals of other states and permits national governments to discriminate against their own nationals.[28] *Walloon* extended social protection only to Walloon residents with the nationality of a Member State other than that of Belgium and permitted Belgium to deny those benefits to residents of Walloon with the Belgian nationality. The dominant perspective in EU citizenship discourse is that reverse discrimination goes against the ideal of equality embodied by citizenship.[29] AG Sharpston in her Opinion in *Walloon* expressed that

[27] See the literature in footnotes 30–33 below.

[28] For the most detailed analysis of reverse discrimination to date: A. Tryfonidou, *Reverse Discrimination in EC Law* (Kluwer Law International, 2009).

[29] Read, for example, H. de Waele, 'EU Citizenship: Revisiting Its Meaning, Place and Potential', *European Journal of Migration and Law* 12 (2010), 319, 329; M. P. Maduro, 'The Scope of European Remedies: The Case of Purely Internal Situations and Reverse

perspective forcefully and eloquently. It is paradoxical, she said, that 'although the last 50 years have been spent abolishing barriers to freedom of movement *between* Member States, decentralised authorities of Member States may nevertheless reintroduce barriers through the back door by establishing them *within* Member States'.[30] Her typification of internal federal boundaries as obstacles to free movement resembles the Court's arguments, but whereas the judges refused to extend coverage also to Belgian nationals, the AG believed that all of Walloon's residents had to have a right to claim protection under the Flemish care insurance scheme. For her, any decision that denies nationals of Belgium eligibility merely because they never exercised the right to free movement would highlight 'the arbitrariness of attaching so much importance to crossing a national border'.[31] Such an outcome would certainly be difficult to square with principles of EU citizenship, which challenges 'the sustainability in its present form of the doctrine on purely internal situations'.[32]

The AG was right in noting the arbitrariness of distinguishing Walloon residents based on whether they have exercised the right to free movement formerly, but failed to recognise that the arbitrary nature of the situation had arisen precisely because of her assumption that the mere prior exercise of free movement rights made non-Belgian nationals resident within Walloon eligible. That is, she overlooked the fact that the situation would never have arisen had she not characterised the borders between decentralised authorities as unacceptable barriers to free movement. This problem also went unnoticed by scholars agreeing with the AG. Van Elsuwege and Adam, for example, believed it to be 'somewhat paradoxical that member states remain entitled to discriminate against their own nationals in a Community that is based on the rule of law and the principle of equal treatment, particularly in the light of the provisions on European citizenship'.[33] To realise the ideal of equality

Discrimination', in C. Kilpatrick, T. Novitz, and P. Skidmore (eds.), *The Future of Remedies in Europe* (Hart Publishing, 2000) 126; C. Jacqueson, 'Union Citizenship and the Court of Justice: Something New Under the Sun? Towards Social Citizenship' *European Law Review* 27 (2002), 260, 281; D. Kochenov, 'Citizenship without Respect: The EU's Troubled Equality Ideal' (2011) 08/10 Jean Monnet Working Paper.

30 *Walloon* (n. 8), Opinion of AG Sharpston, para. 116.

31 ibid., para. 141. She expressed a similar view in Case C-34/09 *Ruiz Zambrano* [2011] ECR I-1177.

32 ibid., para. 140.

33 P. Van Elsuwege and S. Adam, 'The Limits of Constitutional Dialogue for the Prevention of Reverse Discrimination', *European Constitutional Law Review* 5 (2009), 327, 333. See also: C. Dautricourt and S. Thomas, 'Reverse Discrimination and Free Movement of

embedded within EU citizenship, federal divisions of authority must be overcome and a harmonisation of social rights be realised at the expense of local forms of democratic self-governance.[34]

Walloon confirms Carens' claim that conceptions of citizenship tend to regard it primarily as a legal status that is universal and equal and neglect institutional divisions of power and the existence of multiple overlapping and interacting centres of decision making. The case displays a preference for individual free movement rights and the homogenisation of rights over Belgium's constitutional divisions of authority and local self-governance. As will be shown in the following section, differentiation between levels of citizenship accordingly provides a heterogeneous set of rights and obligations attached to each of them respectively.

II Citizenship in a Polycentric Union

In my discussion of the AG's Opinion and the Court's decision and their consequences, I have not yet paid much attention to problematic aspects of the reasoning that led to their conclusions. In this Section, I specify my ideal contours of citizenship in a Union where authority is divided over multiple overlapping centres of decision making. My account differs from more popular assessments of *Walloon*, which show considerably more sympathy towards the conclusions reached by the members of the Court. One line of thought is that the decision was insufficiently attentive to Belgium's federal arrangement, which the EU, in accordance with Article 4(2) TEU,[35] is expected to respect, but still believes that, everything considered, the Court struck the correct balance between competing EU values. There is simply no *a priori* reason to assume that principles of EU citizenship must always give in when encountering the boundaries of Article 4(2) TEU. Van Elsuwege and Adam reasoned that at least occasionally, 'the federal organisation of a member state can be

Persons under Community Law: All for Ulysses, Nothing for Penelope?' *European Law Review* 34 (2009), 433; D. Kochenov, 'Citizenship without Respect: The EU's Troubled Equality Ideal' (n. 29).

[34] I am not the first to suggest that *Walloon* treaded too lightly on national constitutional federal values. See H. Verschueren (n. 14) 283–4; T. Vandamme, 'Case C-212/06, *Government of the French Community and the Walloon Government* v. *Flemish Government*, Judgment of the Court of Justice (Grand Chamber) of 1 April 2008, Nyr', *Common Market Law Review* 46 (2009), 287, 298.

[35] Accordingly, 'the Union shall respect the equality of Member States before the Treaties as well as their national identities, inherent in their fundamental structures, political and constitutional, inclusive of regional and local self-government'.

used as a potential justification for infringing free movement rights under [EU] law',[36] thereby implying that we should speak of infringements to free movement law in these circumstances. Kochenov has gone further, arguing that putting into effect AG Sharpston's suggestions is essential for EU citizenship to realise its full promise.[37]

These arguments are implausible, because all presume some tension between EU citizenship and the division of powers between different governance centres within the EU that does (or should) not exist. In fact, equal citizenship can be realised without challenging the fragmentation of authority between different centres of government, and citizens' mobility does not need to undermine territorial boundaries, between or within Member States. In doing so, I highlight that EU citizenship, due to its two key characteristics – free movement and non-discrimination – is able to contribute to realising two key aspects of polycentric theory. EU citizens' freedom of entry and exit can be operationalised with respect for practices of collective self-governance within these centres, and the system of general rules be enforced so as to overcome barriers to cooperation between them. Based on a different conception, the realisation of EU citizenship entails respect for the substantive decisions by and boundaries between national and local processes of self-governance, and EU citizenship law should concern itself with resolving conflicts between different levels of decision making rather than attempting to unify or diminish the importance of these levels. Following that conception, the principle of non-discrimination on grounds of nationality requires deference to the substantive content of national and local citizenship (subsection A) and through free movement we should seek to connect the different localities in a way that respects self-governance within the EU (subsection B).

A Non-Discrimination on Grounds of Nationality as a Means of Self-Governance

My claim that no tensions exist between the ideal of citizenship equality and divisions of authority requires some nuances, as it is a well-established fact that citizens' substantive rights are not necessarily uniform in polities that divide authority between different centres of government. Within

[36] P. Van Elsuwege and S. Adam (n. 33) 337.

[37] D. Kochenov, 'On Tiles and Pillars: EU Citizenship as a Federal Denominator', in D. Kochenov (ed.), *EU Citizenship and Federalism: The Role of Rights* (Cambridge University Press, 2017).

federations, for example, 'more equality between citizens across the federation almost necessarily implies less freedom ... for the component units'.[38] Still, the ideal of equal citizenship remains. The goal is to embed it within the federation's political structure when determining to whom to extend equal treatment; when powers are retained by the constituting states, equality of treatment is guaranteed within the boundaries of those states with respect to all citizens resident there.[39] The right to non-discrimination on grounds of nationality normally guarantees the same within the EU. A German national resident within Belgium is treated like a Belgian national, which implies, by extension, that the German national resident within Walloon is treated like the Walloon region treats its residents holding Belgian nationality.

This requires a somewhat different perspective on the principle of non-discrimination on grounds of nationality, for commonly we treat it as a constraint on the Member States' political discretion. They cannot enact laws that discriminate against non-national EU citizens. In addition, however, we should also think of that right as constraining the CJEU's discretion. If non-national EU citizens are included within the scope of national or local law and are treated on an equal basis, as if they were national citizens, the judges must not interfere with these decisions and provide 'deference to the states on the substantive content of citizenship'.[40] Note that this does not suggest that decentralisation is almost certainly preferable over centralisation. It is difficult to offer firm conclusions about the ideal division of authority in our societies a-contextually and independently of the matter we seek to regulate.[41] All I argue is that Member States'

[38] P. Dardanelli, 'Federal Democracy in Switzerland', in M. Burgess and A. G. Gagnon (eds.), *Federal Democracies* (Routledge, 2010), 155.

[39] There may be exceptions to that rule and also, within the EU, Member States are sometimes still permitted by secondary legislation to deviate from the right to non-discrimination on grounds of nationality, as is the case, for example, with social assistance. I will not address that issue here. For discussion of recent disputes over access to social assistance, N. Nic Shuibhne, '"What I Tell You Three Times Is True" Lawful Residence and Equal Treatment after Dano', *Maastricht Journal of European and Comparative Law* 23 (2016), 908.

[40] This was also the meaning of nineteenth-century citizenship in the USA, as pointed out by: W. J. Novak, 'The Legal Transformation of Citizenship in Nineteenth-Century America', in M. Jacobs, W. J. Novak, and J. E. Zelizer (eds.), *The Democratic Experiment: New Directions in American Political History* (Princeton University Press, 2003), 88.

[41] Scholars of polycentricity were correct in asserting that '[n]o a priori judgment can be made about the adequacy of a polycentric system of government as against a single jurisdiction'. C. Tiebout, R. Warren, and V. Ostrom, 'The Organization of Government in Metropolitan Areas: A Theoretical Inquiry', *American Political Science Review* 55 (4) (1961), 831, 838.

internal structure and the content of local and national law is in principle for the national centres of decision making, not for the Court, to decide.

At least two reasons speak in favour of bottom-up governance in this context. As McGinnis was correct to note:

> Each institutional component should enjoy a greater sense of legitimacy and a high level of community participation. In addition, because people with access to knowledge of local conditions selected these institutions, they should be more closely adapted to local circumstances, and thus prove more effective in the long run.[42]

First, deference to the substantive content of national or local citizenship means deference to the outcomes realised through political procedures that treat all citizens as equals.[43] Hence, the principle of non-discrimination can and should be recognised as a principle that acknowledges the importance of democratic self-governance. If national decisions incorporate the requirements of the principle of non-discrimination on grounds of nationality, the Court should restrain itself and respect the democratically legitimated content of domestic law, decided on by national and local democratic processes.[44] Secondly, not only do the pressures of harmonisation created by the EU citizenship jurisprudence challenge the self-governing capacity of different communities, they will also preclude citizens from finding solutions to political problems that are best attuned to local circumstances. For a start, ideally there is a certain correspondence 'between the beneficiaries of public goods and services and those who pay for them',[45] which the CJEU challenged in *Walloon* and would have lost completely had all the residents living in the Walloon region entitled to the benefits offered by the Flemish care insurance scheme. More importantly, Belgium's governance structure is designed precisely so that it mirrors the interactions between and diffuses conflicts among the different linguistic communities living within Belgium. We should want the EU to be careful before it intervenes in national governance decisions, not just because it has promised to do so in accordance with Article 4(2) TEU, but most of all because it is not as well placed

[42] M. D. McGinnis, 'Costs and Challenges of Polycentric Governance' (n. 6) 1–2.

[43] Equality sits at the very core of contemporary understandings of democracy. See T. Christiano, *The Constitution of Equality: Democratic Authority and Its Limits* (Oxford University Press, 2008); R. A. Dahl, *Democracy and Its Critics* (Yale University Press, 1991).

[44] A. J. Menéndez, 'European Citizenship after Martínez Sala and Baumbast' (2009) 11/2009 ARENA Working Paper 1, 37.

[45] M. D. McGinnis and M. Hanisch (n. 5) 22.

to decide on the desirable boundaries of the jurisdiction and the shape of the institutions through which national citizens govern themselves.

Citizenship scholars responded to *Walloon* with a plea for harmonising social rights within Belgium and an extension of the Flemish care insurance scheme's scope to all of Walloon's residents, with the purpose of realising equality among Union citizens. The underlying conception of the principle of non-discrimination of nationality is hard to square with the EU's multilevel system of governance. We can see now that this tension disappears once we adopt a different perspective on that principle, according to which it aspires to safeguard self-governance on the local level and serves as a constraint on the discretion enjoyed by the Court. Alike federations, which square a devolution of authority with principles of equal citizenship by guaranteeing equality between citizens within the locality in which they reside, the principle of non-discrimination on grounds of nationality should be interpreted as requiring respect for the substantive content of citizenship as decided upon various processes of self-governance within the Member States.

Joseph Carens was thus correct to argue that recognising the multidimensionality of citizenship is essential for safeguarding the promise of equality that the language of citizenship usually evokes.[46] The ECJ's failure to respect the boundaries of local citizenship produced an unjustifiable discrimination between Belgian and non-Belgian EU citizens resident within Walloon. The appropriate solution to that problem, however, is not, along AG Sharpston's line of thought, to revoke decision-making power from local authorities and harmonise social security coverage within Belgium. Had the members of the Court recognised the plurality of actors involved in the governance of citizenship within the EU and not have sought to deny those a legitimate role in that endeavour, they would have realised equality of treatment between citizens within the locality of residence and have respected the boundaries and powers of lower level decision-making units in Belgium.

B Principles of Free Movement as a Means to Cooperation between Local Government

Interdependencies between these different centres of decision making and levels of government and their inability to tackle collective

[46] J. H. Carens (n. 4) 161.

problems individually may cause them to establish forms of cooperation. As Vincent Ostrom put it, they can 'derive an advantage through the formation of a new public enterprise which could provide a joint service for the larger community of people comprising the several small communities'.[47] Such cooperation can occur under an overarching shared system of rules that is subject to enforcement mechanisms.[48] To regulate relations between the different federal regions of Belgium, the set of overarching rules conditions, for example, which region is responsible for the social welfare of citizens. Belgium, as I explained, employs the principle of *lex loci domicilii* to delineate who is covered by which social arrangement. The EU can be regarded as serving a similar purpose at a higher level, offering an institutional arrangement whereby it can constrain negative externalities resulting from domestic decisions, and realise collective solutions to problems faced by the Member States.

Cross-border mobility is among the most prominent domains shaped by EU regulation. An elaborate set of rules sets out under what conditions free movement of goods, services, capital and persons can take place between Member States.[49] Local communities can benefit from the opening up and reconstructing of borders, being able to attract well-trained and skilled individuals, while local entrepreneurs can sell their goods and services abroad. By forming a new set of institutions with the power to establish a common regime of free movement, smaller communities can achieve results and offer opportunities that they could not realise individually. On the other hand, these collective rules would have diminished companies' and individuals' costs of entry and exit had local and national restrictions been in effect. EU citizens are entitled to vote with their feet and move to where they can enjoy the 'good life'.[50] These shared rules also potentially enhance, in polycentric terms, individuals' ability for

[47] If such cooperation is desirable, different centres of authority, as Ostrom said it, 'derive an advantage through the formation of a new public enterprise which could provide a joint service for the larger community of people comprising the several small communities'. V. Ostrom, 'Can Federalism Make a Difference?' *Publius* (1973), 218.

[48] See, in this Volume, Chapter 1 by J. van Zeben.

[49] See, in this Volume, Chapter 5 by J. van Zeben and A. Bobić.

[50] F. de Witte, *Justice in the EU: The Emergence of Transnational Solidarity* (Oxford University Press, 2015), 61–64. Interesting in this regard is the recent decision of the CJEU in Case C-673/16 *Coman* [2018], in which it obliged Member States to recognise the marital status of same-sex couples.

self-governance, allowing them to move to the country offering the most beneficial regime.[51]

The challenge is finding a durable balance between an EU citizen's individual right to free movement and national processes of self-governance needed to govern our complex societies. Two questions are important in that regard: (1) under what conditions can Union citizens invoke principles of free movement in response to decisions enacted at a lower level of governance and (2) which EU institution is best positioned to define the overarching set of rules and define the limits of national autonomy? Both questions are complex and I can only address them briefly here.

First of all, contrary to the decision in *Walloon*, the Member States and their regions should not be obliged to redesign their policies in order to ensure compatibility with more attractive policies elsewhere, as perceived by individual citizens. In a Union where authority is divided between different levels of government, it is inevitable that entitlement to benefits can be 'dependent on the condition of residence in either a limited part of national territory . . . or in another Member State'.[52] This, to be clear, is no argument against harmonisation, but EU citizens' freedom of entry and exit should not be construed so broadly that losses of opportunity to eligibility for benefits, as a consequence of individual mobility, are earmarked as obstacles to free movement. In addition, citizens may be discouraged from continuing to reside in their current place of residence if another region or country offers more substantive protection of rights, but that cannot be taken to mean that the former undermines citizens' right to residence. For example, the refusal of Member State A to offer the benefits offered by Member State B could discourage nationals of A from continuing to reside there, but Member State A does not obstruct the realisation of the right to move and reside freely thereby.[53] Such or

[51] R. A. Epstein, 'Exit Rights under Federalism' *Law and Contemporary Problems* 55 (1992), 147; I. Somin, 'Foot Voting, Federalism, and Political Freedom', in J. E. Fleming and J. T. Levy (eds.), *Federalism and Subsidiarity* (New York University Press, 2014).

[52] *Walloon* (n. 8) para. 47.

[53] This is the unfortunate position the Court took in Case C-127/08 *Metock* [2008] ECR I-6241, para. 89: 'the refusal of that Member State to authorise his family members who are nationals of non-member countries to join him there would be such as to discourage him from continuing to reside there and encourage him to leave in order to be able to lead a family life in another Member State or in a non-member country'. Following this line of thought, the CJEU decided that the situation constituted a barrier to the right to move and reside freely. This artificial barrier produced reverse discrimination among EU citizens (as it did in *Walloon*) and, similar to the response to *Walloon*, scholars have suggested

similar interpretations of the right to move and reside freely within the Member States might result in an overly broad intrusion into lower levels of self-governance, not least on the national, regional and local level. Thus, while a homogeneous interpretation of EU citizenship might create additional opportunities and choice for the individual, they may bring about new asymmetries across existing lines of political decision making.

More complex and controversial are impediments to free movement that arise out of the application of national substantive standards to mobile citizens. That is, if the right to free movement is an operationalisation of the principle of non-discrimination on the grounds of nationality – and substantive standards are applied to national and mobile citizens indistinctly – the latter may be worse off if also they had to comply with the Member State of origin's rules previously. The principle of mutual recognition intends to protect against such dual burdens.[54] Absent adequate overriding justifications, the political decision-making unit of destination is under the obligation to recognise goods, services, and personal statuses lawfully produced, provided and acquired by the rules of the Member States of origin.[55] It offers an instructive example of the resolution of coordination problems through principles of free movement. Within the field of EU citizenship, the principle of mutual recognition has also been applied to decide which regulatory regime governs the mobile citizen.[56] However, whatever the merits of this principle, by imposing on Member States the obligation to recognise another's laws and constraining it in its application of its own regulatory standards, it restricts the scope for democratically legitimate decision-making processes on lower levels to formulate and apply their own policies.[57] The resolution of such conflicts must rest upon a careful balance between the individual's rights and interests and the concerns of lower levels of

that the appropriate response is the equalisation of rights upwards (which the CJEU partly realised in Case C-34/09 *Ruiz Zambrano* (n. 31)). This ignores that reverse discrimination would never have arisen had the CJEU not considered the situation in *Metock* as a barrier to free movement.

[54] For a recent discussion of mutual recognition, K. Nicolaïdis, 'Mutual Recognition: Promise and Denial, from Sapiens to Brexit', *Current Legal Problems* 70 (2017), 227.

[55] C. Janssens, *The Principle of Mutual Recognition in EU Law* 1st edn (Oxford University Press, 2013).

[56] For a discussion of some relevant case law: M. van den Brink, 'What's in a Name Case? Some Lessons for the Debate on the Free Movement of Same-Sex Couples within the EU', *German Law Journal* 17 (3) (2016), 421.

[57] A. Somek, 'The Argument from Transnational Effects I: Representing Outsiders through Freedom of Movement', *European Law Journal* 16 (2010), 315.

decision making, requiring an adequate valuation of their public policy interests. Unfortunately, the balance struck by the Court often appears skewed towards individual free movement rights.[58] *Walloon* merely serves as another illustration of that phenomenon, the Court deciding that the constitutional division of powers within Belgium could not even be invoked 'to justify the failure to observe obligations arising under [EU] law'.[59] It is thus far from evident whether the prominent role played by the Court and the substantive constraints imposed by its decisions on lower level political processes is compatible with our professed allegiance to democratic self-governance, as it has used EU citizens' rights to freedom of entry and exit to challenge the existence of the different centres of decision making we find within the EU.

It follows that an assessment of whether decisions taken by different centres of decision making within the Member States are compatible with EU law should take place primarily against the legislative framework established within the EU. Applied to the domain of European Union citizenship, decisions taken by lower levels of decision making should be evaluated above all in the light of the different sources of legislation that govern that domain. That justifies the initial challenge brought by the Commission against the care insurance scheme established by Flanders, on the ground that the exclusion of Union citizens working in the Dutch-speaking region or bilingual region of Brussels but residing in another Member State was incompatible with Regulation 1408/71 EEC.[60] Following the amendments Flanders introduced to its scheme however, it complied with the relevant legislative provisions. In such situations, the substantive content of the laws adopted by the different centres of decision making must be deemed valid, a presumption that can be rebutted if national political decisions pose obstacles to the realisation of other norms of EU law. However, any assessment of whether that is the case needs to attach adequate weight to the decisions taken by domestic governance institutions. *Walloon* is compatible neither with this presumption in favour of local self-governance, nor with the principle that national legitimate interests must be weighed seriously in the Court's

[58] F. W. Scharpf, 'Legitimacy in the Multi-Level European Polity', in P. Dobner and M. Loughlin (eds.), *The Twilight of Constitutionalism?* (Oxford University Press, 2010).

[59] *Walloon* (n. 8) para. 58. See also F. Cheneval, Chapter 3 in this Volume, for a more conceptual definition of political decision-making units and their powers and immunities in a polycentric system.

[60] *Décret modifiant le décret du 30 mars 1999 portant organisation de l'assurance soins* (*Moniteur belge* of 9 June 2004) 43593.

legal assessments. Ironically, the Court challenged the ideal of self-governance, central to prominent theories of citizenship and polycentric governance alike, based on its legal construction of EU citizenship. While EU citizenship holds promises for polycentric governance within the EU, in its current shape the drawbacks are far greater.

III The Democratic Rights of EU Citizenship

The analysis so far has highlighted that conceptions of EU citizenship which neglect the EU's multilevel nature threaten self-governance within the EU. I offered an alternative conception that grows out of and respects these different coexisting levels of decision making and construed the principle of non-discrimination on grounds of nationality as requiring deference to the substantive content of national and local citizenship. Furthermore, I argued, we should attempt to use the right to move and reside freely within the EU to overcome territorial boundaries. Finally, I underlined that the principle of self-governance should also guide our assessment of which institutions should enjoy primary responsibility for deciding the EU's course of action. However, whereas my reflections so far highlight how EU citizenship law can be shaped with respect for principles of self-governance, I said little about the position of EU citizens itself in processes of self-governance within the EU. I want to consider that question in this final section.

According to one prominent conception of free movement, it is free movement law itself that constitutes a democratic right of EU citizens. This so-called 'argument from transnational effects' is summarised well by de Witte, who has argued that containing national democratic processes through market integration tackles the most evident externality of democracy: the fact that its norms might affect citizens, interests or institutions that are not represented in the institutional process, did not have a chance to voice their concerns, and that the norms expressed by that institutional process might therefore contain a parochial bias.[61]

Proponents of that argument thus criticise national democratic procedures for their parochial and exclusionary effects.[62] Because the franchise is

[61] F. de Witte, 'Sex, Drugs & EU Law: The Recognition of Moral and Ethical Diversity in EU Law', *Common Market Law Review* 50 (2013), 1545, 1553.

[62] C. Joerges, 'European Law as Conflict of Laws', in C. Joerges and J. Neyer (eds.), 'Deliberative Supranationalism' Revisited (EUI Working Paper No. 2006/20, 2006); F. de Witte, ibid.; M. Maduro, *We the Court: The European Court of Justice and the European Economic Constitution* (Hart Publishing, 1998).

bounded and includes only insiders – those enjoying national or local citizenship –[63] they fear that democratically elected officials decide to the detriment of those who were excluded. On that account, the demos' bounded nature constitutes a significant externality, which can only be overcome by including outsiders' interests in our decision-making processes. Because free movement law allows for one community to be confronted with the value choices taken by another and forces decision making centres to consider whether the application of democratically enacted rules to outsiders will be precluded, free movement accomplishes outsider inclusion and reinforces democracy within the EU.

For various reasons, we should treat the argument from transnational effects critically. First, it takes for granted that democracy's parochial nature – that not all who are affected by democratic decisions are included within electoral processes – is problematic. That is not evident. For example, it is safe to assume that decisions taken by German representative processes affect all EU citizens resident within the EU to some degree at the very least. However, it does not follow that, therefore, all EU citizens should be included within the German franchise. That would have remarkably impractical implications and it seems desirable that German decision makers consider primarily the interests of those primarily affected by their decisions, i.e. citizens and residents of Germany.[64] This is not to say that the cross-border implications produced by national decisions should be neglected and through transnational institutional arrangements, Member States could seek to mitigate externalities produced by domestic decision making. Proponents of the argument regarding transnational effects, however, accept with remarkable ease the suggestion that the transnational processes by which to contain domestic political processes are ideally judicial.[65] The puzzling

[63] It is important to clarify that the boundaries of local and national citizenship can be drawn differently. For example, residence qualifies the boundaries of the local franchise, while nationality governs those of the national franchise. Hence, resident EU citizens are included in the local franchise, but only in national elections if they possess the required nationality.

[64] For some discussion of the principle of All Affected Interests and its limitations, R. E. Goodin, 'Enfranchising All Affected Interests, and Its Alternatives', *Philosophy & Public Affairs* 35 (2007), 40; S. Song, 'The Boundary Problem in Democratic Theory: Why the Demos Should Be Bounded by the State', *International Theory* 4 (2012), 39; R. Bauböck, 'Stakeholder Citizenship and Transnational Political Participation: A Normative Evaluation of External Voting', *Fordham Law Review* 75 (2007), 2393.

[65] According to de Witte, '[t]he notion of constrained democracy is implemented by removing agency, or self-determination, from "the political" sphere, and re-allocating it

element of that argument is that it pretends to extend the scope of democratic processes by granting power to an institution that has wielded its authority so expansively that it likely has done more harm than good to democracy within the EU. Finally, principles of free movement simply do not achieve what the argument around transnational effects credits it with doing. Even if free movement would just be an operationalisation of the principle of non-discrimination on grounds of nationality, outsiders remain excluded from the political process. All it ensures is the equal application of the substantive value choices taken by representatives of those included within the process.[66]

Whether mobile Union citizens should be included within national democratic processes and EU law should draw the boundaries of the national demos differently is a controversial matter. On the one hand, there is little disagreement, so it appears to me, that all Union citizens should be entitled to vote in elections to the European Parliament.[67] Somewhat more controversial, though also not widely contested among democratic theorists,[68] is that EU citizens should be included in the local demos and entitled to vote for and stand in local elections of their community of residence. EU law guarantees EU citizens political rights in municipal elections, even though debate remains about what constitute a 'municipal' election.[69] For example, non-UK EU citizens are entitled to participate in elections to the Scottish parliament, while non-Austrian EU citizens are denied the right to vote in elections to the city council of Vienna, as Austria recognises the city of Vienna, not as a municipality, but as a *Bundesland*.[70] Wholly excluded from the package of EU citizenship rights is the right to vote and stand in national elections

to a different type of government, whether judicial . . . expert-based . . . administrative . . . or the individual (through market structures)'. de Witte (n. 61) 1554.

66 For a persuasive elaboration of the limits of the argument from transnational effects, read: A. Somek (n 57).

67 Article 22(2) TFEU. See also, Council Directive 93/109/EC of 6 December 1993 laying down detailed arrangements for the exercise of the right to vote and stand as a candidate in elections to the European Parliament for citizens of the Union residing in a Member State of which they are not nationals [1993] OJ L329/34.

68 Bauböck (n. 64).

69 Article 22(1) TFEU. See also, Council Directive 94/80/EC of 19 December 1994 laying down detailed arrangements for the exercise of the right to vote and to stand as a candidate in municipal elections by citizens of the Union residing in a Member State of which they are not nationals [1994] OJ L368/38.

70 D. Kochenov, 'Free Movement and Participation in the Parliamentary Elections in the Member State of Nationality: An Ignored Link?', *Maastricht Journal of European and Comparative Law* 16 (2009), 197, 209.

within the Member State of residence. No Member State has opened the boundaries of the national demos to include non-national resident EU citizens and EU law does not require them to redraw these boundaries.

One take on this situation is that denying EU citizens political rights in national elections is an unjustifiable limitation of their right to free movement,[71] but that argument begs the question of whether mobile EU citizens must be entitled to democratic inclusion within their state of nationality or residence. Certain Member States exclude nationals who have left the territory and are resident abroad (for a certain duration) from the franchise.[72] Such policies sit uncomfortably with the right to free movement, but also constitute a clear democratic wrong, because they deprive mobile Union citizens from a say in national elections but also on who represents them in the Council.[73] However, whether mobile EU citizens must be included in the national franchise of their country of nationality or residence remains an open question.

The real question is how to draw the boundaries of the demos from a democratic perspective. The democratic boundary debate is lengthy and complex and I will not seek to offer a full answer to that question here. However, we should adopt a wider conception of local citizenship, which can be different from national citizenship. Membership of local communities changes automatically with a change in residence, as opposed to national citizenship. An Austrian national from Vienna retains her nationality but loses her Viennese 'citizenship' following a move abroad. Since one can solely be a local citizen of one's community of residence (in nested polities one can of course be a member of two or more local communities (e.g. the provincial and municipal community)), levels of governance below the national ought in principle to guarantee political inclusion for all residents.[74]

The situation is different and more complex at the national level. It seems questionable to me to argue that it is a democratic essential to extend the franchise of citizenship to newly arrived migrant Union

71 F. Fabbrini, 'The Political Side of EU Citizenship in the Context of EU Federalism', in D. Kochenov (ed.), *EU Citizenship and Federalism: The Role of Rights* (Cambridge University Press, 2017); D. Kochenov, 'Free Movement and Participation in the Parliamentary Elections in the Member State of Nationality: An Ignored Link?', *Maastricht Journal of European and Comparative Law* 16 (2009), 197.

72 For an overview of different rules on external voting, see Bauböck (n. 64).

73 The different contributors to the following debate appears to share that view: R. Bauböck, P. Cayla, and C. Seth (eds.), *Should EU Citizens Living in Other Member States Vote There in National Elections?* (EUI RSCAS Working Paper 2012).

74 Bauböck (n. 64).

citizens. Visitors and temporary residents, such as jobseekers and students, generally retain strong associative ties with their Member State of nationality and the better solution is to guarantee their political rights at home. On the other hand, the longer the citizen resides in a country of which she is not a national the more legitimate her claim to full democratic inclusion. The permanent exclusion of foreigners from the national franchise violates principles of democratic justice and the EU should seek to remedy such democratic wrongs. The more difficult question is at what point in time foreign EU citizens should acquire full political rights in the host state. It is evident that drawing these boundaries on grounds of someone's duration of residence is somewhat arbitrary, as these criteria serve merely as a proxy for integration. Yet, as Carens points out:

> [i]f we want to institutionalize a principle that gives weight to the degree to which a person has become a member of society and if we expect to have to deal with a large number of cases, we will want to use indicators of social membership that are relevant, objective, and easy to measure. *Residence* and *time* clearly meet these requirements. Other ways of assessing social membership do not.[75]

Two potential avenues thus exist for enhancing EU citizens' democratic standing: the Member States could offer non-national EU citizens a reasonable opportunity to be naturalised (following a specific and not overly exclusive period of residence), or EU citizens could be entitled to vote and stand in national elections once they have acquired permanent residence (currently five years of lawful residence).[76] Both options improve EU citizens' ability to participate in national processes of democratic self-government.[77]

IV Conclusion

According to dominant conceptions of EU citizenship, the Court is justified in challenging national and local practices of self-governance and divisions of authority in order to promote the individual mobility of Union citizens and harmonise their rights. I offer a different understanding of EU citizenship in this chapter, more attuned to the EU's

[75] J. H. Carens, *The Ethics of Immigration* (Oxford University Press, 2013), 165.

[76] Article 16(1) of Directive 2004/38/EC of the European Parliament and of the Council of 29 April 2004 on the right of citizens of the Union and their family members to move and reside freely within the territory of the Member States [2004] OJ L158/77.

[77] For a variety of views on where EU citizens should vote, read: R. Bauböck, P. Cayla, and C. Seth (n. 73).

polycentric nature. The principle of non-discrimination on grounds of nationality must be understood not just as a constraint on the discretion of national decision-makers but should also require European institutions to respect the substantive content of national and local citizenship. In addition, rather than posing a challenge to territorial divisions of authority, the right to free movement should connect and allow for cooperation between the different localities. The Court should not determine the political and social arrangements within the EU based on its best understanding of EU citizenship, but rather, our conceptions of EU citizenship should grow out of these arrangements. That requires a more polycentric understanding of EU citizenship, which recognises the existence of and demonstrates respect for the dispersion of authority within the EU.

8

Self-Organisation of Third-Country Nationals in the European Union: Polycentric Governance by the 'Other'

IRIS GOLDNER LANG*

A discussion of polycentricity in the EU limited to EU citizens would be inherently incomplete as it would exclude the important role of the 'other', i.e. third-country nationals (TCNs). This chapter therefore sets out to identify centres of TCN self-organisation in the EU, specifically those centres that seek to increase their rights, and political and social influence. In keeping with the remainder of this volume, the premise of this exercise is that such centres are an expression, and necessary feature, of the polycentric character of the EU.[1] Moreover, as TCNs are usually excluded from formal political institutions and processes, self-organisation of TCNs points to deeper structural deficiencies and problems in their integration in the host Member States' societies. Also, mapping TCN self-governance underlines the tensions between formal and informal polycentricity.[2] For this reason, this Chapter will primarily refer to 'self-organisation' and not 'self-governance' so as to emphasise the inclusion of informal, as well as formal, processes.

* I am grateful to Josephine van Zeben and Ana Bobić for their valuable comments on the text.

[1] Polycentricity refers to a complex form of governance with multiple centres of decision-making (V. Ostrom, C. M. Tiebout, and R. Warren, 'The Organization of Government in Metropolitan Areas: A Theoretical Inquiry', *American Political Science Review* 55 (4) (1961), 831; E. Ostrom, *Understanding Institutional Diversity* (Princeton University Press, 2005); See also, in this Volume, Chapter 1 by J. van Zeben.

[2] On case studies of political participation of certain refugee groups in Germany, Sweden, and the United Kingdom, see A. Bekaj and L. Antara, 'Political Participation of Refugees: Bridging the Gap, International Institute for Democracy and Electoral Assistance' (2018), available at www.idea.int/sites/default/files/publications/political-participation-of-refugees-bridging-the-gaps.pdf accessed 17 May 2018.

EU law clearly distinguishes between the rights of Union citizens and third-country nationals in the EU.[3] Union citizens are provided with extensive EU-based rights and corresponding mechanisms for their exercise, whereas the status of third-country nationals remains limited, with Member States preserving partial competence to regulate this area.[4] The status of the 'third-country national' is shared between two groups of individuals. The first group refers to highly vulnerable refugees, who are granted a high level of protection based on EU asylum rules, but whose status, nevertheless, remains weak in practice. The second group is much more diverse. It encompasses all non-EU citizens, who are in general granted only a limited set of rights by EU law, when compared to the rights granted to EU citizens.[5] The latter group covers both 'desirable' migrants (e.g. tourists, students, researchers, business people and short-term visitors), TCNs who have a stronger link with the host Member State (such as long-term residents and family members of EU citizens and of legally resident TCNs) and all other migrants; who can be classified as 'non-desirable', among them primarily being non-highly skilled economic migrants, whose volume of admittance remains regulated by Member States. The recent influx of migrants and refugees has magnified pre-existing challenges in EU migration and asylum law, including

[3] On the rift between EU citizens and third-country nationals, see I. Goldner Lang, 'The European Union and Migration: An Interplay of National, Regional and International Law', *American Journal of International Law* 111 (2017), 509, available at www.cambridge.org/core/journals/american-journal-of-international-law/article/european-union-and-migration-an-interplay-of-national-regional-and-international-law/7C8123D7AA60097246CA46E269DFA3BA accessed 28 March 2018.

[4] Based on Article 4(2)(j) TFEU, policies on the area of freedom, security and justice are shared competence between the Union and its Member States. Based on Article 79(5) TFEU, Member States preserve the right to determine volumes of admission of third-country nationals coming to their territories in order to seek work.

[5] Throughout the text, the term 'third-country national' is used as the general term which encompasses all persons who are not Union citizens or EFTA nationals. The term 'migrant' is used to refer to TCNs who move to the EU in order to improve their material and/or social conditions and/or prospects. On the other hand, the term 'refugee' applies to a 'third-country national who, owing to a well-founded fear of being persecuted for reasons of race, religion, nationality, political opinion or membership of a particular social group, is outside the country of nationality and is unable or, owing to such fear, is unwilling to avail themselves of the protection of that country, or a stateless person, who, being outside of the country of former habitual residence for the same reasons as mentioned above, is unable or, owing to such fear, unwilling to return to it' (definition from Article 1A of the Geneva Convention and Article 2(d) of the Qualification Directive 2011/95).

frequent violations of TCN rights.[6] The identification of other decision-making centres and centres of power that can help to become active and involved participants in the EU society could be a vital step in increasing TCNs' awareness and use of their rights and available mechanisms of protections.

This Chapter confirms that TCNs' self-organisation is indeed possible in the EU by showing the paths through which it manifests itself. TCNs' self-organisation can be detected at several levels; some instances of self-organisation are informal and ad hoc, while others are formal, official and more permanent. In some cases, self-organisation is initiated by TCNs themselves – either individually or collectively. In other cases, it is initiated by non-migrant organisations (typically non-governmental organisations (NGOs)), businesses or cities and other local authorities. In these situations, TCNs are either chosen as the target group or beneficiaries of the activities undertaken by these actors, or they are encouraged to directly participate in the activities and/or political processes of these actors.

In order to portray this diverse picture, this Chapter will be divided following the classification of TCNs' centres of power:[7] informal self-organisation (Section I) and formal self-organisation (Section II), which in turn will be divided into three subsections on the role of NGOs, the role of businesses and the role of cities in TCNs' self-organisation. The third Section will determine the causes and objectives for self-organisation of TCNs. It will aim to discern whether TCNs' self-organisation takes place in order to provide for basic needs, to encourage social and political inclusion of TCNs – by empowering them as active participants in social and political processes – or both. As such, the third Section will examine two questions. First, does self-organisation of TCNs aim to supplement or replace certain national and EU processes? Second, is self-organisation of TCNs successful? That is, does self-organisation (significantly) improve the generally weak status of TCNs or do TCNs remain voiceless in certain or all instances where national and EU law or

[6] For a detailed account of the impact of the refugee influx on EU migration and asylum law, see I. Goldner Lang, 'Human Rights and Legitimacy in the Implementation of EU Asylum and Migration Law', in S. Vöneky and G. L. Neuman (eds.), *Human Rights, Democracy, and Legitimacy in a World of Disorder* (Cambridge University Press, 2018), 234–62 .

[7] The analysis of polycentric system does not place an emphasis on the central state level, but rather focuses equally on both state and non-state decision-making centres. In line with this approach, the current Chapter will focus only on non-state forms of self-organisation among third-country nationals.

practice do not protect them? In answering these questions, this research relies on new interviews with relevant stakeholders.[8] The Chapter will conclude by considering whether self-organisation by TCNs can be considered polycentric.

I Informal Self-Organisation

Taking the bottom-up approach, the smallest units of self-organisation of third-country nationals in the EU are third-country nationals themselves. Their self-organisation can take place at two levels: individually and collectively. Both individual and collective self-organisation of migrants and refugees tend to be informal and sporadic. Informal self-organisation is nevertheless an important method of migrant and refugee empowerment, as it improves their generally weak status in EU society, and provides them with valuable information they would otherwise not be able to obtain.

Informal self-organisation of refugees and migrants who came to the EU during the 2015/2016 influx, and of those who are currently arriving, takes place through word of mouth, social media and mass media. Social media and web-based services – in particular Facebook, WhatsApp, Twitter, Skype, Viber and Googlemaps – have played an enormous role in informal self-organisation of migrants in the past several years, both in Europe and worldwide.[9] Some Facebook groups function as public while others require an invitation by the group administrator. Some groups are linked to individual EU Member States, or the individual nationality of third-country nationals while others are transnational. Membership of some of these Facebook groups comprises only migrants and refugees, while others are also joined by representatives of NGOs.

Despite considerable differences between the groups, they all share a significant and multiple empowering impact on migrants and refugees.

[8] The author has conducted a number of interviews with relevant stakeholders and she is particularly grateful to Tamim Nashed from the European Council on Refugees and Exiles (ECRE); a representative from the UNHCR office in Berlin; Max McClellan from the UNHCR Office in London; Sara Kekuš and Vanja Bakalović from the Centre for Peace Studies (CMS) in Zagreb; Sam Koplewicz who, at the time, worked for the Human Rights Watch and other interviewees who preferred to stay anonymous.

[9] For example, see a Facebook page titled 'Karajat Al Mushuntiteen' www.facebook.com/groups/manmano/?ref=group_header accessed 8 June 2018; Facebook group 'I am a Syrian in Lebanon' www.facebook.com/groups/172406933094432 accessed 8 June 2018; Facebook group 'Phone Credit for Refugees and Displaced People' www.facebook.com/groups/1709109339334305/ accessed 8 June 2018.

In the first place, social media facilitates migration by enabling migrants and refugees physically to reach the EU, which would otherwise be much more difficult, if not impossible.[10] Social media and smartphones equip TCNs with the necessary information on travel routes, perils on the routes and destinations, thus making it possible for them to undertake these long and dangerous journeys on their own, at least partly avoiding the use of smugglers.[11] An example of the migrants' and refugees' exchange of information via acquaintances, mobile phones, and social media groups, with the aim to enable and facilitate their transit and journey to the EU (but also their basic needs), was the creation of several national Western Balkans Facebook groups, consisting of both migrants/refugees, and of many grassroots NGOs and activists.[12] Social media also has an important downside, as they create a means for smugglers to advertise their activities. The use of social media for human smuggling and other forms of illegal activities aimed at third-country nationals is the negative or harmful facet of migrants' and refugees' self-organisation, which is a direct consequence of the challenges in migrating to the EU in a lawful and safe way.

Second, once third-country nationals arrive in the EU, their exchange of information through social media enables them to access information they would otherwise not be able to obtain from official sources. Social media equips them with information about the asylum procedure, asylum rights, including family reunification rights, access to food, accommodation, schooling, and other daily needs.[13] Unfortunately, the speed and informal character of social media can lead to the provision of incorrect or false information and thus mislead migrants and refugees

[10] For examples of selected messages exchanged on the Western Balkans Route through Facebook groups, see e.g. REACH, 'Migration to Europe through the Western Balkans: Serbia and the Former Yugoslav Republic of Macedonia', Report, December 2015–May 2016, 23, available at www.reachresourcecentre.info/system/files/resource-documents/reach_report_consolidated_report_on_migration_to_europe_through_the_western_balkans_2015-2016_july_ 2016_0.pdf accessed 22 March 2018.

[11] On the impact of social media on smuggling into the EU, and on the variety of reasons why social media and smartphones are important for refugees, see M. Brunwasser, 'A 21st-Century Migrant's Essentials: Food, Shelter, Smartphone' (*New York Times*, 25 April 2015) www.nytimes.com/2015/08/26/world/europe/a-21st-century-migrants-checklist-water-shelter-smartphone.html accessed 22 March 2018.

[12] See www.facebook.com/groups/nikonijeilegalan/and www.facebook.com/pg/dobrodosli.dragi.imigranti/about/?ref=page_internal accessed 19 April 2018.

[13] See D. McLaughlin, 'Mass migration guided by mobiles and social media' (*The Irish Times*, 9 September 2015) www.irishtimes.com/news/world/europe/mass-migration-guided-by-mobiles-and-social-media-1.2344662 accessed 22 March 2018.

as to their rights at a certain destination. Cases of misinformation via WhatsApp have, for example, been encountered in relation to migrants and refugees arriving to Germany.[14] This often leads to the feeling of disappointment, due to the discrepancy between the third-country nationals' expectations and reality. Another example of spreading misinformation through social media has taken place during the existence of the Western Balkans Route (one of the main migratory routes towards the EU) when social media enabled the dissemination of information that it was impossible to gain asylum in Croatia.[15]

Third, social media enables migrants and refugees to stay in touch with their families and friends from whom they are being separated or with whom they are trying to re-unite. This way, social media plays an important role not only in preserving the emotional and social ties of people on the move, but also facilitates the creation of groups of migrants and refugees who share the same nationality, language, religion, or another common denominator, such as the stage of the asylum process they have reached. The creation of such peer groups – which consist of members who support and help each other – also fosters self-organisation among third-country nationals who share a common background, characteristic, or situation. It also acts as a pull factor encouraging further migration of persons belonging to the same social group.[16]

Finally, social media has an important social, political, and legal function, as all social media directly or indirectly provides information to both third-country nationals and the interested public (such as NGOs and activists) on cases of human rights violations across the EU. The still existent Western Balkans Route Facebook groups would again be a good example of this effect of social media. Another example would be the Facebook Group 'Are you Syrious?', created by a Croatian-based NGO, dedicated to helping refugees and to other humanitarian work – which is regularly publishing information and reports on violations of human rights of refugees both in the EU and third countries such as Turkey.[17]

Word of mouth is another important method of informal self-organisation of third-country nationals. However – unlike social media, which can connect a large number of individuals instantaneously – word

[14] Information obtained from one of the interviewees (see n. 8).

[15] Information obtained from one of the interviewees (see n. 8).

[16] UNESCO, 'Migration as a Development Challenge: Analysis of Root Causes and Policy Implications' (2017) MOST/REPORTS/2017/1, 10, available at: http://unesdoc.unesco.org/images/0024/002470/247089E.pdf, accessed 17 May 2018.

[17] www.facebook.com/areyousyrious/ accessed 28 March 2018.

of mouth requires proximity of individuals and is, therefore, much slower and less far-reaching. Nevertheless, word of mouth continues to be used extensively among third-country nationals who are travelling to the EU and among those who are already residing there. Its usage is especially visible in places where groups of third-country nationals get together, spend time, or live together, notably in reception centres. Reception centres are places where refugees – who are usually in the same stage of the asylum process – spend weeks or months living together in a rather confined space. This enables them to share information about all aspects of the asylum procedure including who are 'good' and 'bad' legal representatives. They also help each other through translation in cases when state authorities are not providing adequate support. Finally, refugees' self-organisation in reception centres is manifest by launching mini businesses – such as cooking food, coffee or tea, and selling it; by providing hairdressing services and cosmetic treatments, etc. – and asking for cash or in kind payment in return.[18] This way, self-organisation enables refugees to acquire trivial things and services on a regular basis, which would otherwise not be available to them or which they would otherwise not be able to afford.

Public squares in certain Member States have – just like reception centres – become spaces of refugees' self-organisation in the past several years. Developments at Victoria Square in Athens stand out as one of the most striking examples of informal self-organisation.[19] Here, hundreds of refugees have been gathering on a daily basis in order to exchange information, charge their cell phones and get food and other resources from NGOs, whose representatives also come to the square.[20] Occasionally, refugees have also resorted to protests as a more political manifestation of informal self-organisation. Two of the most striking examples of refugees' expression of dissatisfaction with their treatment and status was, first, the attempt of two Pakistani nationals to hang

[18] The launching of such mini businesses has, for example, been recorded in the reception centre Porin in Croatia.

[19] See, for example, 'Athens under pressure: city races to clear port's refugee camp before tourists arrive' (*The Guardian*, 26 April 2016) www.theguardian.com/cities/2016/apr/26/athens-under-pressure-city-port-refugee-camp-tourists accessed 12 April 2018; K. Papathanasiou, Afghan Refugees Remain Stranded in Athens' Victoria Square (*Greek Reporter*, 16 September 2015) http://greece.greekreporter.com/2015/09/16/afghan-refugees-remain-stranded-in-athens-victoria-square/ accessed 12 April 2018.

[20] See, for example, the activities on Victoria Square of the initiative 'Solidarity with Refugees in Greece' www.facebook.com/pediontouareos/

themselves at Victoria Square[21] and, second, a hunger strike by Syrian refugees at Syntagma Square in Athens due to delays in reunification with their family members in Germany.[22]

To sum up, informal self-organisation takes place mostly ad hoc and out of dire necessity. It is aimed at satisfying the refugees' basic needs, such as food, shelter, and medicine, and at obtaining valuable information on access to the EU and exercising their rights. Refugees have so far attained these objectives by congregating and using word of mouth, as well as through social and mass media. Informal self-organisation has only rarely taken the form of political protests, such as the cases of attempted hangings at Victoria Square and the hunger strike at Syntagma Square.

II Formal Self-Organisation

The following Section will discuss the role of NGOs, businesses and local authorities – primarily cities – as the drivers of formal self-organisation. This type of self-organisation has been extremely important as a method of giving credibility to TCNs' social and political involvement. As such, formal self-organisation has been an important means of reinforcing third-country nationals' voice and influence across the EU.

The involvement of these actors is all the more important as the EU's competence to promote TCNs' social and political participation remains extremely limited. The competence to adopt integration measures stays with the Member States, whereas the EU can only support Member States' actions.[23] For this reason, the Commission's measures aimed at integration and inclusion of third-country nationals have been limited to soft law measures, encouraging Member States to promote their integration and inclusion.

The Commission's Action Plan on the integration of third-country nationals stands out as the most important EU-level document in this

[21] See T. Kermeliotis, 'Refugees attempt suicide by hanging themselves from tree in Greece' (Al Jazeera, 25 February 2016) www.aljazeera.com/news/2016/02/refugees-attempt-suicide-hanging-tree-greece-160225191001445.html accessed 12 April 2018.

[22] K. Tagaris and D. Kyvrikossaios, 'Refugees in Greece demand transfer to Germany, start hunger strike' (Reuters, 1 November 2017) www.reuters.com/article/us-europe-migrants-greece/refugees-in-greece-demand-transfer-to-germany-start-hunger-strike-idUSKBN1D14UQ accessed 12 April 2018.

[23] Based on Article 79(4) TFEU, the EU can adopt measures 'to provide incentives and support for the action of Member States with a view to promoting the integration of third-country nationals residing in their territories', excluding any harmonising measures.

area.[24] It sets five policy priorities that need to be undertaken at the EU and Member State level in order to support integration of third-country nationals: pre-arrival/pre-departure measures; education; labour market integration and access to vocational training; access to basic service; active participation and social inclusion. The fifth priority entitled 'Active participation and social inclusion' is the most important from the perspective of refugees' self-organisation. Here, the Commission sets out to develop handbooks and launch projects under different EU funds promoting active participation of third-country nationals 'in political, social and cultural life and sports' in the host societies. It also encourages Member States to 'increase third-country nationals' participation in local democratic structures'.[25] The division of the tasks into two groups – the first one setting out the tasks which the Commission undertakes to achieve on its own, and the second one setting out the activities which the Commission only encourages Member States to undertake – reflects the fact that the integration of third-country nationals stays primarily within the Member States' competence.

The EU-level financial instrument used for the purpose of integration and inclusion of refugees is the Asylum, Migration and Integration Fund (AMIF).[26] One of the objectives set by the Fund is the integration of third-country nationals, and its beneficiaries can be Member States' national and local authorities, NGOs, private and public companies as well as education and research organisations. However, the funding rules for AMIF have created significant barriers to AMIF participation for civil society organisations.[27] Also, it is questionable whether the amount available is actually spent for integration purposes, as there is no publicly available data on actual spending patterns.[28]

[24] See, for example, the Commission's Action Plan on integration of third-country nationals (2016) COM 377 final https://eur-lex.europa.eu/legal-content/EN/TXT/?uri=CELEX%3A52016DC0377 accessed 18 April 2018.

[25] ibid., 13.

[26] For the details about the Asylum, Migration and Integration Fund https://ec.europa.eu/home-affairs/financing/fundings/migration-asylum-borders/asylum-migration-integration-fund_en accessed 18 April 2018.

[27] R. Westerby, 'Follow the Money: Assessing the Use of EU Asylum, Migration and Integration Fund (AMIF) Funding at the National Level' (2018) ECRE, 41.

[28] N. Nielsen, 'Athens Mayor Wants Direct Access to EU Migration Fund' (EUobserver, 21 May 2018) https://euobserver.com/migration/141863 accessed 21 May 2018.

A NGOs as Champions of Refugees' Rights

Political inclusion of third-country nationals is not an EU competence, which means that Member States have discretion as to whether to allow for third-country nationals' political participation and other forms of formal self-organisation. National laws frequently exclude third-country nationals from political participation. Within this broader group of people, roughly composed of refugees and (economic) migrants, NGOs have been the most important actors regarding the formal self-organisation of refugees. The involvement of NGOs has been twofold. First, they provide material, legal and other support to refugees. Second, NGOs are crucial in promoting refugees' political and social empowerment by enabling their participation in political processes and other activities carried out by NGOs.

Depending on the type of involvement of NGOs and their relations with refugees, refugees have taken either a passive role of mere beneficiaries of NGOs' activities, or a more active role of active participants in the activities provided by NGOs and in political processes. The majority of NGOs view themselves as 'charity organisations', thus treating refugees as passive beneficiaries of their assistance. NGOs' activities targeted at promoting refugees' active participation have been rare. This is probably partly due to the actual needs of refugees and the logic that one first has to satisfy basic needs before promoting refugees' civic and political rights. NGOs' mandates reflect the problems encountered by refugees in a particular Member State. For example, NGOs in Greece have primarily targeted refugees' basic needs, whereas the work of NGOs in Austria and the Scandinavian countries has also included education and the promotion of inclusive policies and non-discrimination.

Second, the small number of participatory programmes might partly be the result of a mistrust in refugees' skills and capabilities, which could suggest the existence of an unconscious bias and point to the need for a shift in our mindset.[29] It highlights the importance of viewing refugees not only as passive recipients of aid, but as active participants who should be included in all areas of social life, thus preventing their segregation and stigmatisation.[30] Some NGOs have indeed promoted active refugee

[29] This point has been raised in the course of the interview with Tamim Nashed, the Policy Officer on Refugee Inclusion at the European Council on Refugees and Exiles (ECRE). On the importance of learning see also, in this Volume, Chapter 12 by S. Garben.

[30] In order to prevent segregation and stigmatisation, the recent tendencies are to apply the term 'inclusion' instead of 'integration'. For a discussion on the advantages of inclusion,

participation by including persons with a refugee or migrant background in their work. The Greek Forum of Refugees is an example of a network whose members are refugees and which is aimed at providing assistance to refugees in Greece.[31] The Forum also stands out as an example of a multinational network, unlike the majority of other refugees' formal self-organisations which are typically nation-based and do not communicate with each other.

The Greek Forum of Refugees, with the support of the European Council on Refugees and Exiles (ECRE), also created the forum Refugees, Ideas and Solutions for Europe (RISE) in August 2016. RISE is a transnational network aimed at representing refugees across the EU.[32] It consists of approximately 20 network members in 14 different European states, where each state is represented by a national contact point. The objectives of the RISE network are the refugees' social political and economic empowerment, raising awareness about refugee issues among different stakeholders and inclusion of refugees into their host societies.

The Open City Fellowships, initiated by the Open Society Foundations, are another important initiative aimed at promoting refugees' active participation in the host Member State society.[33] The Open City Fellowship Programme is aimed at promoting leadership among refugees and migrants and at supporting their inclusion in the host city of their residence. The Programme functions through collaboration with four partner cities – Amsterdam, Athens, Barcelona and Berlin – and a host organisation in Brussels. It enables people with a refugee or a migrant background to represent their respective communities by improving refugee and migrant integration policy or practice at the city level. RISE and the Open City Fellowships are two rare examples of

in comparison to integration of refugees, see the interview with the ECRE policy officer Tamim Nashed entitled 'Why inclusion rather than integration?', available at: www.ecre.org/why-inclusion-rather-than-integration-interview-with-ecre-policy-officer-on-refugee-inclusion-tamim-nashed/ accessed 18 April 2018. On the finding of school segregation of migrant children, taking place in half of EU Member States, see European Union Agency for Fundamental Rights, 'Together in the EU: Promoting the Participation of Migrants and Their Descendants' (2017), 39, available at: http://fra.europa.eu/sites/default/files/fra_uploads/fra-2017-together-in-the-eu_en.pdf accessed 19 April 2018.

31 http://refugeegr.blogspot.hr/ accessed 19 April 2018.

32 http://refugees.gr/rise/ accessed 16 April 2018.

33 See www.opensocietyfoundations.org/sites/default/files/open-city-fellowship-20170718.pdf accessed 16 April 2018.

transnational self-organisation of TCNs, whereas local and nation-level initiatives remain more frequent. This is, again, due to the fact that the competence to integrate TCNs stays primarily with the Member States.

B *The Role of Businesses in Third-Country Nationals' Self-Organisation*

The link between third-country nationals and the private sector has been twofold. First, there have been examples of good business practices regarding the hiring of refugees and supporting their access to education. Some of these practices have been initiated by businesses themselves, whereas others were initiated and financially supported by a Member State or EU institution. Second, third-country nationals are sometimes successful in starting their own businesses, which in turn hire other third-country nationals.

Private initiatives have taken place in a number of European states[34] as well as transnationally. A number of large companies – including IKEA,[35] Deutsche Telekom, NCC, Accenture, bpost, Scandic hotels, ADECCO, Microsoft, and Goldman Sachs –[36] have committed to fostering refugees' and other migrants' access to the labour market. Some of them are offering jobs to refugees, while others are awarding grants aimed at enabling refugees to start their own businesses, enter university, undergo a language course or vocational training.

Member State initiatives tend to encourage private businesses to hire refugees by offering financial support to the company which employs refugees. The Danish 'integration basic education scheme' (*integrationsgrunduddannelse* – IGU) enables companies to employ refugees in short-term jobs at an apprentice salary for up to two years, while at the same time offering refugees skill development or education courses.[37] In return, companies qualify for a financial bonus. In addition to creating jobs for refugees and thus integrating them into the labour market and their host society, the IGU system creates a twofold benefit for the

[34] For example, see the initiative 'Wir zusammen' in Germany www.wir-zusammen.de/

[35] For the activities taken in this regard by IKEA, see www.architecturaldigest.com/story/why-swedish-design-brands-hiring-syrian-refugees-ikea accessed 17 May 2018.

[36] For the initiative 'Goldman Sachs Gives', see www.goldmansachs.com/citizenship/goldman-sachs-gives/ accessed 17 May 2018.

[37] 'Denmark has new plan to get refugees into work' (*The Local*, 18 March 2016) www.thelocal.dk/20160318/denmark-has-new-plan-to-get-refugees-into-work accessed 1 May 2018.

municipality. First, the municipality saves on welfare payments if a refugee receives income rather than a welfare payment. Second, the municipality receives a results-based bonus from the state when a refugee completes six months of IGU apprenticeship.[38] By January 2018, at least 34 refugees had been engaged in the IGU scheme, but the potential is much higher.[39]

The European Commission has been trying to coordinate the efforts of different private and public-sector stakeholders. In 2015, it launched the 'European Dialogue on Skills and Migration', a platform aimed at fostering dialogue between different stakeholders on issues of labour migration and labour market integration of third-country nationals.[40] On 23 May 2017, at the second meeting of this platform, the Commission launched the 'Employers together for integration' initiative, aimed at promoting employers' efforts to support the integration of refugees and other third-country nationals.[41]

Despite these praiseworthy initiatives, the 2016 employment rate of foreign-born migrants for the whole EU was only 66%, compared with 71.8% for the native-born population.[42] The employment rate for refugees is even lower. In 2014, only 56% of refugees in the EU were employed,[43] whereas the employment rate of refugees in Germany in 2017 stood at only 17%.[44] Some businesses have encountered administrative problems in hiring refugees. In addition, most openings have been for low-skilled jobs, which is partly due to the language barrier and the fact that manual jobs usually do not require language proficiency.

38 'Scrapping refugee apprenticeships could cost councils millions': Report (*The Local*, 8 January 2018) www.thelocal.dk/20180108/populist-move-against-refugee-apprenticeship-programme-could-cost-councils-millions-report accessed 1 May 2018.

39 'Scrapping refugee apprenticeships could cost councils millions': Report (*The Local*, 8 January 2018) www.thelocal.dk/20180108/populist-move-against-refugee-apprenticeship-programme-could-cost-councils-millions-report accessed 1 May 2018.

40 Available at https://ec.europa.eu/home-affairs/what-we-do/policies/legal-migration/european-dialogue-skills-and-migration_en accessed 17 May 2018.

41 Available at https://ec.europa.eu/home-affairs/what-we-do/policies/legal-migration/european-dialogue-skills-and-migration/integration-pact_en accessed 17 May 2018.

42 Eurostat statistics http://ec.europa.eu/eurostat/statistics-explained/index.php/Migrant_integration_statistics_-_labour_market_indicators accessed 1 May 2018.

43 European Commission and OECD, 'How are refugees faring on the labour market in Europe?' (2016) Working Paper 1, available at https://publications.europa.eu/en/publication-detail/-/publication/87a8f92d-9aa8-11e6-868c-01aa75ed71a1/language-en accessed 1 May 2018.

44 G. Chazan, 'Most refugees to be jobless for years, German minister warns' (*Financial Times*, 2017), available at www.ft.com/content/022de0a4-54f4-11e7-9fed-c19e2700005f accessed 1 May 2018.

The end result of offering mostly low-skilled jobs to refugees, though not explicitly or intentionally discriminatory, has been effectively discriminatory in comparison to EU citizens. It is also extremely challenging for refugees to start their own businesses. This is due to a number of challenges faced by refugees, such as language barriers, non-recognition of foreign qualifications, problems in accessing bank loans, insufficient knowledge about the local market, administrative problems encountered in the process of registering the business, discrimination, etc.[45] Nevertheless, there have been examples of successful businesses initiated by refugees in different Member States, who in turn hire other refugees.[46]

C The Role of Cities in Formal Self-Organisation

Cities and other local authorities have been playing an ever-growing role in TCNs' lives and self-organising activities, as the vast majority of TCNs live in urban areas and as TCNs' needs can be best addressed locally.[47] For these reasons, the role of cities in assisting TCNs and in promoting their political participation is expected to increase further in the future. As stated by Georgos Kaminis, the Mayor of Athens, '[the central] government is a very remote instance for those very crucial issues that have to do with integration' of refugees and, for this reason, the 'EU funding needs to be organised in such a way that local authorities are entitled to distribute it'.[48]

[45] For the discussion of different obstacles encountered by refugees who want to establish businesses in Germany, see C. Copley, 'Refugees Bring Entrepreneurial Spirit to Risk-Shy Germany' (Reuters, 2016), available at www.reuters.com/article/us-europe-migrants-germany-entrepreneurs/refugees-bring-entrepreneurial-spirit-to-risk-shy-germany-idUSKCN0VA2D8 accessed 11 June 2018.

[46] For example, see the success stories of the African Cuisine & Bar in Zagreb, Croatia www.africancuisineandbar.com/ accessed 17 May 2018, and of the Taste of Home catering service in Zagreb, Croatia www.okus-doma.hr/en accessed 17 May 2018. See the story of a Syrian family in the UK www.theguardian.com/small-business-network/2017/feb/28/refugees-turned-entrepreneurs-future-business-perserverance accessed 11 June 2018. Also, see the Entrepreneurial Refugee Network in the UK www.wearetern.org/ accessed 11 June 2018.

[47] According to the OECD Study, two-thirds of migrants live in metropolitan areas. The Study found that 'while migrants tend to concentrate in urban areas, however, asylum seekers are more spread across urban-rural areas than are the rest of the resident population.' See OECD Study 'Working Together for Local Integration of Migrants and Refugees' (OECD Publishing, 2018), 24, available at: www.oecd.org/publications/working-together-for-local-integration-of-migrants-and-refugees-9789264085350-en.htm. A survey of migrant integration policies across European cities accessed 12 June 2018.

[48] N. Nielsen, 'Athens Mayor Wants Direct Access to EU Migration Fund' (EUobserver, 21 May 2018) <https://euobserver.com/migration/141863> accessed 21 May 2018; see

The European Commission has been playing a significant role in pulling together relevant stakeholders and promoting integration activities in urban areas. The Partnership on Inclusion of Migrants and Refugees initiative places cities at the forefront of refugee integration activities in the EU.[49] The objective of the Partnership is to promote cities' management of the integration of migrants and refugees. The Partnership has been set within the framework of the Urban Agenda for the EU[50] and it encompasses different types of stakeholders. Key members are five major European cities: Amsterdam (as coordinator), Athens, Barcelona, Berlin and Helsinki. In addition, members include four Member States,[51] the European Commission, the European Investment Bank, organisations of local and municipal governments, and programmes aimed at them (Council of European Municipalities and Regions (CEMR), EUROCITIES and URBACT) as well as refugee-assistance organisations (ECRE and the Migration Policy Group).

The added value of the Partnership is that it targets refugees and other third-country nationals as both beneficiaries of assistance and active participants, thereby promoting their self-organisation. With regard to its latter objective, the Partnership sets forth the establishment of the European Migrants Advisory Board whose members would be the representatives of the host cities and 'first-generation migrants and former refugees holding a status or a European nationality'.[52] The establishment of the Board aims to address the problem that migrants and refugees are typically not directly involved in policy making. The Board, therefore, serves two crucial purposes. First, its objective is to provide an objective viewpoint on the work of the Partnership. Second, it serves to facilitate third-country nationals' civic engagement.[53] The establishment of the Board is linked to the Open Society Fellowships (see above), as the selected fellows automatically become members of the Board.[54]

J. van Zeben, 'Local Governments as Subjects and Objects of EU Law', in E. Fahey and S. Bardutszky (eds.), *Objects and Subjects of EU Law* (Edward Elgar, 2017), and in this volume, Chapter 4 by J. van Zeben and K. Nicolaïdis.

[49] https://ec.europa.eu/futurium/en/inclusion-of-migrants-and-refugees accessed 19 April 2018.

[50] https://ec.europa.eu/futurium/en/urban-agenda-eu/what-urban-agenda-eu accessed 19 April 2018.

[51] Denmark, Greece, Italy, and Portugal.

[52] P. 27 of the Action Plan.

[53] P. 26 of the Action Plan.

[54] P. 27 of the Action Plan.

The establishment of the European Migrants Advisory Board is not the only example of a consultative body that includes representatives of migrants. Such bodies have been established at national, local, or regional level in a number of Member States. Their aim is to foster structured dialogue between migrant groups and national governments and they usually include representatives of the largest migrant groups in that Member State. However, the successful representation of different migrant groups depends on the level of self-organisation of migration communities.[55] Namely, it is expected that the migrants selected for the board represent and successfully network within their migratory group.[56] Consequently – and paradoxically – while third-country nationals' consultative/advisory boards foster third-country nationals' self-organisation, they are, at the same time, conditioned upon the existence of migrants' previous successful self-organisation, which is most often rather low. Such an interrelation between third-country nationals' involvement in consultative boards and their self-organisation – whereas self-organisation is, at the same time, a precondition and the objective of the membership in the board – creates a vicious circle, as it is difficult if not impossible to join an advisory board without self-organising in the first place.

On the other hand, initiatives of individual cities in Europe (and worldwide) show the importance of the role of cities in granting certain rights and access to local services to refugees and other individuals (e.g. undocumented migrants and the homeless) who would otherwise not have these rights based on state-level rules.[57] Paris is one of the European cities taking the lead in developing active citizenship for all its residents, no matter what their status is. The *carte citoyenne* grants to all individuals residing in Paris access to municipal services and enables them to take part in cultural events in Paris and meet with the elected officials.[58]

[55] European Union Agency for Fundamental Rights, 'Together in the EU: Promoting the Participation of Migrants and Their Descendants' (2017), 57–58, available at: http://fra.europa.eu/sites/default/files/fra_uploads/fra-2017-together-in-the-eu_en.pdf accessed 19 April 2018.

[56] For example, see the criteria for the selection of migrants for the European Migrants Advisory Board https://ec.europa.eu/futurium/en/inclusion-migrants-and-refugees/workshop-european-migrant-advisory-board-amsterdam-2-november-2017 accessed 20 April 2018.

[57] For the research on how local governments in Europe welcome and integrate refugees, see 'Cities of Refuge' research project led by B. Oomen, available at: http://citiesofrefuge.eu/ accessed 12 June 2018.

[58] On *carte citoyenne*, see www.paris.fr/cartecitoyenne accessed 12 June 2018; 'New York helps Paris integrate vulnerable migrants after terror attacks' (Apolitical, 19 May 2018)

The Belgian city of Mechelen has started a 'speed dating programme' which fosters migrants' and refugees' integration by pairing each TCN with a city resident and the two sides meet once a week for six months. As stated by the Mayor of Mechelen, Bart Somers, who was awarded the 2016 World Mayor Prize, regular meetings with a designated city resident enable the TCN to learn about the city, practise their language skills and create a human relationship.[59] Through its 'Plan Einstein' the city of Utrecht enables refugees to live in the same buildings as local Dutch people, and offers them language, entrepreneurship and coaching classes.[60] Apart from Utrecht, a number of other cities – such as Amsterdam and Leverkusen – are promoting decentralised housing for asylum seekers.[61] These are worthy initiatives, which show the power local authorities have in promoting refugees' rights and self-organisation, as well as the ability of local authorities to adapt and develop the state-level system for the betterment of refugees.

III Causes and Objectives of Self-Organisation

Two developments associated with migration into the EU can be considered as the crucial causes of migrants' and refugees' self-organisation. First, the refugee influx into the EU in the past several years has put EU asylum law and national practices under strain and brought to the surface a number of its deficiencies. Refugees' self-organisation aims to counterbalance these deficiencies and provide for the basic needs and for civil and political rights of refugees, where such needs and rights are not satisfied and protected by law and/or practice of Member States' authorities.

https://apolitical.co/solution_article/new-york-paris-municipal-id-terror-attacks/ accessed 12 June 2018.

[59] N. Nielsen, 'Belgian mayor invites Orban to migrant diverse town' (EUobserver, 14 June 2018) https://euobserver.com/migration/142078 accessed 14 June 2018.

[60] On 'Plan Einstein', see https://plan-einstein.nl/wp-content/uploads/2018/03/Folder_Engels_def.pdf accessed 12 June 2018. A. Valez, 'Breaking down barriers between locals and refugees in Utrecht' (Euronews, 23 May 2018) www.euronews.com/2018/05/23/breaking-down-barriers-between-locals-and-refugees-in-utrecht accessed 12 June 2018.

[61] On the Startblok housing project in Amsterdam, see www.startblok.amsterdam/en/overview/ accessed 12 June 2018. On the model in Leverkusen, see M. Popp and S. Roebel, 'Asylum Seekers Embrace Alternative Housing' (Spiegel Online, 30 August 2013) www.spiegel.de/international/germany/asylum-seekers-alternative-housing-approach-in-leverkusen-a-success-a-919007.html accessed 12 June 2018.

Second, the rights of entry residence, and access to the labour market of economic migrants as well as their integration and political participation are mostly excluded from EU law. Member States preserve the right to control the number of economic migrants entering their territories, while EU law takes a sectoral approach to migrants, only regulating the rights of certain 'desirable' categories of TCNs. On the other hand, national laws often exclude TCNs from political participation, thus leaving such initiatives to their self-organising activities.

These developments have had three important consequences in terms of TCNs' (both refugees' and migrants') self-organising tendencies. First, TCNs' self-organising activities are targeted at two separate but mutually supportive goals. First, they aim to satisfy TCNs' basic needs, such as food and accommodation. Second, they are the reflection of TCNs' desire not to be marginalised: to become accepted and integrated members of the host society, capable of being treated as equals, of acquiring a job, of building relationships with domestic population and of influencing and contributing to the social and political life of the host Member State. In other words, TCNs' self-organisation can be viewed primarily as a mechanism of supplementing or substituting EU-level or national-level protection of their basic needs and civil and political rights, in cases when these right and needs are not protected by EU/Member States' law and practice.

Second, self-organisation is more likely with regard to categories of TCNs in a particularly vulnerable position (such as refugees) and TCNs who are not granted an extensive set of rights by EU law or national practice. This primarily applies to 'non-desirable' categories of economic migrants who do not qualify as highly qualified employees or intra-corporate skilled transferees. Finally, the frequent exclusion of TCNs from political participation in EU Member States means that self-organisation is typically informal rather than formal.

IV Polycentric Self-Organisation?

This Chapter provides an overview of key developments with respect to the self-organisation of TCNs in the EU. These developments themselves raise important questions regarding the position of TCNs and the sustainability of the patterns of exclusion and marginalisation that came to the surface in many cases. Within the context of this research project, we also need to wonder whether the emerging pattern of formal and informal self-organisation qualifies as polycentric.

In order to answer this question, one needs to ascertain whether the attributes of polycentricity and its institutional essentials are present in different manifestations of formal and informal self-organisation of TCNs, discussed in this Chapter.

All three attributes of polycentricity (multiple independent centres of decision making; continuous competition, cooperation and conflict resolution; and overarching shared system of rules) can, to a certain degree, be detected in the context of TCNs' self-organisation. The existence of 'multiple independent centres of decision making' can be attributed to all the formal manifestations of TCNs' self-organisation: NGOs, private businesses, and cities and other local authorities. These entities have decision-making powers within their respective spheres of activities. The status of informal centres of self-organisation of TCNs is much more complex. However, even though one cannot characterise TCNs' self-organisation via social media, mass media and the word of mouth as centres of decision making in the narrow sense of the word – as their ability to make binding decisions is limited – informal centres of self-organisation reflect choices of their members who share common interests and goals. In this sense, the existence of 'multiple independent centres of decision making' can be attributed both to formal and informal centres of TCNs' self-organisation.

Equally, the existence of 'continuous competition, cooperation and conflict resolution' can be attributed to both formal and informal centres of TCNs' self-organisation. These attributes are visible in the work of NGOs, businesses, and cities, whose efforts in promoting TCNs' rights and self-organisation can be viewed as an endeavour to both cooperate and compete with each other. Similarly, by providing information to TCNs who share common interests, different social media and mass media often compete with each other to get more attention from the same group of stakeholders.

Finally, centres of TCNs' formal self-organisation do function under an 'overarching shared system of rules', albeit one that corresponds to the shared system of rules in the EU only to a limited extent.[62] The overlap is visible in EU-based rules (e.g. those on the funding possibilities for NGOs, private and public companies and national and local authorities from the Asylum, Migration and Integration Fund (AMIF)) but less so in state-based rules which diverge across the EU. Refugees are protected by a number of international legal instruments, most notably the Geneva

[62] Discussed by A. Bobić, Chapter 6 in this Volume.

Convention. They are also protected by EU primary law (TFEU and the Charter) and a number of EU secondary law instruments which stipulate who qualifies for international protection,[63] what are the procedural guarantees in the asylum proceedings,[64] which Member State is responsible for examining an asylum application,[65] and what are the standards of reception of asylum applicants.[66] However, due to the fact that asylum matters are mostly regulated by directives, Member States retain certain flexibility in terms of the form and method of putting in place these rules at the national level. In reality, national practices vary significantly and often deviate from EU rules. Finally, the EU's overarching set of rules is even less applicable to manifestations of TCNs' informal self-organisation, carried out through social and mass media, and especially through the word of mouth.

Furthermore, the EU also sets rules for certain categories of economic migrants (highly skilled workers, seasonal workers, intra-corporate transferees), for family members of EU citizens and legally residing TCNs, for researchers and students, and for TCN long-term residents.[67] However, Member States retain the competence to determine

[63] European Parliament and Council Directive 2011/95 on standards for the qualification of third-country nationals or stateless persons as beneficiaries of international protection, for a uniform status for refugees or for persons eligible for subsidiary protection, and for the content of the protection granted (2011) OJ L 337, 9–26.

[64] European Parliament and Council Directive 2013/32/EU on Common Procedures for Granting and Withdrawing International Protection (2013) OJ L 180, 60–95.

[65] European Parliament and Council Regulation 604/2013 on establishing the criteria and mechanisms for determining the Member State responsible for examining an application for international protection lodged in one of the Member States by a third-country national or a stateless person (Recast) (2013) OJ L 180/31, 31–59.

[66] European Parliament and Council Directive 2013/33 laying down standards for the reception of applicants for international protection (2013) OJ L 180, 96–116.

[67] Rights of third-country nationals are codified in a number of sectoral directives, e.g. on family members of EU citizens (European Parliament and of the Council Directive on the right of citizens of the Union and their family members to move and reside freely within the territory of the Member States amending Regulation (2004) OJ L 158/77), on family members of legally resident third-country nationals (Council Directive 2003/86 on the right to family reunification (2003) OJ L 251/12), on long-term residents (Council Directive 2003/109 concerning the status of third-country nationals who are long-term residents (2003) OJ L 16/44), on highly qualified employees (Council Directive 2009/50 on the conditions of entry and residence of third-country nationals for the purposes of highly qualified employment (2009) OJ L 155/17), on third-country nationals workers legally residing in a Member State (European Parliament and Council Directive 2011/98 on a single application procedure for a single permit for third-country nationals to reside and work in the territory of a Member State and on a common set of rights for third-country workers legally residing in a Member State (2011) OJ L 343/1), on students, pupils, researchers and au pairing (European Parliament and Council Directive 2016/801

the number of economic migrants entering their territories, as well as to adopt rules on integration of TCNs. In conclusion, apart from certain narrow categories of TCNs, such as family members of EU citizens, TCNs are generally granted a much lower level of EU-based rights than EU citizens. Thus, TCNs are only partially subject to an overarching shared set of EU-based rules, and, in this context, can be perceived as 'outsiders' in the EU society.

The existence of institutional essentials of polycentricity (freedom and ability to enter and exit; enforcement of shared systems of rules; and peaceful contestation) in the context of self-organisation of TCNs is highly debatable and at times even non-existent. TCNs are free to enter and exit different self-organising groups discussed in this chapter, such as social media groups, NGOs or businesses. However, the very reason for TCNs' self-organisation is their inability to enter other formal ways of representation available to EU citizens. From this perspective, self-organisation of TCNs is a direct consequence of the lack of this institutional essential.

As regards the TCNs' ability to enforce a shared system of rules, EU law enables TCNs to rely on directly applicable EU rules before national judicial and administrative authorities, and binds national authorities to respect and apply EU law. However, in reality there are at least four problems in this context. First, there are a number of EU-level 'legal gaps' in relation to TCNs, which enable divergent and discriminatory national and local rules and practices. Second, as stated previously, national practices with regard to TCNs often deviate from EU rules. Third, it is difficult to control and monitor national judicial and administrative authorities in order to ensure that they apply EU law to each individual case. Finally, TCNs (and refugees, in particular) are extremely vulnerable, marginalised individuals with scarce means and a weak social position. For all these reasons, the TCNs' ability to enforce the rules that apply to them is often limited to non-existent.

on the conditions of entry and residence of third-country nationals for the purposes of research, studies, training, voluntary service, pupil exchange schemes or educational projects and au pairing (2016) OJ L 132/21), on seasonal workers (European Parliament and Council Directive 2014/36 on the conditions of entry and stay of third-country nationals for the purpose of employment as seasonal workers (2014) OJ L 94/375), on intra-corporate non-EU skilled transferees (European Parliament and Council Directive 2014/66 on the conditions of entry and residence of third-country nationals in the framework of an intra-corporate transfer (2014) OJ L 157/1).

Finally, TCNs self-organisation can be understood as a form of peaceful contestation of their marginalised and discriminated social and legal status. Different forms of both informal and formal self-organisation are an attempt to challenge and resist the system which treats TCNs as outsiders, who are both legally and socially disadvantaged. However, different centres of TCNs' self-organisation do not enable or enforce peaceful contestation between various groups of TCNs. Different groups of TCNs – clustered based on their nationality, religion, language, status, or common interests – generally do not mix with other groups, partly due to a lack of trust. For this reason, there is no or little room for peaceful contestation between different groups of TCNs.

Due to the lack, or incompleteness, of institutional essentials, it is questionable whether self-organisation of TCNs in the EU can be considered sufficiently polycentric. This suggests that polycentric governance in the EU remains reserved for 'insiders' – EU citizens – and a significant and growing number of individuals on the EU territory remains only partially included or even excluded. This points to a structural deficiency within the EU and raises the question whether the EU can be polycentric without including all individuals present on the EU's territory.[68]

[68] For a more detailed discussion on this, see the concluding Chapter of this Volume.

9

Peaceful Contestation

DAMJAN KUKOVEC

Polycentricity implies the diffusion of sovereignty over several levels of governance and numerous institutions.[1] It envisages an explicit role for non-governmental bodies, such as private and community-based organisations and it puts the individual at the heart of society and social construction.[2] Polycentricity presents a normative alternative to federalism, multilevel governance that prioritises self-governance, or individual autonomy,[3] as a goal.[4]

Peaceful contestation plays a special role within the polycentric theory, a role of an institutional essential.[5] This means that peaceful contestation needs to be constantly enabled in a polycentric society in order for the society to be able to maintain its polycentric character. Peaceful contestation is the peaceful challenge of any existing legal and political situation in view of ensuring the values of polycentric theory, particularly self-governance. Polycentric theory and peaceful contestation thus need to be understood dynamically: many decision centres with autonomous and limited prerogatives need to be able to and should in fact constantly contest existing norms and policies as well as their own autonomy and prerogatives. NGOs, cities, individuals, corporations, states or expert groups are just some of the loci of decision making and contestation that are involved in a constant reconfiguration of society. Once this dispersed process of social reconfiguration stops or is limited, the system will revert to another type of pluricentric governance, such as federalism or multilevel governance.

1 See, in this Volume, Introduction by J. van Zeben and A. Bobić, 2.

2 V. Ostrom, *The Meaning of American Federalism: Constituting a Self-Governing Society* (ICS Press, 1991).

3 See, in this Volume, Chapter 3 by F. Cheneval.

4 J. van Zeben (n. 1) 3.

5 P. D. Aligica and V. Tarko, 'Polycentricity: From Polanyi to Ostrom, and Beyond', *Governance: An International Journal of Policy, Administration, and Institutions* 25 (2) (2012), 237, 238; J. van Zeben and A. Bobić (n. 1) 4.

This chapter sets out the notion of peaceful contestation within the framework of polycentric theory. Part I discusses the most important premises of peaceful contestation as addressed in the framework of the polycentric theory, and the notion of 'peaceful' contestation within that framework. Part II discusses the realisation of the goal of polycentricity – self-governance – through peaceful contestation within the framework of the theory of polycentricity. It develops the notion of 'trust-producing conflicts' and the notion of a social actor or 'public entrepreneur', explaining the role of a public entrepreneur with an example of an infringement procedure of the European Commission. Part III concludes. The overall aim of this chapter is to develop an ideal type of peaceful contestation that is needed for the maintenance of a polycentric system, one that prioritises self-governance or individual autonomy.

I Peaceful Contestation within the Polycentric Theory

Peaceful contestation is fundamental to liberal political theory. John Stuart Mill sees constant contestation of opinions as crucial for productive human discourse and the preservation of liberty. This is because it is only through the constant contestation of our opinions that we can begin to sort out what we believe to be true from what we believe to be false.[6] There are several definitions of peaceful contestation in liberal political theory, with several goals of this process in mind, such as the upholding of social discourse and legitimacy.[7] These are not the goals of peaceful contestation per se in a polycentric world. While peaceful contestation is not precisely defined in polycentric theory, there are several elements that the theory offers for its interpretation.

A Contestation in Polycentric Theory

Polycentric theory acknowledges the highly fragmented and decentralised network of sociopolitical relationships and overlapping authority. A polycentric political system is one where 'many officials and decision structures are assigned limited and relatively autonomous prerogatives to determine, enforce and alter legal relationships'.[8] There is a web of

[6] J. S. Mill, *On Liberty* (Longman, Roberts, and Green, 1869).

[7] A. Wiener, *Theory of Contestation* (Springer-Verlag, 2014) 1. (Wiener defines contestation as 'social practices, which discursively express disapproval of norms'.)

[8] V. Ostrom, 'Polycentricity' (Washington D.C. Workshop Working Paper Series, Workshop in Political Theory and Policy Analysis, Presented at the Annual Meeting of

societal actors and identities which is held together by the antagonistic claims based on the actors' self-governance. Various abstract and under-operationalised social ideals cannot be imposed on the participants by an overarching authority. They have to be given content by the web of social actors. The social structure therefore has to allow for the multitude of constantly clashing opinions to exist.[9]

Two broad types of peaceful contestation exist: legal and political contestation. Legal contestation is performed before any legalised bodies and institutions. It can be conducted in administrative procedures, before courts and tribunals as well as before any legalised fora and institutions of international, European Union or national law. Political contestation means participation in the political process, in elections, in parliamentary debates, referenda or in any international, European or national setting that does not perceive its framework or mission as purely legalised. In the context of European Union law, numerous possibilities for peaceful contestation exist. One could imagine enforcement actions, such as the European Commission's infringement procedure or actions to challenge the validity of EU laws, such as an action for annulment. Elections to the European Parliament, a complaint to an Ombudsman, formal or informal contacts with European institutions, or preliminary reference procedures are just some of the forms of peaceful contestation in the European Union.

Polycentric theory aims at a society in which people and organisations constantly contest and produce norms and renegotiate their own legal situation. This simultaneously contributes to constant shaping of the normative predispositions of a social order defined by self-governance, as well as dynamically self-correcting[10] the social order accordingly.

In the European Union setting, this would mean that by constant popular and dispersed contestation of the existing state of affairs, legal and political decisions remain constantly dispersed and articulated in a decentralised and highly democratic manner. Policies and social outcomes would be shaped through the exercise of self-governance by citizens and organisations, organised horizontally, rather than by a hierarchical institutional and social structure. Finally, decisions by actors who are often understood as hierarchically privileged could be constantly challenged,

the American Political Science Association (1972), 5–9; M. D. McGinnis (ed.), *Polycentricity and Local Public Economies* (University of Michigan Press, 1999), 55–6.

[9] P. D. Aligica and V. Tarko (n. 5); M. Polanyi, *The Logic of Liberty* (University of Chicago Press, 1951).

[10] P. D. Aligica and V. Tarko (n. 5) 246.

contested and amended by various social actors and particularly by individuals and their representatives throughout the European Union. In turn, this would lead to a truly polycentric order in which decision makers initially perceived as hierarchically privileged lose, or keep losing, this capacity. This should result in a discursive shift in the European Union from a focus on the binary between the prerogatives of Member States and European institutions, towards the role of the individual in this binary. Rather, individual self-governance should be perceived as the central constitutive element of European Union governance. It would lead to a society in which policies are shaped through the exercise of private autonomy in a polity that places an emphasis on horizontal rather than vertical policy and decision making.

B *When Is Contestation 'Peaceful'?*

Having set out the key features of peaceful contestation in a polycentric system, this chapter will now turn to the question of what it means for contestation to be 'peaceful' in a liberal political system in general and within the framework of polycentric theory in particular. This discussion has several important implications. First, as discussed in Part I, there are several avenues and types of political contestation and some, particularly the more political ones and those where individuals do not directly involve legal institutions, could be perceived as going against the overarching rules of the rule of law. Second, polycentricity encourages individual self-governance, which does not only entail creating, but also breaking, legal relationships. It is important to recognise under what circumstances these types of acts are perceived as peaceful. Third, individuals exercise self-governance in countless different ways, such as to enable self-governance or the policy goals of larger entities such as cities, regions and corporations and even states. From the perspective of the individual, self-governance by larger social units shares the same theoretical underpinnings as cases of individual self-governance.

The content and nature of peaceful contestation in liberal political theory is determined by way of opposition to (imaginary) war-like behaviour.[11] Overcoming the state of nature in which war is waged by everyone against everyone else is an incessant concern of liberal political

[11] Understanding of our social life as a constant struggle is not a part of the polycentric nor general liberal analysis. For the claim that the global society should be understood as a society of constant struggle, see D. Kukovec, 'Hierarchies as Law', *Columbia Journal of European Law* 21 (1) (2014), 131.

theory.[12] This state of nature was not perfectly abolished when liberal institutions were set up. There is a constant possibility of, and there are indeed constant – albeit mostly partial – slippages back into this state that a liberal society needs relentlessly to police.

Such slippages can occur on a 'macro' level and on a 'micro' level. The macro level could be described as an illegal use of force or an all-out war in international relations. Alleviation of war has been European Union's raison d'être from the start. As the prevention of regression to war or to war-like relationships has been the cornerstone of liberal political theory, the fact that the European Union is an inherently liberal construct should not come as a surprise. While the European Union has been successfully spared a war since 1945, numerous dilemmas in the field of international law can serve as examples of what is considered peaceful and within the bounds of the law and what is considered as beyond the law.[13]

The micro level of a slippage into a state of nature occurs through a use of force and self-help that is not sanctioned by the legal system and is often described as 'taking the law into one's own hands'. Examples include retaliatory violence, blood feuds, self-help or another type of behaviour not involving the legal or some other legalised form of dispute settlement and norm contestation. Different legal systems allow for various but always very limited ways of 'legal' self-help in resolving disputes or remedying the wrongs imposed by others. Once those limits are overstepped, one cannot speak about peaceful contestation anymore, but about overstepping the boundaries of peaceful resolution of disputes and going beyond the rule of law.

Countless examples could portray the constant social policing of proper boundaries between peaceful contestation and illegal regression to the state of nature. One could imagine an institution faced with the question of the legality of protests by indigenous people or NGOs against the activities of multinational corporations, or a court policing the boundaries of adverse possession. Claims and demands can be made in pursuit of numerous social goals – justice, an array of human rights,

[12] T. Hobbes, *Leviathan* first published 1651 (Oxford University Press, 2008); J. Locke, *The Second Treatise of Civil Government and a Letter Concerning Toleration* first published 1689 (Blackwell, 1946).

[13] For a discussion on the legitimacy of the Iraq war see e.g. A. Paulus, 'The War Against Iraq and the Future of International Law: Hegemony or Pluralism?', *Michigan Journal of International Law* 25 (3) (2004), 691.

economic profit, provision of common goods and services or self-governance, to name a few.

II Self-Governance through Peaceful Contestation

This section turns to the specificities of contestation that are required for the system to become and stay polycentric. Vincent Ostrom argued that functional polycentric systems do not emerge spontaneously but require the conscious and conscientious practice of organisational artisanship.[14] Design and spontaneous order reinforce one another in the polycentric theory. Design is possible within the overarching rules and within the broader process of the ever-evolving spontaneous order. Therefore polycentric theory should not adopt a laissez-faire approach to social construction, but rather one of careful social engineering.

How should peaceful contestation be organised and constructed in the framework of the European Union? What type of social activity should be encouraged? Polycentric theory resists fiat and centralised decision making. Freedom to make individual and personal contributions to the management of the social system is at the heart of the theory. Social actors should be contesting and participating in social – legal and political – life. Contesting the content of rules is thus at the heart of social construction.

A Self-Governance and Institutional Design

Peaceful contestation is essential for the maintenance of independent centres of decision making as those centres cannot exist or maintain their existence without being able to peacefully contest their own positions. It is a necessary precondition to ensure continuous competition, cooperation and conflict resolution. Without this institutional essential, no maintenance of the system by autonomous individuals and other decision-making centres can be ensured. There are two ways in which Vincent Ostrom addresses rule contestation. First, Ostrom emphasised the importance of access to rapid, low cost, local arenas to resolve conflict among users or between users and officials.[15] If individuals are going to follow rules over a long period, they must institute some

[14] V. Ostrom, *The Meaning of American Federalism* (n. 2) 199–221; M. Fotos, 'Vincent Ostrom's Revolutionary Science of Association', *Public Choice*, 163 (1) (2015), 67.

[15] V. Ostrom (n. 2).

mechanism for discussing and resolving what is or is not a rule infraction. By devising simple mechanisms to get conflicts aired immediately and make resolutions that are generally known in a community, the number of trust-reducing conflicts can be reduced.[16]

Second, peaceful contestation within the polycentric society could not only be understood as an arena of decreasing the number of 'trust-reducing conflicts', but as increasing 'trust-producing conflicts' – conflicts which entail contestation of rules and policies understood as creating the polycentric system itself. Ostrom notes that if individuals or units operating in a polycentric order have incentives to take actions to enforce general rules of conduct, then polycentricism will become an increasingly viable form of organisation.[17] The idea behind 'trust-producing conflicts' is that individuals should be free not only to play the game or have the incentives to self-enforce the rules of the game but also to change those rules in an orderly way.[18] Constant contestation and simultaneous enforcement of general rules of conduct that provide the legal framework for a polycentric order is thus essential for a polycentric system. It is this second understanding of rule contestation that the remaining part of this chapter will address.

How can the goal of self-governance, the main virtue in a polycentric system, be realised in the context of peaceful contestation, so that the system constantly keeps its polycentric nature? A democratic institutional set-up should be understood as a precondition for successful peaceful contestation.[19] At least since the adoption of the Maastricht Treaty, there has been an emphasis on the development of a democratic institutional set-up in the EU. This was pursued through constant expansion of institutional opportunities for citizens to play a direct role in agenda setting or in influencing the actual decision making in the European Union. However, how precisely should the institutional setting change following the insights of the polycentric theory? Polycentric theory's emphasis on self-governance could lead to a simplified conclusion that this theory favours 'private' enforcement over 'public' forms of enforcement.[20]

[16] ibid.

[17] P. D. Aligica and V. Tarko (n. 5) 246.

[18] P. D. Aligica and V. Tarko (n. 5) 247.

[19] See, in this Volume, Chapter 2 by J. van Zeben.

[20] In this sense, see M. D. McGinnis, 'Costs and Challenges of Polycentric Governance' (2005) Paper presented at Workshop on Analyzing Problems of Polycentric Governance in the

One could argue that private enforcement is from a purely conceptual perspective more desirable than public enforcement, as it reflects the wishes of individuals rather than of (possibly unelected) officials or hierarchically privileged institutions. Enforcement of competition law illustrates some of the dilemmas and benefits of private and public enforcement. Private enforcement of competition law occurs through the invoking of Articles 101 and 102 TFEU in litigation between private parties in the courts of the EU Member States, as opposed to public enforcement. Public enforcement refers to proceedings conducted or brought by competition authorities (either the European Commission or the competition authorities of the EU Member States), including such proceedings that are triggered by complaints from private parties to such authorities.[21]

Despite a possible initial perception of the generally beneficial nature of private enforcement, several arguments, independent of the demands of polycentric theory, could be made favouring public enforcement. Wouter Wils, for instance, lists several benefits of public enforcement. First, as to the level of the monetary sanctions (fines or damages), public enforcement has the additional advantage of allowing better control in setting the optimal amount of the sanction. When the sanction consists of damages awarded as a result of private litigation, it becomes virtually impossible to target the optimal amount. Damages will be calculated not by reference to the offender's gain, but by reference to the losses which those plaintiffs who happen to bring claims manage to prove.

Second, private actions for damages are inevitably driven by the private gains and expenses of the parties concerned. These private interests will often diverge from the general interest. Cases that should be brought to clarify the law and generate deterrence in the general interest may never arise through private litigation, because no private party has a sufficient interest to bring an action, or because cases are settled without any clarification of the law. Conversely, private plaintiffs will try to obtain interpretations of the law that are to their financial or commercial benefit, irrespective of their general merit, or to win cases in which they have

Growing EU, Humboldt University, Berlin (available at http://citeseerx.ist.psu.edu/viewdoc/download?doi=10.1.1.529.2214&rep=rep1&type=pdf) accessed 18 October 2018, 2.

21 W. Wils, 'Private Enforcement of EU Antitrust Law and Its Relationship with Public Enforcement: Past, Present and Future', *World Competition: Law and Economics Review* 40 (1) (2017), 3.

large financial or commercial stakes, irrespective of the merit of the interpretation of the law on which the case is won.[22]

Would polycentric theory insist on private enforcement, enhancing self-governance, despite several arguments such as those above in favour of public enforcement? Indeed, polycentricity's requirement that policies and social outcomes are shaped through the exercise of self-governance by citizens and organisations, organised horizontally by constant dispersed contestation of the existing state of affairs, could lead to a conclusion that the enforcement and challenge of European Union norms should be exercised by individuals as fully-empowered agents. In other words, it could lead to a conclusion that individuals should be constantly and, in any situation, empowered to enforce and challenge European Union law directly, without an institutional medium.

The Ostroms' work does not seem to support such sweeping conclusions. Vincent does not argue for a complete transcendence of the public/private distinction or for a reduction or elimination of the public for the benefit of the private; entrepreneurship plays a key role in the private sector since entrepreneurs are the ones who must discover strategies to put heterogeneous factors of production together in new and complementary ways given the availability of resources and technology.[23] The profit motive is the driving force for private entrepreneurs on the market.[24] Elinor Ostrom's work similarly argued that the market and provision of public goods and common-pool resources are importantly different and often complementary. On the other hand, providing and producing public goods and common-pool resources – including public safety; conflict resolution at international, national, regional and local levels; public education; and public health, as well as sustaining natural resource systems – require different institutions than an open, competitive market. Even the market itself is not a viable, independent institution without the presence of effective public property arrangements, courts of law and police.[25]

[22] ibid.

[23] V. Ostrom, *The Meaning of American Federalism* (n. 2) and M. Fotos, 'Vincent Ostrom's revolutionary science of association' (n. 14).

[24] ibid.

[25] E. Ostrom, 'Polycentric Systems as One approach for Solving Collective Action Problems' (2008), available at: http://dlc.dlib.indiana.edu/dlc/bitstream/handle/10535/4417/W08-6_Ostrom_DLC.pdf accessed 4 June 2018. See also, in this Volume, Chapter 5 by J. van Zeben and A. Bobić.

The Ostroms found that the language used by many analysts divides the rich world of institutions into a barren dichotomy of the market versus the state. Markets are considered by most to be open realms where many individuals and firms of diverse sizes and assets compete, whereas the depiction of the public sector is one of a top-down hierarchy with little room for problem solving except by top level government officials. Elinor Ostrom argues that the public sector should encourage human development at local, regional, national, and international levels and enable, encourage and engage actors constantly to contest and reshape the system in an orderly manner; to be polycentric with small units nested in larger systems.[26] In the context of the EU's common fisheries policies, for example, Elinor's work demonstrates the necessity of a constant interaction of scientists, fishing vessels, government agencies and marine conservation groups[27] who communicate, develop their own agreements, establish positions or monitor and sanction those who do not conform to rules. The goal of polycentric contestation is therefore the constant enabling of private and public actors to intelligently and mutually engage.

B *The Notion of 'Public Entrepreneur'*

The principles expounded by the Ostroms are not necessarily aimed at enabling each citizen *directly* to contest any legal or political position or enabling them to enforce the system privately. A complete shift to a private system of enforcement or to a completely dispersed system of legal and political contestation without an institutional medium would thus not find its place within the polycentric theory. Analysis of peaceful contestation within the framework of polycentric theory should address systemic elements of the theory that promote self-governance and advance the cause of enabling of private and public actors to engage intelligently with the public and the private. The development of 'the conscious and conscientious practice of organizational artisanship'[28] requires an analytical focus on ensuring self-governance through an active and knowledgeable social actor who actively and peacefully challenges existing legal and political situations.[29]

[26] ibid.
[27] ibid.
[28] V. Ostrom (n. 8); M. Fotos (n. 14) 24.
[29] See, in this Volume, Chapter 12 by S. Garben.

This analytical turn goes far beyond the question of any particular institutional set-up. Even if the theory of polycentricity offered precise pointers on institutional restructuring, such restructuring would not necessarily achieve a polycentric society. Creation of institutional alleys for contestation does not necessarily mean that citizens will actually use them nor that levels of participation and contestation would be effective and fulfil the requirements of a polycentric system. The direct elections of the Members of the European Parliament, while extremely important for the democratic life of the Union, are just one example of the under usage of avenues of participation in political life.[30] The elections in 2014 witnessed a mere 42.61 per cent turnout. While the low level of participation in direct elections may be a result of indifference – a problem that a system aiming at polycentricity should certainly address – there are other reasons which may prevent the system from keeping its polycentric features in terms of active dispersed decision making.

The European Union's complexity can be said to be one of the main obstacles to its full democratic potential.[31] It is thus vital that individuals and other entities are able to navigate this complex system which requires a lot of resources, organisation and activity by individuals and other actors to make the democratic and polycentric system work at all. It requires active and motivated social actors and a great deal of knowledge of the complexity of the system so that social actors are able to navigate it to exercise their self-governance.[32]

Successful and legitimate exercise of self-governance is, according to the Ostroms, vitally dependent on knowledge and learning. Elinor Ostrom argued that for the creation of all human artefacts, knowledgeable experimenters who know what they are doing are required.[33] Vincent Ostrom's insight into the interplay of design and spontaneous order further explains the fundamental importance of knowledge and learning in the shaping of the polycentric system as well as of peaceful contestation. According to Vincent, design and spontaneous order reinforce one another in the polycentric theory. Design is possible within the overarching rules and within the broader process of the ever-evolving

[30] European Parliament, 'Results of the 2014 European elections' (Europa, 2014), available at: www.europarl.europa.eu/elections2014-results/en/turnout.html accessed 5 June 2018.

[31] D. Kukovec (n. 11).

[32] See, in this sense, V. Ostrom, *The Meaning of American Federalism* (n. 2), 272.

[33] M. Fotos (n. 14) 17.

spontaneous order. The link between spontaneity and design is given by the notion of knowledge and its correlate concepts such as learning.[34]

The process of learning needs to be understood as dynamically as peaceful contestation and the polycentric society itself. For this reason, Vincent Ostrom brings the idea of an experimentalist and problem-solving private entrepreneur to the management of public affairs and to the process of learning. This idea appears to be more important to Ostrom than a particular type of a site or of an agent of contestation. He would argue that effective solving of collective action problems requires opening public as well as private spheres of activities, ranging from the small to the very large.[35] Any actor of society, small or large, should be encouraged to participate in problem solving.[36] Individuals, whose conduct may cause the problem, such as depletion of fish stocks by overfishing, should act collectively rather than individually to solve the problem at hand.[37] All social actors involved in the production of public goods and common-pool resources should thus be understood as 'public entrepreneurs',[38] as decision-making actors motivated by diverse interests, but by common social goals to peacefully contest norms and situations, thus constantly reconstituting a polycentric society by exercising their self-governance.

Public entrepreneurs – individuals, NGOs, cities, corporations, states, regions, or expert groups and countless others – are all loci of decision making and contestation that are involved in a constant reconfiguration of society. Public entrepreneurs are constantly learning from their experience in participating in peaceful contestation. They should thus know the art and science of association and need to conduct their affairs in multi-organisational settings characterised by a culture of deliberation conducted in a spirit of curious enquiry and self-interest.[39] They constitute and maintain dispersed decision making by constantly contesting their autonomy, their prerogatives as well as existing norms and policies. Once this dispersed process of social reconfiguration stops or is limited, the system cannot claim to be polycentric.

34 V. Ostrom (n 8). See also S. Garben, Chapter 12 in this Volume.
35 V. Ostrom (n. 8) 1.
36 ibid.
37 E. Ostrom, *Governing the Commons: The Evolution of Institutions for Collective Action* (Cambridge University Press, 1990).
38 V. Ostrom (n. 8) 2.
39 V. Ostrom (n. 8); M. Fotos (n. 14) 24.

The polycentric theory is therefore conducive to Marc Galanter's portrayal of society as a legal regime in which parties of several different types constantly interact with one another. However, the distinction as set out by Galanter between repeat players, those who constantly participate in contestation and those who are one-shooters and engage with it only once in their lifetime or very occasionally,[40] should be alleviated or at least reduced as much as possible in a polycentric society. Ideally, a polycentric society should be one of horizontal repeat players, involved in a constant process of learning, experimentation and social development by utilising any type and site of peaceful contestation.

C *Public Entrepreneur in a Public Enforcement Procedure*

The European Commission is a repeat player in the infringement procedure under Articles 258 and 260 TFEU. It has the sole power of enforcement of law in the scope of these articles. The infringement procedure could thus be described as the most 'public' form of EU law enforcement. The Commission launches this procedure when a Member State of the Union is alleged to violate a provision of EU law. The nature of the infringement procedure does not mean, however, that other social actors could not be repeat players in the process. This subsection explores how NGOs, individuals, various stakeholders or even other institutions and entities, acting as 'public entrepreneurs', could importantly shape this procedure.

The Commission has a discretion to bring to Court both the infringement procedure under Article 258 TFEU as well as the procedure for penalties under Article 260 TFEU. The procedure follows a number of steps laid out in the EU Treaties, including sending a letter of formal notice requesting further information to the country concerned and sending a reasoned opinion, a formal request to comply with EU law. Finally, the Commission may decide to refer the matter to the Court of Justice.

Both Articles 258 and 260 expressly envisage the Commission's discretion to pursue these proceedings. Commission's discretion is an understandable institutional prerogative, given the limited resources and given that any individual or institution must have some discretion

[40] M. Galanter argues in the context of litigation that there is a continuum between one-shooters and repeat players. See M. Galanter, 'Why the "Haves" Come Out Ahead: Speculations on the Limits of Legal Change', *Law & Society Review* 9 (1) (1974), 95–160.

in pursuing litigation. While the European Commission does have significant resources, particularly in terms of knowledge and manpower, those resources are finite, which warrants granting the Commission discretion in this regard. This is where an essential role of various public entrepreneurs becomes visible. The Commission can identify possible infringements of EU law on the basis of its own investigations, particularly in cases of non-transposition or incorrect transposition of Directives or in cases where informing the Commission is an obligatory step in particular procedures on a national level. In other cases, the Commission is very reliant on the information from the complainants – individuals, NGOs, businesses or other stakeholders who encounter violations of European Union law on a daily basis. Any individual, NGO or other actor can inform the Commission of the alleged violation of EU law. Thus, in the proverbially 'public' form of enforcement action, the main initiative for launching a procedure may actually come from the individual. Only social actors in their daily lives have insight into EU law's operation and performance on a daily basis. The input from an active citizen or another public entrepreneur is thus vital already at the stage of launching the procedure.

Most infringement cases are settled before being referred to the Court and the input of a 'public entrepreneur' at the stage of pre-court settlement is equally important. The orientation to problem solving and solutions which could satisfy various parties are fundamental in this stage. A public entrepreneur needs to inform the Commission about the situation on site, provide photographs, legal reasoning, facts and especially explain the consequences of the alleged infringement. If the Court finds that a Member State has breached EU law, the national authorities must take action to comply with the Court judgment. If, despite the Court's judgment, the EU country still doesn't rectify the situation, the Commission may refer the country back to the Court, proposing that the Court imposes financial penalties, which can be either a lump sum and/or a daily payment. Again, while individuals may only be used as a source of information, or of support rather than being agents themselves, they can play an invaluable and crucial role in articulating the continued infringement on the ground and on providing necessary information.

A public entrepreneur learns and solves problems while participating in the infringement proceedings, even if his ideas and suggestions are not necessarily taken up. Moreover, the European Commission learns with the assistance of other public entrepreneurs in its own role as a public entrepreneur. Individuals' skills, resources, knowledge, the culture of openness to participation, and the actual activity of social actors become more important than precisely regulated institutional settings. In other words, skilful and engaged public entrepreneurs can play a more important role in peaceful contestation than a particular institutional design.

D *An Ideal Type of Peaceful Contestation in Polycentric Theory*

The discussion brings us to an ideal type of peaceful contestation under the polycentric theory. Polycentric peaceful contestation is exercised in a democratic institutional setting which enables constant dispersed decision making. However, hierarchical imposition of particular interpretations of various abstract and underoperationalised social ideals on the participants by an overarching authority cannot be accepted in a polycentric system. Decisions by actors who are often understood as hierarchically privileged can be constantly challenged, contested and amended by various social actors and particularly by individuals and their representatives throughout the Union. This leads to a truly polycentric situation in which decisions, initially perceived as hierarchically privileged, lose, or keep losing, this capacity.

Ostrom argues that Hobbes' state of nature does not account for the human capacity for language and learning used to develop a community of understanding that would oblige members of the community to abide by mutually agreed-upon restraints.[41] A notion of dialogue and peaceful contestation is thus ingrained in the polycentric theory, one where claims of rule of law are dynamically reshaped through a dialogue rather than unilaterally imposed. The dispersion of decision-making capabilities associated with polycentricity allows for substantial discretion or freedom of individuals and for effective and regular constraint upon the actions of governmental officials.[42] Such reasoning enables communities of persons to construct a sovereign who is bound by human law and thus the capacity for self-governance is within the reach of human intelligence.[43]

Social ideals have to be given content by the horizontal web of social actors. The social structure has to allow for the multitude of constantly clashing opinions to exist.[44] 'Public entrepreneurs' – repeat players

[41] M. Fotos, (n. 14) 16
[42] V. Ostrom (n. 8)
[43] M. Fotos (n. 22) 15
[44] P. D. Aligica and V. Tarko (n. 5) 238; M. Polanyi (n. 9)

dispersed throughout the Union – should be able and encouraged to frame their concerns and aspirations peacefully. This certainly includes demands for more self-governance. Peaceful demands to leave a particular legal system, such as the European Union or a nation-state system – or demands to leave any legal relationship on a micro level – need to be acknowledged and treated peacefully.

The contestation in a polycentric system depends on public entrepreneurs who dare to experiment, but also learn from the mistakes made. Knowledge, education, and constant learning and engagement are vital for a successful public entrepreneur and for a polycentric system to thrive. Public entrepreneurs should be dispersed throughout the society and throughout all social layers. This leads to the question of equality of resources in the Union as well as to the question of the mindset of public entrepreneurs, which is beyond the scope of this chapter.[45]

Any social context and setting should be understood as a site of peaceful contestation in polycentric theory, including domains of social life such as art and education or the media or workplace and other settings of economic activity. Marches, politically motivated strikes, discussions and statements on Twitter, Facebook and on other social media, boycotts and other social movements such as the #MeToo movement are all fundamental avenues of peaceful contestation in a polycentric world. Regardless of the type and site of peaceful contestation, citizens need to know the art and science of social association. They need to have 'the habits of heart and mind' to conduct their affairs in multi-organisational settings characterised by culture of deliberation conducted in a spirit of a curious enquiry and self-interest.

It could plausibly be argued that the European Union is governed by a relatively small number of European institutions, state and non-state actors such as NGOs, individuals, corporations, cities and law firms acting as public entrepreneurs. There are many one-shooters, but not many repeat players. This is why institutionalisation and formalisation of the possibilities for the exercise of individual self-governance, as for example described in the infringement procedure, do not stand to deliver a fully polycentric Union. The lack of realisation of the polycentric potential within the scope of peaceful contestation is thus a sociolegal rather than institutional question. It points to the need of further research on the implications of EU law in daily reality and how various actors in

[45] See D. Kukovec, 'Law and the Periphery', *European Law Journal* 21 (3) (2015), 406–28.

the Union experience EU structures and influence actual decision-making.

Questions of legal culture in the Union also come to the fore. Peaceful demands for self-governance need to be met with a peaceful reaction and experimentation should be encouraged and supported. Active, daring and educated public entrepreneurs are crucial, but perceptive institutions prepared to seriously listen to concerns and demands for self-governance are equally indispensable. Culture of responsiveness, education, experimentation and active creation of an empowered individual are all vital components on the road to a polycentric Union. The immense complexity of the Union makes a truly polycentric system hard to achieve or maintain. A public entrepreneur needs to know what she is doing. Polycentricity requires dispersed decision making and it requires democratisation of expertise. The democratic element thus meets the expertise, able to navigate in the system, in the Ostroms' teaching, yet expertise is in fact not evenly spread out in the Union.[46] Complexity further breeds concentration of expertise, repeat players and power.

III Conclusions

Polycentric theory offers a powerful account of ways of improving the political life of a society in general and of the European Union in particular. Peaceful contestation constitutes one of the vital pieces of the puzzle. It needs to be constantly enabled in a polycentric society in order for society to be able to claim this character. Once this dispersed process of social reconfiguration stops or is limited, the system cannot claim to be polycentric.

All social actors involved in the production of public goods and common-pool resources should thus be understood as 'public entrepreneurs', as active, knowledgeable, and daring decision-making actors motivated by diverse interests and common social goals to peacefully contest norms and situations, thus constantly re-constituting and reconfiguring a polycentric society. The European Union, an unprecedented, necessary and cherished historic democratic achievement, should strive to achieve the polycentric ideal type.

The ideal type of peaceful contestation in a polycentric theory prioritises self-governance or individual autonomy and resists a hierarchical

[46] ibid.

social construction. It requires one in which seemingly hierarchical relationships keep being turned into horizontal ones. The ideal type of peaceful contestation in a polycentric world leads to a conclusion that unless peaceful contestation satisfies the conditions of the polycentric theory, the very idea of peaceful contestation in liberal political theory is not realised.

10

Access to Justice in Polycentric Governance

LETICIA DÍEZ SÁNCHEZ

Access to justice refers to the ability of individuals to defend their interests before courts. It comprises formal access rights (*locus standi*) and ability to access justice in a broader sense (economic resources, legal knowledge and motivation to litigate). Ostrom argued that polycentric systems are only sustainable if the laws that have been agreed can be enforced and if there are mechanisms to contest these rules.[1] Access to justice in the EU is a prerequisite to *peaceful contestation*, as courts are one of the mechanisms by which individuals can challenge policies they disagree with.[2] Access to justice in the EU is also essential for *enforcing a shared system of rules.*[3] Since these institutional essentials are already discussed in other parts of this Volume,[4] the present chapter will focus on the function of courts as mechanisms for the management of social conflicts in the EU – both through peaceful contestation and enforcement – and the extent to which individuals have access to these mechanisms.

Access to justice is a prerequisite of polycentric functioning as it reinforces self-governance and allows for constructive and sustainable disagreement within the community. Drawing on Hobbes and Tocqueville, Ostrom sought to explore innovative forms of governance that expanded the ability of individuals to pursue the life they choose for themselves.[5] Claims before courts allow individuals to oppose decisions that violate their interests, an

[1] P. D. Aligica and V. Tarko, 'From Polanyi to Ostrom, and Beyond', *Governance: An International Journal of Policy, Administration, and Institutions* 25 (2) (2012), 237, 245.

[2] A. T. Turk, 'Law as a Weapon in Social Conflict', *Social Problems* 23 (3) (1976), 277. For a more detailed account of peaceful contestation, see, in this Volume, Chapter 9 by D. Kukovec.

[3] See, in this Volume, Chapter 6 by A. Bobić.

[4] See notably, in this Volume, Chapters 1 and 2 by J. van Zeben, and Chapter 9 by D. Kukovec.

[5] See V. Ostrom, *The Meaning of American Federalism: Constituting a Self-Governing Society* (ICS Press, 1991); V. Ostrom, *The Meaning of Democracy and the Vulnerability of Democracies: A Response to Tocqueville's Challenge* (University of Michigan Press, 1997).

aspect particularly important when the claimants are members of collectives that were not taken into account during the policy-making process.[6] At the same time, courts can help channel conflicts that could otherwise spiral out of control,[7] as ordered mechanisms for the acknowledgement and settlement of conflicts prevent disagreements from escalating and threatening the very existence of the polity. For courts to perform these functions, access to justice must be inclusive. All actors that are affected by the decisions adopted in their respective decision centres must hold a chance to challenge these decisions before courts.

This chapter explores the role of access to justice in the EU and the ways in which EU governance increases the opportunities to seek judicial redress. At the same time, it highlights the challenges and limitations to access to justice that polycentric governance creates. A central claim is that accessing the EU judicial system is not only a matter of standing, but also of a wider ability to litigate as well as of ensuring that the interests of individuals that cannot litigate for themselves are defended. By showing litigation patterns in different EU policies, the chapter illustrates that inequalities in access to justice exist between and within social groups, as well as between the interests that privileged applicants defend before the courts. These inequalities highlight inevitable tensions. Polycentric structures increase the self-governance of some individuals but without access to justice, they can also hinder access to courts by marginalised and non-organised groups. In looking for solutions, a choice is to be made between re-enforcing the litigation capabilities of individuals or re-enforcing the tutelage of privileged applicants and public interest groups over under-represented groups.

I Access to Justice in Polycentric Systems

Political systems are founded on common goals and values, but there will always be ineluctable disagreements that give rise to conflicts. Of the many ways in which the system can accommodate conflict, courts have been given an ever-expanding role.[8] The centrality of courts in dealing

[6] See also V. Ostrom, 'Polycentricity (Part I)', in M. D. McGinnis, *Polycentricity and Local Public Economies: Readings from the Workshop in Political Theory and Political Analysis* (The University of Michigan Press, 2002), 60.

[7] V. Aubert, 'Courts and Conflict Resolution', *The Journal of Conflict Resolution* 11 (1) (1967), 40; A. Sarat, 'Courts and Conflict Resolution: Problems in the Mobilization of Adjudication', *The American Political Science Review* 69 (4) (1975), 1201.

[8] R. Hirschl, 'The Judicialization of Politics', in G. A. Caldeira, R. D. Kelemen, and K. E. Whittington (eds.), *The Oxford Handbook of Law and Politics* (Oxford University Press, 2008).

with matters of public policy is particularly prominent in the EU. The European Union comprises such vast constituency that preferences will inevitably differ.[9] However, the EU does not always manage conflicts well during legislative and political processes.[10] The regulatory apparatus of the EU, highly fragmented both vertically (between EU and Member States) and horizontally (between institutions at the EU level), makes it difficult to negotiate and adopt solutions at the policy-making level. Decisions on core moral and political controversies ranging from the effect of EU law to the patentability of human cells have therefore often been moved to the Court of Justice of the EU (CJEU).[11] As a result, the use and abuse of courts has taken a prominent role in the research agenda of EU legal studies.[12]

A Expanded and Restricted Access to Justice

Access to justice refers to individuals who seek access to the judicial system in order to defend their interests.[13] In the EU, traditional approaches to access to justice focus on the *formal* requirements by which public entities (national governments, institutions, regions) and individuals (companies, organisations or citizens) can access the CJEU. Article 263(2) TFEU states that Member States, the European Parliament, the Council and the Commission can always bring action before the CJEU (they are 'privileged applicants'). Pursuant to Article 263(3), the European Central Bank and the European Committee of the Regions have standing only to defend their own prerogatives (they are

[9] This is perhaps a diplomatic way to describe the many conflicts embedded in the governance of the EU. The level of integration that should be achieved, the clashes between different levels of government or the difficulties stemming from partial regulation among different decision centres are some of the conflicts that the EU legal system generates, see D. Chalmers 'The Conflicts of EU Law and the Conflicts in EU Law', *European Law Journal* 18 (5) (2012), 607, 615–6.

[10] M. Dani, 'Rehabilitating Social Conflicts in European Public Law', *European Law Journal* 18(5) (2012), 621, 622–3.

[11] F. de Witte, 'Sex, Drugs & EU Law: The Recognition of Moral and Ethical Diversity in EU law', *Common Market Law Review* 50 (6) (2013), 1545.

[12] A.-M. Slaughter, A. Stone Sweet, and J. H. H. Weiler (eds.), *European Court and National Courts: Doctrine and Jurisprudence. Legal Change in Its Social Context* (Hart Publishing, 1998). M. Claes, *The National Courts' Mandate in the European Constitution* (Hart Publishing, 2006); K. J. Alter, *Establishing the Supremacy of European Law. The Making of an International Rule of Law in Europe* (Oxford University Press, 2003).

[13] R. A. Macdonald, 'Access to Civil Justice', in P. Cane and H. M. Kritzer (eds.), *Oxford Handbook of Empirical Legal Research* (Oxford University Press, 2010).

'quasi-privileged applicants'). The remaining individuals (natural or legal persons, e.g. an individual citizen, a company or a local entity) have very limited standing according to Article 263(4). They can only bring an action against EU legislative acts if they have direct and individual concern,[14] and against regulatory acts[15] if they have individual concern.

The restrictive conditions of access for non-privileged individuals has been a reason for criticism of the EU judicial system.[16] The Court has repeatedly avoided an expansive interpretation of *locus standi* for individual applicants.[17] As a result, there is 'privileged' and 'non-privileged' access to justice: to the former category belong the Member States and EU institutions; to the latter category all the remaining subjects of EU law. Advocates of this restrictive system claim that the limited direct access to the CJEU is compensated by the expansive scope of the preliminary ruling procedure.[18] The preliminary ruling request foreseen in Article 267 TFEU allows national courts to ask the CJEU about the right interpretation of EU law provisions that are relevant for the case they have at hand. Thanks to these referrals some landmark decisions have been issued, including *Van Gend en Loos, Costa* and *Cassis de Dijon.*[19] The preliminary ruling procedure can also be used to ask if secondary provisions of EU law violate the Treaties – this 'indirect' action of annulment has allowed for the review of EU law in cases like *Schrems.*[20]

14 Case 25/62 *Plaumann* & *Co* v. *Commission* [1963] ECR 95.

15 The General Court defined them as 'all acts of general application apart from legislative acts' in Case T-18/10 *Inuit Tapiriit Kanatami* [2011] ECR II-5599, para. 56. On appeal, the Court of Justice confirmed this interpretation in Case C-583/11 P *Inuit Tapiriit Kanatami* [2013], para. 61.

16 A. Arnull, 'Private Applicants and the Action for Annulment under Article 173 of the EC Treaty', *Common Market Law Review* 32 (1) (1995), 7; R. Barents, 'The Court of Justice after the Treaty of Lisbon', *Common Market Law Review* 47 (3) (2010), 709, 7246; P. Van Malleghem and N. Baeten, 'Before the Law Stands a Gatekeeper – Or, What Is a "Regulatory Act" in Article 263(4) TFEU? *Inuit Tapiriit Kanatami*', *Common Market Law Review* 51 (2014), 1216; S. Peers and M. Costa 'Court of Justice of the European Union (General Chamber), Judicial review of EU Acts after the Treaty of Lisbon; Order of 6 September 2011, Case T-18/10 *Inuit Tapiriit Kanatami and Others* v. *Commission* & Judgment of 25 October 2011, Case T-262/10 *Microban* v. *Commission*' *European Constitutional Law Review* 8 (1) (2012), 82.

17 Most famously in C-25/62 *Plaumann* (n. 14).

18 Case C-50/00 P *Union de Pequeños Agricultores* v. *Council* [2002] ECR I-6677, para. 40; Case C-491/01 *British American Tobacco (Investments) and Imperial Tobacco* [2002] ECR I-11453, para. 39. See also, A. Arnull, 'Private Applicants and the Action for Annulment under Article 173 of the EC Treaty', *Common Market Law Review* 32 (1) (1995), 40.

19 Case 26/62 *Van Gend en Loos* [1963] ECR, Case 6/64 *Costa* v. *Enel* [1964] ECR 585, Case C-120/78 *Cassis de Dijon* [1979] ECR 649.

20 C-362/14 *Schrems* [2015] ECLI:EU:C:2015:650.

However, the broad scope of the preliminary ruling request is not always a good alternative to direct access to the CJEU. This procedure depends on domestic rules of standing which, as we shall see below, are not equal in all Member States.

The functioning of the preliminary ruling requests highlights the fact that the daily application of EU law takes place both before EU courts (the European Court of Justice (ECJ) and the General Court) as well as domestic courts. The full justiciability of EU law can only be achieved through the *collaboration* of different units. Domestic courts are required to set aside a domestic provision if it clashes with an EU law obligation. In fact, and unlike other regimes of international law, the EU legal system generates rights for individuals even if their respective Member States have not translated these provisions into domestic legislation.[21] Domestic courts are also allowed (sometimes compelled) to refer a case to the CJEU if the proper interpretation of EU law is not clear.[22] The CJEU, in turn, has the monopoly of interpreting and invalidating EU legislation.[23] On the other hand, courts within the EU also engage in *competition* with each other. Some constitutional courts have opposed the unconditional allegiance to the primacy of EU law with the justification that their own domestic legal systems offer better protection to the citizens. The dispute between the German Constitutional Court and the ECJ known as *Solange I*,[24] in which the German Court threatened to set EU law aside if it did not ensure an effective protection of fundamental rights, resulted in the ECJ recognising the existence of fundamental rights as a general principle of EU law. This was positive for the individual because new avenues for challenging national and EU policies opened up. Karen J Alter has also claimed that competition between domestic courts advanced legal integration in the EU.[25] Many landmark referrals originated in lower courts that saw in EU law the chance to circumvent the restrictive jurisprudence of higher courts and to push for their preferred policy outcome. In doing so, lower courts allowed the ECJ to expand its

[21] Famously, Case 26/62. In addition, the failure to transpose an EU directive into national law triggers the liability of the national government pursuant Case C-6/90 *Francovich* [1991] ECR I-5357.

[22] Case 283/81 *CILFIT* [1982] ECR 3415.

[23] Case 314/85 *Foto-Frost* [1987] ECR 4199 para. 17.

[24] C-11/70 *Internationale Handelsgesellschaft* [1970] ECR 1125.

[25] K. J. Alter, 'The European Court's Political Power', *West European Politics* 19 (3) (1996), 458, 466.

jurisdiction and jurisprudence, making the direct effect of EU law a reality.

These parallel dynamics of competition and collaboration can be seen as expanding access to justice. The expansion of rights in primary and secondary legislation, the direct applicability of EU law and the preliminary ruling procedure have transformed citizens from actors with little leverage into 'political players capable of directly influencing national policy'.[26] For instance, equality interest groups have used EU law to change British legislation by means of strategic litigation.[27] Once the Court declared British legislation to be discriminatory, government and private companies had no choice but to change their gender policies. Similar litigation strategies have taken place in other areas such as competition policy, securities regulation and disability discrimination.[28] Increased access to justice has given consumers, shareholders, victims of discrimination and firms the opportunity to re-regulate domestic legislation through 'adversarial legalism'.[29]

The European Commission has enacted various measures to improve access to justice in order to harness the potential of individuals as enforcers of the EU legal system.[30] There are caveats to this however. Domestic legal systems are still formally independent and, as such, each Member State retains the right to set their own procedural rules.[31] The consequence is that individuals do not enjoy an equal chance of invoking EU law provisions before their own domestic courts, even though all of them might be equally affected by an EU policy. This can happen, first, because Member States have very different systems of adjudication. The bodies that take on 'judicial duties' are not always what we understand as standard courts – they include competition

[26] K. J. Alter and J. Vargas, 'Explaining Variation in the Use of European Litigation Strategies – European Community Law and British Gender Equality Policy', *Comparative Political Studies* 33 (4) (2000), 452, 453.

[27] ibid.

[28] R. D. Kelemen, *Eurolegalism – The Transformation of Law and Regulation in the European Union* (Harvard University Press, 2011).

[29] R. D. Kelemen, 'Suing for Europe – Adversarial Legalism and European Governance', *Comparative Political Studies* 39 (1) (2006), 101, 121.

[30] Following the Council Regulation concerning judicial cooperation in civil matters, the Commission proposed an Access to Justice Directive that was ultimately adopted in 2003. More recently, the Commission has proposed another Directive as regards better enforcement and modernisation of EU consumer protection rules (11 April 2018).

[31] See R. A. Kagan, 'Should Europe Worry about Adversarial Legalism', *Oxford Journal of Legal Studies* 17 (1997), 165, 17983.

authorities,[32] patent bodies,[33] and other ad hoc administrative entities.[34] The CJEU has progressively defined the criteria under which these bodies can be considered as courts and make a referral.[35] Yet many entities that apply EU law in their resolution of disputes have been left out, encumbering the possibility of individual litigants to reach the CJEU.[36]

Another aspect that remains within the discretion of national legislatures are standing rules. As the European Parliament documents, *locus standi* before administrative courts presents enormous differences across countries.[37] The case of regions can serve as an extreme example:[38] when the Commission considers that a project funded through the cohesion funds is not compliant with the conditions of award, financial corrections are imposed. The Court has ruled that regions do not have standing to challenge financial corrections: since the Commission transfers the funding to the Member State and it is for the Member State to deal with the operators, beneficiary regions do not have a 'direct' concern.[39] One could argue that regions could instead bring actions against the Member State's administrative decision *before a domestic court*. Alas, the constitutional setting of some Member States like Italy precludes a region from bringing actions against the central government. The result is that recipients of regional funds (mostly the poorest regions in the EU) do not have access to justice. And this, in turn, reinforces the imbalances in the policy-making process in which richer regions manage to influence EU policies to a greater extent than poor ones.[40]

Lastly, even assuming it would be formally possible for all individuals to defend their interests before national courts, the opportunities brought

32 C-53/03 *Syfait* v. *Glaxo* [2005] ECR I-4609.

33 C-246/05 *Häupl* [2007] ECR I-4673.

34 Like the courts adjudicating on surnames of C-96/04 *Standesamt* [2006] ECR I-3561.

35 Case 246/80 *Broeckmeulen* [1981] ECR 2311.

36 G. Bebr, 'Arbitration Tribunals and Article 177 of the EEC Treaty', *Common Market Law Review* 22 (1985), 489.

37 www.europarl.europa.eu/RegData/etudes/etudes/join/2012/462478/IPOL-JURI_ET(2012)462478_EN.pdf accessed 18 October 2018 at 65.

38 While the ideal objective of cohesion policy would be to assist the worst-off regions, in practice part of these funds go towards wealthier areas. The reasons stem from a logic of 'everybody gets something' (the only way to get richer Member States to fund cohesion policy is to make them see that they also benefit from it) and the fact that richer regions from decentralised countries have got a more sophisticated administrative apparatus and effective lobbying techniques than their poorer counterparts.

39 C-417/04 P *Regione Siciliana I* [2006] ECR I-3881 and C-15/06 P *Regione Siciliana II* [2007] ECR I-2591.

40 L. Hooghe, 'Subnational Mobilisation in the European Union', *West European Politics* 18 (3) (1995), 192.

about by the EU legal system seem de facto restricted to a certain category of citizens. Individuals whose disputes have a cross-border element are more likely to invoke an EU law provision: mobile citizens and transnational companies can use the Treaty freedoms to defend their interests, while non-mobile Europeans seldom can.[41] Moreover, the theoretical capability to access courts does not guarantee de facto access to justice. The enforcement of the law requires 'an informed and vigilant citizenry'.[42] The adoption of decisions in polycentric systems of governance follows complex patterns that not everyone is able to understand and exploit. Only the well-informed and well-resourced individual (worker, consumer, shareholder) will have the time, the resources and the knowledge to litigate and to invoke an EU law provision that can help their cause.[43]

**

Vincent Ostrom reflected on the social and cultural conditions needed for effective democratic governance.[44] Problems of institutional weaknesses, he defended, could not be corrected simply by new institutions – knowledge, skills and trust were also essential elements to become self-governing.[45] These considerations are also relevant for courts, since sociological and economic circumstances constitute obstacles to justice in their own right. Recent 'waves' of access to justice scholarship have progressively mapped barriers to access.[46] They include judicial fees,

41 The application of the market freedoms to 'purely internal situations' has expanded in the past years, especially in the aftermath of the creation of EU citizenship. This expansion nonetheless seems restricted to claims involving double nationality (C-148/02 *Garcia Avello*) and family reunifications (famously, C-34/09 *Ruiz Zambrano*). See N. Nic Shuibhne, 'Free Movement of Persons and the Wholly Internal Rule: Time to Move On?,' *Common Market Law Review* 39 (4) (2002), 731; A. Lansbergen and N. Miller, 'Court of Justice of the European Union European Citizenship Rights in Internal Situations: An Ambiguous Revolution?', *European Constitutional Law Review* 7 (2) (2011), 287.

42 M. D. McGinnis, 'Legal Pluralism, Polycentricity, and Faith-Based Organizations in Global Governance', in M. Sproule-Jones, B. Allen, and F. Sabetti (eds.), *The Struggle to Constitute and Sustain Productive Orders* (Lexington Books, 2008), 45, 51.

43 See also, in this Volume, Chapter 12 by S. Garben.

44 V. Ostrom, *The Meaning of Democracy and the Vulnerability of Democracies: A Response to Tocqueville's Challenge* (University of Michigan Press, 1997), 89–90, 113–114.

45 ibid., 291.

46 M. Cappelletti and B. Garth, 'Access to Justice: The Worldwide Movement to Make Rights Effective: A General Report', *Buffalo Law Review* 27 (1978), 181; J. Bass, F. Zemans, and W. Bogart (eds.), *Access to Justice for a New Century: The Way Forward* (Law Society of Upper Canada, 2005).

delays and complexity,[47] procedures that favour certain types of claims,[48] and, of course, economic disadvantage.[49] Marc Galanter's seminal work showed that wealthier organisations (big law firms, transnational companies) exploit courts to a greater extent than the have-nots.[50]

Besides money, knowledge is a key resource. People need to know that an event goes against their interests and that the legal system is potentially on their side. Non-organised interests (consumers, taxpayers) are generally in a worse-off position than companies in calculating the costs of certain policies and mobilising against them.[51] The act of claiming before courts is, as a result, an exercise that big law firms, Member States with dedicated legal services, transnational companies, sophisticated and wealthy individuals dominate to a much larger extent than the illiterate and the have-nots. There are reasons to believe that polycentric systems increase inequalities in legal mobilisation, as the complexity of multiple decision-making centres makes it yet more difficult for the average person to understand the opportunities that the system brings and the legal avenues to enforce them.

Several strategies emerged to compensate for unequal legal mobilisation. Firstly, there is public interest litigation in which not-for-profit entities defend marginalised sectors of society, often with the overarching goal of achieving policy changes. The phenomenon of public interest law has been prominent in the United States and particularly useful in defending the interests of racial minorities and the very poor.[52] Given the limited standing for non-privileged applicants before the European Courts, the possibilities for public interest litigation before the CJEU are significantly reduced.[53] However, many associations have pursued public interest cases before domestic courts and requested preliminary references to the ECJ, knowing that EU law could help in pursuing their policy objectives. The landmark case *Defrenne* on gender discrimination was

[47] A. Hutchinson (ed.), *Access to Civil Justice* (Carswell, 1990).

[48] D. Black, *Sociological Justice* (Oxford University Press, 1989).

[49] R. A. Macdonald, Access to Civil Justice (n. 13), 514.

[50] M. Galanter, 'Why the "Haves" Come Out Ahead: Speculations on the Limits of Legal Change', *Law & Society Review* 9 (1) (1974), 95.

[51] Famously, M. Olson, *The Logic of Collective Action: Public Goods and the Theory of Groups* (Harvard University Press, 1971).

[52] A. Chayes, 'The Role of the Judge in Public Law Litigation', *Harvard Law Review* 89 (7) (1976), 1281; C. F. Sabel and W. H. Simon, 'Destabilization Rights: How Public Law Litigation Succeeds', *Harvard Law Review* 117 (4) (2004), 1015.

[53] O. de Schutter, 'Public Interest Litigation before the European Court of Justice', *Maastricht Journal of European and Comparative Law* 13 (1) (2006), 9.

possible thanks to a Belgian lawyer who actively sought a woman employed in the airline sector to challenge the airlines' discriminatory retirement policies.[54] More recently, associations for the protection of immigrant's rights have taken over the so-called 'headscarf cases' and given legal support to women dismissed for wearing the headscarf in their workplace.[55] From this perspective, access to justice is enhanced when the EU or the Member States promote the existence of associations for the judicial defence of under-represented interests. Directive 93/13, for example, established the creation of consumer associations at the domestic level with the power to bring actions against practices that breach the Directive.[56]

Secondly, the submission of observations during an ongoing procedure allows for non-party actors to give their views, ideally influencing the outcome.[57] The Statute of the Court grants a right to intervene to 'any other person establishing an interest in the result of any case submitted to the Court'.[58] Thanks to this provision, associations representing specific interest groups can submit observations if the decision could potentially affect the collectives they represent.[59] In *X* v. *Commission*,[60] the International Federation of Human Rights Leagues was allowed to intervene in a case involving the compatibility of the medical examinations undergone by EU civil servants with the right to privacy.[61] However, only EU institutions and Member States can submit their observations during a preliminary reference request: in cases between Member States, in cases between EU institutions or in cases between Member States and institutions.[62] This is not very inclusive, since intervention is granted to the same actors that already enjoy privileged standing before the Court. Expanding the scope of the submissions would be relatively costless

[54] M. Wolferen, 'The Limits to the CJEU's Interpretation of Locus Standi, a Theoretical Framework', *Journal of Contemporary European Research* 12 (4) (2016), 917.

[55] C-157/15 *Achbita* [2017].

[56] Article 7(2) of the Directive 93/13/EEC of 5 April 1993 on unfair terms in consumer contracts, OJ L 95.

[57] In fact, empirical research points out that submissions of Member State have got an impact in Court's decisions, see C. Carubba, M. Gabel, and C. Hankla, 'Judicial Behavior under Political Constraints: Evidence from the European Court of Justice', *American Political Science Review* 102 (4) (2008), 435.

[58] Article 40.

[59] O. De Schutter, 'Public Interest Litigation before the European Court of Justice', *Maastricht Journal of European and Comparative Law* 13 (1) (2006), 9, 31.

[60] Case C-404/92 P *X* v. *Commission* [1994] ECR I-4737.

[61] See O. De Shutter (n. 59).

[62] Article 40(2) of the Statute.

compared to the benefits of having a plurality of views taken into account in the development of the case law. Another possible solution would be allowing citizens to request the submission of observations from the government, a policy only in force in the UK at the moment.[63]

Lastly, diffuse interests represented among groups such as consumers and taxpayers often lack standing before any Court – they are not sufficiently affected by a rule or practice to litigate against it, be it at the national or at the EU level, and most legal systems do not foresee a broad *actio popularis*. In these cases, public institutions become essential not only because they are privileged applicants, but also because as 'repeat players' they have knowledge and means that many individuals and not-for-profit organisations lack.[64] This is an aspect often forgotten and worth remarking, since the legal services of the Commission and Member States should represent their broad constituencies in their litigation strategies; ideally compensating those that do not enjoy access by themselves (such as future generations affected by current pollution or future university students who cannot vote yet).

B Challenges to Courts as Conflict Mediators

The previous Section reflected on the core functions that courts perform in polycentric systems and the importance of understanding who, and under what conditions, can access justice. However, despite their importance and centrality, courts remain limited as arenas for conflict resolution in several ways.

In the first place, conflicts with highly sensitive stakes can be settled but are rarely resolved.[65] The losing party is likely to contest the decision, especially if these decisions are imposed by bodies whose expertise on complex matters or understanding of morally sensitive issues is limited, or perceived to be limited by (one of) the parties.[66] The rich body of

63 M. Malecki, 'Do ECJ Judges all Speak with the Same Voice? Evidence of Divergent Preferences from the Judgments of Chambers', *Journal of European Public Policy* 19 (1) (2012), 59, 612.

64 See M. Galanter (n. 50).

65 B. de Jouvenel, *The Pure Theory of Politics* (Cambridge University Press 1963), 206.

66 A. T. Turk. 'Law as a Weapon in Social Conflict', *Social Problems* 23 (3) (1976), 276, 2856. The impartiality of a third party can be an asset when looking for conflict resolution. However, if the Court seems oblivious to aspects that are of core concern to one or some of the parties (such as the importance of national welfare state institutions vis-à-vis freedom of movement), the parties might precisely understand that the Court is biased (too internal-market oriented, or averse to national welfare traditions). As Turk claims,

scholarship on the role courts adopt vis-à-vis politically sensitive matters falls outwith the scope of this chapter.[67] It suffices to say that courts should not be overly relied on, for many social conflicts are better discussed and more inclusively resolved in the realm of politics.[68] For instance, the conditions of employment of posted workers were not sufficiently clarified in the Posted Workers Directive.[69] When the Court had to resolve these matters in *Viking* and *Laval*, public outrage ensued because the market freedoms had been given priority over social rights.[70] The strong reactions resulted in the legislature having to modify the Posted Workers Directive and thus indirectly limiting the effect of the Court's judgment.[71] As highlighted by Aligica and Tarko, polycentric non-juridical processes can sometimes offer better solutions than courts.[72]

Secondly, the multiplicity of decision centres in polycentric systems means that it can be difficult to assign responsibility for a particular decision. This can also make it difficult to know in which judicial forum to challenge the measure. This is part of the so-called 'problem of many hands' of complex organisations, where citizens do not know the agencies that are responsible for the adoption of relevant decisions and thus cannot hold them accountable.[73] The judicial references on Euro-crisis measures from Portuguese courts serve to illustrate this point. The Eurozone crisis entailed tight macroeconomic governance across countries with excessive levels of debt. Austerity measures ensued, many of them suspicious of violating fundamental rights. Preliminary references from national courts reached the ECJ, questioning the legality of the Memoranda of Understanding (MoU) in the light of the Charter of Fundamental

'[t]he terminology and style of public legal conflict may emphasize instead of correcting the affective and cognitive bias associated with conflict'.

67 N. Komesar, *Imperfect Alternatives: Choosing Institutions in Law, Economics and Public Policy* (University of Chicago Press, 1994).

68 T. Eckhoff, 'The Mediator, the Judge and the Administrator in Conflict-Resolution', *Acta Sociologica* 10 (1–2) (1967), 147, 165.

69 P. Syrpis and T. Novitz, 'Economic and Social Rights in Conflict: Political and Judicial Approaches to Their Reconciliation', *European Law Review* 33 (3) (2008), 411, 416.

70 C-438/05 *Viking* [2007] ECR I-10779 and C-341/05 *Laval* [2007] ECR I-11767.

71 Revised Posted Workers Directive, approved by the Council on 21 June 2018.

72 P. D. Aligica and V. Tarko, 'Polycentricity: From Polanyi to Ostrom and Beyond', *Governance: An International Journal of Policy, Administration, and Institutions* 25 (2) (2012), 237, 240.

73 M. Bovens, *The Quest for Responsibility: Accountability and Citizenship in Complex Organisations* (Cambridge University Press, 1998), 46.

Rights.[74] The Court, however, declared all these references inadmissible because the national legislation was not implementing EU law. At this point it was unclear if the case had failed because the applicants did not establish a sufficient link with EU law or because the MoU were not considered EU law at all.[75] In the recent *Florescu* decision, the Court finally agreed to examine domestic austerity measures under the Charter of Fundamental Rights, stating that the purpose of the measures was to implement the MoU, 'which is part of EU law'.[76] Yet it remains unclear whether the ECJ can rule on the validity of the MoU itself,[77] and if the status of an MoU as part of the EU legal system varies if concluded for balance of payments assistance as opposed to, say, in the framework of European Stability Mechanism or European Financial Stability Facility assistance (since these have an inter-governmental character).[78]

Thirdly, competitive dynamics are not always justice-enhancing. In the quest to maximise their own power, courts carefully adjust their behaviour to the context in which the decision is pronounced and the reactions it will generate on other institutions. This long-term strategy often appears to be at the expense of individuals involved in the case. The CJEU has sought the acceptance of the EU legal system by issuing strong pronouncements often followed, however, by limited practical application to the case at hand.[79] For example, despite boldly creating the primacy of EU law, the Court declared that the Italian privatisation of ENEL did not breach the Treaty, causing Flaminio Costa to lose his case.[80] Defrenne won her case on gender discrimination, but the Court limited the effects of the decision to those workers that had instituted legal proceedings before the date of the judgment.[81]*Köbler* offers an extreme illustration of

[74] Case C-264/12 *Fidelidade Mundial* [2014]; C-665/13 *Via Directa* [2014]; C-566/13 *Assis dos Santos*.

[75] M. Markakis and P. Dermine, 'Bailouts, the Legal Status of Memoranda of Understanding, and the Scope of Application of the EU Charter: Florescu', *Common Market Law Review* 55 (2) (2018), 643, 6501.

[76] C-258/14 *Florescu and others* [2017].

[77] M. Markakis and P. Dermine (n. 75), 656.

[78] ibid., 657. See also A. Poulou, 'Financial Assistance Conditionality and Human Rights Protection: What Is the Role of the EU Charter of Fundamental Rights', *Common Market Law Review* 54 (2017), 991.

[79] T. C. Hartley, *The Foundations of European Union Law* (Oxford University Press, 2014), 75.

[80] Case 6/64 *Costa* v. *Enel* [1964] ECR 585.

[81] Case 43/75 *Defrenne* v. *Sabena* [1976] ECR 455.

unproductive conflict.[82] An Austrian professor who had worked abroad did not have his service recognised to the same extent as professors who developed their careers at Austrian universities. The Austrian administrative court asked the ECJ if this constituted discrimination, but decided shortly thereafter that existing case law on discrimination was not applicable and withdrew the reference request. Mr Köbler then requested damages for an infringement of EU law. The domestic court again made a reference to the ECJ asking whether the behaviour of the administrative court constituted a breach of EU law. The ECJ answered that it did, but it diplomatically added that the violation was not serious enough to trigger the award of damages under the *Francovich* doctrine. As a result, the feud between courts was of little help to Mr. Köbler, who never received a remedy.

Lastly, the multiplicity of communities and decision centres of a polycentric system makes it difficult for courts to be perceived as legitimate in every community. A court whose decisions are not seen as legitimate cannot claim to be the institution in charge of managing conflicts. In fact, the decisions of an illegitimate court risk making conflict more acute – remember, for instance, the famous 'Stop the European Court of Justice!' written by Herzog and Gerken in the aftermath of *Mangold*.[83] Extremely interesting from a polycentric point of view are the effects of judicial decisions issued by domestic courts on other Member States. The German Constitutional Court refused to acquiesce to the Spanish request for extradition of a man suspected of collaboration with al- Qaida,[84] and a court in Schleswig Holstein refused to extradite the Catalan leader Puigdemont, requested by the Spanish Supreme Court under the charges of rebellion. Spanish citizens are thus confronted with judicial decisions affecting sensitive matters, issued by courts from other legal systems. This creates tensions between the different communities involved, ultimately challenging the view of courts as conflicts mediators in a polycentric system.

**

82 Case C-224/01 *Köbler* [2003] ECR I-10239.

83 R. Herzog and L. Gerken, 'Stop the European Court of Justice', EUObserver, 10 Sep 2008, available at https://euobserver.com/opinion/26714.

84 See J. Komárek, 'European Constitutionalism and the European Arrest Warrant: In Search of the Limits of Contrapunctual Principles', *Common Market Law Review* 44 (1) (2007), 9.

The EU legal system has progressively expanded the rights of individuals, and the direct effect of EU law means that these rights can be invoked before national courts. Dynamics of collaboration between judicial centres (especially the preliminary ruling procedure) as well as competition (between national constitutional courts and the CJEU, or between domestic courts) have re-enforced these dynamics of expanding rights. As a result, individuals have additional opportunities to challenge national decisions that hinder their interests as well as having the unique opportunity to subject the decisions of a supranational legislature to judicial review.

The expansion of access to justice is not without caveats, however. Rules of standing distinguish between privileged and non-privileged applicants, meaning that not everyone can access the CJEU directly. Since domestic judicial systems remain autonomous, the chances to reach the CJEU via the preliminary ruling procedure are also different across Member States. In addition, material and cognitive resources needed to claim an EU law right mean that only specific types of individuals (the 'haves' and the knowledgeable) benefit from access to justice.

Courts may not be the best forum to decide on all conflicts that attain to the community, but they remain important mechanisms for individuals to self-govern. The next Section explores how different individuals exploit the EU courts in different policies, showing how this 'unequal access to justice' unfolds in practice.

II Legal Mobilisation at the European Court of Justice

The previous Section showed unequal formal access to justice between privileged and non-privileged applicants, as well as a common lack of standing for certain groups of society or the (economic, cognitive) resources to defend their interests in court. This section offers an empirical illustration of these dynamics. Other works have shown litigation dynamics in securities policy, competition and non-discrimination.[85] This Section focusses on redistributive policies within the EU – including the Common Agricultural Policy (CAP), the European Social Fund (ESF) and the European Regional Development Fund (ERDF) and tax policy – that aim to balance the interests of organised collectives (companies,

[85] R. D. Kelemen, *Eurolegalism* (n. 28); K. J. Alter (n. 25).

Member States) with other, generally non-organised collectives (taxpayers, consumers).

A The Common Agricultural Policy

The Common Agricultural Policy (CAP) sparked most litigation before the CJEU. The CAP dates back to the early years of the European Communities and was established with the twofold aim of increasing food production and improving the living conditions of the farming community (food security and helping rural areas in transiting towards an industrialised economy were key concerns in post-war Europe). The main instruments of CAP were food quotas (which guaranteed a minimum price per food item) and subsidies. The decision as to what products were subsidised was a cause of conflict between Member States, since each of them had different climate and thus specialised in different produce. Besides, high food prices mean that consumers were the ones bearing the cost of assistance to farmers. Since the assistance was proportional to the productivity of the farming unit, big (transnational) agricultural holdings captured a lot of the budget of the CAP. It is no surprise that the CAP became such a conflicting policy, and in fact most of the decisions of the Court developing the 'general principles of EU law' were given in agricultural cases.

When exploring the origin of these cases, an unequal map becomes apparent. It is often assumed that the CAP was designed to benefit the farmers from Italy, France and later Spain; yet more than half of all the preliminary ruling requests originate in Germany (even before the unification of the country).

Private actors (mostly companies and associations) have lodged more direct actions before the CJEU than Member States themselves, despite the fact that, as mentioned above, it is difficult for non-privileged applicants to be granted standing. There is also clear inequality between sectors: dairy and cereal make up most of the cases, and the sugar industry has litigated as much as all other producers of fruits and vegetables together.

One might think that the high number of direct actions lodged by private actors, or individuals, comes from unhappy farmers (imagine here the bucolic image of the rural community with family farming units). But actually most cases stem from sectors dominated by en masse agricultural producers. In fact, the cases where the Court declared for the first time that fundamental rights are part of general principles of EU law were brought by import and export companies from Germany

Table 10.1 *Origin of Preliminary Ruling Procedure by Member State in the CAP*

Preliminary Ruling from	*N*
Germany	403
Italy	139
Netherlands	118
France	107
United Kingdom	52
Belgium	43
Austria	15
Ireland	15
Denmark	11
Greece	11
Spain	7
Luxembourg	6
Hungary	5
Estonia	4
Sweden	4
Latvia	3
Portugal	3
Czech Republic	2
Cyprus	1
Finland	1
Total	**950**

Table 10.2 *Direct Actions by Member States and Private Actors in the CAP*

	Total	Successful	Unfounded
Direct actions by Member States	312	97	239
Direct actions by Private Actors[86]	357	66[87]	205[88]

86 Includes actions for damages, actions for annulment, actions declared inadmissible and cases where decision unnecessary.

87 40 actions for annulment and 26 actions for damages.

88 72 actions for annulment and 133 actions for damages.

Table 10.3 *Litigation by Sector in the CAP (Selected)*

Sector	*N*
Dairy	201
Cereal	146
Beef Meat	115
Sugar	75
Fruit and Vegetables	70

that were unhappy with the way the CAP curtailed their dealing activities.[89]

Consumers have, for a long time, been the most affected by the functioning of the CAP due to artificially high food prices. Their interests, however, are remarkably absent from the nearly 2,000 cases on agricultural policy. No consumer or consumer organisation has ever opposed any of the numerous measures reducing food market supplies and/or artificially increasing price floors. The reasons probably stem as much from the general lack of knowledge on food law as from the restrictive rules on standing. But – whose interests do Member States defend when they bring a case before the CJEU? Big companies have captured a lot of Member State litigation, although national governments have done a relatively good job in representing small-scale farming activities. From 2005 to 2015, Spain only brought three cases to the CJEU.[90] In two of them, the Spanish government litigated the Community's assistance to olive oil and cotton, both sectors where small-scale producers prevail.

Remarkably, on few occasions have the Member States adopted measures for the protection of consumer interests. The only cases where consumers were at the heart of the controversy came about in the 1970s, in the midst of the inflationary crisis. Member States froze maximum prices for some items, which infuriated domestic producers and generated a wave of preliminary reference requests from Italy, Belgium, France and the Netherlands.[91]

[89] Case 25/70 *Einfuhr* [1970] ECR 1161; Case 11/70 *Internationale Handelsgesellschaft* [1970] ECR 1125; Case 38/70 *Deutsche Tradax* [1971] ECR 145.

[90] C-287/02 *Spain* v. *Commission* [2005] ECR I-5093; C-310/04 *Spain* v. *Council* [2006] ECR I-7285; C-24/11 P *Spain* v. *Commission* [2012].

[91] Case 31/74 *Galli* [1975] ECR 47; Case 60/75 *Russo* [1976] ECR 45; Case 65/75 *Tasca* [1976] ECR 291; Case 88/75 *Sadam* [1976] ECR 323; Case 154/77 *Dechmann* [1978] ECR

Table 10.4 *Litigation by Member States and Private Actors in Cohesion Policy*

	N
Direct actions by Member States	57
Direct actions by private actors	68

The CJEU was permissive towards the measures of national governments and considered that their actions did not infringe the price mechanisms. Other than these cases, consumer litigation has been remarkably absent from the CAP.

B Structural Funds

Cohesion policy is supported through several funds, all of them with the ultimate aim of assisting regions that lag behind in terms of social-economic development. The European Social Fund (ESF) focuses on promoting employment, while the European Regional Development Fund (ERDF) tackles general development of the region. Both the ESF and the ERDF are allocated to specific project applications. However, given the different scopes of the funds, each of them is carried out by different actors. The ESF is mostly devoted to measures combatting unemployment and its recipients are generally private entities performing as training centres. The ERDF is spent on big infrastructure development plans, and therefore regions and/or metropolitan areas generally take part in the application process together with other private actors.

When exploring the litigation patterns in cohesion policy, a remarkable aspect that comes out is that only a handful of actions have been brought by the Commission.[92] The reason is that most cases originate in the Commission's decision to suspend aid, and thus the applicants are the Member States or the beneficiaries affected.

1573; Case 223/78 *Grosoli* [1979] ECR 2621, Joined Cases 16 to 20/79 *Danis* [1979] ECR 3327; Case 5/79 *Buys* [1979] ECR 3203; Case 10/79 *Toffoli* [1979] ECR 3301.

92 Case C-336/13 P *Commission* v. *IPK* [2015]; Case C-84/04 *Commission* v. *Portugal* [2006] ECR I-9843; Case C-32/95 P *Commission* v. *Lisrestal* [1996] ECR I-5373; Case C-143/95 P *Commission* v. *Socurte* [1997] ECR I-00001; Case 101/84 *Commission* v. *Italy* [1985] ECR 2629; Case T-168/10 *Commission* v. *SEMEA* [2012].

Almost half of all cases stem from a direct action from private entities (mostly Portuguese). And while regional development is the key aim of cohesion policy, there are only a few cases prompted by regions themselves,[93] although all of them have been declared inadmissible due to lack of standing.[94] This can be contrasted with very high numbers of direct actions from private entities – if standing rules are so strict when it comes to recipients of structural aid, why do private entities reach the threshold while regions do not? Given the different scope, the application process is slightly different in the ESF and the ERDF (the latter deals with much bigger sums of money, and needs of the intermediation of public actors bearing the primary financial burden). The restrictiveness of the Court in appreciating the existence of 'direct concern' when it comes to managing the funds has meant that regions by definition never qualify, while the companies that receive the ESF do even if the differences in managing both funds are subtle. This means that regions' interests are only defended as long as Member States are willing to litigate for them. In Germany, there are procedures by which the *Länder* can compel the federal government to bring a case to the CJEU – but this is not a possibility foreseen in other Member States, like Spain.

C Tax Policy

There has been little tax harmonisation in direct tax matters at the EU level, among other reasons because low-tax jurisdictions were keen to exploit their lower tax systems to attract economic activity. Lack of harmonisation means a great degree of diversity of tax base and rates across Member States. This leads to situations in which a mobile worker or a multinational company with a complex corporate structure might well have to pay taxes twice (double taxation) if all the countries involved claim their respective taxing powers. Often, domestic tax schemes are suspected of breaching freedom of movement and brought to the Court.

EU tax lawyers conventionally divide the case law on direct taxes between individual and corporate tax. Another interesting classification comes, however, when we divide the cases between those that pertain to capital interests and those that do not. Capital here includes corporate tax, individual capital gains (shares, royalties, interests . . .) and taxes on property (as well as their correlated tax credits). Cases that do not relate

[93] Case C-417/04 P *Regione Siciliana* v. *Commission* [2006] ECR I-3881 and Case C-15/06 P *Regione Siciliana* v. *Commission* [2007] I-2591.

[94] ibid.

Table 10.5 *Litigation by Issue in Tax Policy*

Non-capital tax	50	
Capital tax	220	
Other tax	9	
	279	**Total**

to capital tax are those on taxation of (cross-border) workers as well as personal deductions (marriage benefits, child credit, etc.). An overwhelming majority of all direct tax cases are capital-related.

One might think that capital is what free movement is about: multinational companies paying taxes across borders,[95] shareholders moving to another Member State,[96] and people paying taxes for real property they own in another country.[97] However, a significant number of mobile citizens count only on their wages to sustain their living. These individuals, some of which move across borders under precarious conditions, also face obstacles in domestic legislation that are questionable under EU law. The European Commission highlighted some of them, such as the refusal of personal deductions if the individual does not reach a minimum salary threshold in any of the countries where it has worked during the year, or the refusal of tax credits for income taxes already paid in another Member State because the certificates presented are in a foreign language.[98] In other words, there is not a necessary correlation between the type of issues we see litigated before the Court and the potentially justiciable tax problems that actors face in the EU.

The ability of taxpayers to stand before courts (any court) is limited – one cannot spontaneously bring an action against Amazon's tax settlement in Luxembourg, even if the settlement is detrimental to our public budget.[99] Besides, most taxpayers are not particularly knowledgeable about the ins and outs of their tax code nor do they have the time and

[95] Case 270/83 *Avoir Fiscal* [1986] ECR 273.

[96] Case C-9/02 *de Lasteyrie* [2004] ECR I-2409.

[97] Case C-182/06 *Lakebrink* [2007] ECR I-6705.

[98] European Commission, 'Ways to tackle cross-border tax obstacles facing individuals within the EU' Report of Expert Group (2015), available at https://publications.europa.eu/en/publication-detail/-/publication/4bfee942-ca41-11e5-a4b5-01aa75ed71a1/language-en, 213. The Report shows that these obstacles exist both in host Member States (where the person works or carries out a temporary economic activity) as well as in home Member States (where the individual lives and files their tax return).

[99] L. Sugin, 'Invisible Taxpayers', *Tax Law Review* 69 (2016), 617.

economic resources to bring actions that, even if won, will give them little benefit. The inequality of taxpayers' interests before the Court reflects yet another issue: those 'repeat players' that do have standing before the Court, like the Commission, have focused their energies in litigating taxes on shareholders,[100] lottery,[101] and inheritance.[102] That is a choice that could have been otherwise.

**

These findings question the traditional focus that EU lawyers have put on access to justice through *locus standi*. Standing before courts is, of course, essential and the lack of standing of regions seems particularly problematic in the light of cohesion policies specifically designed to enhance the autonomy of backward regions. Yet there are inequalities in legal mobilisation beyond these procedural questions. 'Expanded' access to justice has benefitted large agricultural industries (dairy, cereal, beef meat and sugar), who are understandably well aware of the ways in which agricultural policy affects their interests and the legal mechanisms to challenge both national and EU decisions. Within cohesion, Portuguese companies (and legal firms) are the repeat players par excellence with respect to the annulment procedure against Commission decisions. Corporations and capital owners (shareholders, immovable property owners, heirs) make up for most of the litigation activities in tax policy.

The limited litigation activities of consumers and taxpayers in agricultural and cohesion policies can likely be attributed to both restrictive standing rules and lack of knowledge. The importance of the socio-economic background of the claimant comes to the surface when we observe that actors who enjoy standing present very different claiming patterns. Not all economic sectors litigate the same within the CAP; not all entities affected by financial corrections of structural funds mobilise the same against the Commission's decisions; not all types of taxpayers use the Treaty freedoms against domestic tax policies.

Given these inequalities in standing and resources, it is particularly important to observe which interests privileged applicants (EU

[100] Case C-406/07 *Commission* v. *Greece* [2009] ECR I-62; Case C-521/07 *Commission* v. *Netherlands* [2009] ECR I-4873; Case C-540/07 *Commission* v. *Italy* [2009] ECR I-10983; Case C-487/08 *Commission* v. Spain [2010] ECR I-4843; Case C-493/09 *Commission* v. *Portugal* [2011] ECR I-9247; Case C-284/09 *Commission* v. *Germany* [2011] ECR I-9879; Case C-342/10 *Commission* v. *Finland* [2012].

[101] Case C-153/08 *Commission* v. *Spain* [2009] ECR I-9735.

[102] Case C-127/12 *Commission* v. *Spain* [2014]; Case C-211/13 *Commission* v. *Germany* [2014]; Case C-244/15 *Commission* v. *Greece* [2016].

institutions, national governments) defend during litigation. In agricultural matters, Member States tend to litigate in defence of their own agricultural undertakings. While countries like Spain do a relatively good job in representing agricultural sectors that are not as organised as the 'big four' (dairy, cereal, beef meat and sugar), Member States have taken little action to defend the prerogatives of consumers in decisions that have affected food prices and/or produce supply. The Commission, on the other hand, has been much more active in litigating against domestic tax measures affecting corporations and capital owners than those affecting transnational workers and tax deductions for personal circumstances.

In sum, access to justice in a polycentric EU benefits some individuals, but marginalises others. The resourceful and vigilant citizen finds herself at ease in exploiting the new avenues that the EU judicial system has opened. The have-nots and less knowledgeable struggle to defend their claims in a more complex environment. As a result, the expansion of self-governance that lies at the core of polycentricity seems either limited (because it does not reach all individuals equally) or problematic (because the increase of capabilities for some comes at the expense of others). The next Section continues this analysis on the European Citizens' Initiative, an instrument designed to revitalise democratic participation in the EU but that, again, seems accessible only to already organised and resourceful groups.

III Judicial Review of the European Citizens' Initiative

Since this chapter gives particular emphasis to access to justice of interest groups, special attention must be given to the judicial review of the European Citizens' Initiative (ECI). The ECI is an instrument by which citizens across the EU can invite the Commission to legislate on a particular issue.[103] It needs to be supported by at least one million citizens across a minimum of seven Member States within a period of one year. Despite the high expectations placed on the ECI as an instrument for participatory democracy, the difficulty of mobilising citizens across European borders has resulted in very few proposals actually reaching the threshold.[104] Moreover, ECIs remain subject to institutional

[103] See also, in this Volume, Chapter 5 by J. van Zeben and A. Bobić.

[104] All the ECIs and the signatures collected are made available by the organisation 'ECI Campaign' at http://www.citizens-initiative.eu/eci/open-closed/

mediation throughout the process: at the registration stage, where the approval of the Commission is needed, and when the collection of signatures reaches the threshold, as the Commission enjoys the discretion to follow up on a successful ECI.[105] Litigation has taken place at both these stages, and the discretion of the Commission has been reviewed by the Courts.

The first step for launching an ECI is requesting the Commission to register the initiative. The Commission can refuse if the proposal falls manifestly outside its competences. About half of all ECIs have been declared inadmissible on these grounds, and on several occasions the judges have been called to decide whether the Commission refusal was legitimate.[106] In *Anagnostakis*, the Court of First Instance supported the Commission's decision to reject the registration of the ECI 'One million signatures for a Europe of solidarity'. The Court considered that the Commission's reasons had been adequate, pointing out that a more detailed statement of reasons would have been needed only if the ECI proposal had been more clear and precise in setting the appropriate legal bases.[107] The CFI also rejected the arguments that the Commission had wrongly interpreted Article 136(1) TFEU and the 'principle of the state of necessity'. The Court's criticism of the lack of clarity and precision of the ECI is problematic, for it implies that only citizens, or most likely organisations, with a sophisticated knowledge of EU law can initiate an ECI with some chance of success. The CJEU has confirmed these findings on appeal.[108]

Other decisions have been less sympathetic to the prerogatives of the Commission. In *Minority Safe Pack*,[109] the Court of First Instance found that the Commission had not stated the reasons why the different proposals comprised within the initiative did not fall within its powers. Since the Citizens' Committee was not able to understand which parts of their initiative were beyond the Commission's competences and the

105 M. Dougan, 'What Are We to Make of the Citizens' Initiative?', *Common Market Law Review* 48 (2011), 1807, 1812–13.

106 Case T-450/12 *Anagnostakis* v. *Commission* [2015] and Case C-589/15 P *Agagnostakis II* [2017]; Case T-646/13 *Minority Safe Pack and Others* v. *Commission* [2017]; Case T-529/13 *Izsák and Dabis* v. *Commission* [2016]; Case T-44/14 *Constantini and Others* v. *Commission* [2016]; Case T-561/14 *One of Us and Others* v. *Commission* [2018]; Case T-361/14 *HB and others* v. *Commission* [2017]; Case T-754/14 *Efler and Others* v. *Commission* [2017].

107 Case T-450/12 *Anagnostakis* v. *Commission* [2015], para. 30.

108 Case C-589/15 P *Anagnostakis II* [2017].

109 Case T-646/13 *Minority Safe Pack and Others* v. *Commission* [2017].

grounds leading to that assessment, they were de facto prevented from introducing a new proposal correcting the defects of the previous one. After the judgment, the Commission issued another decision stating which parts of the initiative were admissible and part of the initiative was admitted for registration.

Shortly after that judgment, the organisers of 'Stop TTIP' also challenged the Commission's refusal to register the initiative before the General Court.[110] As suggested by the name, 'Stop TTIP' asked the Commission to reverse its decision authorising the negotiation of the Transatlantic Trade and Investment Partnership (TTIP) and to submit a proposal to the Council not to conclude the Canada Comprehensive Economic and Trade Agreement (CETA). The Commission refused the registration of the initiative also on the grounds that it fell outside its competences. The reasons were that proposals to the Council to authorise the opening of negotiations are not proposals for legal acts per se, and that a citizens' initiative cannot ask the Commission to issue a decision *not to adopt* a legal act. The General Court disagreed with the Commission, pointing out that initiatives with a negative effect such as Stop TTIP have legal effects because they can preclude the modification of EU law intended by these agreements. For the Court, this was an essential aspect of citizens' participation in the democratic life of the EU.

Once an initiative collects the required number of signatures and is formally submitted, the Commission has discretion as to how to act on it. The Commission has (partly) taken action following the 'Right to Water' and 'No to Vivisection' initiatives within existing EU legislation.[111] However, it categorically refused to follow up on 'One of Us', the other initiative that made it to this stage. 'One of Us' requested the adoption of legislation against the destruction of human embryos (including abortion, stem cell research and genetic modification for medical purposes). The Commission issued a Communication that addressed and rejected, point by point, each of the proposals contained.[112] The promoters then sought the annulment of this Communication, arguing that the right not to take action following an ECI had to be interpreted restrictively, that legal and

[110] Case T-754/14 *Efler and Others* v. *Commission* [2017].

[111] A. Karatzia, 'The European Citizens' Initiative and the EU Institutional Balance: On Realism and the Possibilities of Affecting EU Lawmaking', *Common Market Law Review* 54 (2017), 177, 188 and 196.

[112] European Commission, 'Communication on the European Citizens' Initiative "One of Us"', 28 May 2014 COM(2014) 355 final.

political considerations had been mixed in the Communication, that the statement of reasons was insufficient and that the reasoning of the Commission was inconsistent with the previous decisions of the Court protecting human embryos.[113] The General Court confirmed that, although the Commission has discretion to decide how to act upon the ECIs, its Communication was susceptible to judicial review. However, the Court ruled that the Commission could not be obliged to take action following an ECI, for it would deprive it from its 'near-monopoly' of the legislative initiative conferred by the Treaties, a monopoly justified by the Commission's role in promoting the general interest of the EU and its independence.[114] The Court also considered that the Regulation on the citizens' initiative (Regulation (EU) No. 211/2011) does not require the Commission to separate its legal and political conclusions, that the refusal had been properly motivated and that the fact that the Commission follows a different ethical approach to that of the applicants does not mean there is an error of interpretation.

Anagnostakis, Minority Safe Pack and the Stop TTIP *case* evidence that the Commission's decisions, albeit discretionary, can be made subject to judicial review. The European Citizens' Initiative aims at the inclusion of proposals from diffuse and marginalised interests that have not made their way through the ordinary policy-making process. The strong institutional filters of ECIs have questioned the high expectations surrounding its establishment.[115] Judicial review gives citizens a potential second chance to succeed.

As Dougan claims, the framework of the ECI makes it particularly suitable for NGOs and other lobby groups, but ill-equipped to accommodate interests that are not already organised in some manner.[116] Setting up a Citizens' Committee with members in at least seven Member States, translating the proposal into Member States' official languages, and collecting the signatures is only feasible for well-established, resourceful organisations. The requirement that ECIs clearly specify the appropriate legal basis, as decided in *Anagnostakis,* further hinders the capacity of 'spontaneous' initiatives to succeed. Moreover, ECIs can be captured by opinions that contradict the values of most Europeans – as seems to be the case with the 'One of Us' initiative –

113 Case T-561/14 *European Citizens' Initiative One of Us* [2018].
114 ibid., paras. 110 and 115.
115 See A. Karatzia (n. 111), 197.
116 M. Dougan (n. 105), 1833.

thereby potentially leading to a violation of the shared system of rules. The judicial review of the European Citizens' Initiative again expands access to justice for certain actors but seems unavailable to most citizens. In these cases, judicial restraint in the review of Commission decisions regarding ECIs may be appropriate, as this safeguards the shared rules of the polycentric system in the longer term, and indirectly supports the ability of EU citizens to govern themselves.

IV Conclusion

Rules of standing before the CJEU discriminate between privileged and non-privileged applicants. This unequal access to justice should be rebalanced by the expansive scope of the preliminary ruling procedure by which national courts can engage the CJEU in the interpretation of EU rules and, indirectly, the review of secondary EU law. The collaborative scheme between domestic and EU courts has expanded access to justice, whereby individuals can enforce the rights that the EU legal system grants them before national courts. Occasional competitive clashes between courts have also benefitted individuals, for the vigilant role of national courts has increased pressures on the CJEU to further respect (and expand) fundamental rights protection. EU citizens have used this opportunity to push for domestic policy changes in fields like non-discrimination, tax policy or consumer protection.

The polycentric nature of the judicial system within the EU and the corresponding changes to access to justice rules have opened new avenues for individuals to govern themselves, by empowering private actors to question policies (especially national ones) hindering their interests. However, this expanded access to justice does not benefit all actors equally. Procedural rules within domestic judicial systems remain within the discretion of national legislatures. As a consequence, procedures surrounding preliminary ruling continue to differ across Member States, while the ability to litigate depends on matters beyond formal standing, including resources and information.

The findings presented in this chapter show that there are acute differences in legal mobilisation between and within collectives. While these inequalities are sometimes caused by formal restrictions, there are also inequalities within groups that enjoy equal *locus standi*, which results in an under-representation of certain groups. This could be, but is not, resolved by representation of these groups by privileged applicants (national governments and EU institutions). The willingness of the

CJEU to review the role of the Commission in dealing with the European Citizens' Initiative has given hopes to those who saw in ECIs an opportunity for democratic participation. However, the design of ECIs makes them de facto available only to already organised interest groups.

These observations suggest that access to justice in the EU expands the capabilities of some citizens but hinders the mobilisation of those (the have-nots and unsophisticated) who struggle to thrive in an even more complex governance system. It is not immediately clear what the best way of addressing these issues would be. Expanding standing rights and removing informal barriers to justice (increasing economic resources, raising legal awareness) can be costly and ultimately unattainable. Alternatively, promoting more active tutelage of under-represented interests by privileged applicants creates a system of 'self-governance by proxy'. These tensions between individuals' ability to litigate by themselves and institutions' tutelage of citizens' interests are at the core of the EU judicial system. Ultimately, the aim of self-governance that lies at the core of polycentricity is undermined when the empowerment is not equally available to all members of the system.

11

Access to Information in Polycentric Governance

VIGJILENCA ABAZI

For Vincent Ostrom access to information was a self-evident condition for realisation of polycentric governance.[1] The analytical framework that supports this Volume positions access to information as a polycentric prerequisite, explaining more explicitly why it is a necessary condition for the achievement of institutional essentials that characterise polycentric systems.[2] Whilst the literature on polycentric governance makes references to the relevance of access to information, a more in-depth analysis is lacking. Often information exchanges are only portrayed in passing when looking at polycentric governance systems such as in regulatory networks or capital markets.[3] This chapter seeks to remedy this gap by offering observations on the role, requirements, and effects of access to information as a polycentric prerequisite generally and for polycentric governance in the EU specifically.

Access to information has been a salient subject of debate over the last few decades. It is considered a key expression of transparency, which in turn is a precondition for accountability,[4] and a facilitator of public

[1] V. Ostrom, 'Polycentricity' (1972), in M. D. McGinnis (ed.), *Polycentricity and Local Public Economies: Readings from the Workshop in Political Theory and Policy Analysis* (University of Michigan Press, 1999), 60.

[2] See, in this Volume, Chapter 2 by J. van Zeben.

[3] K. Van Boetzelaer and S. Princen, 'The Quest for Co-ordination of European Regulatory Networks', *Journal of Common Market Studies* 50 (5) (2012), 819; M. D. McGinnis, 'Costs and Challenges of Polycentric Governance: An Equilibrium Concept and Examples from US Health Care' (2011) Paper presented at the Conference on Self-Governance, Polycentricity, and Development, Renmin University of China, Beijing.

[4] See A. Meijer, 'Understanding the Complex Dynamics of Transparency', *Public Administration Review* 73 (2013), 429; M. Bovens, 'Analysing and Assessing Accountability: A Conceptual Framework', *European Law Journal* 13 (4) (2007), 447; E. Fisher, 'The EU in the Age of Accountability', *Oxford Journal of Legal Studies* 24 (3) (2004), 495; C. Harlow, 'European Governance and Accountability', in N. Bamforth and P. Leyland (eds.), *Public Law in a Multi-layered Constitution* (Hart Publishing, 2003); J. M. Moncrieffe, 'Accountability: Ideals, Ideas, Constraints', *Democratization* 8 (2001), 26; but see also J. Fox, 'The Uncertain Relation between Transparency and Accountability', *Development in Practice* 17 (2007), 663–71.

participation and deliberation.[5] Over 100 countries have adopted legislation that provides citizens direct access to information.[6] The EU has also been part of this regulatory trend, in part due to the need to address the democratic shortfalls of the EU legal order.[7] Access to information in the EU is stipulated in primary law,[8] and it is also protected as a fundamental right in the EU Charter of Fundamental Rights. EU secondary legislation provides for the 'widest possible access' to documents in the Regulation 1049/01.[9] From a legal perspective, therefore, access to information in the EU has constitutional value, is a fundamental right and is safeguarded through judicial review.[10] Whilst practice does not always match the 'law on the books', access to information is taken seriously in the EU,[11] and new frontiers of transparency are advanced continuously, including in foreign relations.[12]

Building on the attributes and institutional essentials of polycentric governance, this chapter maps the role of access to information as a prerequisite to polycentricity. While the chapter focuses on the context of the EU for the empirical discussion on access to information, the

5 D. C. Mutz, *Hearing the Other Side – Deliberative versus Participatory Democracy* (Cambridge University Press, 2006); M. Bessette, 'Deliberative Democracy: The Majority Principle in Republican Government', *American Enterprise Institute for Public Policy Research* (1980), 102.

6 See Global Right to Information Rating, programme by Access Info Europe and Centre for Law and Democracy. Available online www.rti-rating.org/about/ accessed 9 July 2018.

7 E.g. G. Majone, 'The Credibility Crisis of Community Regulation', *Journal of Common Market Studies* 38 (2002), 273; K. Lenaerts, 'In the Union We Trust: Trust – Enhancing Principles of Community Law', *Common Market Law Review* 41 (2004), 317; K. Lenaerts, 'The Principle of Democracy in the Case Law of the European Court of Justice', *International & Comparative Law Quarterly* 62 (2) (2013), 271; and J. Lodge, 'Transparency and Democratic Legitimacy', *Journal of Common Market Studies* 32 (1994), 343; A. E. Stie, Democratic Decision-making in the EU: Technocracy in Disguise? (Routledge, 2013); V. A. Schmidt, 'Democracy and Legitimacy in the European Union Revisited: Input, Output and "Throughput"', *Political Studies* 61 (2012), 2.

8 Article 1 TEU, Article 15 TFEU.

9 Charter of Fundamental Rights of the EU, Article 42; Regulation (EC) No. 1049/2001 of the European Parliament and of the Council of 30 May 2001 regarding public access to European Parliament, Council and Commission documents [2001] OJ L145/43, Article 1(a).

10 See an analysis of judicial review and case law on access to documents, L. Rossi and P. Vinagre e Silva, Public Access to Documents in the EU (Hart Publishing, 2017).

11 E. O'Reilly, 'The European Ombudsman, EU Institutional Politics of Secrecy and Transparency in Foreign Affairs: A Commentary', *Politics and Governance* 5 (2017), 91–3.

12 See V. Abazi and J. Adriansen, 'EU Institutional Politics of Secrecy and Transparency', *Politics and Governance* 5 (2017), 91.

purpose is to offer insights that are relevant for polycentric governance more generally. In doing so, the remainder of this chapter is structured as follows: it will compare 'traditional' and polycentric approaches to access to information, as well as discuss the key aspects of polycentricity that shape access to information (Section I). These insights serve as the theoretical foundation through which practical requirements for access to information in a polycentric system can be identified (Section II). Finally, the reality of access to information in the EU will be described and its effect on EU polycentric governance discussed (Section III). This analysis shows that the EU falls short of offering access to information in a manner that supports polycentric governance due to issues of 'privileged access' and information asymmetries.

I Comparing 'Traditional' and Polycentric Approaches to Access to Information

Access to information has been analysed by scholars in different disciplines, especially in political science, public administration and law. There is a broad consensus regarding the theoretical importance and instrumental value of access to information for good governance principles, such as transparency, participation and accountability.[13] Notwithstanding serious concerns regarding the ideological drift away from the progressive ideals that underpin access to information,[14] practice has proven these rights to be important for citizens and civil society to scrutinise government action, and a crucial means for parliamentary representatives to exercise their institutional prerogatives.[15]

This Section builds on this existing theoretical and practical framework in order to decipher the role of access to information as a prerequisite of polycentric governance. Towards that aim, first I address the relevance of access to information seen from what can broadly be categorised as 'traditional' approaches to access to information. These approaches are understood to be 'traditional' in so far as they

[13] See R. Corbett, 'The Evolving Roles of the European Parliament and of National Parliaments', in A. Biondi, P. Eeckhout, and S. Ripley (eds.), *EU Law after Lisbon* (Oxford University Press, 2012). But see also V. Abazi, 'Surveillance under a veil of secrecy: Do oversight bodies oversee or overlook?' (2013), available at www.euractiv.com/section/digital/opinion/surveillance-under-a-veil-of-secrecy-do-oversight-bodies-oversee-or-overlook/ accessed 24 October 2018.

[14] D. Pozen, 'Transparency's Ideological Drift', *Yale Law Journal* 128 (2018), 1–50.

[15] See Case C-350/12 P *Council* v. *Sophie in 't Veld* [2014].

reflect established debates on the necessities of access to information and approach the latter from a conceptual framework that focuses on improving democratic governance. Second, I focus on the defining features of polycentricity, particularly self-governance, in order to draw similarities and contrasts of access to information from these different strands, but also to provide details on the aspects of access to information that are relevant for polycentric governance. Ostrom considered 'the role of the individual in democracy [to rely] heavily on responsibility, resilience, ownership, and learning'.[16] This understanding of the role of the individual is both shaped by, and shapes how, access to information should be conceptually understood as well as implemented in practice.

A The 'Traditional' Approach: Accountability and Participation

The most fundamental characteristics of democracy are grounded on the presumption that the flow of relevant information and its proper handling are not obstructed.[17] The importance of access to information is highlighted at varying degrees depending on the normative conception of democracy. Representative, deliberative, and participatory democracy all correlate information with the exercise of power and show various preferences for the question of at what stage of the democratic processes access to information is most necessary.[18] Access to information in non-polycentric systems is viewed as essential in order to ensure that actions of the delegated public authority are in line with the interest of the citizenry.[19] This approach puts emphasis on the role of access to information for accountability, for ensuring that the agent is defending and realising the best interest of the principal. Hence, this rationale of access to information focuses on the vertical relation between the agent and the principal without too much regard of information sharing among citizens or different centres of decision making. From a legal perspective, an access to information policy would qualify as satisfactory for realising accountability as long as there is a clear stipulated right of the individual

16 See, in this Volume, Chapter 1 by J. van Zeben.

17 J. Habermas, *Between Facts and Norms: Contributions to a Discourse Theory of Law and Democracy* trans. edn by William Rehg (Massachusetts Institute of Technology Press, 1996), 269.

18 D. C. Mutz, *Hearing the Other Side* (n. 5); M. Bessette (n. 5).

19 A. Gutmann and D. Thompson, *Democracy and Disagreement* (Harvard University Press, 1996).

to have access to information and such information is only limited under justified exception in the light of protecting other public interests.

Full information is however not expected; even Robert Dahl, who takes as one of the central assumptions of democracy to be that 'all individuals possess identical information', acknowledges that gaps of information can (and actually do) exist.[20] The main goal is to enable citizens to create independent and informed opinions and to do so not through rumour but through accurate information.[21] This is a fundamental aspect of access to information for accountability purposes: providing citizens with a view directly to the information for the decision-making processes. This in turn enables citizens to oversee the exercise of the delegated authority and scrutinise possible abuses of power. Information is indispensable to the obligations to explain and justify public conduct as the main elements of the core meaning of accountability.[22] Democratic debates must 'above all' ensure accountability, which *inter alia* implies that it is essential to know 'the identity of those participating in the debate and, in particular, the terms on which they are doing so'.[23] Otherwise, as John Stuart Mill asked in 1861, how can citizens either check or approve what they are not permitted to see?[24]

Moving beyond passive observation of government actions, access to information enables citizens to make meaningful contributions to decision making and broadens the range of parties who have access to such opportunities.[25] Citizens cannot participate if information lacks or is only available after a considerable passage of time. In *Democracy and Disagreement*, Amy Guttmann and Dennis Thompson argue that if the reasons for certain policies are public then citizens can contribute to making perspectives of agreement broader.[26] In addition, access to information clarifies the nature of disagreement regarding different courses of actions and enables a self-correcting character that ideally would be achieved in a deliberative democracy.[27]

20 R. Dahl, *A Preface to Democratic Theory* (University of Chicago Press, 1956), 70.

21 F. Rourke, *Secrecy and Publicity: Dilemmas of Democracy* (The John Hopkins Press, 1961), 90.

22 M. Bovens (n. 4) 449–50; E. Fisher (n. 4); J. M. Moncrieffe (n. 4).

23 Case C-280/11P *Council* v. *Access Info Europe* [2013], Opinion of Advocate General para. 71.

24 J. S. Mill, *Considerations on Representative Government* (Parker Son and Bourn, 1861), 34.

25 D. C. Mutz, *Hearing the Other Side* (n. 5).

26 A. Gutmann and D. Thompson (n. 19) 95–127.

27 ibid.

At the core of the 'traditional' approaches to access to information is the premise that delegated authority should be held accountable for which the agent must provide information. The main emphasis of this account on access to information is as a *control* tool for citizens to use in order to check whether their representatives protect their interest, whether there is abuse of power and ensuring that consequences will follow if that is the case. Access to information in this framework is usually given after the action (decision-making process, policy) has taken place. Access to information is also seen as an instrument to ensure public participation in decision making. In such cases, access to information is needed during the process, however generally not all information is shared in order to protect other public interests. Hence, within the traditional approaches to access to information, emphasis is either placed on accountability and/or participation, depending on the underpinning democratic rationale for the application of access to information. In other words, whereas, within the accountability framework, access to information is *ex post facto* provided for the full documentation and serves the purpose of control,[28] in the participation framework, information must be shared during the process but it is usually much more redacted and in practice issues often arise regarding de facto privileged participants in decision making.[29]

Access to information in the light of the traditional approaches explained above has the following main features: first, its rationale is based on democratic accountability and participation; second, the focus is on the vertical relation between the principal and the agent and hence the regulatory architecture for this policy is set towards facilitating this relation; third, access is required to as much information as possible, limited only through legitimately justified public interest exceptions, as the aim is to allow citizens to create independent and informed opinions through accurate facts; lastly, information is an instrument of control and rules on access to information ensure that citizens have access to this control.[30]

[28] See in the EU context the rationale of access to information as a control tool and its implications in V. Abazi and E. Tauschinsky, 'Reasons of Control and Trust: Grounding the Public Need for Transparency in the European Union', *Utrecht Law Review* 11 (2015), 78.

[29] See the value of access to information for participation and the latter's legal shortfalls in the EU in J. Mendes, 'Participation and the Role of Law after Lisbon: A Legal View on Article 11 TEU', *Common Market Law Review* 48 (2011), 1849, see also J. Mendes, 'Transparence et Participation: des Principes Démocratiques pour l'Administration de l'Union Européenne', *Revue Française d'Administration Publique* (2011), 101.

[30] The notion of 'control' is broader than accountability and can include both *ex ante* and *ex post* mechanisms of directing behaviour. Accountability is concerned with *ex post* checks. See on these issues: C. Scott, 'Accountability in the Regulatory State', *Journal of Law and*

Do similar aspects of access to information matter from the polycentric governance perspective? How does polycentric governance improve or expand access to information for citizens and/or other stakeholders in a democratic society that should give the outmost expression to self-governance? The next subsection examines access to information as a polycentric prerequisite.

B Enabling Polycentric Self-Governance through Information

In Ostrom's work, access to information is necessary for the realisation of self-governance.[31] However, its precise role and rationale are not elaborated.[32] Below I examine the literature that has directly or indirectly touched upon the issue of access to information in a polycentric system since Ostrom's contribution, in order to draw insights in mapping a polycentric view on access to information. However, as it will become quickly apparent, guidance on the role of access to information thus far has been limited.

To start with, McGinnis deals indirectly with the relevance of information and makes mention of it in several accounts in his explanation of the governance architecture as a higher level of abstraction of network governance, to which he sees polycentricity to be conceptualised as an attribute to this governance architecture.[33] Furthermore, in their analysis of the European Regulatory Networks, Van Botezelear and Princen refer to information in the context of emphasising the importance of information in the non-hierarchal coordination efforts – which may be viewed as an example of polycentric governance within the EU.[34] Other contributions have touched upon the role of information not only with regard to citizens directly, but also how institutions interact in a polycentric setting. For example, in the analysis of national parliaments in the EU, mention is made that national parliaments request and receive information about draft EU legislation directly from the Commission, among other means of information sharing obligations.[35]

Society 27 (2000), 38. For the difference between control and accountability in the EU context, see M. Busuioc, 'Accountability, Control and Independence: The Case of European Agencies', *European Law Journal* 15 (2009), 599.

31 See, in this Volume, Chapter 1 by J. van Zeben.

32 V. Ostrom, 'Polycentricity' (1972) (n. 1) 60.

33 M. D. McGinnis (n. 3) 5.

34 K. Van Boetzelaer and S. Princen (n. 3) 821.

35 L. Besselink, 'National Parliaments in the EU's Composite Constitution: A Plea for a Shift in Paradigm', in P. Kiiver (ed.), *National and Regional Parliaments in the European Constitutional Order* (Europa Law Publishing, 2006), 119.

In his analysis of the role of non-profits in polycentric systems, Bryce notes the importance of transparency and openness for an entity to be effective within a polycentric system.[36] While these concepts are not theoretically developed, Bryce does examine the regulation of transparency and information in US capital markets. This analysis is valuable, but mostly descriptive, and as such does not offer any understanding on *how* such observations on information within the context of capital markets are relevant for polycentric governance more generally.

Within polycentricity scholarship, Aligica and Tarko, and van Zeben, have contributed to expanding the analysis of access to information. Aligica and Tarko consider information paramount not only for the functioning of the polycentric system but also for identifying the members of a particular polycentric system.[37] Since information is an essential component, the lack of it according to Aligica and Tarko could lead to a 'breakdown' of polycentricity. Specifically, if there is no available information relevant to decision making it would actually lead to random decisions, the relation between consequences and rules would be unclear, and a spontaneous order would turn into drift.[38] van Zeben situates access to information as a prerequisite of polycentricity, which means access to information is a feature that affects the realisation and sustainability of each institutional essential, and indirectly the system's capacity for continuous self-governance.[39] Both Aligica and Tarko, and van Zeben, position access to information as a polycentric essential or 'prerequisite' – a building block without which polycentric systems could not function, as the ability to self-govern would be undermined. Specifically, access to information is relevant for citizens' *motivation* to self-govern,[40] for their *capacity* to self-govern,[41] and for their *contribution* to societal

[36] H. J. Bryce, 'Review Essay: Polycentric Governance, Capital Market, and NGOs as Regulatory Bodies: Expanding the Scope of Ostrom's Understanding Institutional Diversity', *Politics & Policy* 40 (2012), 519, 522.

[37] P. D. Aligica and V. Tarko, 'Polycentricity: From Polanyi to Ostrom, and Beyond', *Governance: An International Journal of Policy, Administration, and Institutions* 25 (2) (2012), 255.

[38] ibid., 258.

[39] See, in this Volume, Chapters 1 and 2 by J. van Zeben.

[40] V. Ostrom, 'Some Developments in the Study of Market Choice, Public Choice, and Institutional Choice', in J. Rabin, W. Bartley Hildreth, and G. Miller (eds.), *Handbook of Public Administration* (Marcel Dekker, 1989).

[41] V. Ostrom, *The Meaning of American Federalism: Constituting a Self-governing Society* (ICS Press, 1994).

groups.[42] These distinctive features of polycentricity show the rationale for access to information, which differs from the rationales of traditional approaches explained above, and in turn may necessitate different types of access.

In Ostrom's view, individuals are inherently motivated to self-organise. Yet, to do so effectively they need skills and institutional know-how. This information is not meant to function as a 'control' on the institution, but rather to help the individual to govern itself. This in turn means that for polycentricity, mere access to institutional information is insufficient; access should facilitate knowledge and understanding. Moreover, all individuals should be able to gain access to information equally; a system of access to information that offers asymmetrical access to information would undermine polycentric governance, as cooperation, competition and collaboration would become unbalanced. Lastly, from a polycentric perspective, information also enables the individual to contribute to her societal groups. This links access to information with learning and jointly they foster societal relations that are necessary for individuals to pursue their own goals.

**

Whereas traditional approaches to access to information are driven by accountability and participation, access to information in a polycentric system is much more focused on understanding and knowledge to facilitate self-governance. Access to information is therefore more substantive than mere physical or digital accessibility, and has to facilitate the understanding that is necessary for the purposes of self-governance.[43] Secondly, motivation, capacity and contribution are essential aspects of information for self-governance. This requires access to information for all citizens equally and the understanding of, rather than the mere 'seeing', institutional documents. Access to information also fosters relations that are relevant for individuals in their societal group or in different decision centres. Relatedly, when centres of decision making provide different levels of access to information for different actors, this leads to information asymmetries that limit the ability of the individuals to be in the equal position for self-governance.

[42] See R. Herzberg, 'Commentary on Richard Wagner's "Self-governance, Polycentrism, and Federalism: Recurring Themes in Vincent Ostrom's Scholarly Oeuvre"', *Journal of Economic Behavior & Organization* 57 (2005), 189.

[43] See also, in this Volume, Chapter 12 by S. Garben.

II Parameters for Polycentric Access to Information

Access to information is a prerequisite of polycentric governance insofar as it allows the institutional essentials of polycentric systems to function. This Section will discuss how access to information rules can be shaped in order to ensure this supportive function. It also creates a benchmark against which EU practices regarding access to information can be evaluated.

A Access to Information as a Polycentric Prerequisite

In order for a system to maintain polycentricity, three institutional essentials must be present: first, the freedom and ability to enter and exit; second, the enforcement of shared system of rules; and third, peaceful contestation among different (interest) groups.[44] Access to information facilitates the successful expression of each of these institutional essentials.

Whilst the formal freedom to enter and exit depends *inter alia* on the established rules of particular jurisdictions, the *ability* to enter and exit depends more directly on access to information. Entry and exit may be understood as a shift from one jurisdiction to another, or a shift from one decision-making unit to another. For both of these, the individual must have access to information to make the choice whether to enter or exit. Secondly, when an individual enters a decision centre, information facilitates her ability to self-govern in that new context. Comprehensibility of information is therefore an implied but crucial element of access to information for self-governance. An example of this is the language in which information is presented. Providing information in several languages presents high costs, which may not be supported by the goals of the constituents of the decision-making unit. However, such practical constraints on the flow of information can clearly (negatively) affect an individual's ability to enter and exit.

The second institutional essential is the enforcement of the shared system of rules. In order for such enforcement to take place, citizens must know and understand the rules and their implications. In this respect, it is important to assess which forums of contestation are available to individuals and what type of access to information is possible for individuals during enforcement efforts. If limits to access are foreseen, then safeguards are necessary to

[44] See, in this Volume, Chapters 1 and 2 by J. van Zeben.

ensure that individual's ability is not hindered to the extent that it blocks the enforcement of rights.

The third institutional essential is the peaceful contestation among different groups. Similar to the enforcement of common rules, this institutional essential requires that information is available about the avenues of peaceful contestation, and the rules themselves, if they are to be successfully and appropriately revised. Peaceful contestation gives direct expression to individual's self-governance because it allows for revisions and modifications that are deemed more favourable by the individual for their personal gain or for the gain of their societal group. Information for the processes of peaceful contestation in this regard is also required as it is a factor in individual's incentive to engage in contestation in the first place. Finally, the polycentric requirement of access to justice imposes additional requirements on access to information, in particular with respect to what can be considered justifiable limits to access to information.[45]

The primary role of access to information in a polycentric system is to foster self-governance and in doing so it must specifically address the necessities of motivation, capacity and contribution of the individual. On the other hand, access to information is a prerequisite of polycentricity's institutional essentials and hence the practical manifestation of access to information must help the realisation of freedom and ability to enter and exit, the enforcement of shared system of rules and the peaceful contestation among different groups. This means that a policy that aims to put into practice polycentric access to information must ensure the functioning of the institutional essentials, with a view to achieving motivation, capacity and contribution in self-governance.

B *Effects of Polycentric Governance on Access to Information*

Polycentric governance expands, specifies and advances access to information. Conceptually, it expands our understanding of access to information beyond a tool of control between a principal and agent (as presented in most traditional approaches).[46] Polycentricity gives value

[45] For the argument that in the EU access to information is limited to the extent that does not fully enable the individual to ensure her right of access to justice, see V. Abazi and C. Eckes, 'Closed Evidence in EU Courts: Security, Secrecy, and Access to Justice', *Common Market Law Review* 55 (2018), 753.

[46] G. J. Brandsma and J. Adriaensen, 'The Principal-Agent Model, Accountability and Democratic Legitimacy', in T. Delreux and J. Adriaensen (eds.), *The Principal Agent Model and the European Union* (Palgrave, 2017) 37–8, 42.

to access beyond a formalistic and institutionalised tool by enhancing its role in a societal sense, showing its salience for community building as well as individuals mobility among different communities or decision centres. Furthermore, the emphasis that polycentricity puts on knowledge and understanding also expands the understanding of access to information as it means access is not only about 'seeing' but rather genuinely enabling and increasing the capacity of the individual to self-govern. In policy terms, polycentricity pushes for more specific and broader access to information. For example, comprehensibility is an important demand on access to information that the institutional essential on freedom to exit and enter has. This aspect of polycentricity hence places a higher demand on *what* kind of information, *when* and *how* it should be available to individuals and as such also increased the benefits of learning both at the individual and group level.[47]

Polycentric governance however can also have negative effects on access to information. A greater number of decision centres translates to more points of access for information, which can make it challenging for the individual to identify the 'correct' point of access or to ensure that information has been acquired from all actors involved, as even knowing which centres are involved can be more difficult. This complexity also poses a challenge in formulating access to information rules as it is not intuitive where the burden should be placed: should the individual search for all relevant information herself, or should decision centres proactively provide information? While the latter takes away certain efficiencies and alleviates the burden on the individual, it also creates a (primarily) top-down, rather than bottom-up, flow of information, which may undermine the motivation and ability for self-governance.

Polycentricity also increases the level of information that the individual needs for self-governing. Whereas traditional approaches focus on specific aims, accountability and participation, polycentricity requires learning from the individual for a much higher and more complex aim: *self*-governance. But in an increasing complex world, it is unclear to what extent the individual would be able to sufficiently understand issues that involve increasingly technical and niche information. In this respect, self-governance can initially contribute to inefficiencies in terms of time and potential overlap in expertise. However, taking into account the dynamic nature of polycentric systems, self-governance can also contribute to a learning process resulting in a more targeted approach to access to

[47] See, in this Volume, Chapter 12 by S. Garben.

information, since not all individuals need to have all the information for the system to achieve its set aims. Individuals can also rely on certain safeguards and allies for access to information.

III An Appraisal of Polycentric Access to Information within the European Union

In this Section, I examine how the law and practice of the European Union matches polycentric standards of access to information and what safeguards are in place that can further foster polycentric access to information. Access for individuals may be 'direct' in the sense that individuals file requests for access to public documents, but it may also be realised through intermediaries – institutional actors or civil society organisations – who act as allies in facilitating access for individuals. These allies have a significant role in supporting individuals and mitigating the challenging factors of polycentric governance for access to information.

A Direct Access: The Right of Access to Public Documents

Citizens in the European Union have a fundamental right of access to public documents stipulated in the EU Charter of Fundamental Rights. Since 2001, Regulation 1049/2001, known as the EU Transparency Regulation,[48] creates direct access for citizens and residents in the EU to request documents and enabling them to gain vision and voice in EU decision making.[49] This Regulation prescribes the widest access possible to public documents. It should immediately be noted that there is a difference in terms of access to 'public documents' and access to 'information': the former means access is given to exiting documents. The Regulation provides that a document is 'any content whatever its medium (written on paper or stored in electronic form or as a sound, visual or audio-visual recording) concerning a matter relating to the policies, activities and decisions falling within the institution's sphere of responsibility'.[50] While broad, this interpretation limits de facto access to public documents. 'Access to information' has a broader scope of

[48] Regulation (EC) No. 1049/2001 of the European Parliament and of the Council regarding public access to documents [2001] OJ L145/43.

[49] A. J. Meijer, D. Curtin, and M. Hillebrandt, 'Open Government: Connecting Vision and Voice', *International Review of Administrative Sciences* 78 (1) (2012), 10.

[50] Article 3(a), Regulation 1049/2001.

application as it does not only encompass information in existing documents, but also information about an issue that the institutions need to produce. With respect to the drivers of self-governance, three specific issues arise.

i Motivation: Fostering Understanding and Knowledge

The Transparency Regulation provides access to documents as they are written during different decision-making stages. These documents are often complex and have a policy jargon that is not necessarily easily comprehensible for those outside the remit of EU decision making. This hinders understanding, learning and ultimately self-governance. Similar concerns have been expressed within previous assessments of the Regulation such that it focuses on control and not sufficiently on information that matters for individuals beyond this paradigm.[51]

Moreover, polycentric access to information requires that only justified limitations are applied in restricting information for individuals in order not to impinge on the motivation of the individual or encumber self-governance. On the basis of the wording of Article 4 of the Regulation, distinctions are drawn between 'mandatory' and 'non-mandatory' exceptions.[52] Mandatory exception under Article 4(1)(a) implies that once the relevant circumstances to invoke the exception are established, the institution in question is not required to balance the protected interest against the general public interest in disclosure.[53] By contrast, the exceptions under Article 4(2) require that even if it is established that a protected interest falls under the exception, the

[51] V. Abazi and E. Tauschinsky (n. 28).

[52] Article 4 of Regulation 1049/2001 reads: '(1) The institutions shall refuse access to a document where disclosure would undermine the protection of: (a) The public interest as regards: Public security; Defence and military matters; International relations; The financial, monetary or economic policy of the Community of the Member States. (b) Privacy and the integrity of the individual, in particular in accordance with Community legislation regarding the protection of personal data. (2) The institutions shall refuse access to documents where disclosure would undermine the protection of: Commercial interests of natural or legal person, including intellectual property; Courts proceedings and legal advice; The purpose of inspections, investigations, and audit; unless there is an overriding public interest in disclosure.'

[53] Case T-105/95 *WWF UK* v. *Commission* [1997] ECR II-313, para. 58, and Case T-20/99 *Denkavit Nederland* v. *Commission* [2000] ECR II-3011, para. 39. Case C-266/05 P *Sison* v. *Council* [2007] ECR I-1233, para. 108, paras. 46–48; Joined Cases T-110/03, T-150/03 and T-405/03 *Sison* v. *Council* [2005] ECR II-1429 para. 107, paras. 51–55; Case T-264/04 *WWF European Policy Programme* v. *Council* [2007] ECR II-911, para. 44; Case T-300/10 *Internationaler Hilfsfonds* v. *Commission* [2012] ECR II-0000, para. 124; and Case T-465/09 *Jurašinović* v. *Conseil* [2012] ECR II-000, paras. 47–49.

institution is nevertheless still required to balance if the general interest in disclosure outweighs the necessity for protection. While these exceptions affect the institutional essential of the enforcement of shared rules, they do not create an unjustified limitation for the individual to realise self-governing, although they do affect her knowledge and hence motivation to self-organise.

ii Capacity: Ensuring Equal Access

In addition to *what* kind of information can be accessed and whether that information is comprehensible for individuals, *who* can access information is an important aspect of polycentric access. The Regulation in this regard is one of the most progressive pieces of legislation in access to documents as it allows for access to 'any citizen of the Union, and any natural or legal person residing or having its registered office in a Member State'.[54] Furthermore, the Regulation does not require a person seeking access to a document to state any reasons justifying her request,[55] and will thus not need to demonstrate any particular interest in having access to documents beyond the public interest in transparency. The emphasis on 'public' interest is linked to the fact that this Regulation is meant to provide access to documents that deal with public interest issues and as such excludes access to documents that the individual would like to access in terms of their own file. Whilst access to one's file is also a right in EU administrative law, its rationale differs from a legal regime that links access to information with democratic and accountability processes. While the legal regime foresees access being granted to any citizen or resident, the practice of access to documents shows that a large number of private firms and companies use the Regulation and as such it is not always utilised for learning and self-governance perspectives from citizens. However, departing from the main pattern in practice, in 2016 the European Commission received the most applications directly from citizens, 40 per cent of the entire number of initial applications for access.[56] Yet, there is an asymmetry in where these requests for access to public documents originate from, with

[54] Article 2(1) and (3), Regulation 1049/2001.

[55] Article 6(1), Regulation 1049/2001.

[56] European Commission, Report on the application in 2016 of Regulation (EC) No. 1049/2001 regarding public access to European Parliament, Council and Commission documents, COM/2017/0738 final.

decision centres closer to Brussels leading in the numbers. As the report on access by the Commission shows, 'the largest proportion continued to originate from the applicants within Belgium, followed by Germany and the United Kingdom. France, Spain, Italy and the Netherlands followed, representing more than 5 per cent of all applications each. The applications originating from within the remaining 21 Member States accounted for less than 2 per cent per Member State'.[57] This shows the significant differences between the decision centres in terms of access to EU documents and as such has an effect on the competition between these different centres.

iii Contribution: Societal Groups and Decision Centres

From a polycentric perspective, information should help the individual to contribute to her societal groups, foster relations and pursue goals that benefit the community. As the Regulation is focused on accountability in the principal-agent framework, it does not per se establish mechanisms or disclosures that are aimed at enabling the individual to contribute. Yet, it also does not prevent individuals from using information in a manner that benefits not only them, but also their societal group. In fact, in this regard, the emphasis the Regulation puts on 'public' interest can be said to provide a basis for the individual to access information that serves the community.

**

The Regulation fosters access to information in a manner that could enable self-governance, but some challenges remain. Information asymmetry is the main issue in the application of this legal regime since individuals based in different decision centres do not seek access to the same degree. Additionally, information may be complex and individuals do not have access to information per se but rather to 'documents' which is a narrower category as explained than information. Lastly, it is not the goal of the Regulation to enable the individual to contribute in their societal groups, but the Regulation does focus on 'public' interest and hence indirectly may address this important aspect of polycentric access to information.

In the light of these shortfalls, the following subsection examines what EU safeguards are in place to ensure information flows.

[57] ibid., section 3.4.

B *Access through Allies: Safeguarding Information Flows*

The pressure points for information in polycentric governance include fragmented responsibility among decision centres, the burden of access, increased information and its complexity as well as necessities for more resources on access.[58] Channelling relevant information through intermediaries or 'allies' can alleviate these complicating factors. This Section presents three key allies to individuals with respect to access to information in the EU.

i Civil Society Organisations

Civil society organisations (CSOs) facilitate the flow of information between different decision centres.[59] CSOs – such as AccessInfo Europe, the Swedish Journalist Association and the The Consumer Association–Austria – act on behalf of citizens and aim to acquire information that otherwise might remain undisclosed or go unnoticed in public debates.[60] In the EU, CSOs have been at the forefront of expanding access to information and ensuring that the complexity of the information is reduced, and cost of access to information is lowered. One key way in how the CSOs have addressed the burden of access to information is by working towards rules that ensure access in *all* decision centres. They also report on access to information by identifying good or bad practices and raise awareness in order to increase the ability of individuals to push for direct access to information. The effectiveness of CSOs is undermined by lack of resources and unequal access to information of these CSOs themselves.[61] Bigger and well-established CSOs, especially those based in Brussels, have more knowledge, more access to officials and to decision-making processes. Conversely, CSOs that are established in different decision centres are less likely to participate.

[58] See also, in this Volume, Chapter 2 (III) by J. van Zeben on potential pitfalls of polycentricity.

[59] B. Kohel-Koch, Three Worlds of European Civil Society – What Role for Civil Society for What Kind of Europe?, *Policy and Society* 28 (2009), 47.

[60] Case T -174/95, *Svenska Journalistforbundet* v. *Council* [1998] ECR II-2289; Case T-2/03, *Verein fur Konsumenteninformation* v. *Commission* [2005] ECR II-1121; see also J. Heliskoski and P. Leino, 'Darkness at the Break of Noon: The Case Law on Regulation No. 1049/2001 on Access to Documents', *Common Market Law Review* 43 (2006), 735–81.

[61] See J. Greenwood, 'Organized Civil Society and Democratic Legitimacy in the European Union', *British Journal of Political Science* 37 (2007), 333.

ii Parliaments

Parliaments are arenas of public deliberation and peaceful contestation, and as such, members of parliament stand as intermediaries in obtaining the relevant information for decision making. Yet a weakness in practice persists concerning access to information for parliaments in order for them to be able to be an arena of debate and understanding for citizens. In the post-Lisbon context, the European Parliament (EP) has clear prerogatives provided in primary law to access information, including in issues of foreign policy.[62] These information channels and flows are further detailed in the EP's Rules of Procedure, providing that access to information must be 'immediate, regular and full . . . if necessary on a confidential basis'.[63] Inter-institutional agreements between the EP, the Commission and the Council also provide that information is to be shared 'regularly', 'without delay' and 'immediately'.[64] However, in practice delayed access or no access at all to information for the EP remains a concern. For example, in the recent *Mauritius* case,[65] the Council did not adhere to requirements of regularity and immediacy but delayed sharing information with the EP for more than three months.[66] This creates information asymmetries *within* a decision centre, and MEPs can only partially compensate for the lack of direct access to information by citizens.

Information asymmetries also persist *among* decision centres. A report on this issue that surveyed all 40 national chambers in the EU revealed

[62] See Article 218 TFEU.

[63] Rules of Procedure of the European Parliament, Article 18.

[64] Inter-institutional Agreement of 20 November 2002 between the European Parliament and the Council concerning access by the European Parliament to sensitive information of the Council in the field of security and defence policy [2002] OJ C298/1; Inter-institutional Agreement of 12 March 2014 between the European Parliament and the Council concerning the forwarding to and handling by the European Parliament of classified information held by the Council on matters other than those in the area of the common foreign and security policy [2014] OJ C95/1.

[65] Case C-658/11 *European Parliament* v. *Council of the European Union* [2014].

[66] Another similar instance of the Council not sharing information with the EP is the Pirate-Transfer Agreement with Tanzania, Case C-263/14, *Parliament* v. *Council* [2016]. See S. R. Sánchez-Tabernero, 'The Choice of Legal Basis and the Principle of Consistency in the Procedure for Conclusion of International Agreements in CFSP Contexts: Parliament v. Council', *Common Market Law Review* 54 (2017) 899, explaining how the CJEU utilised the principle of consistency as a supporting argument to the duty to inform the EP specifically in the context of the Common Foreign and Security Policy where oversight powers of the EP are limited.

that not all parliaments have equal access to information.[67] For example, only 27 chambers accessed documents that are sensitive but unclassified, known in the EU document categorisation as *Limité* documents.[68] Only 18 out of 40 national parliaments/chambers accessed a government database containing relevant EU information and documents.[69] Most significantly, only the Austrian *Nationalrat* and *Bundesrat* accessed *EU Secret* and *Top Secret* documents.[70] The 'privileged' position of the latter is related to the fact that this decision centre followed the rigid rules on access to information where exceptions on security or other matters should not be a hindrance for access. Whilst this is positive for this particular decision centre in that it has better standing in contrast to other decision centres, it shows a more general lack of equal access for citizens of different Member States that is important to polycentricity. This level of information asymmetry reduces comprehensibility for individuals and resources become too focused on the pressure for access rather than how access should facilitate self-governance. It also shows the limits of peaceful contestation and the need for individuals to have more direct avenues for enforcing their access rights.

iii Courts

A crucial venue for individuals to enforce rights of access is the Court of Justice of the European Union (CJEU). The Court decides upon the limits of access to information and in this regard has the most consequential role. The Court allows different levels of limitations on access to information and aims to ensure that the relevant right is upheld through the requirement of a statement of reasons. The Court has stated that the degree of precision of the statement of reasons 'must be weighed against practical realities and the time and technical facilities available for making the decision'.[71] Yet, similarly to the Parliament, the Court has struggled with access to information and actors in different decision centres have not always shared information. For example, France refused to disclose official secrets to the Court on the basis of national security

67 COSAC, Report 2012, Developments in European Union Procedures and Practices Relevant to Parliamentary Scrutiny, www.eerstekamer.nl/eu/publicatie/20120422/17_th_bi_annual_report_cosac/document.

68 ibid.

69 ibid., 6.

70 ibid., 5.

71 Case T-228/02 *OMPI* [2006] ECR II-4665, para. 141; Case C-350/88 *Delacre and Others v. Commission* [1990] I-395.

and these objections were raised before the Court although the same information had been shared with the governments of all Member States.[72] The UK also refused to grant the Court access to official secrets for reasons of national security.[73] As a result, the Court has revised its procedural rules in order to access information, although in cases of classified documents it might be able to do so only at the detriment of the individual not having any direct access to the information or to the summary of that information.[74]

**

The lack of access for parliaments and courts leads to these actors trying to safeguard their own access, even at the expense of direct access by citizens and of facilitating their learning and self-governance. Faced with challenges in gaining access to information, both the European Parliament and the CJEU revised their procedural rules to allow for privileged access to information for themselves, even in cases when the same information would not be accessible at all for individuals. For example, the Court revised its rules on access and review of confidential material through its Rules of Procedure. In the Introductory notes to the Rules of Procedure, the Court points out that the revision was driven by the need to 'provide solutions to procedural situations' involving the management of and access to confidential material and information.[75] For the first time in the history of the Court, with these new rules, the Court allows privileged access to classified information for itself and that information can be the basis of a judgment without the individual given even a summary or the gist of the information. This level of lack of access for the individual on the grounds on gaining access to the Court raises serious issues not only for matters of transparency, but also access to justice.

From a polycentric perspective, the main issue with both parliaments and courts is their privileged access to information, which remain undisclosed and possibly fully unknown to the individual. Whilst from an accountability perspective this type of access is sufficient as it serves the

[72] Opinion in Case C-27/09 P, *French Republic* v. *People's Mojahedin Organization of Iran* [2011] ECR I-13427, para. 7.

[73] Case C-280/12 P, *Council* v. *Fulmen* [2013] para. 77.

[74] See V. Abazi and C. Eckes, 'Closed Evidence in EU Courts: Security, Secrecy, and Access to Justice', *Common Market Law Review* 55 (2018), 753.

[75] The draft rules of procedure of the General Court were submitted to the Council in March 2014, see Council document 7795/14, COUR 12, INST 157, JUR 164, see in particular the fifth objective, Chapter 6, Section 3 and Chapter 7.

purposes of oversight, from a polycentric perspective it limits self-governance. Hence, citizens face limitations on access to information and their allies are of little help to elevate their position. This in turn shows that there are gaps in information for the individual in polycentric governance and at least in EU practice, such gaps are dominant in security matters.

IV Conclusion

Access to information has always been considered a condition for the functionality of polycentric governance. However, the exact role, requirements and effects of access to information in a polycentric system remain under-theorised. This chapter shows that access to information enables self-governance by fostering motivation, capacity and contribution. Specifically, this chapter identified that knowledge, understanding, equal access and contribution to societal groups and decisions centres are the building blocks of polycentric access to information. Moreover, as a prerequisite for institutional essentials, polycentric access to information should foster the ability of individuals to enter and exit, to enforce the shared system of rules and peaceful contestation. Polycentric access to information should be implemented to foster comprehensibility; equal access; forum choice; and only justified limitation to access.

Polycentric governance is conditioned by access to information but it also expands, specifies and advances this polycentric prerequisite. It gives value to the accessing of information beyond a formalistic tool or a measurement of control. It expands its power to offer learning and knowledge to individuals, which also shows the deep connections between access to information and learning as two separate prerequisites for institutional essentials. Similarly, by expanding the scope of access to information, polycentricity ensures higher standards of access to justice. Yet polycentricity also negatively impacts access to information due to its characteristics. Polycentric governance, with its many decision centres, results in fragmented responsibility among them and with increased burden on the individual both in finding the correct centre for access and increased complexity and level of information. This in turn means significant resources are necessary for genuine self-governance. Safeguards and allies can help to reduce complexity, increase access and enforce the right of access when other means fail.

Does the law and practice of the European Union match with this polycentric framework on access to information? The short answer is both yes and no. *Yes*, to the extent that the legal framework stipulated in EU law provides high levels of access to information and in doing so facilitates the individual in self-governance. Whilst limitations on the application of the right of public access to documents are a concern, the chapter showed that these as such do not diminish the overall potential for access to information in the EU to deliver on polycentric governance.

No, as in practice two major issues persist. First, information asymmetries are a real challenge. This has negative implications for self-governance, as it leads to individuals across the EU to have different levels of motivation, capacity and contribution. It also affects all institutional essentials: information asymmetries reduce choice for entry and exit and they prevent enforcement of rules to be shared in a manner that allows for equality of information flows. Paradoxically perhaps, information asymmetries both increase and decrease competition between different groups and their capacity in polycentric governance overall. As the example with parliaments shows, when it is revealed that there are asymmetries in accessing information among different parliaments, certain chambers demand more information from national governments, hence overall increasing the capacity of that decision centre. Yet, information asymmetries persist especially if they are not structurally addressed as opposed to ad hoc, leading to less knowledge and understanding within certain decision centres and hence their decreased competition overall in the polycentric system. 'Privileged' access is the second major concern in the EU practice not fully adhering to standards of polycentric access to information. The level of lack of access to information for individuals in these situations negatively affects not only the learning or understanding aspects of information, but the realisation of access to justice.[76]

Challenges of privileged access and information asymmetries are not unique to the EU's polycentric system but rather can be viewed as challenges to polycentric governance generally. The question therefore remains for future analysis as to how polycentric governance can mitigate these challenges and strengthen polycentric access to information as a prerequisite of institutional essentials.

[76] See, in this Volume, Chapter 10 by L. Díez Sánchez.

12

The Capacity to Learn in the Polycentric European Union

SACHA GARBEN*

The capacity to learn is a core *prerequisite* for polycentric governance.[1] If individuals are to successfully self-govern, they need to be able to acquire the necessary skills to do so, which means learning about the existing governance framework (the institutions, the procedures, the rules, the practices) and the existing and impending substantive law and policies.[2] In turn, self-governance through participation in the overarching governance framework fosters further learning, leading to a self-reinforcing dynamic. As such, learning is not only a prerequisite for, but also a *benefit* of a successful polycentric system. Within this process, a distinction can be made between the individual and collective capacity to learn.[3] This distinction is particularly relevant given the unit of analysis applied to self-governance in polycentric systems. This distinction illustrates the

* The views expressed in this chapter are entirely personal and do not reflect the official position of the European Commission.

1 See for full discussion, in this Volume, Chapter 1 by J. van Zeben.

2 See C. Colomb, 'The Added Value of Transnational Cooperation: Towards a New Framework for Evaluating Learning and Policy Change', *Planning, Practice & Research* 22 (3) (2007), 348.

3 In addition, different conceptual distinctions can be made between various learning types, including (i) organisational learning, which concerns process-related behaviour and strategy, (ii) lesson-drawing, concerning instruments, (iii) social learning, which is about world views and ideas, and (iv) political learning entailing understanding others' preferences and selling an argument (see A. Zito and A. Schout, 'Learning Theory Reconsidered: EU Integration Theories and Learning', *Journal of European Public Policy* 16 (8) (2009), 1103). Since all these, and possibly other, forms of learning seem equally relevant for both the capacity to learn as a prerequisite and as a benefit of polycentricity, this chapter will discuss learning generally without endeavouring to analyse it in reference to these distinctions specifically. Furthermore, the definition of learning for this chapter is pragmatic. Learning theory tends to include change of behaviour on the basis of the acquired insights in the concept of learning. Since, for the purposes of polycentricity, it is rather the *capacity* to learn than the measuring of actual learning that is relevant, this chapter will not generally assess the degree of actual learning taking place but instead the potential for it.

tension between Ostrom's methodological individualism,[4] and the practical reality that most self-governance expresses itself through organisation with others, either formally or informally (thus including functional and territorial, governmental and non-governmental entities), which has led most scholars of polycentricity to take these groups, at different levels, as unit of analysis.[5]

The goal of this chapter is to provide a holistic overview of the role of learning in the EU considered from a polycentric perspective. To that end, this chapter explores how the EU currently provides for the capacity to learn in a collective and individual sense, both as a prerequisite of polycentricity and as a potential benefit. Learning as a prerequisite of polycentricity shall be interpreted mainly as learning specifically *about the European Union and self- governance within the EU*, while learning as a benefit of polycentricity on the other hand shall be considered as *general learning* (about other decision-making centres and about the world at large). In line with the self-imposed constraints of this Volume's scope, the core question of how the EU provides for the capacity to learn will be answered through reference to the EU's 'rules' – both its 'overarching system of shared rules' (i.e. its constitution in the more general sense of the term) and its substantive rules (i.e. its legislation and official policies). Nevertheless, in line with polycentricity theory's firm grounding in real world decision making,[6] which necessitates an interdisciplinary and empirical approach, the chapter will seek to imbue the legal analysis as much as possible with relevant insights from other disciplines as well as an awareness of informal practices and practical realities.

I The Capacity to Learn and Polycentric Governance

Individual citizens, as well as groups of individuals that are somehow organised around a governance objective, need to be able to learn about the specific policies of the overarching central level of governance of the polity within which they are nested. This includes also learning about its fundamental set-up and functioning (in polycentric terms: the overarching system of shared rules), in order to be able to

[4] V. Ostrom, *The Meaning of American Federalism: Constituting a Self-governing Society* (ICS Press, 1994), 227, as discussed by J. van Zeben in Chapter 1.

[5] See, in this Volume, Chapter 1 by J. van Zeben.

[6] R. Herzberg, 'Governing Their Commons: Elinor and Vincent Ostrom and the Bloomington School', *Public Choice* 163 (2015), 96.

successfully self-govern (with)in that system. This learning will empower them to make use of the opportunities that the system provides to influence its output. First, it means that they can more effectively (and peacefully) contest the authority, or a specific policy, of the central level when they consider that it leads to excessive centralisation detrimental to their own regulatory autonomy (and thus capacity to self-govern).[7] Secondly, it empowers them to actively use this central level to cooperate with others, in particular with other decision-making centres within the polycentric polity, when they consider that this suits their objectives.

As one of the three prerequisites of polycentric governance, the capacity to learn facilitates the institutional essentials of a polycentric system of freedom of entry and exit, the enforcement of a system of shared rules and peaceful contestation among different (interest) groups in obvious ways.[8] However, the capacity to learn does not only facilitate the freedom of entry and exit, the latter also impacts the former: the freedom of entry and exit puts various decision-making centres in competition with each other (a core attribute of polycentricity), and as will be explained, this may enhance but also limit the collective capacity to learn, depending in part on the extent to which the overarching system of shared rules sufficiently allows for cooperation between the various jurisdictions.[9] The relationship between the capacity to learn and the other prerequisites of polycentricity (access to justice and access to information) is more straightforward. Learning is particularly intimately connected with access to information, as it depends on it, and in turn benefits it.

Apart from being a precondition, the capacity to learn can be considered one of the main *potential benefits* of polycentric governance. The diversity and dynamism, characteristic of a successful polycentric polity, can be expected to foster comparison, entrepreneurship and a destabilisation of entrenched understandings, thereby creating fruitful dynamics that invite and encourage learning in an individual and collective sense. In the words of M. D. McGinnis and E. Ostrom: '[a]mong the positive

[7] See, in this Volume, Chapter 9 by D. Kukovec.
[8] See, in this Volume, Chapter 1II.C. by J. van Zeben.
[9] On the relationship between competition and cooperation in the EU: S. Garben, 'Competition, Cooperation, and Solidarity in EU Law – A Federal Perspective', in P. Chiocchetti and F. Allemand (eds.), *Competitiveness and Solidarity in the European Union: Interdisciplinary Perspectives* (Routledge, 2018).

benefits of polycentricity touted by [V.] Ostrom were such matters as [. . .] generation of a richer body of information available to citizens'.[10] This benefits self-governance and thus polycentricity itself, and its potential to be self-sustaining. Furthermore, learning can be expected to lead to better policy outcomes. While it is important to stress that in polycentric theory, what matters is that the people involved in the governance system set their own goals, and these may not necessarily be the 'best' as judged by external standards of efficiency, effectiveness or quality, it is nevertheless worthwhile to consider these additional potential benefits when analysing a specific system from the viewpoint of polycentricity.

This second dimension of learning as a benefit rather than a prerequisite of polycentric governance does not pertain so much to the existing overarching governance framework, nor the ability of individuals and collectives to operate therein, but rather to (the advancement of) knowledge in a more general sense. This includes institutional and substantive knowledge about the other decision-making centres, but also insights not directly connected to governance issues at all, but instead about the world at large. While this dimension of learning is not often considered as part of 'the capacity to learn' in polycentric theory, to include it would seem to find support in Vincent Ostrom's work, e.g. where it states that 'the future belongs to those whose covenants are bonds of mutual trust grounded in principles of self-governance and who learn to use processes of conflict and conflict resolution to elucidate information, clarify alternative, stimulate innovation, and extend the frontiers of inquiry to open new potentials for human development'.[11] Accordingly, the present chapter considers both dimensions of learning in the context of the EU.

II Collective Learning as a Prerequisite for a Polycentric EU

How do the EU's rules provide for the capacity to learn about its constitutional arrangement and its law and policies, both for collectives and for individual citizens? Our assessment of that question will be based on the assumption that apart from specific provisions made for academic learning, the most important way to learn about the EU's operation and its output is by doing, i.e. to be involved in it. This shows the potentially

[10] M. D. McGinnis and E. Ostrom, 'Reflections on Vincent Ostrom, Public Administration, and Polycentricity', *Public Administration Review* 72(1) (2012), 22.

[11] V. Ostrom, 'Polycentricity', in M. D. McGinnis (ed.), *Polycentricity and Local Public Economies: Readings from the Workshop in Political Theory and Policy Analysis* (University of Michigan Press, 1999), 272.

self-reinforcing dynamic of polycentricity: learning enables self-governance and self-governance fosters learning.[12] As such, this Section maps not only the specific ways in which EU law and policy foster learning about the EU in a direct sense, but also the ways in which the EU provides for the information, consultation and participation of various governmental and non-governmental groups and individual citizens.[13] In this respect, there are a number of privileged actors that derive such rights directly from the Treaties, while others are forced to rely on either formal or informal policies to learn about and operate in the EU decision-making process. Furthermore, as we shall see, some privileged actors are more privileged than others, in that some are provided with significantly more opportunities for learning and self-governance.

A *The Council and National Governments*

Article 10(2) TEU reminds us that 'Member States are represented in the European Council by their Heads of State or Government and in the Council by their governments' and indeed, national governments still play the most important role in EU decision making of any kind, be it in the form the adoption of legislation through the Community Method, through soft law and policy coordination, or through inter-governmental decision making. Of course, these extensive participation rights imply a front row seat in anything EU-related and entail highly privileged access to information, meaning that national governments are in prime position to learn about the EU both institutionally and substantively.

Still, this does not automatically mean that national governments know everything there is to know about the EU, or that they have a boundless capacity to learn it.

First, even for national governments, the EU and its decision-making process are not fully transparent. Individual governments are not always fully aware of the activities or 'agenda' of the other main actors in the decision-making process such as the Commission, the Parliament and the ECB, the CJEU's case law, informal 'agreements' between other national governments or between governments and EU Institutions, and – in the legislative process – the informal negotiations in trilogues.

[12] It should be noted that this may have certain disadvantages, as it throws up hurdles for newcomers who have to 'compete' in the governance framework with actors who can build on their previous experience.

[13] This, once again, demonstrates the intimate link of the capacity to learn with the prerequisite of access to information, and with self-governance more generally.

This may impede their substantive and institutional learning about the EU, and thus limit their capacity for effective self-governance.

Secondly, a national government depends on the quality and quantity of its internal resources, particularly its civil service, to be able to learn effectively about the EU and to operate successfully within it.[14] The capacity of a civil service in this respect is dependent on many different factors, such as the prestige accorded to public service in general and the priority given to EU affairs specifically, the possibilities offered for training and education on the EU, the overall (financial and otherwise) investment in human resources and, more generally, the country's institutional capacity and stability over time.

Relatedly,[15] not all national governments are in the same position when it comes to their experience in EU affairs. Some have been involved in the integration process from the beginning, organically developing their knowledge and skills, while other Member States have joined the project much later, meaning that they have had to absorb much larger amounts of information in a much shorter period of time, and cannot build on the same levels of experience in the negotiation and implementation of new EU law and policy. This is all the more relevant because the EU functions in highly specific ways, through 'endless and numerous multilateral negotiations and coalition building, consensus reaching and

[14] T. Börzel makes this argument through a specific example in EU environmental policy: 'Coalition-building and interest accommodation skills provide a third important source of influence in shaping European policies. The Dutch have a particular reputation for working out complicated, tailor-made compromises which are acceptable to all parties involved (Andersen and Liefferink, 1997, 27–8). But being present in the various networks that prepare and accompany the European negotiation process demands considerable staff-power, expertise and information, which the Member States do not have to the same degree. The German Ministry of the Environment, for instance, counts some 900 employees and the Federal Environmental Agency has another 850 experts working in the field. The Dutch core environmental administration employs about 1,500 people (Hanf and Gronden, 1998, 171). Not surprisingly, German and Dutch experts are omnipresent in the environmental committees and hearings of the various European institutions like the Commission, the Council, the European Parliament, the Economic and Social Committee or the Committee of the Regions'. T. Börzel, 'Pace-Setting, Foot-Dragging, and Fence-Sitting: Member State Responses to Europeanization', *Journal of Common Market Studies* 40 (2) (2002), 193, 200.

[15] While taking due care to avoid generalisation, the Member States that have more recently acceded tend also to be countries with more limited administrative capacity. See T. Verheijen, 'Administrative Capacity in the New EU Member States – The Limits of Innovation?' (2007) World Bank Working Paper Series, Paper No. 115.

linking issues that at first seem non-linkable'.[16] Newer Member States have to learn to 'play this game'.[17]

These structural limitations cannot be overcome completely, but the EU features a range of instruments to mitigate their effects.

Although the information flow between the actors involved in EU decision making is imperfect, this could be said about any multilateral decision-making process. Compared to 'traditional' inter-governmental governance, EU decision making is actually much more transparent and objective, including for national governments. A key element is the involvement of the Commission as an 'honest broker' representing the common interest and counteracting traditional power-play, particularly to the benefit of Member States that are less naturally 'dominant' because of their size[18] or their experience. Furthermore, the Commission is committed to evidence-based governance through its 'Better Regulation Agenda', which requires impact assessments of each legislative initiative.[19] Here is not the place to enter into a detailed appreciation of whether the Commission actually lives up to this important 'neutralising' role, and to what extent it has the legitimacy to 'mitigate' politics in this way, but rather to point out that compared to cooperation between

16 P. Kaczynski, 'The Fifth Enlargement of the EU, Five Years On: The Case of Poland and the Czech Republic', in *Europe Visions 2* (Institut Français des Relations Internationales, 2008), 23.

17 ibid., '"New Europeans" are learning the game on a daily basis, trying to find room for themselves, their interests and objectives. At the same time, they try to define or redefine their interests and objectives. This dynamic situation sometimes leads to defensive situations and it at times takes an inexperienced new member to clumsily veto. Yet, in general they seem to be moving towards a constructive consensual approach. The question is "how" the new members learn their lesson. It seems to be a general process applicable to all (or most) new members, as well as those states that adhered to the EU before. Any new country at first tries to "defend" its national interests: this means that new states apply defensive, not offensive tools. The most visible of them is the veto power. As time passes, state officials learn that vetoing is sometimes counterproductive, sometimes alienating and rarely successful, especially in areas where there is no consensual decision-making. They learn that the veto power is rightly labelled "the nuclear weapon" of EU decision-making. [. . .] [This] lesson that the veto power is absolutely the last resort is to be learnt by all new members, be it Sweden in 1995 or Poland in 2004.

18 See on this point P. Magnette and K. Nicolaïdis, 'Large and Small Member States in the European Union: Reinventing the Balance', *Notre Europe: Research and European Issues*, No. 25 (2003).

19 For extensive discussion, see: S. Garben and I. Govaere, *The EU Better Regulation Agenda: Critical Reflections* (Hart Publishing, 2018). The Better Regulation Agenda is an exercise in policy appraisal, arguably directed at enhancing policy learning. See C. Radaelli, 'Measuring Policy Learning: Regulatory Impact Assessment in Europe', *Journal of European Public Policy* 16 (8) (2009), 1145.

wholly independent jurisdictions, the EU features more safeguards for national governments in their pursuit of self-governance, and their capacity to know and learn.[20]

Secondly, the EU's accession policy prioritises capacity building. In the pre-accession period, the candidate country is required to adapt its institutions, standards and infrastructure to enable it to meet its obligations as an EU Member State. This involves compliance with the Copenhagen criteria,[21] which includes 'administrative and institutional capacity to effectively implement the *acquis* and ability to take on the obligations of membership'. There is close supervision of a candidate's progress by the EU Institutions, and, more importantly, both funding[22] and technical assistance[23] are provided. This should ensure a minimum standard of knowledge and administrative capacity (thus learning and governing capacity) once the candidate becomes an EU Member State.

Post-accession, continuing support in administrative capacity building is available for EU Member States under the EU's cohesion policy (Article 174 TFEU).[24] The European Social Fund, the European Regional Development Fund and the Cohesion Fund all provide investment in

[20] To a certain extent, this is also ensured by the fact that the Commission still includes nationals of all Member States. Declaration 10 on Article 17 of the TFEU underlines this, by stating that 'when the Commission no longer includes nationals of all Member States, the Commission should pay particular attention to the need to ensure full transparency in relations with all Member States. Accordingly, the Commission should liaise closely with all Member States, whether or not they have a national serving as member of the Commission, and in this context pay special attention to the need to share information and consult with all Member States'.

[21] European Council in Copenhagen in 1993.

[22] Currently the EU provides substantial support to the enlargement countries, through the Instrument for Pre-Accession Assistance II, with a level of funds for the period 2014–2020 of €11.7 billion. See European Commission Communication, Enlargement Strategy and Main Challenges 2013–2014, COM(2013) 700 final.

[23] TAIEX is the Technical Assistance and Information Exchange instrument of the European Commission which supports public administrations with regard to the approximation, application and enforcement of EU legislation and facilitates the sharing of EU best practices through workshops, expert missions and study visits. The Assistance is not only open to governmental civil servants but also the judiciary and law enforcement authorities, parliaments, and trade unions and employers' associations. The actual assistance itself is provided by public officials from EU Member States.

[24] The main legal framework is provided by the Common Provisions Regulation for the European Structural and Investment Funds (Regulation (EU) 1303/2013). For a detailed overview and discussion of the EU legal instruments concerning the structural and investment funds, see European Commission, European Structural and Investment Funds 2014–2020: Official Texts and Commentaries, Luxembourg: Publications Office of the European Union, 2015, available online at: http://ec.europa.eu/regional_policy/sources/docgener/guides/blue_book/blueguide_en.pdf

the structures, human capital and systems and tools of the public sector, 'oriented towards more efficient organisational processes, modern management, motivated and skilled civil servants' and is accompanied by the possibility of technical assistance for the implementation of these funds.[25] Furthermore, Member State civil servants can be temporarily seconded to work for the Commission.[26] Such national experts have a dual role in learning: they acquire knowledge and experience on EU issues to bring back home and they bring national knowledge and experience to the European level. That latter dimension can be strategically employed by national governments to influence EU law making and policy making.[27]

Finally, the specific context of the EU Presidency should be noted. The Presidency presents a major challenge for national administrations and at the same time an important opportunity to reinforce the national government's capacity to learn about the EU substantively and institutionally, as well as influence its output. The current system of trio presidencies[28] supports mutual learning among the Member States and their administrations, and while not every Presidency can be considered equally successful, they all provide national administrations with important 'lessons' not only pertaining to the administration of a Presidency specifically, but about EU governance more generally.[29]

[25] http://ec.europa.eu/regional_policy/en/policy/themes/better-public-administration/ accessed 18 October 2018.

[26] European Commission Decision laying down rules on the secondment to the Commission of national experts and national experts in professional training, C (2008) 6866 final.

[27] T. Börzel (n. 14) 199. See also A. Héritier, '"Leaders" and "Laggards" in European Clean Air Policy', in B. Unger and F.V. Waarden (eds.), *Convergence or Diversity? Internationalization and Economic Policy Response* (Avebury, 1994) 278–305, and D. Liefferink and M. S. Andersen, 'Strategies of the "Green" Member States in EU Environmental Policy-making', *Journal of European Public Policy* 5 (2) (1998), 254.

[28] Council Decision of 1 December 2009 laying down measures for the implementation of the European Council Decision on the exercise of the Presidency of the Council, and on the chairmanship of preparatory bodies of the Council, (2009) 322 OJ L 28–34.

[29] For case studies, see e.g. M. Jensen and P. Nedergaard, *EU Precidencies between Politics and Administration, The governmentality of the Polish, Danish and Cypriot Trio Presidency in 2011–2012* (Routledge, 2017); L. Ferreira-Pereira, 'Portugal and the 2007 EU Presidency: A Case of Constructive Bridge-Building', *Journal of Common Market Studies* 46 (1) (2008), 61; P. Humphreys, 'The Fifth Irish Presidency of the European Union: Some Management Lessons' (1997) Committee for Public Management Research Discussion Paper 2; S. Kajnč and M. Svetličič, 'What It Takes to Run an EU Presidency: Study of Competences in Slovenia's Public Administration', *Administrative Culture* 1 (2010), 84.

In conclusion, perhaps unsurprisingly considering the EU's nature as a (very advanced form of) international organisation, notwithstanding some limitations the EU institutional and substantive framework contains many possibilities of participation and learning for national governments, both 'individually' and in their joint manifestation as the Council.

B The European Parliament

Individual citizens organise themselves at the European level through the direct election of the European Parliament (EP). Its involvement in EU decision making is significant, particularly in its exercise of legislative and budgetary functions (Article 14 TEU) and in the election of the Commission President (Article 17 TEU) and has increased substantially and consistently with every Treaty revision. However, this does not mean that the EP's knowledge and capacity to learn about EU decision making is limitless.

First, as with parliaments around the world more generally,[30] MEPs may not possess the necessary qualifications in relation to parliament's key functions (legislative, budgetary), having been elected sometimes at short notice and from all walks of life.[31] Furthermore, there are inherent limits to individual MEPs' capacity to manage the increasing and complex information resulting from the EU's growing range of activities, as well as society's increasing (scientific, economic, legal, political) complexity.[32] Compounding that fact is that the same complexity that makes

[30] K. Coghill, C. Lewis, and K. Steinack, See 'How Should Elected Members Learn Parliamentary Skills: An Overview', *Parliamentary Affairs* 65 (3) (2012), 505; R. Donohue and P. Holland, 'Building Parliamentary Human Capital', *Parliamentary Affairs* 65 (3) (2012), 529.

[31] Interestingly, research suggests that 'the 2004 cohort of new member state MEPs are better educated and more politically experienced' than 'their counterparts from the old member states'. See T. Bale and P. Taggart, 'The Newest of the New? Accession state MEPs: Who They Are and Who They Think They Are' Paper presented to the Federal Trust Workshop on 'the European Parliament and the European Political Space' 30 March 2006, London.

[32] 'The profound differentiation and complexity of modern society is manifested in a number of different features that affect governance. The various processes relating to production, commerce, health, education, industries, service production, etc. are not overseeable. In sum, there is great societal complexity. There is administrative complexity; there is technical and scientific complexity, complexity of social values and lifestyles. The established, formal institutions of government cannot handle this complexity'. S. Andersen and T. Burns, 'The European Union and the Erosion of Parliamentary

issues difficult to handle by parliaments also presents a challenge to the European executive, which is therefore compelled to delegate to specialised bodies, such as agencies, making it even harder for MEPs to access, understand, learn and participate in these areas.

Moreover, there remain a number of important areas where the EP plays only a marginal role, such as economic governance. Indeed, while it is true its powers have progressively expanded, arguably the European integration process has expanded even more and overall there has been a shift to more inter-governmentalism, benefiting the Council to the EP's detriment.[33] Furthermore, even under the Community Method, the EP remains without the right to take legislative initiatives (as it only has the right to request a proposal, Article 225 TFEU).

A number of counterbalancing elements are worthy of mention: MEPs can rely not only on the support of their personal team, which usually consists of several assistants, but also on the expertise of the in-house European Parliamentary Research Service, which produces a wide range of information varying from short briefings to in-depth academic research projects. As Neunreither concludes on the basis of a detailed overview of learning support for MEPs, 'the internal services of the EP [...] have grown over a period of more than 40 years into a widely respected, non-partisan public service, considered by many as a "strong internal bureaucracy". The value of these services, which should be strengthened, is that they are trusted'.[34]

In addition to in-house expertise, MEPs can learn about the technical details of relevant issues through the consultation of stakeholders. While this practice suffers a bad image, as it allows organised interests to 'lobby' the decision-making process, the supply of expertise and information to those in power arguably has its value,[35] provided that there are sufficient

Democracy', in S. Andersen and K. Eliassen (eds.), *The European Union: How Democratic Is It?* (Sage Publications, 1996) 236.

33 C. Bickerton, D. Hodson, and U. Puetter, 'The New Intergovernmentalism: European Integration in the Post-Maastricht Era', *Journal of Common Market Studies* 53 (4) (2015), 703.

34 K. Neunreither, 'Elected Legislators and Their Unelected Assistants in the European Parliament', *The Journal of Legislative Studies* 8 (4) (2002), 57.

35 P. Bouwen, 'Exchanging Access Goods for Access: A Comparative Study of Business Lobbying in the European Union Institutions', *European Journal of Political Research* 43 (3) (2004), 337; P. Bouwen, 'Corporate Lobbying in the European Union: The Logic of Access', *Journal of European Public Policy* 9 (3) (2002), 365; F. Pappi and C. Henning, 'The Organization of Influence on the EC's Common Agricultural Policy: A Network Approach', *European Journal of Political Research* 36 (2) (1999), 257.

guarantees (notably, transparency[36] – confirming its importance as a prerequisite for successful polycentric governance) to prevent or counterbalance the negative externalities of private rent-seeking by these groups and individuals and unequal representation of interests/access to the EU Institutions.[37]

Finally, the EP has been very successful in learning how to wield informal power in areas where its competences are restricted, ultimately to the effect of expanding its formal competences. Héritier has mapped its strategies in this respect, the main ones being (i) the renegotiation of ambiguous institutional rules in its favour, (ii) delaying, (iii) arena linking (withholding consent in one area in return for being given more institutional power in another), (iv) forming alliances with Member States favourable to expanding its powers, (v) invoking CJEU rulings in the hope of being confirmed in its institutional aspirations and (vi) making unilateral first moves in changing institutional rules that other institutional actors face that came with high political cost for returning to the status quo *ante.*[38]

In conclusion, while the EP's important constitutional powers are limited by a number of factors, several practices mitigate these limits, suggesting that overall the EP possesses a very strong capacity to learn.

C National Parliaments

It is often argued that European integration has decreased the influence of national parliaments. The cause of this lies, to an important extent, in diminished control over the activities of (their) national governments in the EU arena,[39] particularly because of a lack of (timely) access to the necessary information, as well as a lack of time and resources to process the amount and complexity of this information.[40] Arguably, this

[36] A. Chambers, 'The Lobbying of the EU – How to Achieve Greater Transparency' (2016) Civitas, available at: www.civitas.org.uk/content/files/Anthony-Chambers-EU-lobbying.pdf

[37] Y. Papadopoulos, 'Cooperative Forms of Governance: Problems of Democratic Accountability in Complex Environments', *European Journal of Political Research* 42 (2003), 474.

[38] A. Héritier, 'The increasing Institutional Power of the European Parliament and EU Policy Making' (2017) 1 EIF Working Paper 2, 3.

[39] A. Moravcsik, 'Why the European Union Strengthens the State: Domestic Politics and International Cooperation', (1994) Harvard University Centre for European Studies, Working Paper No. 52.

[40] For this latter point in relation to economic governance: V. Kreilinger, *National Parliaments, Surveillance Mechanisms and Ownership in the Euro Area* (Jacques Delors Institute, 2016), 51.

situation has been aggravated by the euro crisis, where additional sensitive policy areas have been uploaded to the EU level for (binding and non-binding) executive decision making.[41]

At the same time, the EU and national parliaments have developed ways to improve parliamentary involvement.

First, national parliaments have the right to learn about the EU's (planned) activities. Article 1 of Protocol 1 on the Role of National Parliaments requires the Commission to forward its consultation documents directly upon publication. It shall also forward the annual legislative programme and any other instrument of legislative planning or policy, at the same time as to the EP and the Council. Draft legislative acts are similarly sent to national parliaments (Article 2 of the Protocol). Such timely informing of the legislative agenda allows national parliaments to better control their executives when they act in the Council. As the EP reports, 'most of the [national] parliaments have [. . .] learned how to deal with information overload by designing procedures aimed at sorting documents and by employing clerks to that end'.[42]

Such rights to information and effective processing strategies also put national parliaments in the position to influence the EU agenda directly, expressing their opinions to the Commission on planned or pending initiatives.[43] When it concerns the principle of subsidiarity, this direct involvement is constitutionalised through the so-called 'Early Warning System' provided for in the Protocol on the Application of the Principles of Subsidiarity and Proportionality. This procedure allows national parliaments to express a 'reasoned opinion' on legislative proposals. While their views are not binding, as the Commission remains free to proceed with the initiative even when the threshold for a 'yellow' or 'orange' card is reached, it is nevertheless a powerful tool of involvement. Parliaments seem to be learning to use these powers granted by the Lisbon Treaty, demonstrated by (i) the consistent increase in opinions,[44] and (ii) an

41 On the displacement of the legislative process in economic governance: S. Garben, 'The Constitutional (Im)balance between "The Market" and "The Social" in the EU', *European Constitutional Law Review* 13 (2013), 23.

42 European Parliament, Directorate-General For Internal Policies, *The Role of National Parliaments in the EU after Lisbon: Potentialities and Challenges* (2017), 55.

43 In addition, since 2015, they have informally started to issue 'green cards' where they suggest new legislation to the Commission, with variable success. See European Parliament, Directorate-General for Internal Policies, ibid., 35.

44 While the overall number fluctuates slightly, also in relation to the amount of initiatives taken by the Commission, over time there has been an impressive increase. In 2016, national parliaments issued 620 opinions, representing a 77 per cent increase compared

increased cooperation between national parliaments in this respect,[45] to date amounting to three 'yellow cards'.

Already before the introduction of the Early Warning System, national parliaments had 'gradually learned to play the European game'[46] mainly thanks to mutual learning processes. O'Brennan and Raunio report that 'when designing new scrutiny systems (new Member States), or choosing how to strengthen existing mechanisms of control (old member countries), the national MPs and parliamentary civil servants have learned "best practices" from each other'.[47] The importance of inter-parliamentary cooperation, between national parliaments as well as with the EP,[48] is underlined by Article 12 TEU and specific provisions are made in the Protocol on the Role of National Parliaments in the EU. In accordance with its Article 10, a Conference of Parliamentary Committees for Union Affairs shall promote the exchange of information and best practice and organise inter-parliamentary conferences on specific topics, in particular to debate matters of common foreign and security policy.[49]

Finally, in the context of European economic governance, it has been reported that national parliaments are learning to scrutinise their executives and the EU level. In the context of the European Semester, the EU's yearly cycle of economic policy coordination, one third of national parliaments has 'adopted new rules or laws that codify parliamentary

to 2015. Looking solely at reasoned opinions, their number increased from 8 in 2015 to 65 in 2016, an increase of more than 700 per cent. European Commission, *Report on Relations between the European Commission and National Parliaments 2016*, COM/2017/0601 final.

45 I. Cooper, 'A Yellow Card for the Striker: National Parliaments and the Defeat of EU Legislation on the Right to Strike', *Journal of European Public Policy* 22 (10) (2015), 1406.

46 J. O'Brennan and T. Raunio, 'National Parliaments Gradually Learning to Play the European Game?', in J. O'Brennan and T. Raunio (eds.), *National Parliaments within the Enlarged European Union – From 'Victims' of Integration to Competitive Actors?* (Routledge, 2007).

47 ibid., 274.

48 Cooperation between the EP and national parliaments has already yielded some results, such as in the case of the European Citizens' Initiative where as Fasone and Fromage report, 'the lowering from one third to one fourth of the Member States for the final threshold of countries from where signatures have to be collected derives from a joint attempt of national parliaments and the EP'. See C. Fasone and D. Fromage, 'National Parliaments and the EU Commission's Agenda: Limits and Recent Developments of a Difficult Partnership', in C. Fasone, D. Fromage, and Z. Lefkofridi (eds.), Parliaments, Public Opinion and Parliamentary Elections in Europe (EUI Working Papers MWP 18/2015), 37.

49 For full discussion: D. Fromage, 'A Mapping of Recent Trends in Interparliamentary Cooperation within the EU', in C. Fasone, D. Fromage, and Z. Lefkofridi (eds.), ibid., 21.

involvement' and '*de facto* and more often than quantitative data suggest, surveillance procedures have become part of domestic politics over the last years'.[50]

As such, while it remains true that national parliaments are in a disadvantaged position for participation and learning in European integration, there is significant potential to improve their situation especially since the Lisbon Treaty, which national parliaments are currently learning to do.

D Regional Authorities

The most important way in which regional authorities can participate and learn about the EU is through the Committee of the Regions, an advisory body of the Union established in 1994. Article 300 TFEU provides that it shall consist of 'representatives of regional and local bodies who either hold a regional or local authority electoral mandate or are politically accountable to an elected assembly'. The members are completely independent. The Treaties provide that the Committee shall be consulted by the EP, Council and Commission in a number of areas, such as transport, employment, social policy, education, health, trans-European networks and the environment. It may issue an opinion on its own initiative in cases in which it considers such action appropriate.

The effectiveness of this constitutional role for the Committee of the Regions has been questioned, as it appears that the EU Institutions 'do not always read the opinions and are consequently often unaware of what the [Committee] propose[s]'.[51] However, as Hönnige and Panke note, the Committee can raise its profile and impact 'through extracurricular activities (e.g. seminars, participation in hearings, circulation of additional information)'.[52] This means that there is some further scope for the Committee to learn how to increase its opportunities to participate in EU decision making. It benefits from a privileged position which enhances its capacity to learn, but this has not yet been exploited to the full extent.

50 V. Kreilinger, *National Parliaments, Surveillance Mechanisms and Ownership in the Euro Area* (Jacques Delors Institute, 2016), 52.

51 C. Hönnige and D. Panke, 'Is Anybody Listening? The Committee of the Regions and the European Economic and Social Committee and Their Quest for Awareness', *Journal of European Public Policy* 23 (4) (2016), 624.

52 ibid.

E Social Partners

Representatives of management and labour (i.e. the Social Partners) both on the national and European level can benefit from EU funding for projects intended to create awareness and instil knowledge about the EU and its opportunities for social dialogue, and for their activities more generally.[53] Such capacity-building clearly enhances their capacity to learn. In addition, the Social Partners benefit from a privileged position under the Treaties. Article 152 TFEU recognises the importance of, and encourages, social dialogue as an important form of self-governance, and the TFEU's Social Title contains specific provisions for the information, consultation and participation of the Social Partners in EU decision making.

Article 154(2) TFEU lays down the obligation of 'first stage' consultation with social partners, where the Commission has to consult management and labour on the possible direction of Union action before it puts forward a proposal. This allows the social partners to influence the Commission's policy from the beginning, rather than in reaction to a pre-defined approach. Article 154(3) TFEU provides the 'second stage' consultation, concerning the actual content of the envisaged proposal. The consultation shall take place as regards initiatives in all areas having social implications, which includes e.g. trade, the internal market and transport.[54]

Article 155 TFEU provides the infrastructure for social partners to self-regulate the matters covered by Article 153 TFEU, including through the adoption of binding agreements to be implemented by the EU legislator. It thereby provides a unique additional law-making process in the EU legal order, where the Commission's usual monopoly on legislative initiative does not apply. It could be called the EU 'Social Method' of law making, in contrast to the traditional 'Community Method'.[55]

While it is true that a number of Member States accord an even more prominent role to social partners in labour market regulation, and that from their point of view EU action in these areas may thereby replace their regulatory autonomy, on balance it should be concluded that the EU framework fosters their capacity to learn in important ways.

[53] See European Commission, *Vademecum - Commission Support to EU Social Dialogue* (2017), 24.

[54] Article 2 of Commission Decision 98/500/EC of 20 May 1998.

[55] S. Garben, 'The Constitutional (Im)balance between "the market" and "the social" in the EU' (n. 41).

F Non-Governmental Organisations

Non-governmental organisations, other than trade unions and employer/business representatives, have to make do with either more general or more informal mechanisms of learning. They can make use of the standard EU information and consultation mechanisms, such as public consultation exercises. In recent years, in the context of the Better Regulation Agenda, the Commission has demonstrated a commitment to inviting public views systematically on new initiatives. This provides NGOs with information about the possibility of a proposal and its potential content, and the option to express their views. However, the actual contribution to participatory democracy of these exercises has been doubted, as there is little evidence of the input being taken on board in the subsequent development of the initiative and because public consultations tend to feature a limited number of 'usual suspects' in terms of participants: the NGOs already well-connected in the 'Brussels bubble'.[56] Public consultations thus seem to serve as information platforms where the Commission publicises its policy intentions, rather than a genuine participatory mechanism. Still, such information is highly valuable in itself in its contribution to the capacity to learn.

Perhaps more effective in terms of actually influencing the output of EU decision making is 'lobbying' MEPs – a practice which, as discussed above, suffers from a bad image but can be instrumental in learning and self-governance, both for parliamentarians and NGOs. Experienced NGOs know the ways to maximise their influence, for instance by providing MEPs sympathetic to their cause with fully fledged amendments to be introduced in the legislative procedure.[57] Less experienced NGOs have to learn how to play this game, for which they can to a certain extent rely on informal mutual learning. The justifiability of these practices is to an important extent dependent on transparency, and for this reason the EP and Commission have established a register.[58] Transparency also allows less experienced NGOs to learn about the lobbying efforts of other NGOs, both those that are politically aligned to their cause and those opposed.

[56] M. Dawson, 'Better Regulation and the Future of EU Regulatory Law and Politics', *Common Market Law Review* 53 (2016), 1219.

[57] T. Venables, 'Tips for the Would-be European Lobbyist' (2008), European Citizen Action Service, p. 16.

[58] Agreement between the European Parliament and the European Commission on the transparency register for organisations and self-employed individuals engaged in EU policy making and policy implementation (2014) 277 OJ L 11–24.

The EU provides financial support to civil society organisations for certain projects. For instance, NGOs working in the area of social inclusion, gender equality and equal opportunities can receive support through the European Social Fund. While TAIEX funding for technical assistance[59] in an enlargement setting is not open to NGOs, research has nevertheless reported on important mutual learning practices, where experienced NGOs serve as policy 'teachers' or 'exporters' of policy lessons.[60]

In sum, the formal and specific possibilities that the EU framework provides for learning and participation for NGOs are very limited.[61] To a certain extent, this forces these actors to rely on more 'informal' mechanisms, such as 'lobbying' the European Parliament.

III Individual Learning as a Prerequisite for a Polycentric EU

The EU's role regarding individual learning about the EU is much more limited compared to collective learning. This is mainly due to the fact that education is considered an area of national autonomy, with only a limited and supporting role for the EU. In particular, the EU's legislative competence in the area of education is closely circumscribed. Although it is true that especially through the use of other legal bases and via the case law of the CJEU an 'EU higher education law and policy' has developed over the years,[62] this indirect European integration has focused mainly on mobility rights and opportunities. The content of education, especially at primary and secondary school level, remains the responsibility of Member States (and the relevant subnational governmental and non-governmental actors). Although a majority of Member States have integrated learning about the EU into their curricula and teacher training programmes, disparities between and within Member States continue to exist and EU topics primarily constitute a small part of the curriculum that a given teacher has to deliver.[63] Studies show that beyond the very

[59] Technical Assistance and Information Exchange Instrument of the European Commission (n. 23).

[60] See, for instance, in the area of environmental protection: E. Bomberg, 'Policy learning in an enlarged European Union: environmental NGOs and new policy instruments', *Journal of European Public Policy* 14 (2) (2007), 248.

[61] See in this regard, the analysis on their limited access to justice by L. Díez Sánchez in this Volume, Chapter 10.

[62] S. Garben, *EU Higher Education Law: The Bologna Process and Harmonization by Stealth* (Kluwer Law International, 2011).

[63] A. Dunne *et al*, 'Learning Europe at School', *ICF GHK Report for European Commission DG EAC* (2013), available at: https://publications.europa.eu/en/publication-detail/-/pub

basic facts, knowledge about the EU amongst young people aged 14 is very low: only 35 per cent of students correctly know who votes to elect members of the EP.[64]

That being said, the legal basis of Article 165 TFEU does specifically provide that the supporting action which the EU is allowed to take should focus, *inter alia*, on a European dimension in education.[65] There are various EU policies that deserve mentioning in this regard.

The Europe for Citizens programme, managed by the Education, Audiovisual and Culture Executive Agency, aims to help the public understand the EU, its history and diversity, and to foster European citizenship and improve conditions for democratic and civic participation at EU level.[66] It provides operational and action-specific grants, to public bodies and non-profit organisations, along with two main orientations. The first is support of activities related to European remembrance, specifically 'to reflect on the causes of totalitarian regimes in Europe's modern history (especially but not exclusively Nazism which led to the Holocaust, Fascism, Stalinism and totalitarian communist regimes)'.[67] The second strand accommodates activities that cover civic participation, 'projects and initiatives that develop opportunities for mutual understanding, intercultural dialogue, solidarity, societal engagement and volunteering at Union level'.[68] Furthermore, the Jean Monnet programme, through which the EU funds university chairs in EU studies[69] as well as a number of education institutions of European interest such as the College of Europe and the European University Institute, contributes to individual learning about the EU at a more advanced stage. The Commission has set up an online Teachers' Corner with concrete

lication/83be95a3-b77f-4195-bd08-ad92c24c3a3c/language-en accessed 18 October 2018.

64 IEA, *ICCS 2009 European Report Civic knowledge, attitudes, and engagement among lower-secondary students in 24 European countries* (2010).

65 See also K. Grimonprez, 'The European Dimension in Citizenship Education: Unused Potential of Article 165 TFEU', *European Law Review* 39 (1) (2014), 3.

66 Council Regulation (EU) No. 390/2014 of 14 April 2014 establishing the 'Europe for Citizens' programme for the period 2014–2020, (2014) 115 OJ L 3–13.

67 ibid.

68 ibid.

69 Regulation (EU) No. 1288/2013 of the European Parliament and of the Council of 11 December 2013 establishing 'Erasmus+': The Union programme for education, training, youth and sport (2013) 347 OJ L 50–73.

examples of learning material that can be used in lessons on the EU,[70] and a Kids' Corner that informs children about the EU.[71] The Commission's Visitors' Centre and the Europe Direct network inform teachers, children and students about the EU and the Back-to-School project allows EU officials to visit schools to inform pupils about EU issues.[72]

A 2013 study for the European Commission showed that existing policy tools and programmes such as Europe for Citizens and Jean Monnet could be put to better use to enhance learning about Europe in schools, through focusing on teachers (which has a multiplier effect), the prioritisation of activities whose core purposes go beyond the development of content/material (which quickly goes out of date and is less easily absorbed than learning-through-doing), proactive advertisement of funding opportunities for education stakeholders and strengthening existing networks that have expertise on the EU and that collaborate with schools.[73] The European Parliament, citing the 2013 study, issued a resolution on Learning EU at school[74] calling on the Commission to continue its support for efforts to develop and promote an EU dimension in education, reinforcing the message that EU action in this area should become more pro-active and more dynamic, moving beyond the provision of documents and materials, and direct interaction with those who come to visit the EU Institutions.

It should be mentioned that more indirectly, as is the case with collective learning about the EU, the possibilities to be informed and participate in the EU decision-making process also foster individual learning. The Treaties feature several individual rights to information, consultation and participation in the EU decision-making process, such as the Citizens' Initiative and the right to petition the EP,[75] and the general right to access to documents.[76] Furthermore, citizens vote directly for the European Parliament. Moreover, especially in an economic capacity, citizens dispose of important free movement rights that

70 http://europa.eu/teachers-corner/home_en>.

71 http://europa.eu/kids-corner/index_en.htm>.

72 See Answer given by Commissioner Navracsics to a Question by MEP C. Ţapardel, E-002657/20, available at www.europarl.europa.eu/sides/getAllAnswers.do?reference=E-2017-002657&language=EN.

73 A. Dunne *et al.* (n. 63).

74 Resolution of 12 April 2016, 2015/2138(INI).

75 Discussed in further detail in this Volume by L. Díez Sánchez, Chapter 10.

76 Discussed in further detail in this Volume by V. Abazi, Chapter 11.

they can invoke directly in the pursuit of the self-governance of their lives.[77]

It thus transpires that in spite of its limited legal competence, the EU features a number of policies and rights that benefit the capacity for individual learning. However, it is doubtful that at present they serve to sufficiently connect the EU to average non-mobile individual citizens. Data from 2017 shows that 57 per cent of EU citizens feel they are not well informed about European matters and 50 per cent of Europeans believe that their voice does not count in the EU.[78] Only 42.61 per cent of EU citizens, and only 27,8 % of 18–24-year-olds, voted in the last European Parliament elections, representing the lowest voter turnout since 1979.[79]

**

Drawing together the threads of analysis of Sections III and IV, it would seem that for individuals that are somehow already ‘activated’, in that they have organised themselves into a collective and/or because they have made use of their EU free movement rights, the EU framework provides many opportunities to further develop this learning about the EU. It is true that generally speaking, the more institutionalised the authority, the more rights and opportunities the EU framework offers for information and participation, but even for non-governmental bodies and individual citizens there are options. By contrast, for those individuals that are not already ‘activated’, the EU contains limited tools to enhance their learning capacity. This may be at the heart of the EU’s legitimacy problem[80] and may also be preventing it from successful polycentric governance.

IV Learning as a Benefit of EU Polycentricity

As discussed, learning is a prerequisite to achieving and maintaining polycentricity. At the same time, when successful, one of the greatest benefits of a polycentric system is its potential for continued learning. The inter-jurisdictional diversity characteristic of federal, multilevel or polycentric systems has since long been associated with significant policy benefits because of the possibility of collective learning that these settings

77 See, in this Volume, Chapter 5 by J. van Zeben and A. Bobíc.

78 Standard Eurobarometer 88, Autumn 2017: ‘Public opinion in the European Union’.

79 As cited by the European Parliament in its Resolution of 12 April 2016, 2015/2138 (INI).

80 A. Føllesdal and S. Hix, ‘Why There Is a Democratic Deficit in the EU: A Response to Majone and Moravcsik’, *Journal of Common Market Studies* 44 (2006), 533.

inherently provide.[81] The simple fact that different jurisdictions will feature different policy and regulatory solutions to similar problems can be expected to allow for a certain degree of comparison and as such inter-jurisdictional learning. Furthermore, it 'hedges our bets [...] against the risk of bad policy'.[82] In addition, multiplicity of government not only prevents potentially bad policy being made on a large scale but allows learning from mistakes and the integration of acquired insights into subsequent initiatives. As such, it is considered to facilitate policy experimentation and innovation, particularly in systems with a shared political, economic and social space, such as the EU.[83] These dynamics are central to the idea of 'laboratory federalism'[84] and similarly central to polycentric governance.

While the scholarship underlying laboratory federalism provides some convincing advantages to polycentric governance, parts of the theory and the assumptions on which it rests are incomplete from a polycentric perspective, and parts are contestable. The remainder of this chapter will discuss the overlaps and differences between laboratory federalism and polycentric theory (A) and set out some observations regarding polycentric learning in the EU (B).

A *Laboratory Federalism and Polycentric Theory*

First, the concept of 'laboratory federalism' is to a certain extent premised on the idea that objectively optimal regulatory solutions exist. However, it is unlikely that there is an objectively optimal solution to any regulatory problem, independent of time, place and other context, and taking all interests concerned equally into account. The definition of a given regulatory problem and the appreciation of the potential solution(s) is inevitably complex and subjective. Even technical questions, such as for instance food safety standards, cannot be resolved only by reference to scientific, objective expertise, as is epitomised in (discussion concerning)

[81] For a discussion of the ways in which polycentric theory is distinct from federalism and from multilevel theory see, in this Volume, Chapter 1 by J. van Zeben.

[82] D. Halberstam, 'Federalism: A Critical Guide' (2011) 251 University of Michigan Public Law Working Paper 16.

[83] This shared space also makes it more likely that people are willing to share positive externalities. See V. Vanberg and W. Kerber, Institutional Competition among Jurisdictions: An Evolutionary Approach', *Constitutional Political Economy* 5 (1994), 193.

[84] In a multilevel system of jurisdictions, non-centralised public policies would lead to a process of experimentation with new policies. The term was coined by W. Oates, 'An Essay on Fiscal Federalism', *Journal of Economic Literature* 37 (1999), 1120.

the precautionary principle in EU law. All acts of regulation, as well as omissions of regulation, are ultimately political decisions weighing the costs and benefits of certain courses of action, and the inevitable trade-offs involved between different interests, at a given time and place. The essence of polycentricity is precisely that it aims not at objective outcomes but rather at subjective procedures: the goals set by the people within the polycentric system. This reflects a democratic imperative: regulation is not (only) about finding the most effective and efficient responses to problems even if they would in theory be available, but about the expression of moral choices of a given people, which tend to be intimately connected to their sociocultural identities. These choices may even go against 'rational' solutions as judged by external standards.

Relatedly, we can reasonably assume that there are limits to the transposability of insights acquired in relation to a regulatory solution in one jurisdiction. A high degree of inter-jurisdictional diversity is notably likely to impede a useful mutual learning process, since the successes and failures of certain initiatives may be closely connected to differences at micro-, meso- and macro level (or, in polycentric terms, at the operational, collective choice and constitutional level). Paradoxically, the more complex a given regulatory problem is (e.g. unemployment), the more it would seem in need of a mutual learning process, but the more difficult it will be to 'compare notes' between different jurisdictions precisely because of the complexity of the issues and how they interplay with the system as a whole (in the example of unemployment, a wide range of socio-economic and constitutional issues on which jurisdictions are likely to differ).

The standard account of laboratory federalism tends to overlook governance by non-governmental actors. Injecting insights of polycentric theory into laboratory federalism, a strong case can be made that comparison and learning are just as relevant and potentially beneficial for non-governmental governance by (groups of) individuals. On the one hand, it could be hypothesised that in comparison to governmental authorities, these actors dispose of fewer resources to engage in such mutual learning (in particular, they may lack information about the non-governmental decision-making centres in other jurisdictions as these are less likely to be subject to transparency requirements and to have a higher sociocultural-linguistic specificity). On the other hand, to actively engage in 'cross-border' collaboration among peers may be a less sensitive exercise for non-governmental actors. Informal networks of this kind should be included into accounts of laboratory federalism which they often are not.

In addition, laboratory federalism implicitly focuses on collectives and thereby overlooks the position of the individual citizen, who is at the heart of polycentric theory. Individuals actually play a central role in the dynamics of laboratory federalism. The improved information base provided by a multijurisdictional setting not only benefits governments, but equally individuals. It allows them to learn about other decision-making centres generally, and importantly also about alternatives. Such a comparison enables the questioning of perceived inevitabilities, destabilises entrenched understandings and challenges realities which are taken for granted. Better informed and critical individuals make up a more dynamic and demanding citizenry. The individuals may very well become 'activated' and organise (perhaps even across jurisdictions), and they may furthermore 'activate' their authorities: confronting governments with the discovered and imagined alternate realities and prodding them into action. In any event, it allows individuals to make more informed choices. To repeat the words of M. D. McGinnis and E. Ostrom: '[a]mong the positive benefits of polycentricity touted by [V.] Ostrom were such matters as [. . .] generation of a richer body of information available to citizens'.[85]

Finally, in theorising the benefits of policy experimentation in a polycentric polity, it should not be overlooked that – paradoxically – the same regulatory competition that drives experimentation and learning, also threatens to limit the jurisdictional regulatory autonomy (i.e. the power of collective self-governance) that is a prerequisite for it. As Halberstam has noted, when the incidents of regulation fall heavily on one entity while the benefits fall on another or on citizens more generally, mobility of the objects of regulation limits the exercise of public power.[86] This explains why redistributive policies are difficult to maintain at the level of local government, as the US Supreme Court recognised in upholding federal unemployment laws.[87]

The 'exercise of public power' affected should be understood broadly, including self-regulation by non-governmental collectives (e.g. by

[85] M. D. McGinnis and E. Ostrom, 'Reflections on Vincent Ostrom, Public Administration, and Polycentricity', *Public Administration Review* 72 (1) (2012), 22.

[86] D. Halberstam (n. 81) 19. For a contribution contesting the existence of regulatory competition, see M. Kahan and E. Kamar, 'The Myth of State Competition in Corporate Law Making', *Stanford Law Journal* 55 (2002), 679.

[87] Ibid.

representatives of management and labour in the form of collective agreements). Unless one adheres to the specific political economic ideology that equals such competitive processes to learning processes and considers the outcomes thereof as necessarily the 'best solutions', one has to regard this restriction of the collective power of self-governance at the jurisdictional/regional/local level as an important limitation to the theoretic possibility of laboratory federalism and the collective capacity to learn (as well as the democratic and social legitimacy) of highly decentralised polycentric systems. This also provides an argument for centralised policies in order to compensate (as much as possible) this loss of subcentral regulatory power. In polycentric terms, the overarching system of rules should ensure the appropriate balance between competition and collaboration between the various independent decision-making centres, and the rules concerning entry and exit are especially crucial in that regard.

In sum, learning through trial and error and competition – as first advocated in laboratory federalism – can be a tangible benefit from polycentric governance. The dynamics described by laboratory federalism that result from inter-jurisdictional diversity, allowing for comparison and – combined with the freedom of entry and exit – leading to both inter-jurisdictional competition and collaboration which in turn allow further learning, fit polycentric theory well, and can easily be expanded to include the importance of non-governmental collectives and particularly individual citizens. The main difference is that the standard account of laboratory federalism seems to consider the main advantage of these dynamics to be that they would lead to objectively 'better' policy, whereas polycentric theory considers the main value to lie in the enriched body of information available to citizens and thus the enhanced capacity for self-governance. The question that remains is what concrete possibilities do we see within the EU to achieve these benefits of polycentric learning?

B Polycentric Learning in the EU

First and foremost, in a number of areas, particularly where direct legislative powers are lacking, polycentric learning processes are a core governance method. The prime example is the Open Method of Coordination (OMC), which is not mentioned expressly in the Treaties but provided for in an indirect way where the TFEU refers to 'the organisation of exchange of best practice' in the provisions relating to employment, social policy, health, research and technological development, and industry. The OMC has been explicitly examined in the context of (the themes raised by) laboratory federalism. Indeed, the OMC specifically aims at improving the information base available to national decision makers and encourages them to learn from the experience of others. As Gornitzka's notes, the OMC assumes that despite different traditions, significant systemic differences, and lack of legal means of integration, Member States can learn from each other and improve their policies, implying that the organised and routinised interaction between Member States will give more effective learning than bilateral or unorganised policy import or mimicry.

Furthermore, economic policy coordination carries many of these features of non-binding targets and peer review and could therefore similarly be argued to constitute a mutual learning process. In any event, economic governance now taking place through the European Semester has largely absorbed the most important features of OMC in the areas of health, social and employment policy. More than the OMC as such ever did, 'new' economic governance is becoming a central element of EU governance.

However, while these methods seem specifically designed to allow for polycentric learning, the effectiveness of new governance in these respects depends on a number of key factors. In the current EU, these are not sufficiently guaranteed.

First, it is not a given that Member States will actually use these processes as a forum for learning. For one, considering the lack of binding, prescriptive measures, the uptake of the process and the steer delivered therein cannot be guaranteed. This is one of the major criticisms levelled against the OMC, and while the European Semester has partially addressed these concerns through a more coercive model (particularly due to the possibility of sanctions and fines in the context of the macroeconomic imbalance and excessive deficit procedures), the uptake of country specific recommendations has been estimated to still be low. Of course, 'mutual learning' should be defined more broadly than those instances where national policy is actually amended because of acquired insights, but it remains a valid point that there is no guarantee that Member States will actually learn through new governance.

Secondly, in a similar way, there is no guarantee that Member States will 'play fair' and will not use new governance methods to play infamous 'two-level games' whereby they use the European level to push their own agenda. As Moravcsik has argued, 'international cooperation redistributes domestic power in favour of national executives by permitting them to loosen domestic constraints imposed by legislatures, interest groups, and other societal actors'. This applies with particular force to in-transparent, inter-governmental fora such as the OMC and the Semester.

Thirdly, from a polycentric perspective, EU new governance does not sufficiently guarantee the inclusion of relevant non-governmental organisations in the learning process. For instance, in matters concerning employment and social policy, the Social Partners should be included, which is not sufficiently the case in the context of the European Semester process. This is all the more important in the light of the preceding observation, namely that care needs to be taken that European-level mutual learning processes is not used to exclude other 'democratic' actors through the excessive empowerment of national executives.

Perhaps most importantly, to what extent new governance genuinely facilitates mutual learning in a polycentric sense depends on how the parameters of the process are defined. As has been stated about the OMC, '"[b]enchmarks" are a type of optimal policy displaying an implicit preference for convergence while limiting the incentives for states to experiment and compete'. The European Semester is notably problematic from this perspective, because rather than an open, reflexive information gathering and exchange, the process instead serves mainly to prescribe specific reforms to be undertaken, often with a view to limit national regulatory autonomy, from the viewpoint of economic criteria. The central level (the Commission and the Council) decides on 'optimal' policies to be implemented by the Member States. The difference here with full legislative harmonisation seems to only lie in the non-binding nature of the measures, but that hardly makes it a successful exercise in collective learning. This is all the more problematic considering the broad scope of application of the process, which includes many areas that ostensibly belong to sub-central decision-making competence, such as minimum wages, pensions, health care and education.

Finally, it has been argued that the rationale of new governance is to overcome the limits on EU legislative competence: a complementary form of governance for when 'harmonization is unworkable but mutual recognition and the resulting regulatory competition may be too risky', for instance 'to encourage the Member States to coordinate sensitive policy areas that are being eroded by the rulings of the Court'. An example would be the EU voluntary tax code, designed to prevent a race to the bottom in taxation, providing an incentive for Member States to reconsider their policies if they cause negative externalities for others. However, when used in areas subjected to heavy regulatory competition, it is highly doubtful whether it can really stop such dynamics. For instance, regulatory competition on corporate taxation is still very much an issue, in spite of new governance's attempts to mitigate it. In polycentric terms, it seems that a fundamental imbalance between competition and cooperation between independent decision-making centres cannot be effectively addressed through a non-binding collective learning process.

This brings us to a final point. To reiterate, a polycentric system's overarching set of shared rules must ensure the appropriate equilibrium between cooperation and competition among the independent decision-making centres, and the role of the possibilities for entry and exit is fundamental in this regard. As a general rule, it would seem that the wider the formulation of rights to free movement of economic factors and citizens, the more this encourages inter-jurisdictional competition and therefore begs the need for (some degree of) cooperation. Sometimes this will have to take the form of binding legislation in order to be fully effective, as the foregoing example on taxation suggests. In the EU, as also discussed in Chapter 5, economic free movement rights are very extensive and can be argued to lead to significant degrees of regulatory competition, to such an extent that can be argued to unduly limit the regulatory autonomy of the national level (to the detriment of self-governance and learning). While the EU's overarching system of shared rules provides many EU competences to cooperate i.e. adopt binding legislation in the internal market and by extension a virtually unlimited range of other policy areas, the exercise thereof often results in full or maximum harmonisation measures, pre-empting further national action. Such standardisation has the effect of foreclosing ongoing concurrent decision making and therefore forecloses mutual learning. From the perspective of polycentric learning, it would be more desirable if, where centralised binding action proves necessary to mitigate competition, the common action left scope for ongoing concurrent decision-making.

The main possibility for such common action that nevertheless leaves scope for continued decentralised action and thus learning, is through the adoption of minimum harmonisation measures (where the EU only sets a baseline standard from which Member States may deviate 'upwards'). The Treaty provisions granting EU competence in a number of areas, such as social and environmental policy, limit EU action to such minimum harmonisation. However, through the use of the internal market legal basis in these areas, the EU nevertheless often uses full harmonisation, in the interest of free movement and market integration. It could be argued that from the perspective of polycentric learning, this practice should be revised. This could for instance become a part of the Impact Assessment of EU legislation required under the Better Regulation Agenda, which more generally expresses a commitment to 'reflexive governance', subsidiarity and staving off excessive centralisation. Apart from the standard question in impact assessments whether a 'soft law' initiative has been considered as an alternative, impact assessments could question whether minimum instead of maximum harmonisation would lead to a more satisfactory balance between the various economic and non-economic, central and decentral, European and national interests.

V Conclusion

This chapter has provided a first exploratory venture into the role of learning in the EU as a polycentric system. As such, it has investigated to what extent the EU framework guarantees learning about the EU as a prerequisite for polycentric governance and has explored to what extent it allows the potential benefits of polycentricity for mutual learning to be exploited. The assessment has tentatively suggested that while the EU framework makes various, generous dispositions for learning about the EU, these mainly benefit governmental bodies and a limited number of privileged non-governmental organisations. The possibilities for non-privileged NGOs and, perhaps most importantly, for individual citizens are more limited in scope and effectiveness, especially concerning individuals acting in a non-economic capacity. Further research is necessary to (dis)confirm these impressions, but our initial assessment indicates that this is a shortcoming that may be preventing the EU from successfully maintaining polycentric governance.

As regards learning as a benefit, polycentric theory enriches the concept of 'laboratory federalism'. It does so particularly, analytically, by recognising the importance of non-governmental collectives and, normatively, by reconceptualising the main expected benefit of mutual learning as the production of an enriched body of information available to citizens (enhancing capacity for self-governance) instead of the achievement of the best policy.

Notwithstanding several promising Treaty provisions, such as the existence of 'new governance' mutual learning processes and a limitation on the EU's legislative competence to set maximum standards in a range of areas, several factors limit the materialisation of improved learning through polycentricity in the EU. In particular, EU new governance as currently used is not a genuine mutual learning process but instead threatens to limit subcentral regulatory autonomy and policy experimentation due to an overly prescriptive and centralising approach. A similarly excessive centralisation takes place in the areas where the Treaties prescribe minimum harmonisation, mainly through the use of the internal market legal basis which instead promotes full standardisation, foreclosing mutual learning. If these findings are confirmed by further research, the policy implications are clear: (i) regardless of its limited competence in the area of education, the EU needs to foster individual learning about EU governance and the EU more broadly, and (ii) the EU needs to reconsider its centralising approach both in the context of its (internal market) legislation and new governance, finding a better balance between unity and diversity.

CONCLUSIONS

Pathways to Polycentricity

JOSEPHINE VAN ZEBEN AND ANA BOBIĆ

There is an old joke, in which a man is driving through the countryside, lost. He stops his car in a small village to ask a local for directions. The local responds by saying: 'You want to get *where*? Oh, to get there, I wouldn't start from here.'

This Volume reflects the collective efforts of a group of scholars with different disciplinary backgrounds and areas of EU expertise. Together, they undertook the first steps in verifying the EU's potential for polycentric governance. In establishing ideal practices for EU polycentricity, the Ostroms' legacy provided the only available starting point. Yet, we found that however rich a theory, Vincent and Lin Ostrom's polycentricity, developed in urban America, does not easily translate to complex multilevel systems such as the EU's. As a result, this Volume's journey took us from theory to practice and back again.

These conclusions provide an overview of our findings with a view to present a new starting point for EU polycentricity and point to some of the most exciting sights observed along the way.

I Theoretical Foundations: Polycentric Attributes, Institutional Essentials and Prerequisites

The first part of the Volume travels from theory to praxis: it presents the theoretical foundations and main characteristics of polycentric theory so as to facilitate its application to the European Union. The most important step in creating this theoretical framework was the identification of the attributes by which to recognise a polycentric system, the institutional essentials that ensure its maintenance and the prerequisites needed in turn for these institutional essentials to function successfully (van Zeben, Chapter 1).

The central aim of Vincent Ostrom's polycentricity is to create a self-governing society, governed by rules and the rule of law, but where the monopoly of authority does not lie with the government.[1] The EU has fundamentally changed the position of national governments within Europe, making this aim seem especially fitting as a normative approach for the future of EU governance. In order to demonstrate its added value vis-à-vis existing theories of EU governance and integration – including multilevel governance, constitutional pluralism, multilevel constitutionalism and federalism – polycentricity's descriptive value was also demonstrated (van Zeben, Chapter 2).

A rudimentary application of the blueprint of polycentric attributes, essentials and prerequisites to the EU showed that there were several theoretical concepts that required further elaboration in order to successfully translate to the EU setting. Firstly, the concept of self-governance, and its relationship with competence-competence and *demoicracy*, was developed further so as to incorporate issues of agency and related claims to self-government by political communities, rather than individuals. This richer understanding of self-governance also accommodates Ostrom's emphasis on horizontal relationships. This translates into an ideal system where horizontal connections make up all or most of the institutional manifestations of the *demoi* in joint consultation or decision-making bodies, and they in turn exercise horizontal checks and balances on each other (Cheneval, Chapter 3).

Table 1 *Attributes, Institutional Essentials, and Prerequisites of Polycentric Systems*

Attributes	(i)	Multiple independent centres of decision making
	(ii)	Continuous competition, cooperation and conflict resolution
	(iii)	Overarching shared system of rules
Institutional essentials	(i)	Freedom and ability to enter and exit
	(ii)	Enforcement of shared system of rules
	(iii)	Peaceful contestation among different (interest) groups
Prerequisites	(i)	Access to information
	(ii)	Capacity to learn
	(iii)	Access to justice

[1] V. Ostrom, *The Meaning of American Federalism: Constituting a Self-Governing Society* (ICS Press, 1994), 242.

Similar to the challenge of developing polycentric theory to accommodate EU reality, two quintessentially European concepts needed to be studied through the lens of polycentricity. First, the practice of the EU principle of subsidiarity is contrasted with the aims of subsidiarity in polycentric governance. This analysis shows that EU subsidiarity cannot accommodate self-governance sufficiently, and that debates regarding subsidiarity within polycentricity are not specific enough to constitute a principled approach. This leads to the introduction of the principle of polycentric subsidiarity, which allows for the inclusion of self-governance, horizontality and organic change within subsidiarity assessments (van Zeben and Nicolaïdis, Chapter 4).

Second, the EU's internal market is analysed as a polycentric system – both on its own merits, and as a polycentric part of the EU's larger whole. Vincent Ostrom's polycentricity is not limited to a reconsideration of governmental systems; a truly polycentric society must incorporate its principles in all societal arenas, including its market system. The analysis of the EU's internal market shows important inequalities in market participants' abilities to access the processes surrounding institutional essentials and prerequisites, endangering the crucial dynamic equilibrium of polycentric governance. It also shows the complications of 'nested' polycentric systems, or polycentric arenas of life, interacting with each other (van Zeben and Bobić, Chapter 5).

II Institutional Essentials and Prerequisites in EU Polycentricity

The second part of the Volume maps EU praxis back on the theory of polycentricity: how, if at all, does EU governance incorporate the institutional essentials and their prerequisites in order to maintain polycentricity?

Polycentric systems have three identifying attributes – multiple independent centres of decision making, continuous competition, cooperation and conflict resolution between centres, and an overarching shared system of rules. The importance of the overarching shared system of rules is self-evident insofar that it provides the framework in which the system's institutional essentials play out. Perhaps surprisingly, neither Vincent nor Lin Ostrom ever gave a precise definition of the sort of *legal* rules needed to ensure polycentric functioning. In order to give greater definition to the EU's framework, Bobić proposes a definition of the shared system of rules through incorporating the findings of transnational constitutional legal theory. In defining the system's substance and enforcement (the latter being an institutional essential), it becomes clear that the EU's shared system of rules displays a lack of emphasis on self-governance – apart from that of the Member States. This is logically accompanied by a lack of rules concerning institutional essentials and prerequisites that would enable and/or encourage such self-governance (Bobić, Chapter 6).

The subsequent discussion of polycentricity's institutional essentials – the freedom and ability to enter and exit, enforcement of the shared system of rules, and peaceful contestation among different (interest) groups – analyses various areas of EU law through a new lens.

An analysis of EU citizenship – key in allowing for free entry and exit *within* the EU – shows that its current interpretation privileges individual free movement and the homogenisation of rights over national constitutional divisions of authority and local self-governance. A polycentric conception of Union citizenship is proposed, respecting divisions of power between different centres of decision making: EU citizens' freedom of entry and exit can be operationalised with respect for practices of collective self-governance within these centres and the system of general rules be enforced so as to overcome barriers to cooperation between them (van den Brink, Chapter 7). As to broader entry and exit *to* the EU, it becomes clear that there is limited formal support for the self-governing abilities of third-country nationals (TCNs) but that TCNs' self-organisation is nevertheless possible and can be detected at several levels, mostly informal and ad hoc. This shows that polycentric governance in the EU remains reserved for 'insiders' – EU citizens – with a significant and growing number of individuals within EU territory only partially included or even excluded (Goldner Lang, Chapter 8). Finally, the importance of the 'public entrepreneur' – an active, knowledgeable, and daring decision-making actor motivated by diverse interests and common social goals – for the possibility for peaceful contestation in the EU is identified, together with encouragements and obstacles to public entrepreneurship (Kukovec, Chapter 9).

In order to maintain these institutional essentials, three prerequisites need to be in place – access to justice, access to information, and learning. In detailing the importance of these prerequisites for polycentric processes, our contributors underlined polycentricity's dynamic nature by showing that polycentricity likewise affects access to justice, information and learning.

Unequal access to justice in the EU, defined broadly to include issues of standing as well as resources, occurs between and within social groups, and extends to the indirect representation of interests by privileged applicants. Importantly, while polycentric structures can increase the self-governance of certain actors, they can also hinder access to courts of marginalised and non-organised groups (Díez Sánchez, Chapter 10). Similarly, the role that access to information plays as a polycentric prerequisite is provided with more detailed theoretical basis. Once theorised, it becomes clear that EU practice falls short of offering access to information in a manner that supports polycentric governance due to issues of 'privileged access' and information asymmetries (Abazi, Chapter 11). Learning, perhaps the most taxing obligation and important prerequisite of individual engagement with polycentric governance, is analysed as an individual and collective process. The main beneficiaries of the EU capacity building in this are governmental bodies and a limited number of privileged non-governmental organisations. The possibilities for non-privileged NGOs and, perhaps most importantly, for individual citizens are more limited in scope (Garben, Chapter 12).

III There and Back Again – Views from the Road

The starting point of our journey was Vincent and Lin Ostrom's work on polycentric governance, hoping it would lead us to a vision for a polycentric European Union. Our intuition regarding the EU's polycentric potential has been confirmed but remaining obstacles have also become clear(er). This Volume is therefore not the end of our journey but 'proof of concept' with much work remaining for future travellers. Let us conclude with some of the most exciting routes for continued exploration.

A European Itineraries

i Complexity and Fragmentation

Polycentric systems are in a state of continuous dynamic equilibrium, maintained by active participants at various levels. This creates a level of complexity that poses practical challenges for institutional design, which in turn calls for further theoretical development.[2] Complexity needs to be

[2] E. Ostrom drew on insights from Simon in observing that 'where one begins a search to improve the performance of a complex system ... makes a substantial difference in the quality and speed of the search process'. See E. Ostrom, *Understanding Institutional Diversity* (Princeton University Press, 2005), 270; H. A. Simon, *Sciences of the Artificial* 2nd edn (Massachusetts Institute of Technology Press, 1981).

addressed as a feature of (processes within) the system, and as a feature of the information needed to meaningfully participate in the system. In this respect, the prerequisites of learning and access to information have emerged as the crucial building blocks where more progress is needed for polycentricity and self-governance to thrive.

Remaining puzzles regarding complexity involve what path to take in order to ensure both qualitatively and quantitatively meaningful information flows; how to equip people with skills to participate in certain decisions; how to allow for efficient differentiation in skills without precluding movement of people between groups; and how to allow for differentiation in linguistic and cultural backgrounds while maintaining a common core of shared information to ensure the system of rules remains 'shared'?

These puzzles show the close connection between complexity and fragmentation. Fragmentation may be viewed as a positive – particularly in these times of 'taking back control' – allowing for different preferences to come to the fore. However, without the glue of values set out in Article 2 TEU, including importantly solidarity – to hold these different pieces together – the whole may not be more than the sum of its parts. Polycentric systems need to strike the balance between fragmentation and solidarity, which may be harder under conditions of high complexity. That said, attempts to 'simplify' the European Union through the concentration of powers and processes at the EU level have arguably been equally unsuccessful.

ii Vertical and Horizontal Relationships

As a system of governance, the EU displays many unique features. Attempts to pigeonhole it as traditionally international or 'national' have clearly failed, but finding tools and terminology that step away entirely from these benchmarks has proven equally difficult. Vincent Ostrom's emphasis on self-governance in the absence of a governmental authority monopoly would seem to fit well with the EU's system given the sharing of sovereignty between the EU and the Member States. However, self-governance in the Ostromian sense requires horizontal relationships (between individuals and between government at different levels) to be considered equal to, and at times more important than, vertical relationships (between government and individual, or different levels of government). The continued centrality of the Member States, even as their monopoly might be weakened, prevents this dynamic from taking root; there is a continued dominance of vertical over horizontal relationships, reflected in every institutional essential and prerequisite. Moreover, this vertical relationship is almost invariably top-down, limiting the input that higher levels of decision making receive from local institutions. This is particularly clear in the EU's practice of subsidiarity, which we suggest should be replaced with polycentric subsidiarity, in order to allow for a more inclusive practice in terms of relevant decision-making centres at all levels, as well as a bottom-up definition of policy goals, and associated organic change to self-governing institutions.[3]

Exciting questions remain concerning methods to ensure increased diagonal relationships (between different actors across different levels); balancing bottom-up goals and preferences with overarching solidarity, efficiency and effectiveness; formally and practically broadening the types of actors included in decision making at the EU level; and, considering the need and possibility for safeguards in case of horizontal transfers of sovereignty.

B Global, and Local, Travels

By analysing the EU through a polycentric lens, polycentric theory has moved away from its birthplace in the context of US metropolitan government,[4] and beyond the excursions into global problems such as climate change, approached from a bottom-up perspective.[5] This move has necessitated a rethinking of certain building blocks of polycentric theory, specifically through the identification of attributes, institutional essentials and prerequisites. This helps facilitate inquiries into the polycentric pedigree of other transnational polycentric systems, as well as comparisons between polycentric systems functioning at different scales.

Even as these specifications may provide us with a better starting point, much important work remains. While ambitious in its scope and inclusive in its contributors, the dominant approach in this volume is a legal one. This has often meant a focus on formal rules to the exclusion of informal processes. At the same time, it has also shown that the Ostroms' use and definition of 'rules' may require further nuance in order for it to translate successfully to the realm of legal scholarship. The difficulties

[3] See in detail Chapter 4 by J. van Zeben and K. Nicolaïdis.
[4] V. Ostrom, C. Tiebout, and R. Warren, 'The Organization of Government in Metropolitan Areas: A Theoretical Inquiry', *The American Political Science Review* 55 (1961), 831.
[5] E. Ostrom, 'A Polycentric Approach for Coping with Climate Change' (2009) World Bank Policy Research Working Paper 5095, available at http://documents.worldbank.org/curated/en/480171468315567893/pdf/wps5095.pdf

that we encountered in combining polycentricity as a theory of governance with the EU as a legal system (as well as a system of governance) present a fertile starting point for further interdisciplinary research collaboration.

Similarly, drawing out the relationships between institutional essentials and prerequisites has exposed a feedback effect between them: prerequisites are not only important in their facilitation of institutional essentials, they are also shaped by the polycentric system in which they function. For example, in order for the shared system of rules to be enforced, individuals must be able to learn about the rules and related processes so as to ensure possibilities for peaceful contestation, and access to justice. This in turn benefits the continuous dynamic development of the rules through individual-led change. However, the process of continuous change also complicates learning, which then undermines the ability to contest and question rules. These feedback effects require further attention, particularly with a view on maintaining certain core certainties within a complex, ever-changing, system.

**

In the 1990s, Vincent Ostrom wrote that

> The future belongs to those whose covenants are bonds of mutual trust grounded in principles of self-governance and who learn to use processes of conflict and conflict resolution to elucidate information, clarify alternative, stimulate innovation, and extend the frontiers of inquiry to open new potentials for human development.[6]

In the same publication, he emphasised that this future need not, and should not, centre on national governments, and that the developments in Western Europe at the time were already demonstrating exactly this.[7] Thirty years later, this Volume considered whether the polycentric vision on which Ostrom based his conclusions can be used to describe the EU's status quo and may eventually act as a vision for the EU's future.

The contributors to the Volume aided our travels towards EU polycentricity by showing how the EU qualifies as a polycentric system in their areas of focus, while simultaneously enriching polycentric governance theory by expanding its key theoretical characteristics with different practices. The result of these efforts is a rich collection of writings that advances our understanding of EU polycentricity and points to several

[6] V. Ostrom, The Meaning of American Federalism (n. 1) 272.
[7] ibid., 8.

roads that may be taken. In keeping with polycentricity's dynamic complexity and the Ostroms' push for scholarly and methodological interdisciplinarity,[8] these roads may need to be travelled simultaneously and, in order to do so successfully, in the company of others.

This inquiry has raised at least as many questions as it has answered. It has become clear that the potential for self-governance exists but that the institutional framework to support it need to be strengthened. Moreover, the demand for self-governance at individual, local, regional and national level is such that it is hard to imagine a sustainable future for the EU that does not head this call. This presents challenges – politically, legally and pragmatically – of complexity and fragmentation. In order to face these challenges, the EU would do well to remember its ambitious and innovative roots and make use of the technological changes that make its people ever more connected and informed, rather than revert to the perceived safety of national monopolies.

[8] A. R. Poteete, M. A. Janssen, and E. Ostrom, *Working Together – Collective Action, the Commons, and Multiple Methods in Practice* (Princeton University Press, 2010).

INDEX

Printed in the United Kingdom by TJ Clays Ltd.